The Luther Myth

The Luther Myth

The Image of Martin Luther from Religious Reformer to Völkisch *Icon*

PATRICK HAYDEN-ROY

OXFORD
UNIVERSITY PRESS

OXFORD
UNIVERSITY PRESS

Great Clarendon Street, Oxford, OX2 6DP,
United Kingdom

Oxford University Press is a department of the University of Oxford.
It furthers the University's objective of excellence in research, scholarship,
and education by publishing worldwide. Oxford is a registered trade mark of
Oxford University Press in the UK and in certain other countries

© Patrick Hayden-Roy 2024

The moral rights of the author have been asserted

All rights reserved. No part of this publication may be reproduced, stored in a retrieval system, transmitted, used for text and data mining, or used for training artificial intelligence, in any form or by any means, without the prior permission in writing of Oxford University Press, or as expressly permitted by law, by licence or under terms agreed with the appropriate reprographics rights organization. Enquiries concerning reproduction outside the scope of the above should be sent to the Rights Department, Oxford University Press, at the address above.

You must not circulate this work in any other form
and you must impose this same condition on any acquirer

Published in the United States of America by Oxford University Press
198 Madison Avenue, New York, NY 10016, United States of America

British Library Cataloguing in Publication Data

Data available

Library of Congress Control Number: 2024941348

ISBN 9780198930266

DOI: 10.1093/9780198930297.001.0001

Printed and bound by
CPI Group (UK) Ltd, Croydon, CR0 4YY

Links to third party websites are provided by Oxford in good faith and
for information only. Oxford disclaims any responsibility for the materials
contained in any third party website referenced in this work.

Acknowledgments

There were a number of institutions and people whose support was instrumental in bringing this work to completion. The study was underwritten by my home institution, Nebraska Wesleyan University, through two year-long sabbatical leaves that provided the time to complete the research and writing of it. In addition, the travel abroad residency in Berlin was in part subsidized by the Dave Peace Fund endowment of Nebraska Wesleyan, which provides faculty development funds for members of the Department of History. Dave Peace is a long-time friend of Nebraska Wesleyan's History Department, and his financial support, as well as enthusiasm for history in all its shapes and sizes, is much appreciated. In addition, Nebraska Wesleyan's faculty development funds provided further financial support for my work. The staff of the Staatsbibliothek zu Berlin: Preußischer Kulturbesitz provided much help in accessing many of the hard-to-find sources at the center of the study. The Theologische Fakultät of the Humboldt University of Berlin provided visiting scholar credentials and additional support for research in their libraries; I am particularly grateful to the librarians of the Fachbibliothek for their assistance. I would like, in particular, to thank Prof. Dr. Judith Becker of Theologische Fakultät for her kind support during the work on the study. Among my colleagues in the History Department at Nebraska Wesleyan, I would especially like to thank Dr. Meghan Winchell, who has provided enthusiastic support and advice along the way. At Oxford University Press, Matthew Cotton, Thomas Stottor, and Nadine Kolz have all assisted in bringing the manuscript through the publication process. Finally, I would like to highlight the help of my wife, Dr. Priscilla Hayden-Roy, who has been an essential conversation partner during the development of this study, and who read through, critiqued, and corrected the entire manuscript. I'm particularly grateful to her for her work on the German translations in the text, which were much improved by her interventions. As always, whatever shortcomings that remain stem from my authorship.

Contents

Introduction	1
1. Luther, the "Most German of All Germans"	6
2. Luther Goes to War	28
3. The Reborn Luther	46
4. Luther's "German Hour"	79
5. Luther, the National Socialist	104
6. Luther [and] *der Führer*	131
7. Luther the Anti-Semite (?)	156
8. Luther the Heathen	199
9. Luther the Perpetrator?	222
Conclusion	247
Bibliography	255
Index for The Luther Myth	271

Introduction

This study deals with Martin Luther not as a historical individual but rather as a cultural symbol during the 1920s and '30s in Germany. Of course, capturing the "real" Luther has been a fraught enterprise ever since he emerged on the historical stage in 1517. Even during his lifetime, Luther's image was part of the struggle for public support by both the incipient movement for reform and its opponents, something Luther himself recognized and acknowledged.[1] And over the centuries, different profiles of Luther emerged within the context of the times: the prophet, the rebel, the man of faith, the advocate of freedom of conscience, among others.[2] For the first couple of centuries the images played out more directly from the religious controversies and forces unleashed at the time of the Reformation. Beginning, however, in the nineteenth century, a transposition took shape under the influence of emergent German nationalism, which shaped a Luther whose meaning defined and reinforced a German national identity in the making. This remaking of the image of Luther was less involved with his significance as a

---

[1] "Tzum ersten bitt ich, man wolt meynes namen geschweygen und sich nit lutherisch, sonder Christen heyssen. Was ist Luther? ist doch die lere nit meyn. Szo byn ich auch fur niemant gecreutzigt. S. Paulus i. Corint. iii. wolt nit lyden, das die Christen sich solten heyssen Paulisch oder Petersch, sondernn Christen. Wie keme denn ich armer stinckender maden sack datzu, das man die kinder Christi solt mit meynem heyloszen namen nennen? Nitt alszo, lieben Freund, last uns tilgenn die parteysche namen unnd Christen heyssen, das lere wir haben. Die Papisten habenn billich eynen parteyschen namen, die weyl sie nit benuget an Christus lere unnd namen, wollenn auch Bepstisch seyn, szo last sie Bepstisch seynn, der yhr meyster ist. Ich byn unnd wyll keynisz meyster seyn. Ich habe mitt der gemeyne die eynige gemeyne lere Christi, der alleyn unszer meyster ist. Matth. Xxiii" (First of all I would ask that one would leave my name out of it and call oneself not Lutheran but Christian. What is Luther? Really the teaching is not mine, and also I wasn't crucified for anyone. St. Paul in I Cor. 3 won't abide that Christians call themselves Pauline or Petrine, but rather Christians. How has it come to pass that, stinking sack of maggots that I am, the children of Christ should be named with my hopeless name? Let's not, my good friends; let us bury the partisan names and call ourselves Christian, which is whose teaching we have. The papists have a partisan name, because they are not content with the name and teaching of Christ; they want to also be papists, so let them be papists, who is their master. I am and don't want to be anyone's master. I have with the community the one common teaching of Christ, who alone is our master. Matth. 22). "Ein treue Vermahnung zu allen Christen, sich zu hüten vor Aufruhr und Empörung." *D. Martin Luthers Werke: Kritische Gesammtausgabe*. Vol. 8. (Weimar: Hermann Böhlau, 1889). 685. Hereafter WA with volume number.

[2] For an example of how complex the translation of even the most well-documented elements of Luther's life is, see Thomas Kaufmann, *"Hier Stehe Ich!" Luther in Worms-Ereignis, mediale Inszenierung, Mythos* (Stuttgart: Anton Hiersemann, 2021). See also Ernst Walter Zeeden, *Martin Luther und die Reformation im Urteil des deutschen Luthertums: Studien zum Selbstverständnis des lutherischen Protestantismus von Luthers Tode bis zum Beginn der Goethezeit*, Vol. 1: *Darstellungen*; Vol. 2: *Dokumente* (Freiburg i.B.: Herder, 1950); and Heinrich Bornkamm, *Luther im Spiegel der deutschen Geistesgeschichte*. 2nd ed. (Göttingen: Vandenhoeck & Ruprecht, 1970).

religious reformer, and framed him as the champion and embodiment of German national unity and rebellion against foreign influences. This image grew and expanded across the nineteenth century, reaching many of its mature features with the four-hundredth anniversary of Luther's birth in 1883.[3] Chapter 1 of the study will deal with the emergence and development of this image of Luther.

The central question addressed by the study involves not just the projection of Luther's image, but the larger question of how his image interacted with and facilitated the success of racial nationalism in Germany during the 1920s and '30s. While the image of the nationalist Luther rested comfortably in the political environment of the Second Empire, World War I and the collapse of the old regime brought a new inflection point for the reception of this nationalist Luther, creating an image of Luther whose characteristics framed a piety that was susceptible to the attractions of radical racial nationalism that was a main focus of resistance to the Weimar Republic. As will be made clear in the main chapters of the study, the conception of Luther that emerged from World War I provided sustenance for a theology that supported *völkisch* nationalism, and a politics that affirmed charismatic authoritarian leadership and bellicose German nationalist resentments. Over time it increasingly provided legitimation for the growing anti-Semitism of German culture and politics and, in the 1930s, the policies of the Nazi State. In this sense, the "Luther Myth,"[4] as the title would have it, follows the lineage of Ian Kershaw's seminal study, *The Hitler Myth*,[5] in considering how the cultural legacy of this image of Luther facilitated the success of the Nazi regime by legitimating its main ideological underpinnings. The widespread view of Luther helps explain the general receptivity of the German Protestant churches and its membership to the appeal of the Nazis and Hitler as its leader. As the most current research has made painfully clear, the German Protestant church was an especially useful and cooperative tool in the coming of the Nazis to power, and once the regime was established provided continuing sources of legitimation for the regime. Of course, the German Protestant church was not a monolith, and there were serious divisions between its parts, which also translated into differing dispositions when it came to evaluating the meaning of Luther and the

---

[3] For a discussion of the mythic projections of Luther that had cultural currency in the nineteenth century, see Hartmut Lehmann, "Anmerkungen zur Entmythologisierung der Luthermythen, 1883–1983." *Archiv für Kulturgeschichte* 68 (1986): 457–77, esp. 473–6.

[4] Hanjörg Buss, in his overview of Reformation celebrations of the nineteenth and twentieth centuries, notes the following: "In dieser Zeit wurden Luthers 'Kampf gegen Rom', seine Bibelübersetzung ins Deutsche, schließlich die Person des Reformators selbst zu einem 'deutschen' Mythos" (In this era, Luther's "struggle against Rome," his bible translation into German, finally the person of the Reformer himself, became a German myth). Hansjörg Buss, "Deutsche und Luther Reformationsjubilaen im 19. und 20. Jahrhundert." In *Luther: zeitgenössisch, historisch, kontrovers*, ed. Richard Faber and Uwe Puschner (Frankfürt a.M.: Peter Lang, 2017): 29–46; 29.

[5] Ian Kershaw, *The Hitler Myth: Image and Reality in the Third Reich* (Oxford: Oxford University Press, 1987).

relationship to National Socialism.[6] However, despite such differences, in the main the view of Luther was a central cultural component that shaped the German Protestant embrace of racial nationalism, Hitler, and the Nazi regime. And when it came to the Nazi policies towards the Jews, Luther was used to affirm the prejudicial treatment of the Jews and ultimately helped enable the murderous actions of the regime. It should be noted that almost none of the shaping or styling of Luther in support of racial nationalist or National Socialist politics came from the action of the Nazi leadership, who, with a few exceptions, remained uninterested in the legacy of Luther. Rather, it was from inside Protestantism that the development of this image of Luther was crafted in the 1920s and '30s, building off the legacy of the nineteenth century, but developing and extending its features into a potent unifying structure within German Protestantism. The study will trace the development of this image, its main features during the 1920s and '30s, the way it facilitated the cooptation of German Protestantism within racial nationalist politics, and ultimately the role it played among Protestants in legitimating the rule of the Nazis.

In many ways the study takes its lead from Kershaw's study of Hitler referenced above. Protestants in the 1930s were at pains to emphasize the parallels between Luther and Hitler, and they were not without some basis upon which to build. As noted by Kershaw, right-wing politics during the Second Empire longed for a charismatic leader who would embody and lead the German nation, which parallels in striking ways the projection of Luther's image in the Second Empire and into the 1920s with its emphasis on the possibilities of his living presence as an source to revive an authentic German identity and revive its national fortunes; many of the attributes associated with Hitler by his followers and the propaganda of the Party map onto the features attributed to Luther, and by association contributed to the susceptibility of Germans for Hitler's cult of leadership. In this way the "Luther myth," though having its own dynamic, helps explain the elective affinity between broad elements within German Protestant Christianity and racial nationalist politics leading up to and into the Nazi regime.

In tracing the development and influence of Luther's image in the Weimar and National Socialist eras, some of the continuities and disjunctures of German history are thrown into relief.[7] Certainly the development of Luther's image across

---

[6] See Manfred Gailus, *Gläubige Zeiten: Religiösität im Dritten Reich* (Freiburg i.B.: Herder, 2021): esp. the sections titled "1933 als religiöses Erlebnis" (15–25), and "Die Protestanten—ein vielstimmiger, dissonanter Chor" (26–38).

[7] For an overview of the lineage of the "German" view of Luther, see the two articles by Georg Schmidt: "Der 'deutsche' Luther." In *Luther: Zankapfel zwischen den Konfessionen und Vater im Glauben*, ed. Mariano Delgado and Volker Leppin (Stuttgart: Kohlhammer, 2016): 163–81, and "Luther und die Freiheit seiner 'lieben Deutschen.'" In *Der Reformator Martin Luther 2017*, ed. Heinz Schilling (Oldenbourg: De Gruyter, 2014): 173–94. He provides an excellent contextualization of the question of Luther's influence on the cultural characteristics of Germans that militates against an overly one-dimensional narrative of meaning and influence.

the nineteenth and into the twentieth centuries highlights how nationalist sentiments evolved over this time, from liberal dreams of a Germany unified around a state that embodied their ideal of freedom, to a Germany unified by blood and iron, and yoked to the Prussian monarchy, to the Germany of World War I and its crucible of nationalism, to the unloved Weimar Republic, whose travails opened the door for the dynamic authoritarianism of National Socialism. Across all these changes the image of Luther adapts and evolves, responsive to the sentiments that were activated by the broad experiences of Protestant Germans with their state. Luther provides a microcosm in which to observe the landscape of sensibility that marked different stages along the way. The image of Luther, associated as it was in this era with a larger German identity, was especially responsive to changes in the *Zeitgeist*. In fact, Luther was frequently experienced as a spiritual presence whose influence pervaded the *Zeitgeist*; it is a distinguishing feature of the relationship to Luther across this period that he is not viewed as a figure of the past, but as someone who lives on in the collective mentality of the day, embodying it as well as providing resources for its enlivenment. This assumption explains the proclivity to project onto Luther the sensibilities of the day, to use him to ground a sense of German identity. It is also this tendency that explains the peculiarly ahistorical qualities of his image, as if he wasn't a personage of a past age, but someone who continued to live on in the present.

The vehicle for conveying this image of Luther was, given the media of this era, primarily the printed word, though public monuments, dramatic performances, historical sites, sermons and speeches were all conveyances of importance. In addition to media, Luther was especially the subject of public celebrations, carried out on the anniversaries of his birth in 1483, death in 1546, and life deeds, especially the date in 1517 conventionally understood to mark the onset of the Reformation with the vividly imagined posting of the Ninety-Five Theses. Celebrations of 1817, 1883, 1917, 1933, and 1946 will provide a rich vein of material with which to observe the development of his image, frequently associated with political developments which give unique texture to the content. Though historical and theological scholarship provide a window into the development of Luther's image, there is also a wealth of more popularized literature, from scores of published sermons and public speeches meant for a broader audience, popularized retellings of the great man's life in picture books, plays, and public observances. The market for such material was seemingly insatiable, and provides a window into popular conceptions of Luther across the entire period. Beyond the literature of the past, Luther has been and continues to be the object of scholarly inquiry, and much of what is treated in this study has been the subject of study. In particular, Hartmut Lehmann has published individual articles on the various aspects of the reception of Luther in the nineteenth and twentieth centuries, and I wish to acknowledge how much this study has benefited from his work—my footnotes bear frequent witness to his scholarship. In general, the celebration of the five-hundredth anniversary of the Reformation in 2017 led to another explosion of Luther studies, and this study, coming in its wake, had benefited greatly. Though no one has pulled the image of Luther together as is done in this study, it could not have been put together as I do without the enormous interest Luther has generated within the scholarly world.

Finally, I want to provide some notes for the reader about a specific challenge in entering the mindset of the people and culture that are the object of this study. The nineteenth and first half of the twentieth centuries saw the emergence and expansion of *völkisch* nationalism within Germany, and it left a deep imprint on German Protestantism. Throughout the study, you will encounter certain words peculiar to this mindset that I have left untranslated. First of all, the base word *Volk*.[8] While in conventional translation this is typically rendered as "people," this English word does not at all capture the resonances of the word as it was used in the era under study. The word contains within it a number of assumptions that are missing in English. Perhaps most importantly, it assumes that the *Volk* are not just a collection of individuals who have come together under some common political, social, or religious community. Rather, the *Volk* is something spiritual that inheres in the makeup its members; there are various *Völker* and they are constituted differently in their essence, or being. The origins of this way of thinking go back to the eighteenth century in Germany, particularly the work of Johann Gottfried Herder (1744–1803), but by the late nineteenth century and the advent of Darwinian biology, and in its wake Social Darwinism, the concept of the *Volk* came to be racialized, so that *völkisch* nationalism in the Wilhelmine Empire and beyond was a racialized nationalism that defined being German as a matter of genetic inheritance, though still with a spiritual superstructure. A certain vocabulary surrounds this mindset, and presents challenges for translation. For instance, *völkisch* authors frequently use the word *Deutschtum*, which references the whole of the German *Volk*. I have translated this in the study as "Germanity," which, while not a conventional English word, captures, I think, this idea of "German humanity" as a unique entity well. Most words related to the base word *Volk*, and there are a wealth of them, such as *Volkstum, Volkheit, Volkgenossen, Volkgeist*, among others, I have left untranslated and relied on the contextual discussion to decipher. The literature concerning Luther in this era is heavily imbued with this *völkisch* mindset, which tends toward a mystical definition of German identity, and is often difficult to render into the conventional language of English, and this in itself is part of the cultural imagination that projected this image. I have sought to render it as transparently but authentically as possible in the study.

The Luther Myth: The Image of Martin Luther from Religious Reformer to Völkisch *Icon*. Patrick Hayden-Roy, Oxford University Press. © Patrick Hayden-Roy 2024. DOI: 10.1093/9780198930297.003.0001

---

[8] See the article "Volk, Nation, Nationalismus, Masse." In *Geschichtliche Grundbegriffe: Historisches Lexikon zur politisch-sozialen Sprache in Deutschland*, ed. Otto Brunner, Werner Conze, Reinhart Koselleck. Vol. 7 (Stuttgart: Clett-Cotta, 1992): 141–431, esp. 347–420.

1
Luther, the "Most German of All Germans"

The making of Luther's image stretches back five hundred and more years now, back to his first appearance as a public figure, and certainly many durable features of his public profile were crafted in his lifetime, and persisted thereafter: nailing the Ninety-Five Theses to the church door in Wittenberg, throwing the papal Bull into the fire in 1520, standing before the Reichstag in Worms in 1521, among others. Luther was a media sensation from his first public exposure, and the association of the Reformation with the new media of printing was symbiotic. He was a figure to be reckoned with across the centuries. It was, however, the changes that came with the Enlightenment and the Napoleonic Wars in Germany that transposed his public image, moving him from the world of the Church and religious culture to become a symbol of Germany and Germanity,[1] especially among a developing Protestant middle class. The nationalism engendered by the successes of German armies during the Wars of Liberation sees the idea first broached of a uniquely German deity associated with the *völkisch* German virtues, within which Luther as a fighter for freedom can be situated.[2] As the century progresses, the aspirations of liberal-minded Germans for political reform of absolutist state structures is connected to possibilities of a unified German national state, at least in the period leading up to the short-circuited revolution of 1848.[3]

The failure of political reform eventually brought nationalist energies to focus on the successful geo-political machinations of Otto von Bismarck (1815–1898), whose adept use of diplomacy and warfare brought about the unification of Germany under the leadership of Prussia, giving the new German state a preponderant Protestant population and profile. This newly united German "Empire" was greatly in need of unifying symbols and ideals, a role some thought Luther fulfilled. Beginning at the start of the century, and then building across the

---

[1] As noted in the introduction, I have used the neologism "Germanity" to translate the word "*Deutschtum*," a word that attains the status of conventional language in German in the course of the nineteenth century and into the twentieth century. Though typically translated as "Germanness," I do not find that adequate to capture the resonance of the word within *völkisch* rhetoric, where it is deployed to define the spiritual essence of the German *Volk*, a German type of humanity.

[2] See Gerhard Graf, *Gottesbild und Politik: eine Studie zur Frömmigkeit in Preußen während der Freiheitskriege 1813–1815* (Göttingen: Vandenhoeck & Ruprecht, 1993): 72ff. for a discussion of Ernst Moritz Arndt and the shaping of a nationalist understanding of God in the context of the Wars of Liberation.

[3] See the discussion in Thomas Nipperdey, *Deutsche Geschichte 1800–1866. Bürgerwelt und starker Staat* (Munich: C. H. Beck, 1985): 286–313.

decades into the Second Empire, Luther takes on the status of "the most German German," one who embodies all of what supposedly characterizes the archetypal German.[4] As a composite projected by different interest groups, there are numerous idiosyncratic interpretations of this theme. And there are far too many other "Luthers" to fully trace the development of the image in a brief space. The chapter will capture certain key elements of the "most German" Luther, and suggest the means through which this image was disseminated in the public sphere, especially in the period after German unification. This will provide a basis for understanding the remarkable embrace of Luther that will mark the First World War, and especially the celebration of the four-hundredth anniversary of the Reformation in 1917. To get there, it makes sense to go back one hundred years and look at the emerging symbiosis of religion and politics that comes into some focus with the celebration of the three-hundredth anniversary of the Ninety-Five Theses in 1817.[5]

The Luther image that is projected in 1817 draws on a number of pre-existing sources. One is the understanding of the Reformation, and by extension Luther, that comes out of the Enlightenment in Germany, where it becomes a commonplace to see the Reformation as freeing the people from the yoke of superstition and the power of the Roman Church. History writing of the eighteenth century in Germany represented Luther apart from confessional and dogmatic issues typical of previous eras. For instance, in the works of Johann Lorenz Mosheim (1693–1755) Luther is represented in the image of the Enlightenment, as someone who fought for freedom in his rebellion against the Church, who modeled Christian virtues, and embodied the *pater familias*. His stand for freedom of conscience, based on an appeal to reason, did battle with medieval superstition, and paved the way for the freedom of knowledge overall.[6] This idealized image of Luther marks a secularizing of his significance which will be received and built upon in the nineteenth century, and becomes part of the stereotypes that are taken into the common culture.[7]

---

[4] See the suggestive article by Hartmut Lehmann, "Martin Luther als deutscher Nationalheld im 19. Jahrhundert." *Luther: Zeitschrift der Luthergesellschaft* 55 (1984): 53–65.

[5] Looking back one hundred years later, Hermann Scholz noted, "Am bedeutsamsten ist dann die Jubelfeier des Jahres 1817 geworden. Wir kennen und ehren sie als die Geburtsstunde der preußischen Union, dieser *magna charta* evangelischer Einheit im Geiste evangelischer Freiheit. Durch jene Feier ging ein Aufschwung, eine frohe Begeisterung, ein Hoffen und Sehnen besserer Zeiten auf." (The celebration of the 1817 has become most significant. We recognize and honor it as the hour of birth of the Prussian Union, this *magna carta* of evangelical unity in the spirit of evangelical freedom. A fresh impetus, a joyous enthusiasm, a hope and longing for better times went through this festive event). *Was wir der Reformation zu verdanken haben: Zur Vierhundertjahrfeier der Reformation* (Berlin: Verlag des Evangelischen Bundes, 1917): 8.

[6] Harold Bollbuck, "Martin Luther in der Geschichtsschreibung zwischen Reformation und Aufklärung." In *Luthermania: Ansichten einer Kultfigur*, ed. Hole Rößler (Wiesbaden: Harrassowitz, 2017): 47–68; 66–7.

[7] For a discussion that highlights literary, historical, and theological shifts in the understanding of Luther in the German Enlightenment era, see Albrecht Beutel, "Martin Luther in Urteil der deutschen

The figure of Luther as the progenitor of freedom gains additional associations during the era of the Napoleonic Wars. Johann Gottlieb Fichte (1762–1814) invokes Luther in his influential *Reden an die deutsche Nation* (Speeches to the German Nation), published in 1808, where he sees the enactment of freedom in Luther's inner self as a model for future ages:

> After he [Luther] had now won the first struggle of the anxiety of the conscience that was caused by his bold tearing away of himself from the whole faith, all his expressions are full of jubilation and triumph about the freedom gained by the children of God, which no longer sought salvation outside itself or beyond the grave, but was equivalent to the eruption of the immediate feeling. He has become in this the model of all future ages and for us brought it all to completion. You also see here an essential feature of the German spirit. When he just sought, he found more than he sought; for he was caught within the stream of enlivened life, that runs away through itself and is swept away with itself.[8]

Fichte's abstract representation of Luther's freedom of conscience that came with his understanding of God's grace reflects one of the most fundamental elements of the image of the Luther as it will develop across the nineteenth century with its idealization of this inner, spiritual event. Luther's understanding of faith is not simply an element of his life, but a spiritual achievement that resonates across the ages. His Christian freedom is secularized, and becomes the type of freedom that is inherited by ages to come, and which, as Fichte would have it, is especially resonant for Germans.

Though Fichte will not put decisive emphasis on this entwining of Luther's spiritual heroics with nationalist identity, Ernst Moritz Arndt (1769–1860) will make this a signature feature of his interpretation of Luther. Writing in 1814 in the wake of the defeat of Napoleon's Army, which enflamed nationalist sensibilities, he concludes a long section of his *Ansichten und Aussichten der Teutschen Geschichte* ("Views and Perspectives on German History") by noting the degree to which what drove Luther, his "all penetrating and inflammable Spirit," came at a time in the past not ready for it. But, Arndt asserts, his current age is ripe: "But peace be upon your ashes, great German man! and may the earth cover your flaws, and

---

Aufklärung: Beobachtungen zu einem epochalen Paradigmenwechsel." In *Martin Luther: Monument, Ketzer, Mensch*, ed. Andreas Holzem and Volker Leppin (Freiburg: Herder, 2017): 215–46.

[8] "Nachdem er nun die ersten Kämpfe der Gewissensangst, die ihm sein kühnes Losreißen von dem ganzen Glauben verursachte, bestanden hatte, sind alle seine Äußerungen voll eines Jubels und Triumphs über die erlangte Freiheit der Kinder Gottes, welche die Seligkeit gewiß nicht mehr außer sich und jenseits des Grabes suchten, sondern der Ausbruch des unmittelbaren Gefühls derselben waren. Er ist hierin das Vorbild aller künftigen Zeitalter geworden und hat für uns alle vollendet. Sehen Sie auch hier einen Grundzug des deutschen Geistes. Wenn er nur sucht, so findet er mehr, als er suchte; den er gerät hinein in den Strom lebendigen Lebens, das durch sich selbst fortrinnt und ihn mit sich fortreißt." Heinrich Bornkamm, *Luther im Spiegel der deutschen Geistesgeschichte*. 2nd ed. (Göttingen: Vandenhoeck & Ruprecht, 1970): 223.

may Christian love cover your mistakes! may God awaken in us in this age—which must be the last years of laziness and catalepsy—a brave, faithful, and pious man, of German sensibilities like you, all passing through God and the *Volk*! Thus, again, your memory revives!"[9] This somewhat cryptic gush of emotion connecting Luther's spiritual inspiration with the revival of the German *Volk* in the aftermath of its victories over the reviled French anticipates the powerful combination of nationalist enthusiasm and idealized Luther "influence" that will mark his image going forward. Enlightenment associations of Luther with freedom, the nationalist upwellings of the Wars of Liberation, and the heroic image of Luther's great Reformation actions will come together in the celebration of the three-hundredth anniversary of the Ninety-Five Theses in 1817.

Sermons and public addresses held during this celebration picked up on this complex of associations and expanded upon them; Luther is portrayed as the liberator from political servitude in the field of faith and thought, the one who bound the tyrants, the savior of the people, freeing them from profound enslavement.[10] With this formula the Reformation and Luther's actions dealt not simply with issues of religious truth, but held significance for the ennoblement and liberation of humanity. The issue was not so much what did Luther teach, but what did his actions and words symbolize within a larger schema of human development.[11] The implications of the Reformation, in this perspective, involved the development of a set of secularized values useful for the economic progress of society, and the creation of the corresponding household of solid German burgers.[12] His steadiness, moral earnestness, industrious labor, and devotion to family were highlighted. For the most part the implications of his rebellious actions were circumscribed in ways that avoided calling into question obedience to the duly authorized authorities. As with Enlightenment portrayals of Luther, it is noteworthy that this image has little to do with any specific religious or doctrinal issue, and plots the events of Luther's life and his virtues onto early nineteenth-century bourgeois sensibilities and the general socio/political landscape.

The valorization of Luther contained within these works is remarkably general and distanced from anything specific to his life or teachings in particular.[13] This broad construction of him as a symbol defines an essential element in the development of the nineteenth-century view of Luther, in that it projects onto him

---

[9] "Doch Friede sei mit deiner Asche, großer teutscher Mann! und deine Mängel bedecke die Erde und deine Fehler die christliche Liebe! uns aber erwecke Gott in diesen Zeiten, welche die letzten Jahre der Faulheit und Starrsucht sein müßten, einen muthigen, gläubigen und frommen Mann, teutsch gesinnt wie du und durch Gott und das Volk alles hindurchführend! So lebe dein Gedächtniß wider auf!" *Martin Luther in der deutschen bürgerlichen Philosophie 1517–1845: Eine Textsammlung.* Werner Schuffenhauer and Klaus Steiner, eds. (Berlin: Akademie-Verlag, 1983): 381.
[10] See the discussion of Lutz Winckler, *Martin Luther als Bürger und Patriot: Das Reformationsjubiläum von 1817 und der politische Protestantismus des Wartburgfestes* (Lübeck, Hamburg: Matthiesen, 1969): 20–1.
[11] Winckler, *Bürger und Patriot*, 22.   [12] Winckler, *Bürger und Patriot*, 25–6.
[13] Winckler, *Bürger und Patriot*, 30–4.

attitudes, characteristics, and implications that are only loosely connected to the historical personage. This remaking of him as symbol is emblematic of the developments of the nineteenth into the twentieth century. Further, this secularized image of Luther exists in 1817, as will be the case going forward, with more traditionally minded projections, which emphasize the religious significance of his life and acts, and which reside in an awkward relationship with the image influenced by Enlightenment ideals.[14] It is worth noting, as well, that some rulers within the German lands were reluctant to highlight the celebration of 1817 for fear of disturbing the Catholic part of their population, and some of the public addresses reflect this concern.[15] Luther was not fully disentangled as yet from the specifically theological controversies of the sixteenth century to serve as a symbol of unity; for just this reason, Goethe suggested moving the date of the three-hundredth anniversary celebrations back to October 18, and the victory over Napoleon at Leipzig, which all Germans could celebrate.[16]

Though most of the celebrations took place on the traditional date of October 31, the most striking episode of the 1817 celebration, and for the development of the image of Luther most instructive, was the celebration held at the Wartburg on the anniversary of the Battle of Leipzig, a couple of weeks prior to the widespread celebrations. The event involved the *Burschenschaften*, the nationalist movement among university students that had sprung up in the wake of the Wars of Liberation and led to the formation of corporative student societies. It was the first of these societies at the University at Jena that instigated the national meeting at the Wartburg. The 350–450 or so student participants came preponderantly from Jena, but also from across the German-speaking states; almost every German university was represented.[17] By combining in the event the recent memory of victory over Napoleon's army with the celebration of the onset of the Reformation, and doing so in one of the most "holy" sites of Luther's career, where he rendered the New Testament into living German, the students' celebration connected with a rich set of possible meanings. The Napoleonic Wars, and particularly the victory of German armies over the Grand Armée at Leipzig, was a unifying event for Germans as a whole, and the context for the first stirrings of a German nationalist religiosity that would resonate across the nineteenth century.

The Wartburg celebration provided the opportunity to connect this nationalist religiosity with the figure of Luther, who famously translated the New Testament

---

[14] Winckler, *Bürger und Patriot*, 40–3.
[15] Wichman von Meding, "'Jubel ohne Glauben?' Das Reformationsjubiläum von 1817 in Württemberg." *Zeitschrift für Kirchengeschichte* 93 (1982): 119–60.
[16] Hartmut Lehmann, "Martin Luther und der 31. Oktober 1517." In *Luthergedächtnis 1817–2017*, ed. Hartmut Lehmann (Göttingen: Vandenhoeck & Ruprecht, 2012): 16–34; 22–3.
[17] See the "Einladungsschreiben der Jenaischen Burschenschaft an die protestantischen Universitäten Deutschlands. An die Hochschulen zu Berlin, Breslau, Erlangen, Gießen, Göttingen, Greifswald, Heidelberg, Kiel, Königsberg, Leipzig, Marburg, Rostock, Tübingen." *Das Wartburgfest am 18. Oktober 1817. Zeitgenössische Darstellungen und Urkunden*, ed Hugo Kühn. (Weimar: Alexander Duncker Verlag, 1913): 11.

into German during his Wartburg exile.[18] The figure of Luther as a German nationalist broached at the Wartburg Fest brings into focus a set of associations with him that will become dominant in the course of the 1800s. Using strikingly emotion-laden language, the addresses at the Wartburg fest portrayed Luther as an eternal memorial to German bravery (*Mut*), German power, German honor, one who inspired the Germans with his words and heroic deeds.[19] This theme is announced in the opening speech to the collected students by Jena philosopher Jakob Friedrich Fries (1773–1843):[20] "German youth! You stand on consecrated soil. What consecration? It was here that Luther, that man of God, gave the German word of eternal truth to the German *Volk*!—and sparked the struggle, the bloody struggle for spiritual freedom and the equality of citizens!"[21] He follows this inspirational opening by situating Luther's actions within their long-term influence:

> This herald also took hold, alarmingly, of the rough, yet healthy energy of our forebearers and led them to faith. Soon, however, in the place of heavenly truth and earthly justice and love stepped the rule of the Roman monks, who covered over the truth with their dead speech and sold the comforts of faith for money. Many witnesses of God, upon whom was outpoured the spirit of truth and justice, fought against the power of darkness and died, until finally the spirit of truth freed our places of learning from the power of the monks, and paved the way for the victor, who at Wittenberg cursed the law of the monks and the monk's crown of atonement and brought devotion and truth to the *Volk* in their living language. And wherever Luther's victorious call sounded, there awoke a free spiritual life in service to truth and justice! The herald that propelled him, also propelled through him all the power of the *Volk* of the last centuries toward the education of the German spirit and toward all unbinding of thought, all equalization of the rights of citizens, beginning with what happened in the Netherlands up to the free states in North America.[22]

---

[18] Winckler, *Bürger und Patriot*, 48–52.   [19] Winckler, *Bürger und Patriot*, 56.
[20] Fries was one of the main sponsors of the *Burschenschaft* at Jena. A decided liberal and nationalist, he would later be removed from his professorate at Jena and have a publication ban placed on him as a result of his actions at Jena and elsewhere. See Lüder Gäbe, "Fries, Jakob Friedrich." In *Neue Deutsche Biographie*. Vol. 5 (Berlin: Duncker & Humboldt, 1961): 608ff.
[21] "Deutsche Jünglinge! Ihr steht auf dem Boden der Weihe. Welcher Weihe? Von hier gab Luther, der Mann Gottes, das deutsche Wort der ewigen Wahrheit dem deutschen Volk!—Und entzündete den Kampf, den blutigen Kampf um Geistesfreiheit, Bürgergleichheit!" "Rede an die deutschen Burschen. Zum 18. October 1817. Von Hofrath Fries." In *Das Wartburgfest am 18. Oktober 1817*, 50.
[22] "Beängstigend hat dieser Verkünder auch unsrer Vorfahren die rauhe, doch gesunde Kraft ergriffen und sie zum Glauben geführt. Aber an die Stelle himmlischer Wahrheit und irdischer Gerechtigkeit und Liebe trat bald römische Mönchsherrschaft, verhüllte die Wahrheit in ihre todte Sprache und verkaufte Glaubenstrost um Geld. Viel Zeugen Gottes, über die der Geist der Wahrheit und Gerechtigkeit ausgegossen wurde, kämpften gegen die Macht der Finsterniß und erlagen, bis endlich der Geist der Wahrheit unsre hohen Schulen von der Macht der Mönche befreyte und so dem Sieger den Weg bahnte, der zu Wittenberg der Mönche Recht, der Mönche Entsündigungskrone verfluchte und dem Volke in seiner lebendigen Sprache Andacht und Weisheit brachte.—Und wohin

12   THE LUTHER MYTH

This divinely inspired force for spiritual ennoblement and political liberation for the *Volk* provided a heady brew for the gathered students, leading into an exhortatory call to stand and fight with Luther for the extension of such liberation to all within the German fatherland.

The keynote address by Heinrich Riemann (1793–1872, student from Jena and one of the founders of the *Burschenschaft*,[23] puts an even sharper focus onto Luther. Announcing the goals of the gathering, he identifies above all the communal project of disinterring the image of the past to inspire their souls, creating from the power of this past image living actions for the present. To that end he directs them to the image of Luther:

> In the fulness of time God awakened from within the dark walls of an Augustinian cloister a man who was to proclaim a better teaching, who would tip over the money-lender tables of the Roman church, freeing the world of the most shameful of all shackles, the shackles of the spirit. Armed with great virtue and qualities, Luther stepped forth, full of trust in God and fear of God, without fear of humans, shaking with enormous power the Roman stones down to their foundations, boldly putting forward the statement that faith is a free thing to which no one can be forced, for each must face their own danger in how they believe, and must see for themselves that they believe rightly. Through his undoing of this great abuse, he worked for the good of all *Völker*, but most of all for his German *Volk*, for whom he translated the Holy Scripture, to whom he gave the German church service, to whom he opened up the inexhaustible treasures of their language. This accomplishment alone has already made him immortal. Don't criticize him as if he brought forth the division and conflict within his *Volk*; his opponents were guilty of that, who didn't deign to recognize divine and human law. Therefore he should be praised by us as the first and greatest man of his time, as the man of God and of the *Volk*, whose name lives inextinguishably in the heart of his *Volk*, just as iron and stone can preserve him.[24]

Luthers siegender Ruf erscholl, da erwachte freyes Geistesleben im Dienste der Wahrheit und Gerechtigkeit! Der Verkündiger, der ihn trieb, trieb durch ihn alle Volkskraft der letzten Jahrhunderte zu deutscher Geistesbildung und zu aller Entfesselung des Gedankens, aller Ausgleichung der Bürgerrechte, von dem an, was in den Niederlanden geschah bis zu den Freistaaten in Nordamerika!" *Das Wartburgfest am 18. Oktober 1817*, 51.

[23] Like many who participated at the Wartburg, Riemann would later suffer legal prosecution as a result, being briefly imprisoned by Prussian authorities, though he went onto a long career as pastor and advocate for liberal ideals. See Peter Hoffmann, *Heinrich Arminius Riemann. Lehrer, Pastor, Demokrat* (Friedland: Steffen, 2006). Available online at https://www.burschenschaftsgeschichte.de/pdf/hofmann_riemann.pdf

[24] "Als aber die Zeit erfüllet war, da erweckte Gott aus den dunklen Mauern eines Augustiner-Klosters einen Mann, zu verkünden eine bessere Lehre, umzustürzen die römischen Wechslertische, die Welt zu befreien von den schmählichsten aller Fesseln, den Geistesfesseln. Ausgerüstet mit großen Tugenden und Eigenschaften, trat Luther auf, voll Gottvertrauen und Gottesfurcht, ohne Menschenfurcht; erschütterte mit Riesenkraft den römischen Fels bis in seine Grundfesten, kühn aufstellend den Satz: daß es ein frei Ding sei um den Glauben, darzu man niemand könne zwingen,

We see with these speeches at the Wartburg the broaching of a Luther whose religious work epitomizes a German spiritual sensibility that is captured in language and in the image of the *Volk*, an image that has the power to inspire youth to fight for freedom and truth. Other speeches in 1817 extend this sense of Luther, depicting him as the progenitor of a German national revival and embodiment of an idealized German type through his religious rebellion against the errors of the Roman Church. Christian Wilhelm Spieker (1780–1858), Professor of Theology at Frankfurt/Oder, captured this vividly in an address he gave in 1817:

> Of all the *Völker* of the earth none are more worthy of the character of Luther or understand the Reformation better than the German *Volk*; for Luther is a man of the *Volk* and his work Germanic. Only a people so free, noble, pious, and brave as ours could have nurtured a Luther. He is German in work and deed, in sensibility and spirit, in public and domestic life, in his virtues and shortcomings. He belongs to us; he is our pride and joy. The German language and German faith have in him their most solid foundation.[25]

The idea of Christianity having different national characteristics had become a commonplace in the early nineteenth century. Spieker took this further in attributing to Luther, and, by extension, the German people, not only a distinctive religiosity, but a religiosity that exceeded that of other people in its receptivity to the Reformation and in its virtuousness. This idea of a strong affinity between the spirit of the German *Volk* and the inner spirit of Christianity, embodied in Luther's words, deeds, and identity, will form a cornerstone within the continuing celebration of him as the "most German" German. And in emphasizing Luther's virtues and his role in the development of German as a language, Spieker and Riemann remove him from the doctrinal and theologically controverted context of the Reformation, and appeal to a broader sense of German pride and patriotism.[26]

---

denn einem jeglichen liege seine eigne Gefahr daran, wie er glaube, und müsse jeder sich sehen, daß er recht glaube. Durch Abschaffung vieler großen Mißbräuche wirkte er wohlthätig für alle Völker, am meisten aber für sein deutsches Volk, dem er die heilige Schrift, dem er den Gottesdienst deutsch gab, dem er den unendlich reichen Schatz seiner Sprache aufschloß. Schon dies Verdienst hat ihn unsterblich gemacht. Tadelt ihn nicht, als habe er seines Volkes Zwietracht und Zerrissenheit herbeigeführt, das war die Schuld seiner Gegner, die göttliches und menschliches Recht anzuerkennen verschmähten. Darum soll er auch von uns gepriesen werden als der erste und größte Mann seiner Zeit, als der Mann Gottes und des Volks, des Name unverlöschlicher in seiner Volkes Herzen lebt, als Erz und Stein ihn aufbewahren können." *Das Wartburgfest am 18. Oktober 1817*, 57–8.

[25] "Von allen Völkern der Erde wird keines den Charakter Luthers richtiger würdigen und den Geist der Reformation besser verstehen, als das Deutsche; denn Luther ist ein Mann des Volks und sein Werk deutscher Art. Nur ein so freies, edles, frommes, und tapferes Volk als das unsrige, konnte einen Luther erzeugen. Er ist deutsch in Wort und That, in Sinn und Gemüth, im öffentlichen und häuslichen Leben, in seinen Tugenden und Fehlern. Er gehört uns an; er ist unser Stolz und unsere Freude. Deutsche Sprache und deutscher Glaube haben an ihm ihre festeste Stütze." Winckler, *Bürger und Patriot*, 56–7.

[26] On shaping of Luther as a figure useful for building nationalist sentiment see the comments of Friederike Krippner, "Der 'deutscheste Mann unserer Geschichte.' Luther im nationalen Diskurs zu

This overtly patriotic take on Luther was able in the context of 1817 to reside together with liberal calls for reforms to secure political and cultural freedoms as well as more tradition-minded pieties. In all the year 1817 marks a number of departure points for the development of Luther's image going forward. The variety of possible meanings attributed to Luther reflects the variety of uses to which his image could be put. The trajectories reflect the contemporary forces at work, from the Luther who could embody enlightenment ideals of progress and freedom, the Luther who embodied the ideals and virtues of the emerging nineteenth-century model burger, the Luther who embodied nationalist German ideals and sensibilities—the man of the *Volk*—and even the one who could stand for political reform, as well as the traditional man of faith. All these projections of his meaning found a place in 1817, and interacted in a somewhat confusing mélange. For the most part they were projected with little attention to the actual writings or historical context of his life, but rather served exhortatory purposes for the audiences of the celebration. This highlights a continuing feature of Luther's image, which is as a free-floating signifier who may be put to work for any number of purposes. To the extent that German liberalism and German nationalism worked together in the course of the nineteenth century, these two versions of Luther could work in tandem, but the events of the second half of the century would diminish the utility of a Luther who stood for political, as opposed to spiritual, freedom, and greatly enhance the dissemination of Luther as the ideal symbol of a spiritualized German nationalism, adding new dimensions along the way.

The ubiquity of Luther as symbol in the nineteenth century can be seen in the engagement of some of the most significant philosophical and literary figures with his meaning. In his *Vorlesungen über die Geschichte der Philosophie*, G. F. W. Hegel (1770–1831) gave the Reformation and Luther's place within it the status of bringing into being the spiritual foundations of the modern world. Within his larger philosophical structure, the Reformation and Luther's actions represented the beginning of the freedom of the spirit that was the basis for the subjective self and its freedom of will and conscience. Luther symbolizes the world-historical turn of the spirit that for Hegel was the departure point for the modern world. And because Hegel yoked this spiritual evolution to the outward world of politics as it was unrolling in the nineteenth century, Luther himself becomes a symbol whose significance is related to such changes. The almost mystical significance that later commentators will come to attach to the symbol of Luther, the disembodiment of his symbol from his actual historical existence, follows from the treatment Hegel makes of Luther.[27] And the association of him

---

Beginn der 19. Jahrhundert." In *Das Imaginäre der Nation. Zur Persistenz einer politischen Katagorie im Literatur und Film*, ed. Katharina Grabbe et al. (Bielefeld: transcript Verlag, 2012): 105–30; 107–9.

[27] For an orientation to Hegel's treatment within the larger development of Luther's image in the nineteenth century, as well as selections from his writings, see Heinrich Bornkamm, *Luther im Spiegel der deutschen Geistesgeschichte*. 2nd ed. (Göttingen: Vandenhoeck and Ruprecht, 1970): 31–5;

as spiritual embodiment of the German national state sets the stage for his use in the later nineteenth century.

Contemporary to Hegel's idealist image of Luther, Heinrich Heine (1797–1856) painted a literary portrait of Luther which is philosophically much less high-flown, but attributes to Luther some equally significant characteristics which reflect the development of Luther's profile into the middle of the nineteenth century. Heine was intrigued by Luther, and commented on him in many of his writings.[28] In his *Zur Geschichte der Religion und Philosophie in Deutschland*, written during his time in Paris, he sought to explain the unique attributes of Luther that made him, according to Heine, "not just the greatest, but also the most German man of our history."[29] He explains this with reference to the way Luther reconciled in his person seemingly fundamental contradictions: the dreamy mystic with the practical man of action; a scholastic word chopper and a God-possessed prophet; he could swear like a fishmonger's wife or be as soft as a sensitive maiden.

> He was a complete human, I'd like to say, an absolute human, in which spirit and materiality were not divided. It would be as erroneous to term him a spiritualist as it would a sensualist. How should I put it, he had something primal, ungraspable, miraculous, as we find it by all providentially chosen men, something eerily naïve, something doltishly clever, something sublimely narrow-minded, something invincibly demonic.[30]

As with the Enlightenment, Heine praises Luther for breaking the chains of the medieval Church, creating the circumstances with his appeal to conscience and reason for the demystifying of the world, along with which has come the progress of the natural sciences. He highlights further not only this freedom of thought, but also the gift of the German literary language which came with the translation of the Bible into German. He notes how this literary language was disseminated in a bible which even the common people had and from which they learned: "this circumstance will, if it comes to a revolution in Germany, have as a result really

---

249–58. See also the comments of Michael Basse, "Luthers Geschichtsverständnis und dessen Rezeption im Kontext der Reformationsjubiläen von 1817 und 1917." *Lutherjahrbuch* 69 (2002): 47–70; 61–2.

[28] See Johann M. Schmidt, "Heine und Luther: Heines Lutherrezeption in der Spannung zwischen den Daten 1483–1933." *Heine-Jahrbuch* 24 (1985): 9–79.

[29] "…daß Luther nicht bloß der größte, sondern auch der deutscheste Mann unserer Geschichte ist." In *Martin Luther in der deutschen bürgerlichen Philosophie, 1517–1845: eine Textsammlung*, ed. Werner Schuffenhauer and Klaus Steiner (Berlin: Akademie Verlag, 1983): 394.

[30] "Er war ein kompletter Mensch, ich möchte sagen, ein absoluter Mensch, in welchem Geist und Materie nicht getrennt sind. Ihn einen Spiritualisten zu nennen wäre daher ebenso irrig, als nennte man ihn einen Sensualisten. Wie soll ich sagen, er hatte etwas Ursprüngliches, Unbegreifliches, Mirakulöses, wie wir es bei alle providentiellen Männern finden, etwas Schauerlich-Naives, etwas Töpelhaft-Kluges, etwas Erhaben-Borniertes, etwas Unbezwingbar-Dämonisches." Schuffenhauer and Steiner, 394.

remarkable implications. Freedom will be able to be spoken everywhere, and its language will be biblical."[31] He ends his excursus on Luther by noting his cultural significance, whose hymns are the Marseilles of the Reformation, the inspirational power of which are still felt to the present.

Heine's piece is shot through with irony, but nevertheless captures the power of Luther's image by the 1830s and its association as a monument of German identity. It is instructive the time he spends on Luther as a means of explaining Germany to his French audience. It is instructive, as well, to note how Heine, the converted Jew and expatriate German (at the time), would be so drawn to the confounding figure of Luther. Heine's attraction to Luther, and his perception that Luther stands in a tradition of "altgermanischen Pantheismus" ("old-Germanic pantheism"), reflects the malleable nature of Luther's image in the course of the nineteenth century, being made over as both an advocate of political freedom and freedom of thought.[32] The nationalist profile he draws of Luther—"the most German of all Germans"—will later be a catch-phrase in the works of lesser authors whose crude remodeling of Luther into the emblem of the bigoted patriot will be used to attack the enlightened values associated with the converted Jew Heine and his literary legacy.

In addition to philosophical and literary expositors of the mythic Luther, the nineteenth century saw a flood of public memorials that embodied the stereotyped great man image.[33] The first of these, and as it were the first non-noble public statue in Germany, was dedicated in Wittenberg in 1821. This statue, and the other public representations of Luther, signify the increasing civic and public significance of his image; unlike previous eras, his image is not contained in

---

[31] "Dieser Umstand wird, wenn bei uns die politsche Revolution ausbricht, gar merkwürdige Erscheinungen zur Folge haben. Die Freiheit wird überall sprechen können, und ihre Sprache wird biblisch sein." Schuffenhauer and Steiner, 397.

[32] See the comments of Markus Winkler, *Mythisches Denken zwischen Romantik und Realismus: Zur Erfahrung kultureller Fremdheit im Werk Heinrich Heines* (Tübingen: Max Niemeyer Verlag, 1995): 135-6.

[33] For a suggestive discussion of the development of the cult of personality in nineteenth century that provides background to the mentality animating a public cult of "great men" see Thomas Kaufmann, "Protestantisch-theologische Wurzeln des 'Personenkultes' im 19. Jahrhundert?" In Thomas Kaufmann, *Aneignungen Luthers und der Reformation: Wissenschaftsgeschichtliche Beiträge zum 19.-21. Jahrhundert* (Tübingen: Mohr Siebeck, 2022): 36-57. Kaufmann points out the tension between a mentality that affirms the ennobling effects of cultic remembrances of the great, which grows out of the increasing skepticism about orthodox soteriology and the divine status of Jesus, and conservative Protestant affirmation of a more biblically grounded anthropology of humanity rooted in traditional Protestant religiosity. One striking feature of the development of Luther's image in the nineteenth century is how dominant the "great man" image became in competition with the conservative Lutheran focus on his theological legacy. See pages 48–54. As we will see, by the start of the twentieth century, conservative Lutheran circles will have imbibed the rhetoric of Luther the secular hero, for the most part. In addition, Kaufmann points out that only with Luther do we find artifacts and places associated with him continually preserved and used as remembrances to honor his legacy from the sixteenth clear through into the nineteenth century. In this sense, the expansion of his cult of remembrance in the nineteenth century rested upon an existing body of places and practices. See pages 44–8.

churches, but inhabits the public square, and is connected with the larger history of the German people. The figure itself represents what will become a somewhat static portrayal across the century, as a berobed Luther stands engaging the viewer with a stolid expression, the German Bible held prominently in his hands, and his left foot placed forward in a solid stance.[34] Such public statuary had previously been the reserved for nobility and crown, not non-noble subjects; with the 1821 Wittenberg statue, the Prussian crown actually intervened to require a housing (*Baldachin*), which made it look more like the statuary within a "sacred" structure, suggesting the crown's awareness of how such a non-noble symbol might potentially be in competition with their own symbolic centrality. Though other public statuary won't be dedicated until the 1860s, after German reunification in 1871 there will be a flood of Luther statues, some of monumental scale, which trace the expansion of his symbolic presence.[35] Other testaments to the increasing power of Luther's public presence can be seen in the commemorative artifacts of the mid-1800s: from porcelain pieces with scenes of or from the life of the great Doctor, to "living" commemorations where sites associated with his life were restored as homes for troubled youth in Weimar and Erfurt, the restoration of sites key to the heroic or exemplary aspects of his life, such as the Wartburg in Coburg, or the Luther House in Wittenberg, to the monumental revision of the *Schlosskirche* in Wittenberg[36] or the herculean attempts to publish Luther's works with the Erlangen Edition and then finally, beginning in 1883, with that most epic of all editions, the *Weimarer Ausgabe*, intended itself as a major stimulant to further engagement with Luther.[37]

---

[34] See Albrecht Geck, "Luthererinnerung im Zeichen von Aufklärung und Emanzipation." In *Ketzer, Held und Prediger: Martin Luther im Gedächtnis der Deutschen*, ed. Marcel Nieden (Darmstadt: Wissenschaftliche Buchgesellschaft, 2017): 83–117; 116.

[35] See Tim Lorentzen, "19. Jahrhundert Nationale, konfessionelle und touristische Errinnerugskulturen." In *Ketzer, Held und Prediger: Martin Luther im Gedächtnis der Deutschen*, ed. Marcel Nieden (Darmstadt: Wissenschaftliche Buchgesellschaft, 2017): 119–69; 156-63. Also Jutta Schuchard, "Luther auf dem Postament: Gedanken und Überlegungen zu Lutherdenkmälern." In *"Der fühlt der Zeiten ungeheuren Bruch und fest umklammert er sein Bibelbuch…": Zum Lutherkult im 19 Jahrhundert*, ed. Hardy Eidam and Gerhard Seib (Berlin: Schelzky & Jeep, 1996): 73–88; and Christian Tümperl, "Zur Geschichte der Luther-Denkmäler." In *Luther in der Neuziet*, ed. Bernd Moeller (Gütersloh: Gerd Mohn, 1983): 227–47.

[36] On the various commemorative sites that were restored and served to capture Luther's legacy see Martin Steffens, *Luthergedenkstätten im 19. Jahrhundert. Memoria-Repräsentation-Denkmalpflege* (Regensburg: Schnell & Steiner, 2008).

[37] In the forward to the first volume, published in 1883, we find the following: "Denkmale von Erz sind dem Reformator in Wittenberg und Worms errichtet…. Wir gehen an einen anderen Bau, zu dem er selbst den Stoff geliefert. 'Luthers Werke,' sagt der Nestor der jetzigen Kirchenhistoriker, 'sind so gut ein deutsches National Denkmal als der Kölner Dom'" (Monuments of metal for the Reformer have been erected in Wittenberg and Worms…we are starting another edifice, to which he contributed the material itself. '*Luther's Works*', says the Nestor of church historians, 'are just as much a national monument as the Cologne Dome'). *D. Martin Luthers Werke: Kritische Gesammteausgabe*. Vol. 1 (Weimar: Hermann Bölhau, 1883): XV. At the end of the foreword the editor dedicates the edition to the "Herzen und Leben unseres Volkes!" (XXII).

The development of history writing in the nineteenth century, associated especially in Germany with the figure of Leopold von Ranke (1795–1886), took up the evolving image of Luther. Ranke himself put great weight in his account of the Reformation on the world-historical significance of Luther's actions, seeing the Reformation as the dividing line between medieval and modern, somewhat similarly to Hegel. Looking back in 1875 to his monumental work on the Reformation, he noted: "I believed that in History of the Reformation I had brought to consciousness that act of the German spirit, through which the nation had most clearly documented its inner unity."[38] By the time we get to this comment, profound changes in the outward circumstances of Germany as a political entity had taken place with German unification under the leadership of Prussia and Otto von Bismarck. What had long been anticipated and longed for among many German liberals came to fruition, though not under the force of liberal political ideals, but the blood and iron of warfare. The force of the victory over France led to the proclamation of a new Empire under the crown of the Hohenzollern. In the emerging field of historical "science" in the nineteenth century, the formation of nation states was viewed, whether in England, France, or the United States, as the teleological end point of the purpose of history itself, as reflected in Ranke's comment above. And among liberal Protestant leaders, the coming of the new state was greeted with enthusiasm.[39]

What is of particular note for the developing image of Luther is the degree he becomes utilized as an image to what defines the "spirit" of this new German state and its people. While the Hohenzollern ruler was now crowned the Kaiser of the new German Empire, the new state lacked a central identity; aside from Prussian military prowess, the new state had need of symbolic integration, a role to which Luther would be deployed. In addition, Protestantism itself was divided between liberal and conservative wings.[40] This integrating role for Luther becomes abundantly clear in the celebration in 1883 of the four-hundredth anniversary of his birthday. This provided the basis for an outpouring of speeches, books, public displays, and commemorative monuments (among them the Weimar Edition

---

[38] "Ich glaubte in der Geschichte der Reformation den Akt des deutschen Geistes zum Bewußtsein gebracht zu haben, durch welchen die Nation ihre innere Einheit am meisten dokumentiert hatte." Quoted in Bornkamm, *Luther im Spiegel...*, 48. Bornkamm notes, however, that Ranke meant this not metaphysically but historically.

[39] Frank Becker, "Protestantische Euphorien 1870/71, 1914, 1933." In *Nationalprotestantische Mentalitäten*, ed. Manfred Galius and Hartmut Lehmann (Göttingen: Vandenhoeck & Ruprecht, 2005): 19–44. In addition, see the article of Günter Brakelmann, "Der Krieg 1870/71 und die Reichsgründung im Urteil des Protestantismus." In *Kirche zwischen Krieg und Frieden. Studien zur Geschichte des deutschen Protestantismus*, ed. Wolfgang Huber and Johannes Schwerdtfeger (Stuttgart: Ernst Klett Verlag, 1976): 293–320. Brakelmann notes, page 305, how the victory of the German armies and the Hohenzollern crown over France was perceived in sermons delivered at this time as a victory of evangelical freedom over French Catholicism, of Luther over the Pope.

[40] See the discussion of Martin Greschat, "Der Held der Nation: Die Gestalt Luthers im Kaiserreich." In *Luther in Seiner Zeit*, ed. Martin Greschat and Günther Lottes (Stuttgart: W. Kohlhammer, 1997): 107–26.

noted above) that overshadowed by far anything so far seen in the nineteenth century.[41] Though there were a variety of images of Luther that got projected during the celebration of his birthday,[42] there was a strong nationalist theme that ran through almost all of them. The celebration took place not only in the context of the recent reunification, but also with the still resonating *Kulturkampf* against the influence of Catholicism in the new Germany. The Hohenzollern were Protestants and head of the Prussian unified Protestant church, and the celebration was authorized and carried out under the aegis of Wilhelm I.[43] Protestant religiosity was viewed by the crown as an integrating identity feature of the Empire, and a cornerstone of their own legitimacy as rulers. This ideal of political and religious symbiosis was given strong expression in the famous Luther lecture commemorating his four-hundredth birthday delivered by Heinrich von Treitschke and published in his *Preußische Jahrbücher*.[44]

Trieitschke's treatment of Luther is worth some extended study, not because it is typical for the celebration in 1883—he gives voice to the liberal nationalist Protestant view—but because it embodies so many of the features of the image of Luther that will become staples of later eras; as Hartmut Lehmann notes, Treitschke's Luther has a remarkably long life.[45] Treitschke was Ranke's successor as Professor of History in Berlin, and as such represents the lineage of nineteenth-century historical scholarship in Germany. Like Ranke, his focus is on the political development of the nation, but his work now deals with a German nation that has come into being as an imperial, Protestant-dominated state. In 1883 Treitschke had just recently set off a public debate about the place of Jewish citizens in the Second Empire with a piece in the *Preußische Jahrbücher*, of which he was editor, which called into question the impact of Jews on the new Germany, questioning their place in this new German nation, and famously stating that "the Jews are our misfortune (*Die Juden sind unser Unglück*)."[46] His 1883 lecture on Luther shared in the same nationalistic spirit, though in this instance the anti-Semitic

---

[41] Hans Düfel, "Das Lutherjubiläum 1883." *Zeitschrift für Kirchengeschichte* 95 (1984): 1–94. In addition to the Weimar Edition of Luther's work, which provided continuing stimulus to scholarly engagement, it is noteworthy that the *Verein für Reformationgeschichte* was also founded in 1883.

[42] Hartmut Lehmann, "Das Lutherjubiläum 1883." In *Luthers Bleibende Bedeutung*, ed. Jürgen Becker (Husum: Husum Druck und Verlagsgesellschaft, 1983): 93–116.

[43] Hans Düfel, "Das Lutherjubiläum 1883," 27.

[44] Heinrich von Treitschke, "Luther und die Deutschen." *Preußische Jahrbücher* 52 (1883): 469–86.

[45] Harmut Lehmann, "'Er ist wie selber: der ewige Deutsche': Zur langanhaltenden Wirkung der Lutherdeutung von Heinrich von Treitschke." In *"Gott mit uns": Nation, Religion und Gewalt im 19. und frühen 20. Jahrhundert*, ed. Gerd Krumreich and Hartmut Lehmann (Göttingen: Vandenhoeck & Ruprecht, 2000): 91–103. Greschat, "Der Held der Nation," notes that the national liberal viewpoint was refuted in some publications in 1883 as betraying the specifically religious significance of Luther and his theological legacy. But he also notes that in the years that followed, even when celebrating such a legacy of faith, the ideas and vocabulary of the nationalist Luther are integrated into their presentation. See pages 119–20.

[46] *Preußische Jahrbücher*, November 1879.

tones remain beneath the surface,[47] as he sought to define Luther as one whose person and actions bless Germany, and who embodied in himself the fundamental qualities of the true German. He consistently frames Luther in explicitly nationalistic political/cultural terms, starting by noting the recent unveiling of the massive Germania monument, which leads him to reflect on the course of German history, and the lack of heroes whose deeds could inspire all Germans. In a sense his talk will turn Luther into an epic memorial, depicting him, like the Germania, as a monumental symbol of German unity and nationhood.

He followed this opening by reflecting on Luther and his deeds, showing how those who are still immune to his greatness are missing his relevance for all of Germany, not just for the Protestants. Treitschke was clearly involved in mythmaking with a purpose, aware of the lack of integrating symbols for the new unified Germany.[48] Into this void steps Luther, whom Treitschke portrays as a hero for true Germans of every stripe. The tragedy of Luther, says Treitschke, is that he came too soon, with an Emperor who was a foreigner and couldn't feel the pull of his rebellion:

> There he stood as the leader (*Führer*) of the nation, heroic as their saint of the *Volk* (*Volksheiliger*), their valiant Michael..., with him it seemed truly as if all the elemental powers that were at work in the deeply aroused nation—the earnest faith of pious hearts, the bold inquiry of the young sciences, the national wrath of the knightly nobility against the foreign clerics, the resentment of the mistreated peasants—united into a mighty stream, powerfully upsurging and washing away all the Roman presence out our state and our church.

But the time was not right, and when the Spanish Emperor rejected his call, the Germanic spirit of uprightness would not allow them to follow against the will of their ruler, and the movement did not gain the support of all the Germans, tragically falling into division instead of unity.[49] To those who came after he appeared smaller than his heroic self as a result of the tragic divisions that followed his death, such that he seemed simply a pious pastor and house father who created a

---

[47] Obviously defining this new Germany as embodied in the person of Luther is in itself suggestive that anyone not stamped by his faith, broadly defined, is an outsider. Treitschke makes some motions, as we will see, to suggest that Catholics might be broadly included; he makes no such gestures in the direction of German Jews, though does not highlight anything concerning Luther's anti-Jewish sentiments, either.

[48] "Luther und die Deutschen," 469–70.

[49] ...da stand er vor Kaiser und Reich als der Führer der Nation, heldenhaft wie ihr Volksheiliger, der streitbare Michael...da schien es wirklich, als sollten alle die elementarischen Kräfte, die in der tief erregten Nation arbeiten, der Glaubensernst der frommen Gemüther, der Forschermuth der jungen Wissenschaft, der Nationalhaß des ritterlichen Adels wider die wälschen Prälaten, der Groll des mißhandelten Bauern, sich zu einem mächtigen Strome vereinigen und gewaltig aufwallend alles römische Wesen aus unserem Staate, unserer Kirche hinwegschwemmen." "Luther und die Deutschen," 470–1.

sectarian church named after himself. Treitschke states that only the historical scholarship of the nineteenth century has recovered the true greatness of his person:

> Only the historical studies of our century found again the heart to understand the whole Luther, the center of his person, in whose soul almost all the new ideas of an abundant century powerfully reverberate; they stand now at a great enough distance in order to judge the indirect consequences of his destructive and constructive actions, in order to take stock of and thankfully acknowledge all the seeds of a new culture that he planted unconsciously, as is the wont of the genius, in the German soil, noting how truly he fulfilled his words: "for my dear Germans was I born, them will I serve."[50]

He noted that the Germans even while pagans had a sense of a coming new Christian world, though the form of faith that came with the Roman Church was never fully suited to their sensibilities, with its one faith housed under the universal structure of the papacy; the logic of medieval theology and the good works channeled through the sacraments of the Church could never provide peace for the active conscience of the Germans. Similarly, the world-denying piety of the cloister never satisfied the German active spirit with its joy in the good things of this world. This mismatch of spiritual structures combined with the outrage of the corrupt Church of the late Middle Ages, which preached ascetic rigors but embraced grotesque excess, such that Rome was the most reprobate city of all Christendom, served to unite all Germans in hatred against the foreign (*wälsch*) presence.[51]

Treitschke accentuates the contrast between the foreign faith of the Roman Church and Luther's religion of conscience, embodied in his protest against false faith and articulated in *On the Freedom of the Christian*, which was at the same time a freer and more rigorous conception of the moral life. By framing the Reformation in this fashion, Treitschke makes Luther's religious revolution a revolution of the German spirit against foreign intrusions. "It is certain Luther's deeds were a revolution, and since religious belief rooted itself in the inner core of the heart of the *Volk* (*Volksgemüthes*) consequently it penetrated all that exists

---

[50] "Erst die historische Wissenschaft unseres Jahrhunderts hat sich wieder das Herz gefaßt, den ganzen Luther zu verstehen, den centralen Menschen, in dessen Seele fast alle die neuen Gedanken eines reichen Jahrhunderts mächtig wiedertönten; sie steht ihm fern genug, um auch die mittelbaren Folgen seines zerstörenden und aufbauenden Wirkens zu würdigen, um alle die Keime einer neuen Cultur, die er ahnungslos, nach der Weise des Genius, in den deutschen Boden senkte, wahrzunehmen und dankbar zu erkennen, wie treu er sein Wort erfüllt hat: 'für meine Deutschen bin ich geboren, ihnen will ich dienen.'" "Luther und die Deutschen," 472.

[51] "Luther und die Deutschen," 473–4.

more than any political upheaval of recent history."[52] By creating such a faith, he made Christianity fit for the German self.[53] And in doing so, Luther also forced the old faith to reform, such that, Treitschke suggests, sensible German Catholics of the present have more in common with the Evangelical faith than with their Spanish co-religionist—it is clear he wants to situate Luther as a reformer for all Germans, and not just the progenitor of the Protestant church in Germany, which makes more sense rhetorically than historically.[54]

The political dimensions of Luther's work are made more manifest as Treitschke turns to consider the consequences of Luther's political philosophy, his setting the power of the state above the church in the secular sphere. Luther broke the power of the priests, says Treitschke, and as a consequence rulers, both Catholic and Protestant, freed themselves from the political overlordship of the crowned priests. From this outward transformation came the political theory of the sovereign state. In this century the states of Europe built themselves into new, free national societies with secular national legal orders, most successfully in those parts of Europe where the Reformation of faith triumphed.[55] And no state benefited more than Germany. Though Luther couldn't envision it, notes Treitschke, the long-term political effects of his actions brought about the new German Empire that now has emerged from Prussia's development.[56] And while the political unity of Germany came from the north, Luther's great act of creating a German literary language with his bible drew from the culture of South Germany and its vernacular, showing that German unity stands on the legacy of its many parts, brought together in Luther.[57] Treitschke is at pains to show how almost all that flows forward to the modern day that is of value in Germany owes a debt to Luther; even the more recent work of German Jesuits is indebted to him, at least to the extent they use the language of Luther.[58] And while he acknowledges the patriarchal nature of the sixteenth century, he also notes how Luther benefited women by making the household, marriage, and children once again honorable, elevating the role of women in society.[59] As a closing testament to the revolution of domestic life, he engages in a sentimental recreation of the idealized

---

[52] "Gewiß war Luthers That eine Revolution, und da der religiöse Glaube im innersten Kerne des Volksgemüthes wurzelt, so griff sie in alles Bestehende tiefer ein, als irgend eine politische Umwälzung der neuen Geschichte." "Luther und die Deutschen," 475.

[53] "Sie [die Reformation] schenkte unserem Volke die Form des Christenthums, welche dem Wahrheitsdrange und der unzähmbaren Selbständigkeit der deutschen Natur zusagt..." (It [the Reformation] provided our *Volk* the form of Christianity which appealed to the longing for truth and the untamable independence of the German nature...). "Luther und die Deutschen," 476.

[54] "Luther und die Deutschen," 476. Given the recent traumas of the *Kulturkampf*, it seems highly likely Catholic Germans would find in Treitschke's formula just another example of their being pushed to the side of German society and its identity. See Greschat's comments, "Der Held der Nation," 118–19.

[55] "Luther und die Deutschen," 478–9.
[56] "Luther und die Deutschen," 480.
[57] "Luther und die Deutschen," 480–1.
[58] "Luther und die Deutschen," 482.
[59] "Luther und die Deutschen," 482–3.

Luther household, with Christmas celebrations, hearty sessions around the table, and the domesticating influence of the good wife who provides solace amidst the travails of life.[60]

In the end, he emphasizes the way Luther's identity merges with that of the German people:

> The precious inheritance that Luther left behind for our *Volk* remains indeed his very person and the living power of his divinely inspired sensibility. No other new nation has ever seen a man who took every word from the lips of his fellow countrymen and so embodied in his habits, mannered and unmannered, the innermost being of his people. A foreigner might indeed in all incomprehension ask how it is such perplexing contradictions might be able to reside together in one soul: this power of destructive wrath and the inwardness of pious faith, such elevated wisdom and such childlike simplicity, so much deeply spiritual mysticism and so much lust for life, such boorish coarseness and such tender heartedness…. We Germans find in all this no mystery, we say simply, "that is blood from our blood."[61]

With his final paragraphs, Treitschke seeks to pull together the central threads of his encomium, which is that the evangelical faith of Luther is truly a Germanic form of belief out of which flows the central features of German character and state formation, providing a core for the current German Empire in its sensibilities and political order, despite the reality that a not insignificant portion of inhabitants of the state are not Protestants. He highlights the parallels between Luther's time and the present, insisting that the most recent events, by bringing into being a German state, provide the fulfillment of everything that was let loose by Luther in the sixteenth century, such that to be German is to participate in the spiritual essence of a Germanity that is defined by Luther. He ends by anticipating a time when all Germans will be united around the spirit of freedom that is defined by Luther's heroic image.

---

[60] "Luther und die Deutschen," 483. This sort of sentimental idealization of Luther's household as the embodiment of the "German" domestic space was ubiquitous in the literature of the era. Greschat notes how little relevance this would have had for working-class Germans whose increasing attraction to Marxian socialism was observed with alarm among Protestants of all stripes; "Der Held der Nation," 117–18.

[61] "Das köstliche Vermächtniß, das Luther unserm Volke hinterlassen hat, bleibt doch er selber, und die lebendige Macht seines gottbegeisterten Gemüths. Keine andere der neueren Nationen hat je einem Mann gesehen, der so seinen Landsleuten jedes Wort von den Lippen genommen, der so in Art und Unart das innerste Wesen seines Volkes verkörpert hätte. Ein Ausländer mag wohl rathlos fragen: wie nur so wunderbare Gegesätze in einer Seele zusammen liegen mochten: diese Gewalt zermalmenden Zornes und diese Innigkeit frommen Glaubens, so hohe Weisheit und so kindliche Einfalt, so viel teifsinnige Mystik und so viel Lebenslust, so ungeschlachte Grobheit und so zarte Herzensgüte…. Wir Deutschen finden in Alledem kein Räthsel, wir sagen einfach: das ist Blut von unserem Blute." "Luther und die Deutschen," 484.

Treitschke's piece draws together the strands of Luther's image that had been developing across the last century and connects them to the new reality of the Second Empire. His treatment of Luther will resonate in the decades that follow. He taps into a heroic narrative of Luther that connects with the needs of the time. While he himself was associated with the national liberal element of Second Empire Protestantism, his message had appeal within a Protestant church that was divided by theology and regional structures; Luther could represent a unifying symbol of Protestant identity and provide a sense of connection between their faith and the lived experience of German unification and its new national identity.[62] For the new German state, Treitschke's Luther affirms its providential destiny, and encourages the loyalty of a significant element of the population. For Germans as a whole, he provides an affirmation of the superiority of their moral heritage and national character. Treitschke's Luther serves the needs of a nation coming into being, providing a founding father who is both a prophet and a living national monument. The worshipful enthusiasm of the writing defines the genre of Luther myth-making yet to come, creating from the figure of Luther a living spiritual force whose mystical presence from across the ages will hold a continuing power for German Protestants over the decades to follow. Treitschke's work demonstrates, as well, how the projection of Luther's image stems from the most educated portions of German culture. While the rhetoric of the piece has the patina of learned scholarship, it heroizes its subject, using appeals to sentimentality and nativist pride that rest on emotionally manipulative language. In this, too, it anticipates the direction of a good part of the literature on Luther that will become increasingly abundant, especially with the coming of the First World War and its aftermath. In general, Treitschke's Luther authenticates the Second Reich as the providential fulfillment of the German idea that has developed since the time of the Reformation; Luther provides the bridge between the events of the deeper past and the developments of the present, a symbol of the political religion of the state that defines much German nationalism of the Second Reich.[63]

The proliferation of memorials in the Second Empire attests to the usefulness of Luther's symbolic meaning with the political needs of the crown and state. A flood of public statuary stems from 1883 and afterwards, such that public representations of Luther came to adorn city landscapes across Protestant Germany. The development of Wittenberg as a "*Lutherstadt*" epitomizes the forces at work that project Luther into the public sphere. Though always a site strongly

---

[62] For an overview of Protestantism and the new German Nation, see Thomas Nipperdey, *Religion im Umbruch: Deutschland 1870–1914* (Munich: C. H. Beck, 1988): 92–100.

[63] See the article of Peter Walkenhorst, "Nationalismus als 'politische Religion?' Zur religiösen Dimension nationalistischer Ideologie im Kaiserreich." In *Religion im Kaiserreich: Milieus-Mentalitäten-Krisen*, ed. Olaf Blaschke and Frank-Michael Kuhlemann (Munich: Chr. Kaiser Verlag, 1996): 503–29, esp. 517–20. See also the discussion of Thomas Nipperdey, *Deutsche Geschichte 1866–1918*, Vol. 1: *Arbeitswelt und Bürgergeist* (Munich: C. H. Beck, 1990): 486–95.

associated with Luther, it was only in the nineteenth century that the structures associated with his life were restored and styled to capture his new meaning. This is particularly the case with the unification of Germany, when after 1871 the Hohenzollern crown took a deep interest in the city of Luther. They sponsored and financed the restoration of the Luther House in Wittenberg, which takes the form of a museum of remembrance, and the restoration/recreation of the *Schloßkirche* in Wittenberg. This interest stemmed both from the desire to associate themselves as benefactors with a part of Prussia that had only been annexed at the start of the 1800s, and to emphasize the connection of crown and altar that was one of the most powerful legitimating elements for their authoritarian rule. By highlighting their connection to the center of Luther's legacy they symbolized the sacral sources of their authority. The strong association of Luther with the system of authoritarian rule of the Second Empire would have significant implications when it fell apart at the end of World War I; as a consequence, it would be almost impossible for Protestants to accept the legitimacy of the Weimar Republic.[64] Of course it was not only the political use of Luther that expanded his presence in the public sphere. Middle-class German society in the nineteenth century embraced public monuments and celebrations, and desired direct participation as a symbol of their agency in public life, such that the 1883 Luther celebration in Wittenberg had two settings, one sponsored by the monarchy and attended by elites, and another, held about a month later, that gave outlet for mass public participation in torchlight marches and other public events.[65]

Beyond the growth of his status as a national symbol, Luther was also taken up into the growing movement of racial anti-Semitism that became especially influential at the turn of the century.[66] In the writings of Houston Stewart Chamberlain (1855–1927) and Arthur Bonus (1864–1941), Luther was given a central role in the development of a Christianity that was racially tuned to the Germanic soul. Bonus, for instance, in describing the aim of his own project of

---

[64] For the development of Wittenberg in the period from 1883 to the present, see the incisive study of Silvio Reichelt, *Der Erlebnisraum Lutherstadt Wittenberg: Genese, Entwicklung und Bestand eines protestantischen Erinnerungsortes* (Göttingen: Vandenhoeck & Ruprecht, 2013): esp. 28–121. See also the intriguing article by Stefan Laube, "Lutherbrief an den Kaiser—Kaiserbrief an die Lutherhalle." In *Lutherinszenierung und Reformationserinnerung*, ed. Stefan Laube and Karl-Heinz Fix (Leipzig: Evangelische Verlagsanstalt, 2002): 265–86. He notes the strong association between crown and Luther, 276: "So ist gerade kurz vor dem Ersten Weltkrieg einer zeitspezifischen Grundtatsache, der immer engeren Verschränkung zwischen Lutherkult und Kaiserverehrung, Rechnung zu tragen, so dass sie am Ende kaum mehr voneinander zu unterschieden waren" (Thus shortly before the First World War one must take into account a time-bound fundamental fact, the ever closer entanglement between the cult of Luther and the honoring of the Kaiser, such that in the end they are scarcely to be distinguished from one another).

[65] Reichelt, 43–8. On the development of Luther celebrations as an expression of public, civic culture, see Johannes Burkhardt, "Reformations- und Lutherfeier: die Verbürgerlichung der reformatorischen Jubiläumskultur." In *Öffentliche Festkultur: Politische Feste in Deutschland von der Aufklärung bis zum ersten Weltkrieg*, ed. Dieter Düding et al. (Hamburg: Rowohlt, 1988): 212–36.

[66] For an overview, see Gottfried Maron, "Luther und die 'Germanisierung des Christentums.' Notizen zu einer fast vergessenen These." *Zeitschrift für Kirchengeschichte* 94 (1983): 313–37.

adapting Christianity for the new age, connects this project to the work of Luther in the Reformation:

> With full consciousness we take up the developments that Christendom achieved in the Martin Luther's Germanification; one need only to read a few pages of Luther to breathe in this atmosphere of defiance and fullness of power.[67]

Bonus was just one of a number of advocates around the turn of the century who sought to bring about a renewal of Christianity by completing the changes that they saw first instigated, but not fully realized, by Luther in the sixteenth century, drawing on the *völkisch* nationalism of the earlier nineteenth century, and combining it with racialist theories taken from popularized Darwinian biology and the hyper-nationalism of the late nineteenth/early twentieth centuries. Even more powerful was the work of Houston Stewart Chamberlain, whose *Grundlagen des neunzehnten Jahrhunderts* ("Foundations of the nineteenth century")[68] posited a master theory of historical development around the factor of race. The work was a best-seller, and made Chamberlain famous, to the extent that he became a close confident of Emperor Wilhelm II, who was deeply influenced by his theories.[69] Chamberlain saw in a Judaized medieval Catholicism a foreign religious antitype that imposed itself on Germans; beginning in the thirteenth century, and coming to a head with Luther's rebellion against the Church, this anti-Germanic spiritual tyranny was broken, and Luther became the political hero of the Germans for his heroic acts. "The separation from Rome, which Luther pursued his whole life with such passionate boisterousness, was the most powerful political revolution which could ever take place. Through it this man became the crux of world history."[70] As we will see, this racial nationalist take on Luther will work its way into the German Protestantism through the influence of figures such as Chamberlain and Bonus, being taken up by theologians such as Reinhard Seeberg, who will give it a central place in his textbook on the history of dogma.[71] Chamberlain's work, in particular, has a seminal influence on National Socialism, and will shape the perspectives of the German Christians

---

[67] "Wir knüpften mit vollem Bewußtsein an die Wendung an, die das Christentum in Martin Luthers Germanisierung gewonnen hatte, eine Stimmung, deren Trotz und Kraftfülle zu atmen man nur einige Seiten Luther zu lesen braucht." Quoted in Christopher König, *Zwischen Kulturprotestantismus und völkischer Bewegung. Arthur Bonus (1864–1941) als religiöser Schriftsteller im wilhelminischen Kaiserreich* (Tübingen: Mohr Siebeck, 2018): 92.

[68] Houston Stewart Chamberlain, *Grundlagen des neunzehnten Jahrhunderts* (Munich: Bruckmann, 1899).

[69] For an overview of his life, see the discussion in Barbara Liedtke, *Völkisches Denken und Verkündigung des Evangeliums. Die Rezeption Houston Stewart Chamberlain in evangelischer Theologie und Kirche während der Zeit des "Dritten Reichs"* (Leipzig: Evangelische Verlagsanstalt, 2012): 28–108.

[70] Quoted in Liedtke, *Völkisches Denken*, 103–4.

[71] Maron, "Luther und die 'Germanisierung des Christentums,'" 324–5.

(*Deutsche Christen*) in the 1930s. And while in part this view of Luther develops from within the Protestant church with the work of figures such as Bonus and Seeberg, it projects Luther's significance apart from his theological legacy, seeing in him a racial nationalist whose rebellion sets in motion the realization of the racial character of the German *Volk*. This idea of Luther will gain broad dissemination in the 1930s.[72]

The ultimate result of the nineteenth-century development of Luther's image leading up to the First World War saw his transformation from a religious reformer to a central symbol of German national identity, whose image and legacy provided legitimacy for an authoritarian system of government, at least among middle-class Protestants. In general, Luther's symbolic presence loomed over and was strongly associated with the state system and public sphere of Wilhelmine Germany, setting the stage for the problematic history of this image in the period following World War I and the collapse of the Second Empire. In addition, the associations of Luther with racialized German identity politics first emerge in this period, anticipating developments to come. It is the traumas of World War I and its impact on German nationalism and religiosity that will transpose his image further, and create a new context within which are amplified the associations made in the course of the nineteenth century. As with politics and society as a whole, the impact of the war will greatly inflame the nationalistic and belligerent features of Luther's image, and connect him to the crisis of Germany's national existence.[73]

The Luther Myth: The Image of Martin Luther from Religious Reformer to Völkisch *Icon*. Patrick Hayden-Roy, Oxford University Press. © Patrick Hayden-Roy 2024. DOI: 10.1093/9780198930297.003.0002

---

[72] See in particular Chapters 5 and 7.
[73] See the comments of Greschat, "Der Held der Nation," 121–6.

2
Luther Goes to War

World War I set into motion forces whose destructive power would unfold across the course of the twentieth century. In its immediate effects, it threw the entirety of the German nation into a massive conflict that would disrupt the social, economic, cultural, and political continuities of the Second Empire, and also greatly enhance certain features of that landscape, particularly those connected to racial nationalism and belligerent patriotism.[1] Luther provides a microcosm of those features of political culture, as he will be drawn into the conflict as a living symbol of Germany's fighting spirit, as an embodiment of its national virtues, especially those related to warfare, as a cultural symbol of German unity of purpose, and, in the later travails of the war, as a figure from whom could flow salvation for a nation in crisis. His image will emerge from the war having taken a form within Protestant religiosity that will set the stage for his further deployment in nationalist Protestant circles as the symbol of resistance to the post-authoritarian Weimar state. In particular, the celebration of the four-hundredth anniversary of the Reformation in 1917 will provide a focal point for the distillation and projection of an image of Luther that will resonate in the decades to follow.

The outbreak of the war in 1914 was received by most Germans, as was the case in other European states, with enthusiasm. The prospect of war seemed to provide an ideal opportunity to fulfill goals of national identity and destiny long frustrated. It was common wisdom that the war would be brief, decisive, and restorative. German elites, especially intellectual elites, embraced the war from the start, and served to popularize the war as the struggle for survival against the forces that sought to enslave and diminish a powerful German nation.[2] For the Protestant church, the war seemed tailor-made to reverse the slide of the German

---

[1] As Thomas Nipperdey writes: "Der Erste Weltkrieg ist mehr als das bloß chronologische oder nur dramatische Schlußstück der Geschichte des deutschen Kaiserreichs. Er ist die 'Urkatastrophe' unseres Jahrhunderts für Europa, für das Welt und auch für Deutschland" (The First World War is more than the mere chronological or just the dramatic closing act of the history the German Empire. It is the 'primal catastrophe' of our century for Europe, for the world, and also for Germany). Thomas Nipperdey, *Deutsche Geschichte 1866–1918*, Vol. 2: *Machtstaat vor der Demokratie* (Munich: C. H. Beck, 1993): 758.

[2] The collection of speeches delivered by German academics beginning from its very outset, *Aufrufe und Reden deutscher Professoren im Ersten Weltkrieg*. Klaus Böhme, ed. (Stuttgart: Reclam, 1975), highlights this rabid promotion of the war effort as a righteous national cause. Prominent among these voices was the Berlin theologian Reinhard Seeberg, whose repeated advocacy of maximalist German aims for the outcome of the war reflect the popularity among Protestants of a militant German geopolitics.

population as a whole away from their traditions of faith, and so, as with almost every segment of German society, it was greeted with enthusiasm.[3] Almost immediately the church used its spiritual influence to encourage Germans to rush forward into the conflict with faith that the war was blessed by God. Not surprisingly, Luther was a major source through which to channel such messages.[4]

Though the initial plans of the German military for a quick victory did not come to fruition, the war soon expanded and quickly transformed into the grinding violence of the trenches; it took some time before a more pessimistic, though not necessarily realistic, set of prospects took hold. In that early context, Luther served to advocate the tools through which victory would be achieved. The image of Luther received from the nineteenth century was readymade for deployment in the war: his unique "German" virtues now represented the superiority of German cultural identity over and against those of the enemies; his manly challenge to the oppressing Roman Church now defined a fighting spirit that animates the spirit of Germany in its current just war against its oppressors; his faith in God provides Germans with a heritage and a faith that will see them through to victory—it is no coincidence that "A Mighty Fortress" was used among the frontline soldiers as a means to inspire them in their endeavor. If one looks at the primary descriptors that were used in sermons of this era, one sees the overwhelmingly militarized image that was projected onto him: passionate, loyal, wrathful, heroic, defiant, a leader, powerful, manly, hammer-wielder.[5] In all, the nineteenth-century nationalist Luther was restyled in the war to accentuate those elements of his image that were most suited to the current hour. With the turn of affairs that become manifest by 1917, the commemoration of the four-hundredth anniversary of Luther's Ninety-Five Theses took on a more desperate tone, accentuating and intensifying much of what had developed with the image of Luther in the previous hundred years.

The celebration of the four-hundredth anniversary of the Reformation in 1917 took place in an environment of escalating crisis and also hopes. The destructive force of the conflict could no longer be denied, given the slaughter of the great battles of 1916 at Verdun and the Somme. The winter of 1916–17, the so-called Turnip Winter, brought starvation to Germany, and the economic hardships that came with the British blockade radicalized Germany's war strategy. Unrestricted

---

[3] See, for instance, the piece by Paul Althaus, "Der Krieg und unser Gottesglaube II." *Allgemeine Evangelisch-Lutherische Kirchenzeitung* XXVII (July 2, 1915): 629.

[4] For an evaluation of the substance of German war sermons, see Wilhelm Pressel, *Die Kriegspredigt 1914–1918 in der evangelischen Kirche Deutschlands* (Göttingen: Vandenhoeck & Ruprecht, 1967); for the use of Luther see 83–97.

[5] For an excellent exploration of the use of Luther in the context of World War I, see Dietz Bering, *Luther in Fronteinsatz: Propagandastrategien im Ersten Weltkrieg* (Göttingen: Wallstein Verlag, 2018). Bering provides an inventory of the terms applied to Luther in the over five hundred sermons he studied, and identifies these terms as the most popular among the many applied to him. See also the article by Andrea Hofmann, "Martin Luther in First World War Sermons." *Kirchliche Zeitgeschichte/Contemporary Church History* 31 (2018): 118–30.

submarine warfare, intended to inflict on England the hardships being suffered by the Germans, had the predictable result of drawing the United States into the conflict. Though on the Eastern Front the Russian Revolution drew Russia out of the war, the long-term prospects for victory did not look promising. In that context, the general solidarity among the main parties broke down, and particularly parties of the left and moderate center were no longer willing to support endless war credits without some softening of the goals for the conflict. Those advocating a diplomatic solution found little receptivity among the military, crown, or nationalist-minded Germans, who advocated a "victory peace," the geopolitical proportions of which expanded with the degree of sacrifice that had been extracted from the German populace. This split led to a more authoritarian military regime, and a fracturing of solidarity among the German people as a whole. In this context, many Protestant leaders supported the crown, military, and right-wing nationalist politics, and the character of the Luther celebration in the fall of 1917 reflected this political environment, though it also elicited a wide-ranging theological debate about Christianity and pacifism that revealed deep and persisting fissures within the German Protestant world.[6]

Given the crisis of 1917, the widespread and extensive public celebrations that marked earlier centenaries fell through—even Wittenberg cancelled its event at the last minute. As noted by Gottfried Maron, however, the lack of public celebrations was compensated for with the enormous outpouring of other material, especially printed works, of every imaginable sort.[7] The publications were designed to connect with just about every possible audience, and they seem to suggest a Protestant church deeply uncertain of its connection to the people and the *Zeitgeist*. While much of what was published is repetitious and lacks any distinctive literary or even rhetorical worth, many of the publications reflect the abundance of meanings that could be attached to Luther's person in this context. A publication that reflects this variety especially well was put out by the Evangelical-Social Press Agency for the Province of Saxony. It collects together fifty-four contributions from authors of many sorts, from military and political

---

[6] For a discussion and documents that highlight the stance of factions within German Protestantism, see Günther Brakelmann, *Der deutsche Protestantismus im Epochenjahr 1917* (Witten: Luther Verlag, 1974): esp. chs. II and III.

[7] Gottfried Maron. "Luther 1917. Beobachtungen zur Literatur des 400. Reformationsjubiläums." *Zeitschrift für Kirchengeschichte* 93 (1982): 177–221; 179, "Nicht die Feiern, sondern *die literarische Produktion ist das eigentliche Charakteristikum dieses Gedenkjahres*. In diesem Bereich hat man allerdings weniger den Eindruck von Stille und Selbstbesinnung als den eines übergroßen Lärms. Es scheint, als wolle man die äußere Beschränkung durch eine gewaltige Materialschlacht kompensieren" (Not the celebrations, but *the literary production is the real characteristic of this year of remembrance*. In this area one has indeed less the impression of calm and stocktaking as an enormous racket. It seems as if they want to compensate for the public restrictions though a powerful material onslaught). For an overview bibliography of works about Luther and the Reformation published during this period see Günther Brakelmann, *Protestantische Kriegstheologie 1914–1918* (Kamen: Hartmut Spener, 2015): 271–85.

leaders, church officials, theologians, as well as a number of a laypeople, men and women. Titled *What Luther means still for us today!: a collection of contemporary original expressions, treatises and poems from the 400th commemorative year of the Reformation*,[8] it provides a telling overview of the meaning of Luther, as suggested in the introductory note:

> The four-hundredth celebration of the Reformation calls awake in an entirely unique sense the memory of the man whose undying *Sturm und Drang* song, "A Mighty Fortress is our God," has long become the common possession of our brothers at the front, without distinction of their confessional loyalties, and has enflamed them to truly superhuman deeds in action and patience. And if we at home bravely persevere, then it is not the least the spirit of Martin Luther, who binds and holds us closely together with the heroes in our striving towards that one high goal: through struggle and victory, death and tears, to help the German being achieve new life and liberating recognition in the world.[9]

The author notes how Luther wanders through the lands of Germany, and despite having passed on, yet he still lives because he is the embodiment of conscience, the man bound to God and human freedom, who will guide the Fatherland, now so severely oppressed, on the path that alone leads to proud heights.[10] The language used here captures how Luther will be portrayed throughout the work: the one who will bring together all Germans through his spiritual presence, whose power crosses confessional boundaries, and encapsulates the qualities that will see Germans through the crisis and to victory.

The various articles follow up with an array of topics that project this idea of the living presence of Luther in all aspects of German life and spirit. The titles themselves convey quite a bit of the emphasis of the volume, and represent the general trends of the whole genre during the 1917 celebration. Above all there is the emphasis on his Germanness: "Luther and the German Spirit; Luther the German Leader; Luther the creator of the new Germany; Luther the German

---

[8] Evangelisch-Sozialien Preßverband für die Provinz Sachsen, *Was Luther uns heute noch ist! Eine Sammlung von zeitgenössischen Original Aussprüchen, Abhandlungen und Gedichten im 400 Gedächtnisjahr der Reformation 1917* (Halle, 1917).

[9] "Die vierte Jahrhundertfeier der Reformation ruft in ganz besonderem Sinne das Gedächtnis des Mannes wach, dessen unsterbliches Sturm- und Dranglied: 'Ein feste Burg ist unser Gott' schon längst gemeinsamer Besitz unserer Brüder im Felde, ohne Unterschied der Konfession, geworden ist und sie zu schier übermenschlichen Taten im Wagen und im Dulden entflammt hat. Und wenn wir daheim tapfer durchhalten, so ist es nicht zuletzt der Geist Martin Luthers, der uns im Ringen um das eine hohe Ziel mit den Helden innig verbunden hält: durch Kampf und Sieg, Tod und Tränen dem deutschen Wesen zu neuem Leben und befreiender Geltung in der Welt zu verhelfen." *Was Luther heute…*, 5.

[10] "Luther wandert durch die deutschen Lande. Er ist gestorben, aber er lebt…. Das verkörperte Gewissen, der Mann der Gottgebundenheit und Menschenfreiheit, hat er unserem jetzt so schwer bedrängten Vaterlande die Wege ermöglicht und gewiesen, die allein zu stolzer Höhe führen." *Was Luther heute…*, 5.

Father of the Family; Luther, the most German of all Germans; Luther the People's Instructor; Luther goes through the German land; Luther and the German Nation; Luther in German Spiritual Life; Luther the Educator of the *Volk*; Luther Spirit—German Spirit; Luther, a True German Man; The Greatest German Man; The Most German of all Germans [again!]; Luther the German."[11] Many of the pieces appeal to the emotions—theological rigor is in short supply—and there is a good deal of poetry in the volume, much of it epic in its vocabulary, or emphasizing the personal significance of Luther's life and "spirit" for the contemporary crisis of the German people. Emblematic of this strain is the poem by Kurt Warmuth, Pastor and Licentiate in Dresden,[12] "der deutscheste Deutsche":

> Luther, the most German man of the Germans
> You move before us in holy battle
> Thanks to you, O Luther!
>
> You gave us Germans the Holy Word
> That gives us support and a safe haven at home and in the field
> Thanks to you, O Luther!
>
> [You] gave us the brazen song to sing
> That like the angel of the Lord before us goes
> Thanks to you, O Luther!
>
> You impressed upon us with your example
> To be German means to be true to your conscience
> Thanks to you, O Luther!
>
> Let us hold your image before our eyes
> Fear the Lord and nothing else in this world!
> Thanks to you, O Luther!
>
> Luther, you fight together with the *Volk* and the troops
> Lead us to victory! To the Lord God be honor
> He gave you to us, Luther![13]

---

[11] "Luther, und die deutsche Geist; Luther der Deutschen Führer; Luther, der Schöpfer Neudeutschlands; Luther, der deutsche Familienvater; Luther—der deutscheste Deutsche; Luther der Volkspädagoge; Der Luther geht durchs deutsche Land; Luther und die deutsche Nation; Luther im deutschen Geistesleben; Luther der Volkserzieher; Luthers Geist—Deutscher Geist; Luther, ein echter deutscher Mann; Der größte deutsche Mann; Der deutscheste Deutsche; Luther der Deutsche." Listed in the *Inhalt, Was Luther heute...*, 181-4.

[12] Born 1872.

[13] "Luther der Deutschen deutschester Mann,/ Du ziehst im heiligen Kampf uns vorn— / Dank dir, o Luther! // du gabst uns Deutschen das göttliche Wort, / das uns daheim und im Feld Halt und Hort— / Dank dir, o Luther! // Gabst uns zu singen das eherne Lied, / Das gleich dem Engel des Herrn vor uns zieht— / Dank dir, o Luther! // Prägtest uns fest durch dein Vorbild es ein: / Deutsch sein heißt: treu dem Gewissen sein— / Dank dir, o Luther! // Hast durch dein Bild uns vor Augen gestellt: / Fürchtet den Herrn und sonst nichts auf der Welt! / Dank dir, o Luther! // Luther, du kämpfst mit im Volk und im Heer, / Führst uns zum Siege! Dem Herrgott sei Ehr:/ Er gab dich uns, Luther!" *Was Luther heute...*, 166.

The poem captures the tone of many pieces, with its mixture of pious formula combined with exhortatory emphasis on the virtues of the German self, connected in the end with a stirring patriotic appeal.

More than one piece in the collection ends by quoting the last line of "A Mighty Fortress" grotesquely out of context, "Das Reich muß uns doch bleiben."[14] This is instructive, not only for its connection to the military situation of 1917, and the defense of Germany's territory, but also because the attempts of the political left in 1917 to bring about a more Parliamentary driven German governance structure were being stoutly resisted by Protestant nationalists. This tone of overblown and bellicose religious nationalism inhabits almost every piece in the collection. It is striking, also, how seamlessly by this point in time such specifically national liberal Protestant emphases on Luther's political and national significance are integrated with his religious teachings.

"Luther the Creator of the New Germany" by Theodor Birt, Professor at Marburg,[15] offers just such an example of the merging of politics and religion in the image of Luther in the context of 1917. The general thrust of his piece is not only the actions of the historical Luther in creating a new Germany in the past, but the potential for his spirit to inspire the creation of a victorious Germany in the present. He starts with a rush of enthusiasm:

> He struck down an entire historical age and tore open the doors to a new one. Luther strikes me like a colossal Roland. Look across the entirety of all of history: this son of a peasant, with nothing but his living word and his German Bible, overshadows in impact and as a stabilizing force all our statesmen and kings. He gave us the "Reformation." Why do we use this foreign word? A "recreation" [*Umschaffung*] is what he gave us, not only of the church, but of the German being in its entirety.[16]

From this he moves to treat faith, not as something private and inward, but as the animating spirit of all that happens in the workplace, in social life, as a christening of work: "For piety works itself into this world. The sanctity of work! Every tradesman, whether tinker or tailor, does his duty as a *Volk* comrade (*Volksgenosse*): that is his priestly office on earth. To serve the whole of society is now the service

---

[14] In the most widespread English translation this is framed as "The Kingdom's ours forever." Put literally it reads "The empire must nevertheless remain ours." In the context of 1917, the quote was meant to connect the meaning of a Mighty Fortress to the wartime struggle of Germany.

[15] Born 1852, Professor of Classical Philology and also author of books of popular literature.

[16] "Ein ganzes Zeitalter zerschlug er und riß die Tore auf für ein neues. Luther wirkt auf mich wie ein Rolandkoloß. Man blicke die Weltgeschichte entlang: an Wucht und mittragender Wirkung übertrifft dieser Bauernsohn, der nichts hatte als sein lebendiges Wort und die deutsche Bibel, all unsere Staatsmänner und Könige. Er gab uns die 'Reformation.' Warum aber dies fremdländlische Wort? Eine 'Umschaffung' gab er uns, nicht nur der Kirche, sondern des ganzen deutschen Wesens." *Was Luther noch…*, 25.

of God."[17] This "this worldly" interpretation of Luther's purpose leads into further reflections on how Luther unleashed Germanity (*Germanentum*) from its shackles and gave it freedom, such that now humanity is the measure of all things. This, in turn, enables the sciences to be set upon an open path.[18]

From there it is on to the creation of the German world, both through his giving back to Germany its language, but also his striving politically and economically to save Germany from the foreigners. He advocated a strong German imperial unity in united faith and a new liberating message. "What miraculous thoughts of super-Bismarckian greatness!"[19] And while it took some time, that wasn't his fault. Eventually his ideas came to fruition through Prussia, where Protestant Germany took up its heroic achievements, fully realized in the new Empire. And even the Catholics were drawn along, whether they wanted to be or not, and came together without confessional restraints in the new Empire. He closes by connecting this all to the current crisis:

> And we welcome the fact that even now as the World War oppresses us, Luther's vivid memory, powerfully inhaled and mightily and wonderfully restorative, rises swiftly before us anew! The old heroic lay tells us of Walther of Aquitaine, who stood entirely alone and unconquerable against the twelve predatory Burgundians. Just such a Walther is also Luther, and so the Germans stand today still fearless in struggle against the superpowers. That is the calling of the Germans: Germany the land of protest against Satan. Standing up for truth and justice against all the world, that is Germanity and Lutheranism: The world may despise me, God does not! Here I stand, I can do no other, God help me.[20]

---

[17] "Denn die Seligkeit zieht schon in das Diesseits ein. Weihe der Arbeit! Jeder Berufsmensch, ob Schuster, ob Schneider, tue als Volksgessose seine Pflicht: das ist schon Priestertum auf Erden. Der Gesamtheit dienen ist schon Gottesdienst." *Was Luther noch...*, 25.

[18] "Die unbändige Kraft des Germanentums, die lang gebundene, entlud sich plötzlich in diesem Menschen, und das Reich, ganz Europa krachte in den Fugen unter seinem Wort. Unbändig darum auch sein Wahrheitssinn. Freiheit des Urteils! Der Mensch soll wieder 'das Maß aller Dinge' sein; unbevormundet prüfe er selbst jede Meinung, ob sie fallen muß oder nicht. So öffnete Luther den Wissenschaften für immer freie Bahn, und wer ihnen dient, muß es ihm ewig danken" (The irrepressible power of Germanity, which was for so long bound, unloaded itself suddenly in this man; and the Empire, all of Europe creaked in its joints under the weight of his words. Irrepressible, too, was his sense of truth. Freedom of judgement! Humanity shall once again be 'the measure of all things.' No longer under tutelage, humanity itself now is to test every opinion, judging whether it shall stand or fall. Thus Luther set the sciences forever onto an open path; whoever is dedicated to them has to give Luther eternal thanks). *Was Luther noch...*, 25–6.

[19] "Welch wundervoller Gedanke von überbismarckscher Größe!" *Was Luther noch...*, 26.

[20] "Wilkommen ist es uns, daß eben jetzt in dem Weltkrieg, der uns bedrängt, Luther Errinerungsbild stark atmend und mächtig und wundervoll ermutigend vor uns neu emporsteigt! Das alte Heldenlied erzählt uns von Walther von Aquitanien... der ganz allein unüberwindlich gegen die zwölf raubgierigen Burgunden stand. Solch Walther war auch Luther, und so steht auch heute der Germane furchtlos im Kampf gegen die Übermacht. Das ist der Beruf des Deutschen: Deutschland das Land des Protestes gegen das Arge. Das Trotzen für Recht und Wahrheit gegen eine Welt, das ist Deutschtum und Luthertum: mag die Welt mir zürnen, Gott zürnt mir nicht! Hier stehe ich, ich kann nicht anders, Gott helfe mir." *Was Luther noch...*, 27.

The piece exemplifies vividly the degree to which Luther's identification with Germany in all its meanings has been merged. The author uses anti-clerical language to affirm the identification of Luther with the world of labor, science, politics, and geo-political struggle, positing what in almost any other context would be a preposterous attribution of agency to the actions and "spirit" of one long-dead person. But in the context of 1917, such claims for Luther took on the role of both religious exhortation and patriotic appeal, aimed to an audience where such rhetoric had the flavor of received truth. Another exemplary feature of the piece is its assumption about the immediate relevance of the past, where the actions of Luther four hundred years prior are perceived to connect with and be manifest in the events and circumstances of the present, so that the author attributes to Luther the ultimate cause for Germany's unification, the triumph of science, and also the solution to the crisis that faced Germany in 1917. This immediacy of Luther, his relevance to the modern situation will be a fixed feature of the literature in the decades that follow. While there is a performative aspect to the literature of this collection, especially the poetry, there is also an authenticity of emotion, a religious devotion that forms a distinguishing feature of the genre.

Another work of 1917, *Vom Geiste Luthers des Deutschen* (*On the Spirit of the German Luther*) by Karl König, at the time pastor in Breman,[21] captures the full proportions of the spiritual meaning attributed to Luther, a meaning that comes close to equating his significance with that of Jesus. By inflating Luther's status as prophet, space is opened for creating out of him a nearly godlike potency. While the notion of Luther as a prophet has a long history going back to the sixteenth century, with König's work, as with many of this era, Luther is both the prophet and embodiment of national and racial characteristics whose sacral significance demonstrates how God infuses his grace into and through a sacralized racial/ethnic community.[22] He begins his work by noting how the struggle of the prophetically fated individual enacts the inner struggle of the people:

> This experience of the <u>Völker is</u> also at the same time the experience of the great individual. Indeed each struggles in their own way for the new future of their

---

[21] König was born in 1868 in Thuringia, and trained at Jena. He held a number of pastorates, and in the 1930s was a member of the German Christians and National Socialist Party member after 1937. See the publication of his great granddaughter Almut König, "Der Krieg von der Kanzel." *Studia Germanistica* 19 (2016): 45–52. Online at https://dokumenty.osu.cz/ff/journals/studiagermanistica/2016-19/SG_19_4_Konig.pdf [accessed 8/4/22]. In addition, König was a long-time associate of Arthur Bonus, and supported many of Bonus' initiatives from the early 1900s up into the 1930s. See Christopher König, *Zwischen Kulturprotestantismus und völkischer Bewegung* (Tübingen: Mohr Siebeck, 2018).

[22] Distinguishing racial from ethnic nationalism in much of the literature of this time is difficult. On the one hand, the attributes of Germanness are defined in spiritual terms, yet they are connected then to *volkisch* identity, often claimed, as König will do, with blood. There is no rigorous differentiation of spiritual qualities from qualities that are grounded in the material self.

Volk, bringing together the centuries-long past into a new creation in their own person and action.[23]

Luther is however the greatest of the Germans. If we wish to, if we must secure perpetually our deepest German character and being, then it happens best in him.[24]

The eternally present past is captured here, as the characteristics of past "great" individuals are present in the inner structures of being possessed by the national/racial community. In this way Luther's spirit is not just an inspirational phrase to present an ennobling example but is meant more literally as an indwelling spirit whose presence can be experienced through participation in his life, actions, and teachings.[25]

As Luther experienced salvation, he set up a model for all those who participate in the German national spirit:

In this regard we must emphasize that Luther's salvation is not a case of secondary experience or an "imitation of Christ"; what we're dealing with here is an original creative act of God in the soul of this greatest of all Germans.[26]

König parallels those great experiences of God's saving grace grasped by Luther with his status as the greatest German, such that what happens to Luther, not unlike Christ on the cross, becomes the possession of those who grasp onto his life and actions:

Indeed there is an elective and essential affinity of the sons of God here on earth only when each of them discovers themselves in others, each his God in the God of another. Humans find themselves only when they find it in God; they find their brother in another human only when they find their God in their brother. All deep and true community among humanity is divine community.... And just that is the community between Luther and Jesus, as it is between us and Luther, between us and Jesus.[27]

---

[23] "Dies Erlebnis der Völker ist aber zugleich das Erlebnis der großen Einzelnen. Auch sie kämpften ja, ein jeder in seiner Weise, um die neue Zukunft ihres Volkes und fassen jahrhundertelange Vergangenheit zu neuer Schöpfung in ihrer eigenen Person und Tat zusammen." Karl König, *Vom Geiste Luthers des Deutschen* (Jena: Eugen Diederichs, 1917): 2–3.

[24] "Luther aber ist der Größte der Deutschen. Wollen und müssen wir uns immer wieder unseres tiefsten deutschen Habens und Seins versichern, so geschieht es am besten an ihm." König, *Vom Geiste Luthers*, 3.

[25] König, *Vom Geiste Luthers*, 6.

[26] "Dennoch müssen wir betonen, es handelt sich bei der Erlösung Luthers nicht um ein Nacherlebnis oder gar um eine 'imitatio Christi', eine Nachahmung Christi; es handelt sich um einen originalen Schöpfungsakt Gottes in der Seele dieses größten Deutschen." König, *Vom Geiste Luthers*, 28.

[27] "Aber es gibt ja auch eine Wahl- und Wesensverwandtschaft der Gottessöhne hienieden nur dadurch, daß jeder von ihnen im anderen sich selber, jeder seinen Gott im Gott des anderen wiederfindet. Es findet ein Mensch sich selber nur dadurch daß er sich in Gott, er findet den Bruder im Menschen nur dadurch, daß er seinen Gott im Bruder findet. Alle tiefe und wahre Gemeinschaft

He follows that remarkable passage by saying: "In Luther Christendom experienced for a second time what it first experienced in Jesus of Nazareth, which, however, it had displaced into heaven to such a degree, that only a little remained and was accessible here on earth."[28] So with Luther, one had access to the experience of Christ in more tangible human form.

And as that experience is made accessible through the Word of God in German, it enacts in the spiritual core of the German a communion of the individual self with the racial community:

> And just this came about with Luther. In him piety and *Volkstum* were joined in a firm covenant before God. He enclosed his German *Volk* in his whole love, and became for them the great prophet. To the hundredfold fractured and tattered Germanity (*Deutschtum*) he gave, in his own person, the inner image of German being, and through his bible translation he gave them a German [language] so colorful and supple, so full of rhythm, soul and power, that it prevailed over all the other dialects, and became, in the face of all tribal divisions, the means to achieving German unity, up to and including the unified German empire.[29]

König emphasizes the material consequences of this spiritual effect, connecting the inwardness of this experience of Luther's faith with the outward world of *Volk*, nation, and society:

> Whoever as a result of our portrayal is able to appreciate what Luther revealed in profound and liberating fashion about the agency of God in creation, they know also that the *Volkstum* must be integrated into piety, and that its realization is a holy duty and a holy joy. For this belongs to true piety, that we listen with clear, alert, reverent ears to the creative Word that speaks distinctly and clearly from the depths of our own physical as well as spiritual being, out of "the divine creation that is created within us." And when it happens that this creating Word of God says "give heed and be on guard, you're dealing with your essence and your blood that I have given to you and that I will sustain, ennoble and raise

---

unter Menschen ist Gottgemeinschaft.... Und eben das ist die Gemeinschaft zwischen Luther und Jesus, wie sie es ist zwischen uns und Luther, zwischen uns und Jesus." König, *Vom Geiste Luthers*, 31–2.

[28] "In Luther hat die Christenheit zum zweiten Male das erlebt, was sie zum ersten Male in Jesus von Nazareth erlebt, aber dermaßen in den Himmel versetzt hatte, daß auf Erden nur noch wenig davon verblieben und zu finden war." König, *Vom Geiste Luthers*, 33.

[29] "Und ebendies geschah in Luther. In ihm schlossen Frömmigkeit und Volkstum ihren festen Bund vor Gott. Er hat sein deutsches Volk mit seiner ganzen Liebe umfaßt und ist ihm selber der große Prophet geworden. Er hat dem hundertfach zerrissenen und zerschlissenen Deutschtum in seiner eigenen Person das Anschauungsbild deutschen Wesens und durch seine Bibelübersetzung ein Deutsche gegeben, so farbig und gelenkig, so voll Rhythmus, Seele und Kraft, daß es über alle Dialekte zum Siege kam und gegenüber aller Stammeszerrissenheit das Mittel zur deutschen Einheit bis hin zum einigen Deutschen Reich geworden ist." König, *Vom Geiste Luthers*, 185–6.

up in you," so it is that I heed this inner call, indeed heed it despite the danger of breaking with everything which up until now has counted for religion according to the church, so certain that it is religious, that it is from God, and so certain that the national striving in us is a divine work and creation. And just because it is so and not otherwise, there strikes through all great patriotic movements always the flame of religion which gives it its full radiance and power. Neither God or religion reside and create in empty rooms of abstraction, but create, effect, bring into being, energize, radiate in flesh and blood, marrow and limbs, spirit and soul. Whoever would separate religion from nationality, they split God apart from his creation, and then all creation may see what will become of her and her national strivings without God.[30]

Though König does not sort out the implications of this theological claim, he anticipates what will be made out of Luther's teachings in the 1920s and '30s, where a theology of creation ostensibly drawn from Luther will affirm notions of racial nationalism, claiming it to be the most profound realization of Luther's revelation of God's action within humanity. It takes little imagination to conceive of how such ideas will fit into the religious culture of German Protestantism in the aftermath of the war, when Luther's "prophetic" calling will be associated with notions of blood identity and mystical nationalism.[31] And he is quite specific, as well, that the fulfillment of this mystical nationhood was envisioned by Luther as a "free national Imperial Germany."[32]

---

[30] "Wer das, was Luther über das Schaffen Gottes in der Kreatur zum tiefsinnigen und befreienden Ausdruck gebracht hat, in unserer Darstellung nachzufühlen vermochte, der weiß, daß auch das Volkstum in die Frömmigkeit mit einbezogen werden muß, und daß seine Wahrung heilige Pflicht und heilige Freude ist. Denn dies gehört zur wahren Frömmigkeit, daß wir allenthalben mit hellen, wachen, ehrfürchtigen Ohren auf das schaffende Wort hören, das aus der Tiefe unseres eigenen leiblichen, wie geistigen Seins, aus 'der Kreatur Gottes, die in uns geschaffen ist,' hell und deutlich redet. Und wenn das dies schaffende Wort Gottes sagt: Gib acht und wehr dich, es handelt sich um dein Wesen, deine Art, dein Blut, das ich dir gab, und das ich in dir erhalten, veredlen und emporgestalten will: so ist dies, daß ich diesem inneren Rufe folge, ja ihm folge zumnächst selbst auf die Gefahr hin mit allem zu brechen, was bisher in Kirchensinne für Religion gegolten hat, so gewiß religiös, so gewiß es von Gott, und so gewiß der nationale Drang in uns ein göttlich Werk und Schaffen ist. Und eben weil es so und nicht anders ist, schlägt durch alle großen vaterländischen Bewegungen stets auch die Flamme der Religion und gibt ihnen erst volle Glut und Kraft. Weder Gott noch Religion wohnen und weben im luftleeren Raum der Abstraktionen, sondern schaffen, wirken, wesen, treiben, glühen in Fleisch und Blut, Mark und Bein, Geist und Seele. Wer das Religiöse vom Nationalen trennen will, der sondert Gott von seiner Kreatur, und dann mag die Kreatur zusehen, was ohne Gott aus ihr und ihrem nationalen Drange wird." König, *Vom Geiste Luthers*, 188–9.

[31] "Hier und nirgendwo anders liegt die Erklärung dafür, daß Luther alle tiefen der deutschen Volksseele aufgewühlt und nicht ein Kirchenmann neben anderen, sondern ein Feuerzeichen, Wegführer und Prophet der deutschen Nation und zugleich der genialste Neuschöpfer des christlich-religiösen Lebens für diese Erdkugel geworden ist" (Here and nowhere else lies the explanation that Luther, stirring up all the depths of the soul of the German *Volk*, was not one churchman among others, but a fire alarm, guide and prophet of the German nation, and at the same time the most ingenious new creator of Christian religious life for entire globe). König, *Vom Geiste Luthers*, 194–5.

[32] "Luthers deutsches politisches Ideal aber war das nationale deutsche Kaiserreich." König, *Vom Geiste Luthers*, 196.

While König's work articulates in its fullest form the unbridled racialized nationalism of the Luther literature from 1917, and captures nicely its advocacy for a Luther who prophesized the sort of state formation that came in the late nineteenth century, and whose legacy was now in a deep crisis, he avoids any overt anti-Semitic themes in his nationalist rhetoric. And, for the most part, explicit anti-Semitism is not prominent in the literature from the Reformation celebration, though not surprisingly, given the overwhelming emphasis on the Germanness of Luther's faith, which itself is exclusionary, a few works give voice to it. Most noteworthy is a multi-author work, *Deutschchristentum auf rein-evangelischer Grundlage. 95 Leitsätze zum Reformationsfest 1917* (German Christendom on a pure evangelical foundation: 95 Thesis for the Reformation festival 1917).[33] The basic notion of the work is that Luther brought the German Christian faith only so far in freeing it from the embrace of Rome. They propose with their theses to now bring it full circle by addressing the presence of Judaizing elements in Christianity, especially the Old Testament. They work with the notion, expressed widely in the literature of 1917, that Christianity is the religiosity that is most suited to the German inner being, referencing not only the figure of Luther, but also recent racial science. They propose a thorough purging of non-"German" content from all aspects of the church's life. And because Christianity is so essential as part of what constitutes Germany's identity, the elimination of the poisonous influence of Judaism is pressing concern. Though this work is something of an oddity in the overall literature of 1917, it suggests the affinity of the mentality reflected in much of this literature for a call of this sort, and the connection of this mentality to the later blooming of Christian anti-Semitism in the German Christian movement of the 1930s is obvious, where Luther will again be used to promote its legitimacy.[34]

The focus here on the nationalist themes of the literature of 1917 reflects its overwhelming prevalence. Even liberal-minded theologians such as Adolf von Harnack and Ernst Troeltsch were caught up in the nationalist enthusiasm that marked the start of the war, and in Harnack's case the theme worked its way into his contribution to the 1917 celebration.[35] While much of the literature is popularizing, it was mostly written by pastors and laity with extensive academic and

---

"Freiheit also von römischer Tyrannei, ein freies, deutsches Kaiserreich, das war Luthers Ideal" (Freedom from the tyrany of Rome, a free, German Imperial Empire, that was Luther's ideal). König, *Vom Geiste Luthers*, 198.

[33] von Hauptpastor Friedrich Andersen in Flensburg, Professor Adolf Bartels in Weimar, Kirchenrat D. Dr. Ernst Katzer in Oberlößnitz bei Dresden, Hans Paul Freiherrn von Wolzogen in Bayreuth. Leipzig: Theodor Weicher, 1917.

[34] See Maron, "Luther 1917," 194–6. See Chapter 7 (pp. 165–7) for a fuller treatment of Andersen et al.'s work.

[35] For Harnack, see Maron, "Luther 1917," 183, and for Troeltsch, Christian Albrecht, "Zwischen Kriegstheologie und Krisentheologie. Zur Lutherrezeption im Reformationsjubiläum 1917." In *Luther Zwischen den Kulturen: Zeitgenossenschaft—Weltwirkung*, ed. Hans Medick and Peer Schmidt (Göttingen: Vandenhoeck & Ruprecht, 2004): 482–99; 495.

theological training, and even among the most eminent theological minds of the time this German nationalist theme predominates. That is not to say there was no dissent from this dominating theme. Ernst Troeltsch, in particular, in his contribution to 1917 celebration, called into question the equation of Christianity and Germanity, and suggested the necessary separation of the two, which coheres with his work prior to the outbreak of the war. In this regard, he is one of the few in the Protestant church who supported a negotiated peace, as was being suggested by the Vatican and the United States in late 1916 and 1917, rather than a "victor's peace" (*Siegesfrieden*), which was being loudly demanded my most Protestants. And Troeltsch was one of the few whose mindset would come to affirm a republican solution to Germany's ruling system after the war.[36] More typical of the viewpoint of academic theologians during the war years was the perspective of Paul Althaus, at this point at the beginning of his academic career, and serving as a medic and then pastor in Poland during the course of the war. Althaus' background and disposition are suggestive of the sources for the nationalistic emphasis of the Luther literature of 1917. He is of the generation born into the recently created German Empire and raised in an environment of heightened patriotism.[37] Raised in a strongly nationalist household, and deeply influenced by the pietistic Bethel "inner mission" movement, he came naturally to a view of the world that saw the Second Empire as the fulfillment of a specifically German formation of church and state; he and those like him were the inheritors of the image of Luther that had developed across the nineteenth century. His experience during the war as pastor to German Lutherans in city of Lodz in what had been Russian-ruled Poland impacted him deeply and shaped his nationalist perspective.[38] Althaus's work from 1917, *Luther und das Deutschtum* (*Luther and Germanity*),[39] shows how deeply the concept of a German Christianity was also rooted in the scholarly conception of Luther. While Althaus' work is more carefully constructed than other works treated above, it reflects the same spirit of German nationalism, and anticipates the future course of his scholarship and popular publications in the 1920s and '30s.[40]

---

[36] See Albrecht. "Zwischen Kriegstheologie und Krisentheologie," 495–7.

[37] For a work that looks at Althaus from this generational perspective, see Tanja Hetzer, *"Deutsche Stunde": Volksgemeinschaft und Antisemitismus in der politischen Theologie bei Paul Althaus* (Munich: Allitera Verlag, 2009): esp. 11ff. For an overview of this generational theme see Friedrich Wilhelm Graf, *Der heilige Zeitgeist: Studien zur Ideengeschichte der protestantischen Theologie in der Weimar Republik* (Tübingen: Mohr Siebeck, 2011).

[38] See Hetzer, *"Deutsche Stunde,"* 50–2. For Althaus, see the excellent biography of Gotthard Jasper, *Paul Althaus (1888–1966): Professor, Prediger und Patriot in seiner Zeit* (Göttingen: Vandenhoeck & Ruprecht, 2013). For some other examples of the forces shaping significant theologians of this generation see two articles by Thomas Kaufmann, "Die Harnacks und die Seebergs. 'Nationalprotestantische Mentalitäten' im Spiegel zweier Theologenfamilien." In *Nationalprotestantische Mentalitäten*, ed. Manfred Galius and Hartmut Lehmann (Göttingen: Vandenhoeck & Ruprecht, 2005): 165–222; and "Werner Elert als Kirchenhistoriker." *Zeitschrift für Theologie und Kirche* 47 (1996): 193–242.

[39] Paul Althaus, *Luther und das Deutschtum* (Leipzig: Deichertsche Verlagsbuchhandlung Werner Scholl, 1917).

[40] See Chapter 3 (pp. 69–78).

He begins in his introduction with the emotionality and overblown rhetoric typical of the period:

> No one can love Luther so dearly as we Germans. He is the "secret Emperor" of the Germans.... For he was one of us...German in his struggles and anger, German in the delicacy of his feelings for children, animals, and flowers. Childlike and soft and wonderfully tender, and then possessed of a manly defiance like no other, from the deepest integrity of his conscience and yet with a mighty, royal freedom of his being, that is the German Luther.

Like many other works, he highlights Luther's "German Peasant's Blood" (*deutsche Bauernblut*), emphasizing his status as a man of the people. Only foreigners or those Germans who have taken up foreign ways wouldn't connect with Luther.[41] He emphasizes, as well, Luther's battle against the foreigners who oppressed Germans, and adds, "one thing Luther sure wouldn't be today and that is **neutral!** He would stand by his *Volk* and fight against the enemy, whose type he so strikingly recognized and described." He continues:[42]

> The image of Luther is a precious gift of God to our whole *Volk*. Luther means present-day power. Just as C. F. Meyer as a German could confess, "he breathes deep in our breast." That is the greatest thing one can say of a person, that he

---

[41] "Niemand kann Luther so lieb haben wie wir Deutsche. Er ist der 'heimliche Kaiser' der Deutschen. Seines Lebens Segen ist weit über die Grenzen unseres Volkes hinausgegengen. Aber nirgends kann der deutsche Prophet so verstanden werden wie in Deutschland. Wie einen Bruder lieben wir ihn. Denn er war unser, 'ein jeder Zoll ein deutscher Mann' (C. F. Meyer), deutsch in seinem Ringen und Zürnen, deutsch in der Sinnigkeit seines Gemütes unter Kindern, Tieren und Blumen. Kindlich und weich und wundersam zart—und dann wieder von einem Mannestrotz ohnegleichen, von tiefstem Gewissensernste und doch von mächtiger, königlicher Freiheit seines Wesens, das ist der deutsche Luther. Aus deutschem Bauernblut entsprossen hat er zeitlebens nichts anderes sein wollen als ein Sohn des Thüringer Volkes. Grob und derb wie ein deutscher Bauersmann blieb er allwege. Mit breiten, lauten Bauernschuhen kann er in seinen Schriften einhertreten. Es gibt Leute, welsche und angewelschte Deutsche, denen er nicht fein genug, denen seine Gestalt zu bäurisch, sein Poltern zu barbarisch ist—von Kaiser Karl V. und den feinen Gelehrten jener Tage an bis heute" (Nobody can love Luther the way we Germans do. He is the "secret emperor of the Germans." The blessings of his life have gone out well beyond the boundaries of our *Volk*. But the German prophet can be understood nowhere so well as in Germany. We love him like a brother. Because he was ours, every inch a German man (C. F. Meyer), German in his struggles and anger, German in his sensitivity of his understanding for children, animals, and flowers. Childlike and tender and wonderfully delicate— and then again from a manly defiance like no other, out of the deepest earnestness of his conscience, and yet from a mighty royal freedom of his being, that's the German Luther. He sprang from German peasant blood, he wanted his whole life to be nothing other than a son of the Thuringian *Volk*. He always remained rough and earthy like a peasant. With broad and noisy peasant shoes he is able to step into his writings. There are people, foreigners and deracinated Germans, for whom he is not refined enough, who find his type too peasantlike, his bluster too barbaric—from Emperor Charles V and the refined scholars of his day all the way up to ours). *Luther und das Deutschtum*, 3.

[42] "Wie hat Martin Luther unser deutsches Volk lieb gehabt! Wenn er sah, wie sein Volk von Welschen gedrückt, geschunden und verachtet wurde, dann schwoll ihm die Zornesader gar gewaltig und deutscher Grimm donnerte durch seine Anklageschriften. Eines würde Luther auch heute gewißlich nicht sein: neutral! Er würde im Kampfe gegen die Feinde, deren Art er so treffend erkannt und ausgesprochen hat, zu seinem Volke stehen!" *Luther und das Deutschtum*, 3–4.

lives on as the deepest power of the *Volk*'s soul, indeed has become a part of the *Volk* soul (*Volksseele*). There lives on in all of us something of Luther, in the inner core of our being, there where we find conscience and God and eternity.[43]

Note the emphasis on a collective soul that connects the *Volk*, an idea that will be central to the development of Althaus' theology.

Having established the breadth and depth of Luther's importance for the inner meaning of what it is to be German, he moves into a more detailed exploration of the exact features of the German being he is referencing. He starts with his understanding of sin and grace, but then turns to specific inner characteristics of the German self, such as the importance of the conscience, of faithfulness, trust, and obedience. He contrasts this with the characteristics of other "*Völker*" such as the Italians, whose stamp was set on the medieval Church with their polarity of either indulgent worldliness or an unconditional fleeing from the world. This is a mentality entirely foreign to Germans, who have a hearty, open joy in God's creation, and manly pleasure in the orders of community and people, and a will to shape them, though this is held in tension with a yearning for the eternal and unseen.[44] This typologizing of national spiritual characteristics will carry over into Althaus' work as a theologian, as will the idea of orders of creation and the need for specifically German sort of society and politics.[45]

The second half of his work also reveals one of the motives behind this typologizing of German Christianity using the person of Luther. Here Althaus addresses the debate that was ongoing at the time with those who were advocating a specifically "German religiosity" (*Deutsche Frommigkeit*), which they saw embodied in figures other than Luther, particularly the spiritualists of the sixteenth century and following. Althaus is at some pains to carefully assert the Lutheran type of religiosity, as he defined it, as that which encompasses best the characteristics of the German spiritual type, and hence the truly native religiosity for the Germans. Though the specifics will change in the 1920s and '30s, this debate about what constitutes the true German type of religiosity will continue to shape the way

---

[43] "So ist die Luthergestalt ein herrliches Gottesgeschenk an unser ganzes Volk. Luther bedeutet gegenwärtige Kraft. Wie C. F. Meyer als Deutscher bekannt hat: 'Er atmet tief in unsrer Brust.' Das ist das Größte, was man von einem Manne sagen kann: daß er als tiefste Kraft in seines Volkes Seele weiterlebt, ja ein Stück Volksseele geworden ist. In uns allen lebt in den altarkammern unseres Wesens, da wo es um Gewissen und Gott und Ewigkeit geht, etwas von Luther fort." *Luther und das Deutschtum*, 4–5.

[44] "Die orientalischen, aber auch die romanischen Völker schwanken vielfach zwischen genuß-freudigstem Aufgehen in der Welt und der rücksichtslosesten Weltflucht.... Dem deutschen Sinne liegen die Extreme fern. Deutsch ist die offene herzliche Freude an Gottes Welt, das männliche Wohlgefallen an den Ordnungen von Gemeinde und Volk, der männliche Wille, die Welt zu gestalten; Deutsch ist aber auch das Ungenügen an der sichtbaren Welt der Natur und des geschichtlichen Lebens, die klare Einsicht in die Unzulänglichkeit des Diesseits und die Sehnsucht nach einer ewigen Welt des Unsichtbaren." *Luther und das Deutschtum*, 16.

[45] See Hetzer, "*Deutsche Stunde*," 54–7.

Luther is defined and typified over the next decades, both within popular religious debates and in more structured theological scholarship. In this sense, while Althaus' 1917 piece is a relatively minor work, it anticipates the direction both of his theological career and his response to nationalist movements in Weimar and beyond.

One feature of almost all the works of the 1917 celebration is the emphasis on combativeness. There is a strong element of exhortation in the pieces that the war was still to be won; what was of necessity was the will to fight to the end, to take on the enemies and defeat them—hence the repeated emphasis on Luther's exemplary fighting spirit. This reflects the overall disposition of Protestants in 1917–18. Though there is recognition that the war effort is in a critical phase, there is little recognition of the growing unlikelihood of armed victory. Protestant voices advocated expansive goals for a German victory, more expansive now that so much sacrifice has been exacted from the German people.[46] That Germany would win such a victory was little questioned, and solidarity with the military and political leadership was the general order of the day. It is striking that even in the very end phase of the war, October and November 1918, there was little recognition of the dire situation of the German military effort, or that the military leadership by the start of October was informing the civilian government of the hopelessness of the situation, and the need bring an end to the conflict before the total collapse of the front lines. As a result, the events at the end of the war—the abdication of the Kaiser, the unconditional surrender (though most did not recognize the proportions of that surrender in the armistice), and the proclamation of a republic came as a wholesale shock among middle-class Protestants of all stripes.[47] The ascension of socialists to the leading figures of the new state was greeted by conservative Protestants with abhorrence, the collapse of the military effort with incomprehension, and a sense of a world falling around them marked the general sense of doom. What sense could be rendered from the situation relied on concepts of divine punishment for the failures and sins of the leaders, and fed into the soon to be articulated "stab-in-the-back theory."[48] Nevertheless, the messages of faith that were conveyed in the 1917 Reformation celebration resonated still. A letter from the end of November 1918 to the editor in the periodical *Christliche Freiheit* (Christian freedom) from a war widow gives a sense of how religious faith made sense of the moment:

---

[46] See the selection of documents highlighting the overwhelmingly aggressive tone of Protestant commentary in Brakelmann, *Der deutsche Protestantismus im Epochenjahr 1917*, 95–143. See also Brakelmann's discussion of Reinhard Seeberg's theology of war, in particular his expansionist goals for a German victory; Günter Brakelmann, *Protestantische Kriegstheologie im 1. Weltkrieg. Reinhold Seeberg als Theologe des deutschen Imperialismus* (Bielefeld: Luther Verlag, 1974): 73–104.

[47] See the selection of documents in Martin Greschat, ed. *Der Deutsche Protestantismus im Revolutionsjahr 1918–1919* (Stuttgart: W. Kohlhammer, 1997): 16–87.

[48] Greschat, ed., *Der Deutsche Protestantismus*, 12.

I'm just coming now from the Lutheran church—I must extend my hand to you, Dr. Traub—and give my thanks. For six months now foreign soil covered over my husband's body. "The highest good of a man is his *Volk*" was his motto, and it stands on his grave. In your words my most beloved was resurrected for me. He fell in the belief in Germany's victory! His soul lives on. We may have lost the war—it is a bitter pill—but no one can rob me of my belief in our Germanity. A new Germany will be born out of need and suffering—we are its agents! The kingdom's ours forever! *Heil*![49]

One can find in such sentiments a sense of the dominant mindset of the majority of German Protestants during the 1920s; a grudging acceptance of the existing circumstances coupled with a hope to bring back some version of societal formation that corresponds to their deeply religious nationalistic sense of identity, connected here with the person of Luther.

A commentary in the Protestant monthly *Die Dorfkirche* (the village church) from December 1918 profiles how this belief in "Germanity" was translated into a political formula:

Yes, in the German personality, in which the German soul has found herself and her right within her freedom from all the world, in this most inward ethical freedom lies the roots of the German body politic. Luther established it [this freedom], when he gave to the German soul the inner freedom in high duty and responsibility before her inner divine law, and upon [this freedom] first staked the entire existence of the German state. The image of Luther before the Emperor and Empire is rooted in the blood of us all.... The goal of a true social state, which the entire soul of the German *Volk* desires, can't arise from any kind of democratic theory.... It can grow only out of the physical German *Volkstum* of history...

...We know, that the greatest path of God goes directly through innocent suffering.... Alone in our God we still hope, in his will we believe. For the sake of the destiny of the German *Volk* we believe, for the sake of the unfulfilled divine promises we believe, which resonate for us in all the great God-given things within German people; for the sake of the goals for which God created it in the beginning, and for which there is for no other *Volk* in the world. It is not a belief in rights, but a belief in history, which sees in world historical events and in all

---

[49] "Eben komme ich aus der Lutherkirche—ich muß Ihnen die hand geben, Herr Doktor Traub—ganz fest, und Ihnen danken. Seit sechs Monaten deckt welsche Erde meines Mannes Leib. 'Das höchste Gut des Mannes ist sein Volk' war sein Wahlspruch, so steht es auf seinem Hügel. In Ihren Worten ist mir mein Liebster wieder auferstanden. Er fiel im Glauben an Deutschlands Sieg! Seine Seele lebt. Mögen wir den Krieg verlieren—es ist bitter schwer-den Glauben an unser Deutschtum kann mir keiner rauben. Ein neues Deutschland wird geboren werden aus Not und Leid—wir sind seine Träger! Das Reich muß uns doch bleiben! Heil!" Greschat, ed., *Der Deutsche Protestantismus*, 34.

the *Volker* and spiritual realities of creation the revelation of the will and purposes of God.[50]

We'll see in the Weimar era this ideal of an organic German society that grows from the soil of the German *Volkstum* takes hold within Lutheran theology, such that it provides a religious basis for embracing the next system of authoritarian rule that comes in the 1930s. While the 1920s will be marked by a "renaissance" within the study of Luther that will take scholars more deeply than ever into his writings, it will remain captured, for the most part, by the Luther image cast by the nationalism of the nineteenth century and the Great War, and by the notion that the answers for the crisis of Protestantism and Germany as a whole lie with an ever deeper engagement with the figure of the German Luther and faith grounded in his legacy and being. This will set the stage for the next great public celebration in 1933 of Luther, which will be carried out in an entirely transformed political environment. The image of Luther inherited by the 1920s undergirds the resistance of the Protestant church as a whole to the new German democracy, and its increasing attraction to racial nationalist and authoritarian systems of rule.[51]

The Luther Myth: The Image of Martin Luther from Religious Reformer to Völkisch Icon. Patrick Hayden-Roy, Oxford University Press. © Patrick Hayden-Roy 2024. DOI: 10.1093/9780198930297.003.0003

---

[50] "...Ja, in der deutschen Persönlichkeit, in der die deutsche Seele sich selbst und ihr Recht in ihrer Freiheit von aller Welt gefunden hatte, in dieser innersten sittlichen Freiheit liegen die Wurzeln des deutschen Staatslebens. Luther hat sie gelegt, als er der deutschen Seele die innere Freiheit gab in der hohen Pflicht und Verantwortung vor ihrem inneren göttlichen Gesetz und darüber zunächst das ganze staatliche Dasein Deutschlands aufs Spiel setzte. Die Luthergestalt vor Kaiser und Reich steckt uns allen im Blute.... Dies Ziel eines wahrhaft sozialen Staates, wonach die ganze deutsche Volksseele verlangt, kann nicht aus irgendeiner demokratischen Theorie hervorgehen.... Nur aus dem leibhaftigen deutschen Volkstum der Geschichte kann es erwachsen.... Wir wissen, daß gerade die größten Wege Gottes durch unschuldiges Leiden gehen.... Allein auf unsern Gott noch hoffen wir, an seinen Willen glauben wir. Um der Bestimmung des deutschen Volkes willen glauben wir, um der unerfüllten göttlichen Verheißungen willen, die uns in allem Großen, Gottgebenen im deutschen Volke entgegenklingen, um der Ziele willen, zu denen Gott es von Anfang an geschaffen und für die kein ander Volk in der Welt da ist. Es ist kein Rechtsglaube, sondern ein Geschichtsglaube, der in den Weltereignissen und in allen Völker- und Geistesschöpfungen Offenbarungen des Willens und der Zwecke Gottes sieht...." Greschat, ed., *Der Deutsche Protestantismus*, 50–1.

[51] On this point, see the comments of Klaus Scholder: "Faßt man den deutschen Protestantismus der Weimarer Zeit als geistig-politische Gesamterscheinung ins Auge, so treten jene Strömungen, die wir eben behandelt haben, stark zurück. Weder den Religiös-Sozialen, noch den Liberalen, noch der dialektischen Theologie gelang es in den Jahren zwischen 1918–1933, einen tiefergehenden Einfluß auf die Kirche selbst zu gewinnen. Diese Kirche blieb vielmehr, aufs Ganze gesehen, auch nach dem Kriege das, was sie vor seinem Ausbruch gewesen war: konservativ und Deutsch-national" (If one considers German Protestantism of the Weimar Era as a spiritual/political phenomenon, then those tendencies that we have just treated retreat decisively into the background. Neither religious socialism, nor liberalism, nor dialectical theology succeeded in the years between 1918–1933 to win a deeply penetrating influence on the church itself. This church remained much more, looked at as a whole, also after the war, what it was before its outbreak: conservative and German-nationalist). Klaus Scholder, "Neure deutsche Geschichte und protestantische Theologie." In *Die Kirchen zwischen Republik und Gewaltherrschaft: Klaus Scholder Gesammelte Aufsätze*, ed. K. O. v. Aretin and Gerhard Besier (Berlin: Siedler Verlag, 1988): 75–97; 87.

3
The Reborn Luther

The end of World War I left behind a broken and bewildering landscape. Though Germany did not experience the physical destruction of France or Belgium, the war destroyed the old order without providing the stable basis for something new. And while Germany experienced a revolution that brought into being new political structures, the Weimar Republic, it did so in a way that left in place the mindsets that had been shaped over the course of the last hundred years; the new system lacked legitimacy in the eyes of many who came under its rule. Even among the socialists who populated the mass political parties that provided the popular legitimacy for the initial changes of structure there was division and uncertainty about the path forward; to many of them the revolution seemed incomplete, and not a few looked to the model of Russia's recent revolution for a guide to what theirs should accomplish. So, while the left side of political spectrum carried forward the constitutional changes, a significant portion of their support was based on expectations of a more fundamental economic revolution to accompany the political revolution. But just such sentiment alarmed many in the political middle and right of the spectrum. Playing on the fears of the specter of Bolshevism and a red menace provided a solid basis for political parties that looked at best with suspicion on the new republic.

Even more debilitating in the long run was the association of the new regime with the signing of the Versailles Treaty, with its war guilt clause that justified the military, territorial, and economic penalties that were exacted from Germany. Though there was little that unified post-war German society, most were convinced that the treaty was an indictment of Germany's honor, and roundly rejected it as the basis for enduring peace. As a result, though the leaders of the new Republic had little choice, they reaped the blame for having put the nation's signature to the Treaty. This provided the basis for an enduring fantasy that Jews and socialists, archenemies of the true Germany, had used the war for gain and profit, and then stabbed the military and imperial leadership in the back in order to consolidate their position in the post-war state. Such ideas proliferated among right-wing parties and become the ammunition that would be used against Weimar all the way through its short history. Though far-right (and -left) rejectionist parties did not dominate electoral politics until late in Weimar's history, the impact of their rhetorical attacks undermined the legitimacy of the state, which struggled to find a place in the sentiments of its citizens. And in the first years of the Republic, political violence and economic turmoil plagued public affairs, and added to the sense of crisis and betrayal. Though greater equilibrium would be achieved toward the middle of the 1920s, the Great Depression at its end would tip German politics back into crisis, leading in the end to the seizure of power by the Nazis. Within this climate of upheaval, Luther would be held up as a figure from whom could emerge the spirit of a new Germany, a rallying point for those for whom the Weimar system offered no sense of connection or identity. In this way, Luther was reborn as a figure both of resistance to the spirit of the current age, but also one whose meaning and inner spirit could inspire a revival of the German being.[1]

Stirrings of this "Luther Renaissance," as its academic expression came to be named, were already present at the end of the war, as noted in the previous chapter. Luther as the carrier of German identity had already been loudly trumpeted in the literature of 1883 and 1917. But after the war this idea was given a more tangible institutional form, and also became deeply rooted in the scholarship of Protestant church history that would unfold in the 1920s, a good portion of which would explore Luther not as an artifact of a past world, but as an enduring spiritual reality to be reanimated for the benefit of present and future. The sensibility and forces at work driving this forward can be seen with the foundation and development of the Luther Society (*Luther-Gesellschaft*), which was established in the waning days of the war, and came to its first flowering during the 1920s.[2]

The idea for such a society was rooted in the idealist philosophy and historical literature that gave form to the image of Luther in the nineteenth century. Hegel's notion of a spiritual lineage of ideas that were associated with the emergence of different epochs of modern history, and which precipitated into the state forms of the nineteenth century, situated Luther as the spiritual ancestor of the German self. Nationalism of the nineteenth century shaped that into the secularized Luther whose spiritual rebellion against Rome became a metaphor for the freeing of the German spirit from foreign influences and the basis for a new German epoch. Though Luther continued to represent also an explicitly Christian spiritual significance, his place in the public square of nineteenth- and early twentieth-century German life was as a national symbol, at least among middle-class Protestant Germans and their cultural mouthpieces. It was clear in the context of the First World War how central this idea of the "German" Luther had become, even among conservative Protestants. So, it makes perfect sense that at the end of the war someone distant from traditional Lutheran religiosity, Rudolf Eucken

---

[1] For an interesting example of the aspirations of Protestant theologians for their agency as expositors of Luther in addressing the crises of the age, see the discussion of a sermon held by Friedrich Gogarten in 1920 in Friedrich Wilhelm Graf, *Der heilige Zeitgeist: Studien zur Ideengeschichte der protestantischen Theologie in der Weimar Republik* (Tübingen: Mohr Siebeck, 2011): 5–6.

[2] For an overview of the founding and development of the society, see *Die Luther-Gesellschaft 1918–2018*, ed. Johannes Schilling and Martin Treu (Leipzig: Evangelische Verlagsanstalt, 2018): esp. Stefan Rhein, "Wittenberg und die Anfänge der Luther-Gesellschaft," 9–33.

(1846–1926), philosopher at the University of Jena, popular author and Nobel Prize winner for literature, and a man of broad religious views, but who also had connections, however, with the Protestant Lutheran establishment, would become the instigator of a new society that would concern itself with the legacy of Martin Luther in its broadest configuration.

Eucken had, in his philosophical writings, come to perceive Luther as one of the "great thinkers" whose *Lebensanschauungen* (life perspectives) marked him as a prophet of a universal religion that stands above and beyond any narrow confessional or timebound expression of religious truth.[3] Eucken developed his view of Luther within the larger schema of his philosophy over time, and in his work *Die Lebensanschauungen der grossen Denker* (the life perspectives of the great thinkers), new editions of which he published repeatedly from the 1890s up through World War I, he came to engage increasingly with Luther. It was particularly the end of the war that brought him to view Luther in a new light, seeing in him a specifically German and deeply inner understanding of freedom that stood in contrast to the world view that informed the culture of the Western powers.[4] Eucken wasn't especially concerned with Luther's theological arguments, and he considered his biblicism to be anti-modern, but he saw him as someone who had recognized an essential challenge to the human self, that is, how to find a sense of freedom within, and had come to find a resolution in a deep understanding of God that provided a model for the modern self in crisis. It was this sense of Luther's central importance as an emollient for the crisis of the times that led Eucken to publish in 1917 a notice calling for the creation of a newly conceived Luther Society,[5] followed in early 1918 by a public notice, in this instance edited with the help of Lutheran theologian and pastor Theodor Knolle.[6] He called on the society to devote itself to the Luther who was "not only the reformer of the church, but of the entire world," noting the full breadth of themes that should

---

[3] For an discussion of Eucken's philosophy and its application to Luther, see Uwe Dathe, "Reform des Glaubens? Reform der Kirche? Reform des Lebens!: Rudolf Euckens lebensphilosophische Luther-Interpretation." In *Luther Denken: Die Reformation im Werk Jenaer Gelehrter*, ed. Christopher Spehr (Leipzig: Evangelische Verlagsanstalt, 2019): 221–38. See pages 226–8 for a discussion of his philosophy of religion as it applies to Luther.

[4] Rudolf Eucken, *Die Lebensanschauungen der grossen Denker: eine Entwicklungsgeschichte des Lebensproblems der Menschheit von Plato zur Gegenwart*. 12th ed. (Leipzig: Veit, 1918). The work was first published in 1890 and went through 18 editions up through 1922. Between 1911 and 1918 Eucken came to his fullest view of Luther. See the discussion of Dathe, "Reform des Glaubens?," 228–30.

[5] Rudolf Eucken, "Aufruf zur Gründung einer Luthergesellschaft." In *Deutscher Will: des Kunstwarts* 31 (1917): 182–4. See the reproduction in *Die Luther-Gesellschaft 1918–2018*, 335–7.

[6] Knolle was at this time a pastor in Wittenberg, and is a good example of the connections between Eucken and the traditional Lutheran establishment in Wittenberg. In addition to being instrumental in the founding of the Luther Society, Knolle would continue over his long career to be an influential member, both as editor of its journals and as a scholarly contributor. See Chapter 8 (pp. 210–12) for his contributions in the controversy surrounding Arno Deutelmoser. For an overview of Knolle's activity with the *Luther-Gesellschaft*, see Andreas Pawlas, "Mit Luther durch aufgewühlte Zeiten- Theodor Knolle und die Luther-Gesellschaft." In *Luther-Gesellschaft 1918–2018*, ed. Johannes Schilling and Martin Treu (Leipzig: Evangelische Verlagsanstalt, 2018): 83–128.

engage its efforts: his relationship to nature, to the life of children, to art, to state and society, and to economic issues.[7] Clearly the founding spirit brought by Eucken reflected his expanded sense of what the engagement with Luther could involve beyond his place in the idealist lineage of Germany's spiritual development.

Though Eucken only led the new society briefly, his contributions to the first volume of the *Lutherjahrbuch*, which remains to this day the flagship publication of the Luther Society, provide a full view of his own expansive sense of Luther's significance for this new world, and also what would animate the profound engagement of scholars with Luther in the 1920s and '30s. He opens the journal with a brief contribution explaining the purpose of the society in sweeping terms:

> We ask ourselves, why do we need Luther today? And we answer with a brief word: because his solid faith, his enormous power, his unshakable trust in God are indispensable for us, in order to save us from the monstrous dangers in which we find ourselves. We stand now in a severe spiritual crisis, and we need urgently great personalities, we need the primal power which Luther opens for us. To be clear, we mean by such a crisis not the world war, although it has moved our spirit in the deepest way, rather we think above all of the spiritual danger that threatens us with a vast lowering of our entire life circumstances and which damages in the deepest way the entirety of our culture with all of its world-historical achievements.[8]

He concludes his short piece with even greater emphasis:

> For us Germans it is of pressing concern that the true spirit of Luther work again in us, driving out all that is false, and rejuvenate us through its rule. Only on that basis can come a solid confidence, a fearlessness, a joy in life in the midst of dangers and emergencies... if the Luther Society is founded in this spirit, then can Luther once again become a savior for us Germans.[9]

---

[7] "Luther war nicht nur ein Reformator der Kirche, sondern der ganzen Welt." The notice is reproduced by Rhein, "Wittenberg und die Anfänge der Luther-Gesellschaft," 14.

[8] "Weshalb, fragen wir, bedürfen wir heute Luther? und wir antworten mit kurzem Wort: weil sein fester Glaube, seine riesenhafte Kraft, sein unerschütterliches Gottvertrauen uns unentbehrlich ist, um uns von den ungeheuren Gefahren zu retten in denen wir uns befinden. Wir stehen jetzt in einer schweren geistigen Krise, und wir bedürfen dringend großer Persönlichkeiten, wir bedürfen ursprünglicher Lebensquellen, wie Luther sie uns eröffnet. Wir denken bei solcher Krise zunächst nicht an den Weltkrieg, obwohl er unsere Gemüter aufs tiefste bewegt, wir denken an erster Stelle an die geistigen Gefahren, welche uns mit einem starken Sinken unseres gesamten Lebensstandes bedrohen und das Ganze unserer Kultur mit all ihren weltgeschichtlichen Leistungen aufs tiefste schädigen." Rudolf Eucken, "Weshalb bedürfen wir einer Luther-Gesellschaft." *Lutherjahrbuch* 1 (1919): 5–8; 5.

[9] "Für uns Deutsche bedarf es dessen dringend, daß wieder der echte Luthergeist kräftig auf uns wirke, alles Scheinhafte austreibe und verjüngend in unseren Seelen walte. Nur von da aus kann uns wieder eine feste Zuversicht, eine Unerschrockenheit, eine Fröhlichkeit des Lebens inmitten aller der

Later in the same volume he added a second essay more specifically elucidating what he had in mind:

> We require such men who seize their whole *Volk* in the manner of the Old Testament prophets and infuse in them a strong longing for the spiritual and divine life. For us Luther is just such a man. As he created out the depths of our German essence, so he can also with primal power bring back to life and elevate the present day; for us he isn't just a historical great, but he works by the power of the life that fills him like an immediate force of the present. Let's take a look now at the main points where Luther's striving touches closely the tasks and demands of the present day.[10]

The article follows with seven parts, each emphasizing a feature of Luther's life and thought that Eucken finds exemplary for the present and its crisis. Among the other prescriptions which he sees connected to this infusion of Luther is a rejection of Enlightenment reason, a call for decisive commitment, a belief that God will aid the Germans in their struggles, and a belief in not just a spiritual but a moral salvation, which will be the basis for a revival of the nation—political systems and programs cannot be the source of national salvation. He concludes by calling for the spirit not only of Luther's love and faith, but also his holy wrath to meet the present-day challenges.[11]

The article reveals a number of perspectives that will inform Luther scholarship of the era that follows. His rejection of the Enlightenment and liberal tradition of rationality and secularism, the instrumental use of Luther as the antidote for the spiritual, moral, and material ills of the present, the idea that commitment to Luther means not just faith but also action, all this feeds into aspects of the "Luther Renaissance." Eucken was no theologian, nor was he especially well versed in Luther's writings, but his enthusiasm for Luther as a powerful living presence from whom could come the salvation from the crisis of the present captures exactly what animates the Luther studies of the 1920s. Eucken's stay as head of the society came to an end in 1919, a result not only of his age, but also the frictions that inevitably emerged between his broad philosophical and cultural

---

Gefahren und Nöte kommen.... Wenn in diesem Geist die Luther-Gesellschaft entstehen wird, kann Luther abermals ein Erretter für uns Deutsche werden." Eucken, "Weshalb," 8.

[10] "Wir bedürfen solcher Männer, welche nach Art der alttestamentlichen Propheten ihr ganzes Volk ergriffen und ihnen ein starkes Sehnen nach dem geistigen und göttlichen Leben einflößten. Ein solcher Mann ist uns Luther. Wie er aus der Tiefe unseres deutschen Wesens schuf, so kann er auch mit ursprünglicher Kraft die Gegenwart beleben und erhöhen; er ist uns keineswegs nur eine geschichtliche Größe, sondern er wirkt kraft des ihn erfüllenden Lebens wie eine unmittelbare Macht der Gegenwart. Sehen wir nun, an welchen Hauptpunkten Luthers Streben sich eng mit den Aufgaben und Forderungen der Gegenwart berührt." Rudolf Eucken, "Luther und die geistige Erneuerung des deutschen Volkes." *Lutherjahrbuch* I (1919): 27–34; 28.

[11] Eucken, "Luther und die geistige Erneuerung," 33–4.

viewpoints, and the more specifically confessional commitments and financially austere habits of most of the rest of the leadership of the new Society.[12]

Another article in this first volume of the *Lutherjahrbuch*, "Luther und der deutsche Staatsgedanke" by Arnold E. Berger (1862–1948), extends and deepens this idea of Luther's restorative power for the crisis of the times. Berger starts by describing the fifteenth and sixteenth centuries as the age when the German *Volk* came to itself, and began to free itself from the fetters of foreign language and culture. In that context Luther emerged:

> In this creative, roiling, spiritually youthful time, shaken by intimations of a great future Luther emerged, and indeed with a watchword that must strike at the heart of the times. For because he called the age to rebirth from within, to a spiritual new becoming, he uncovered for it not only the secret of its destiny, but also he showed the way to become master of its perplexing disquiet; that is, by the simple devotion to the saving power of the Gospel and the answer it offers to humanity's highest question, the question of the meaning of our life, to the purpose and substance of the divine world order.[13]

It is this sense of the existential relevance of Luther for the times that infuses much of the engagement of the 1920s; to study Luther isn't to look to the past, but to make what was eternal in the great individual of the past living again. And this is not simply a question of individual comfort in a difficult time, as is common with Christian piety. Berger has a much broader field of significance for Luther. He attributes to Luther a huge agency in bringing about a fundamental reorientation of the relationship of spiritual to worldly authority, whereby the church was set in the inner person, and much of what the church had taken as its proper sphere in the outer world—law, schools, the regulation of human relations—ended up in the hands of the state. According to Berger, Luther envisions a society where, with the right ruling order, the true faith can be much more; "namely a practical Christendom, acting out of a love of neighbor for the sake of God's love,

---

[12] See the discussion of Rhein, "Wittenberg und die Anfänge der Luther-Gesellschaft," 9–33. Eucken instituted as part of the Society's activities a series of Luther evenings, with readings and vocal solos by Eucken's daughter. Though these were intended as fund raisers, they frequently failed to make back the costs of the affair, and were looked upon with skepticism by other members of the Society's board.

[13] "In dieser schöpferisch erregten, seelisch jungen und von Ahnungen einer großen Zukunft erschütterten Zeit trat Luther auf, und zwar mit einer Losung, die sie mitten ins Herz treffen mußte. Denn indem er sie zur Wiedergeburt von innen heraus, zum seelischen Neuwerden aufrief, enthüllte er ihr nicht nur das Geheimnis ihrer Bestimmung, sondern er wies ihr auch den Weg, um ihrer rätselhaften Unruhe Herr zu werden: in der schlichten Hingabe an die erlösenden Kräfte des Evangeliums und die aus ihm zu gewinnende Lösung der höchsten Menschheitsfrage, der Fragen nach dem Sinn unseres Lebens, dem Zweck und Inhalt der göttlichen Weltordnung." Arnold E. Berger, "Luther und der deutsche Staatsgedanke." *Lutherjahrbuch* I (1919): 34–56; 35–6.

Christian service to one's brother, and with this 'a preview or foretaste of the true blessedness of heaven'."[14]

This leads him to describe what constitutes the "deutsche Staatsgedanke (German idea of the state)," distinguishing it from those forms which mark Western, democratic, capitalistic society, and extolling a Germanic organic order in which the power of the authorities rests on the implicit will of the *Volk*, bound together by ties of mutual obligation grounded in a divinely ordained order. He highlights features of Luther's thought that correspond to such a definition, and then discusses how the development of the German state in the nineteenth century, and in particular the Prussian state and its order during the time of Bismarck, represented this German and Luther-conforming state formation.[15] Always, he notes, this German state order has been disrupted by the incursion of foreign elements with their natural law and cosmopolitan ideas, which necessitated struggle, "never more passionately and successfully than with Luther's great spiritual relation, Bismarck."[16] And while the structure may have now been destroyed, the foundation on which it rested is still there, the unshakable belief in the ethical and religious power of the people—"the spirit lives on in us all, and our fortress is God."[17]

---

[14] "...das weltliche Regiment kann aber, wenn es im rechten Glauben geübt wird, doch noch viel mehr sein, nämlich praktisches Christentum, handelnde Nächstenliebe um der Gottesliebe willen, christlicher Bruderdienst und somit 'ein Vorbild (oder ein Vorahnen) der rechten Seligkeit im Himmel.'" Berger, "Luther und der deutsche Staatsgedanke," 39.

[15] Berger, "Luther und der deutsche Staatsgedanke," 40–52.

[16] "Nur unter schweren Kämpfen ist es gelungen, diese Erneuerung des deutschen Staatswesens aus seinen bodenständigen Kräften Schritt um Schritt durchzusetzen, immer wieder gestört durch den Einbruch fremdländischer Gedanken naturrechtlicher Herkunft und weltbürgerlichen Gepräges, mit denen niemand leidenschaftlicher und erfolgreicher gerungen hat als Luthers großer Geistesverwandter Bismarck" (Only with great struggle has it succeeded, step by step, to accomplish this renewal of the German state through its native powers, again and again disrupted by the invasion of foreign ideas rooted in natural law and a cosmopolitan character, with which no one wrestled more passionately and successfully than Luther's great spiritual relation, Bismarck). Berger, "Luther und der deutsche Staatsgedanke," 53. This association of Luther with Bismarck had become a stock formula in the Luther literature of the late nineteenth and early twentieth century, with a number of works written based on the notion of the fundamental affinity between the two great uniters of Germany. See, for instance, Herman von Bezzel, *Luther, Bismarck: von Dr. von Bezzel* (Munich: Müller & Fröhlich, 1917). For a more recent discussion of Bismarck's connection to Luther and Lutheranism, see Rudolf von Thadden, "Bismarck—ein Lutheraner?." In *Luther in der Neuzeit*, ed. Bernd Moeller (Gütersloh: Gerd Mohn, 1983): 104–20.

[17] "Der von ihm geschaffene kühne und stolze, wenn auch innerlich noch unfertige Bau des neudeutschen Kaiserreichs ist unter dem Druck eines ungeheuren Schicksals nach kaum fünfzigjährigem Bestande wieder in den Staub gesunken. Aber so gewiß Luther und Bismarck ewig unter uns leben werden, so unerschütterlich glauben wir auch an die religiösen und sittlichen Kräfte unseres Volkes, die bei jenem Bau geholfen haben. Zwar sind sie heute tief gebeugt, betäubt und gelähmt, doch nicht gebrochen: 'Das Haus mag zerfallen—was hat's denn für Not? Der Geist lebt in uns allen, und unsere Burg ist Gott'" (The bold and glorious, if inwardly incomplete structure of the new German Empire created by him sank into the dust under the weight of a horrific fate after scarcely fifty years of existence. However, just as Luther and Bismarck will live among us eternally, so also we believe unwaveringly in the religious and ethical forces of our *Volk*, which helped in this construction. While they are profoundly bent, deadened, and paralyzed today, they are not broken. 'The house may

He envisions what this order would look like:

> Just our forebearers on the eve of the Reformation or the Wars of Freedom, so we also are inspired (*beseelt*) by the confidence in Germany's rebirth based on the emergence of a new national organic society (*Lebensgemeinschaft*) from within and from below. We must succeed in creating the state structure which, as an authentic expression of the most noble life force and determinations of the will of our *Volk*, guarantees the self-determination and expression of the German spirit (*Geistes*) in the world. It can only grow out of a new consciousness of the ethical sovereignty of the German state idea, which as ever has something significant to say to the world. For its undeniable superiority over the Roman, British and Slavic ideas rests upon its inborn belief in the holiness of the state order, which reigns over us all, promoting and directing us as an undying spiritual-ethical corporative identity and historical incarnation of the essence of the nation, and yet at the same time it wins a living form in the existing current body of the *Volksgenossenschaft* and becomes real, acting at the same time transcendently and immanently.[18]

This mystical ideal of an organic Germanic state order leads him to a final prophecy about the fulfillment of the historical destiny of the German state idea:

> A people who understands itself in this way, however, needs for the sake of its preservation a powerful, independent, guiding (*führenden*) ruler who is conscious of his high responsibilities, who is free of the current partisan desires and opinions of the moment, acting often in conscious opposition to them, recognizing with a sharp eye and resolutely discerning the common good; who above all, as a strong protector of social justice and national sense of community, takes the subversive (*zersetzendes*) edge off the class struggle and gains the courage to take into himself the contradictory desires and bring them together into a unitary action until finally, as Luther, concerning similar hopes, onetime

---

crumble—what would that matter? The spirit lives on in all of us, and our fortress is God'). Berger, "Luther und der deutsche Staatsgedanke," 53.

[18] "Wie unsere Vorfahren am Vorabend der Reformation oder Befreiungskriege, so beseelt auch uns die Zuversicht auf Deutschlands Wiedergeburt, auf das Werden einer neuen nationalen Lebensgemeinschaft von innen heraus und von unten herauf. Ihr muß es gelingen, die Staatsform zu schaffen, die als vollwertiger Ausdruck der edelsten Lebenstriebe und Willensbestimmtheiten unseres Volkes die unerläßliche Selbstdarstellung und Selbstbehauptung des deutschen Geistes in der Welt sicher verbürgt. Sie kann nur erwachsen aus einer neuen Besinnung auf die sittliche Hoheit des germanischen Staatsgedankens, der der Welt noch immer Bedeutsames zu sagen hat, denn seine unleugbare Überlegenheit gegenüber dem romanischen, britischen und slawischen ruht auf dem ihm eingeborenen Glauben an die Heiligkeit der staatlichen Ordnung, die als unsterbliche geistig-sittliche Gesamtpersönlichkeit und geschichtliche Verkörperung des Wesens der Nation fordernd und richtend über uns allen thront und doch zugleich in den jeweils gegenwärtigen Gliedern der Volksgenossenschaft lebendig Gestalt gewinnen und Tat werden möchte, transzendent und immanent zugleich wirkend." Berger, "Luther und der deutsche Staatsgedanke," 53–4.

said, "the time comes that God gives again a true hero or miracle man, under whose guidance everything goes better or as well as could be found in any book; who will either alter the law or master it, so that the land becomes green and blooms with peace, discipline, security, justice, such that it might be termed a healthy regime; and consequently during his life he is most highly feared, honored and loved, and after his death praised eternally."[19] May the heralds of returning health also soon appear for our sickened time, and may the bond between the German state idea with the ethical spirit of Christendom prove anew its constructive power.[20]

As we will see, this ideal of the *Führer* as described by Berger actually tracks the description of Luther in the literature of the Luther Renaissance and other popular representations of him that will come forward in the 1920s and '30s. And this coupling of Christian ethics with spiritual renewal and a coming "heroic" leader informs much political thought that will emerge out of the reengagement with Luther that marks the Luther Renaissance, and will form the basis for much of the enthusiasm among Protestants for the coming of the National Socialist regime.

While the *Lutherjahrbuch*'s first volume provides a broad sense of the aspirations that will inform the turn to Luther in the 1920s, the most important specifically scholarly impetus for a new engagement with Luther came from the studies of Karl Holl (1866–1926), Professor of Church History and Systematics in Berlin, whose work was seminal for a generation of Luther scholars and initiates. Holl is himself a figure of great interest apart from his writings on Luther. He came out of the liberal Protestant tradition, and made his name initially as a patristics scholar. Two passageways in his life transformed his theological perspective, the first his encounter with Luther, which had the effect similar to Luther's own "Evangelical breakthrough," and the second his experience of World War I. Holl emerged from these two intertwined passages transformed, dedicating his later theological

---

[19] On Luther's idea of the *Wundermann* see Patrick Hayden-Roy, "Unmasking the Hidden God: Luther's *wundermänner*." *Lutherjahrbuch* 82 (2015): 66–105.

[20] "Ein so sich verstehendes Volk aber bedarf um seiner selbsterhaltung willen einer starken, ihrer hohen Verantwortlichkeit bewußten, selbständig führenden Obrigkeit, die frei von den jeweiligen Parteiwünschen und Tagesmeinungen, oft genug diesen bewußt entgegen, das gemeine Beste scharfblickend erkennt und entschlossen wahrnimmt, die vor allem als strenge Hüterin sozialer Gerechtigkeit und nationalen Gemeinschaftsgefühls dem Klassenkampf seine zersetzende Schärfe nimmt und den Mut gewinnt, die auseinanderstrebenden Willensrichtungen an sich zu ziehen und zu einheitlichem Handeln zusammenzuballen, bis endlich—wie Luther aus gleichartigem Hoffen einmal gesagt hat—'die Zeit kommt, daß Gott wieder einen gesunden Helden oder Wundermann gibt, unter dessen Hand alles besser gehet oder je so gut, als in keinem Buch stehet; der das Recht entweder ändert oder also meistert, daß im Lande alles grünet und blühet, mit Friede, Zucht, Schutz, Strafen, daß es ein gesund Regiment heißen mag, und dennoch daneben bei seinem Leben aufs höchste gefürchtet, geehret, geliebt und nach seinem Tode ewiglich gerühmet wird.' Möchten auch unserer krank gewordenen Zeit die Vorboten wiederkehrender Gesundheit bald erscheinen und der Bund des deutschen Staatsgedankens mit dem sittlichen Geiste des Christentums seine aufbauende Kraft von neuem bewähren." Berger, "Luther und der deutsche Staatsgedanke," 55–6.

career to the study of Luther, which brought him great fame and made him a leading figure in the theological struggles of post-World-War-I Protestantism. From his faculty seat in Berlin, he trained the next generation of scholars who would maintain a significant influence in Protestant church history and systematics in Germany up through the 1960s. And this despite the fact that he died suddenly in 1926.[21] Holl's encounter with Luther exemplifies vividly the powerful effect Luther's life and writings exercised in the era following World War I.

Though he had written on Luther previously, Holl's decisive encounter with Luther came in 1910 with an essay on Luther's lectures on Romans, which marked a turn in his scholarship and his theological understanding.[22] It is instructive that Holl came to his study of Luther's lectures on Romans from 1515, which were newly edited and available, already having worked out his own understanding of justification—it was not the reading of Luther that first gave stimulus to his ideas, but rather that reading Luther's lectures on Romans integrated and provided answers to questions that he had already formulated. This exemplifies the degree to which Holl's treatment of Luther was driven by his engagement with present-day concerns: as Eucken had foretold, Luther was the means for resolving the ills of the era. Though the primacy of textual study and the guiding principles of Rankean historicism are instrumental in the scholarly methodology of the Luther Renaissance, fundamentally Luther is a vehicle to establish and legitimize a prescriptive definition of religiosity and faith that responds to the perceived crisis of the age, a resolution to the existential crisis of the self in its relationship to God and creation.[23] Holl's Luther is a distinctive construction that reflects Holl's own experience and intellectual concerns as they unfolded in a time of personal and societal crisis.

What was it about Luther that would prove so compelling to Holl, and then to a generation of scholars who would follow? For one, the majority Luther's extensive corpus was now available through the Weimar edition. And the breadth of those writings, combined with the already powerful presence of Luther in German cultural consciousness, as well as Luther's engagement with fundamental issues of religious truth and meaning, provide the basis for this "renaissance." For Holl and others, Luther modelled the existential hero, who, facing a fundamental crisis of being, finds within himself the path to affirm his self, and a truth that structures his moral being, which he then puts into action in his life's work. Holl finds in Luther a life experience that may be extensively and sophisticatedly explored through Luther's vast web of writings, enabling Holl to work out the

---

[21] For the most current biographical portrait of Holl's life see Heinrich Assel, "Karl Holl 15 Mai 1866, 23 Mai 1926." In *Karl Holl: Leben—Werk—Briefe*, ed. Heinrich Assel (Tübingen: Mohr Siebeck, 2021): 17–132.

[22] See the discussion of Assel, *Karl Holl*, 45–9.

[23] See the discussion of Heinrich Assel, *Der andere Aufbruch: Die Lutherrenaissancce* (Göttingen: Vandenhoeck & Ruprecht, 1994): 81–8.

meaning of questions that are raised not just by his discipline of theology, but also by a historical crisis that swept away what he believed were essential elements of German civilization. Through Luther he constructed the theoretical basis for a new understanding of the self, from which could emerge—note the similar hope articulated in Berger's essay on Luther's idea of the state—a new basis for German society.

It is noteworthy that this was done not through a direct exercise in systematic theological construction, but mediated through the person and writings of Luther. Given the philosophical and theological developments of the nineteenth century, and the impact of the war on the liberal theological tradition out of which Holl emerged, the theological legacy of the recent past seemed a dead end; even scripture itself as an object of faith was compromised by the corrosive effects of nineteenth century biblical scholarship. This crisis of faith that emerged from the nineteenth century, and made itself felt as never before with the world war, explains the turn to Luther not just as an object of study, or an inspirational ancestor, but as a model for ones' being and a bringer of revelation. As engaged with by Holl, Luther is not an individual of the past who writings could be mined for insights, but the religious man par excellence, whose existential encounter with the eternal God played out in an inner drama the results of which provide a way forward for the modern interlocutor who can mine the essential ingredients of this exemplary spirit. Like Luther, who in Holl's telling of the tale came to his lectures on the book of Romans in 1515 having already developed a sense of the true nature of God's justification, Holl also encountered Luther's writings in a similar state, and found resonant in Luther's experience the key to his own vision. The Luther Karl Holl extricates from Luther's early writings is preponderately a product of the needs of Holl's own life and times. What gives his work its larger significance was the enthused reception with which it was eventually greeted and the many scholars who were shaped by its substance.

However, between 1910 with his essay on Luther's Roman's lectures and the publication of his best-selling collection of Luther essays in 1921, Holl experienced the war. Like most of the German professoriate Holl embraced the war fully, and eventually came to identify with some of the most extreme nationalistic elements among his colleagues.[24] A letter from August, 1914 gives a sense of his mindset at the start of the war:

> And what does Rade [Martin Rade] mean when he says that we should conduct a short war with England? Doesn't he realize that a war with England that doesn't

---

[24] For a sense of the unbending nationalism of almost all of the German professoriate, especially in Berlin, see the collection of public addresses in *Aufrufe und Reden deutscher Professoren im Ersten Weltkrieg*, ed. Klaus Böhme (Stuttgart: Reclam, 1975).

come to a really actual battle will leave us forever in the cramped position with which we have lived for the last twenty years? We have to have space in relation to England, and since England isn't going to grant that on its own free will, consequently we have to fight for it to the death. How refreshing it would be instead of such hot air to have the manly words of Luther.[25]

With this perspective he opened up to a consideration of the war as a working out of God's order of creation, which, if he didn't connect directly to Luther, he viewed as in keeping with his principles:

Whoever themselves has not grasped in these times the simple fact that some *Volker* grow and as a result need more space, and others age and consequently no longer entitled to their entire location, whoever doesn't sense that this is God's order of creation (*Schöpfungsordnung*), and on the other hand closes their eyes to the fact that no *Volk* out of good will give up what they have when they don't have to, with these I don't argue any longer.[26]

He would argue this point again in a public way in a piece written in 1917 for the *deutschen evangelische Gemeindetages* (German evangelical congregational congress), with social-Darwinistic considerations justifying expansive war connected to the idea of a divine order of creation, a position that would have influential force within the thinking of many who came after Holl.[27] While Holl does not engage in the same orgy of Luther patriotism that was the staple of the 1917 celebration, his Luther is a product of the war and defeat and the ensuing sense of spiritual crisis resulting from the conviction that Germany had lost any firm foundation for its civilization. Holl's Luther is a man for the times.

While many of Holl's essays on Luther were published prior to or during World War I, it was not until after the war in 1921 that these works, together with a few other pieces he produced, would be reedited and released, bringing him

---

[25] "…Und was meint Rade, daß wir einen <u>kurzen</u> Krieg mit England führen sollten. Ahnt er nicht, daß ein Krieg mit England, in dem es nicht zum richtigen tätlichen Kampf kommt, uns immer in der beklemmten Lage lassen wird, in der wir seit 20 Jahren leben? Wir müssen Luft haben gegenüber England und da uns England das freiwillig nicht gewähren wird, so müssen wir eben darum bis in den Tod kämpfen. Wie erfrischend waren gegenüber solchem Geschwätz die männlichen Worte Luthers." Quoted in Assel, *Karl Holl*, 61–2.

[26] "Wer selbst in dieser Zeit die einfache Tatsache nicht begriffen hat, daß von den Völkern die einen wachsen, darum mehr Raum brauchen, die andern altern, darum nicht mehr auf ihre ganze Stellung ein Anrecht haben, wer nicht empfindet, daß das Gottes Schöpfungsordnung ist, andererseits die Augen demgegenüber verschließt, daß kein Volk Gutwillig aus den Raum, den es einmal hat, weicht und auch nicht zu weichen braucht […] mit dem streite ich mich überhaupt nicht mehr." Quoted in Assel, *Karl Holl*, 62.

[27] See "Luthers Anschauung über Evangelium, Krieg und Aufgabe der Kirche im Lichte des Weltkriegs." In *Gesammelte Aufsätze zur Kirchengeschichte III: Der Westen*, ed. Karl Holl (Tübingen: Mohr Siebeck, 1928): 147–70, esp. 162.

enormous public recognition and setting in motion the "Luther Renaissance."[28] His *Gesammelte Aufsätze I: Luther* would become the second best-selling theological book of the inter-war years (behind Karl Barth's *Commentary on Romans*), and, along with Barth's dialectical theology mark one of two major departures in Protestant theology of the 1920s, such that Heinrich Assel titles his landmark study of the Luther Renaissance *Der Andere Aufbruch* (the other awakening).[29] Though the volume was a collection of essays, and not a unitary study, Holl had reworked much of the material for the publication of the collection, and the ideas interweave from one piece to the next. And it is the multi-valent quality of the work, its embeddedness in Holl's own experience and its emphasis on Luther's experience, and the open-endedness of the ideas he broaches that explains its seminal and creative impact on the theology of the Weimar era and beyond.[30]

At the heart of his representation of Luther is the contention that what distinguishes Luther's understanding of justification, and by implication his whole concept of the human relationship to God, is a distinctive understanding of the conscience (*Gewissen*). According to Holl, for Luther the conscience is the fulcrum for the whole spiritual drama of salvation that unfolds with humans' response to the living reality of the divine—Luther's religion is *Gewissensreligion*.[31] For

---

[28] The following essays were published in *Gesammelte Aufsätze I*: "Was verstand Luther unter Religion?" (what did Luther understand by religion?)—given as an address for the Reformation celebration and originally published in 1917 and then reedited for this volume; "Die Rechtfertigungslehre in Luthers Vorlesung über den Römerbrief mit besonderer Rücksicht auf die Frage der Heilsgewißheit" (the teaching on justification in Luther's Lectures on the Letter to the Romans with particular attention to the question of the certainty of salvation)—originally published in 1910 and reedited for the second edition in 1923; "Die Neubau der Sittlichkeit" (the new construction of ethics)—delivered as a lecture in 1919 and first published in this form in 1921; "Die Entstehung von Luthers Kirchenbegriff" (the development of Luther's concept of the Church)—first published in 1915; "Luther und das landesherrliche Kirchenregiment" (Luther and the territorial rulers' Church order)—first published in 1911; "Luthers Urteile über sich selbst" (Luther's judgment of himself)—a lecture delivered in 1903; "Luther und die Schwärmer" (Luther and the enthusiasts)—first published in the second edition of 1923; "Die Kulturbedeutung der Reformation" (the cultural meaning of the Reformation)—lecture first delivered in 1911 and again in 1918; "Luthers Bedeutung für den Fortschritt der Auslegungskunst" (Luther's significance for the advancement of the art of translation)—lecture delivered in 1920. The essays were edited from their original form for the 1921 or 1923 editions of the *Gesammelte Aufsätze I*.

[29] See Friedrich Wilhelm Graf, *Der heilige Zeitgeist*, 64, for the publication history of Holl's first volume of *Gesammelte Aufsätze*.

[30] See the discussion in Assel, *Der andere Aufbruch*, 33–41.

[31] "Luthers Religion ist **Gewissensreligion** im ausgeprägtesten Sinne des Worts. Mit all der Eindringlichkeit und persönliichen Bedingheit, die einer solchen zukommt. Wie sie aus seiner Gewissenserfahrung bestimmter Art, aus dem von Luther in eigenartiger Schärfe erlebten Zusammenstoß eines zugespitzten Verantwortungsgefühls mit dem als unbedingt, als schlechthin unverrückbar geltenden göttlichen Willen hervorging, so ruht sie als Ganzes auf der Überzeugung, daß im Bewußtsein des **Sollens**, in der **Unwiderstehlichkeit**, mit der die an den Willen gerichtete Forderung den Menschen ergreift, **das Göttliche sich am bestimmtesten offenbart**. Und zwar um so klarer und unzweideutiger, je tiefer das Sollen den Menschen erregt und je schärfer es sich von den 'natürlichen' Lebenswünschen des Menschen abhebt. Es ist für Luther ein grundlegender Satz, daß nicht das vom Menschen selbt 'Erwählte', das frei von ihm Erdachte, sondern das ihm **durch eine höhere Ordnung Auferlegte, das Gemußte**, den Stempel des Göttlichen an sich trägt" (Luther's religion is a **religion of conscience** in the strongest sense of the word. Including all the urgency and personal relativity

Holl, what drove Luther's dynamic of faith was his encounter with the living reality of God's holy commands and the duty of humans to fulfill them to make themselves holy, coupled with the realization of the fundamental inability to do just that. When we go into ourselves and explore our response to the demands of the just God, what motivates us is a desire to achieve holiness not for its own sake, but for our own selfish benefit, which Luther saw in itself as sin. According to Holl, what marked Luther as exceptional was his deep understanding of the human self, and its duty yet inability to meet the just commands of God.[32] But, Holl contends, Luther did not just fall into despair, but the encounter with the judging God led him to recognize as well that a just God must somehow provide a path for the human self to be reconciled, that the demand that one ought to fulfill the demands of God implied the possibility of doing so. In a gamble that goes against the natural instincts of the human self, one believes that the goodness and love of God must mean there is some way to be made right with God. It is with this mindset that Holl believes Luther encountered the letter of Paul to the Romans, and the contention there that the just live by faith, that humans do not justify themselves by what they do, they do not prove themselves to God, but rather it is God who, despite the insufficiency of the human will and self, justifies sinful humans.[33] And this did not mean that there was some cancellation of human sinfulness, but rather that one no longer has to define oneself in relation to God according to what one cannot do, but rather now is freed from the inward curve of the self, the "I-ness" of our natural being, to live and act in the consciousness of the God who is love. But this concept of God is dynamic, since the wrath of God through which he judges humans and the world is always active at the same time that love is what defines the divine character. Humans live in the consciousness and the reality of this dynamic God.[34] The fundamental insight itself came, Holl emphasized, from Luther's experience, and was then confirmed and given fulness with his encounter with scripture. This primacy of experience over scripture is a signature feature of Holl's representation of Luther.

Another aspect of Holl's view of Luther involves the active agency of God within creation. Luther, Holl says, sees the good and the ill of the created order as aspects of God's active being. Luther does not deny that this raises paradoxical issues when considering the being of God, but that is just what those created by

---

associated with such a thing. Just as it emerged out of his specific type of experience of conscience, out of the collision, experienced by Luther with unique sharpness, between a heightened sense of responsibility and the unconditional, absolutely unshakeable divine will, so it rests as a whole on the conviction that in the consciousness of the **ought**, in the **irresistibility** with which the demand directed at the will seizes the person, **divinity reveals itself most decisively**. Indeed, it becomes clearer and less ambiguous, the more deeply the "ought" arouses the individual, the more sharply it sets itself apart from the 'natural' human desires of life. For Luther it is a fundamental proposition, that not what humans 'choose', what they freely invent, but rather what is **imposed on them by a higher order, the 'must,'** is what carries the seal of the divine within it.). *Gesammelte Aufsätze*, 35.

[32] *Gesammelte Aufsätze*, 15–27. [33] *Gesammelte Aufsätze*, 29 and following.
[34] *Gesammelte Aufsätze*, 237–42.

God should expect of a God who goes beyond their ability to understand. God is both revealed and hidden, defined by his love, but hidden behind the masks within creation where we cannot fathom his divine purpose or will.[35] It is this dimension of the divine being that necessitates a heroic faith, and conviction that the demands of God that we fulfill his commands are not cancelled out by grace—God's will is real, and humans owe God a response to it.[36] This conception of God and humanity has implications for thinking about, among other things, the world of power. The state and its rulers hold their authority intentionally from God as a check on the destructive instincts of humanity; when viewed as love, God does this to protect the weak and vulnerable, and to serve that order as a Christian is itself an obedience to God's commands and a realization of his love; but when viewed as his wrath, the horrors of war and destruction can be seen as his rod of punishment, or a mysterious working out of his providential purpose—his comments during the war justifying Germany's expansionist aims noted above fit into this category. In the essay collection, which reflect his wartime

---

[35] "Der Glaube an die göttliche **Alleinwirksamkeit** war nicht ein Lehrstück, das Luther nur äußerlich aus Paulus übernommen hätte; er ruhte bei ihm auf persönlicher Erfahrung. Aber was er in sich selbst wahrgenommen hatte, weitete sich ihm aus zu einer allgemeinen Betrachtung und wandelte sein ganzes Weltbild. Die Welt erschien ihm jetzt nicht mehr wie den Griechen und der Scholastik als eine ruhende Ordnung. Er schaute sie als begriffen in nie rastender Bewegung, und auch ihre Ordnung sah er in jedem Augenblick neu erzeugt. Dadurch wird ihm die Lebendigkeit Gottes erst im eigentlichen Sinn anschaulich. Denn Gott war es, der als der 'unruhige Treiber' die Dinge unaufhörlich zum Wirken drängte und ihr Ineinandergreifen schuf; die ganze Welt war ein ununterbrochenes Zeugnis seiner nie versiegenden Schöpferkraft. Luther gewahrt deshalb die göttlich Allmacht nicht wie die Scholastik nur in den außerordentlichen Begebenheiten, mit denen Gott die von ihm gesetzte Ordnung durchbrach. Der gewöhnliche Gang der Welt ist ihm bereits das größte Wunder. Und die Allmacht ist ihm nicht die unendliche Fülle von **Möglichkeiten**, die Gott frei zu seiner Verfügung hat, sondern die in der Gestaltung der wirklichen Welt sich betätigende unendliche Macht. Er sieht sie offenbar werden an jeder Stelle und in jedem Augenblick. Alle Kreaturen sind Gottes Larven und Mummenschanz, Masken, unter denen er sich verbirgt, Werkzeuge, mit denen er arbeitet" (The belief that **God worked all in all** was not a teaching that Luther would have adopted in a superficial manner from Paul; it came to him out of personal experience. And what he found true within himself expanded out into a general way of seeing and transformed his entire worldview. The world no longer appeared to him as it did to the Greeks and the Scholastics as a static order. He saw it caught up in a never ceasing movement, and its order he saw newly generated in each blink of an eye. In this way for the first time the vitality of God was made transparent in reality. For it was God who was the "restless driver" who pushed things persistently into action and created their engagement with one another; the entire world was a continual testimonial to his inexhaustible creative power. Thus Luther became aware of divine omnipotence not just in extraordinary occurrences, as the Scholastics had, when God intervened in the divinely ordained order. The usual course of the world was for him the greatest miracle. And this omnipotence is not for him the infinite wealth of **possibilities** that God had at his disposal, but rather the infinite power at work in shaping of the real world. He sees it being revealed in every place and every moment. All creatures are God's veils and mummery, masks behind which he hides himself, tools with which he works). *Gesammelte Aufsätze I*, 45–6.

[36] "Aus der Tatsache, daß Gott **Wille** ist—der den Menschen **allmächtig** umfassende, aber seine Güte ihm schon durch die Gabe des Lebens und noch mehr durch die ihm eingepflanzte höhere Gestimmung erweisende Wille—, folgert Luther zunächst das Einfache und Grundlegende, daß der Mensch Gott den Dienst der Religion **schuldet**" (From the fact that God is **Will**—a will that encompasses humans **all powerfully**, but which demonstrates its goodness through the gift of life and even more through the higher vocation planted within them—Luther deduces first of all the simple and fundamental fact that humans **owe** God the service of religion). *Gesammelte Aufsätze I*, 52.

experience, this leads to additional problematic considerations of how God's active agency in the created order translates into the specific crisis of post-war Germany and its possible resolution.

In the aftermath of the war, Holl had come to see Germany's failure as a sign of God's judgment on the Germans.[37] As noted above, during the war Holl had begun to view the war itself as part of the *Schöpfungsordnungen* (orders of creation) within which God's agency was worked out. And to the extent that Germany's struggle could be seen as part of a struggle for self-preservation, a justifiable attempt to gain the space needed for its growing population, this could justify the extensive violation of the commandment not to kill others that comes with the war, making of it a higher obedience to the mysterious will of the hidden God. Given that state formations and national (or racial) struggles could be seen as part of the providential working out of God's agency, it made sense that after the war Holl would seek to connect Luther's understanding of faith and teachings on Christians in the world to the immediate needs of the day. For Holl, if there was a remnant who had the faith that Luther represented, who were strong in this living faith in God, that would be the basis for turning what was crisis into the foundation for a new society.[38]

In his post-war essays, Holl has Luther advocating the agency of these strong ones in faith to serve as creative forces to school and guide the church and society to a new realization of itself. And this may occur in ways that seem at odds with the nature of love, but reflect the agency of the hidden God in time:

> In Germany there remains preserved as a legacy of Luther the conviction about an ethical goal for history, the belief in an absolute, that even at the price of happiness should be desired for itself and realized for its own sake, the capability to grasp even the grizzliest and most repellent thing nevertheless as a means through which the meaning of history unfolds, and at its deepest the insight that history in truth is not the work of humans but of the power that controls them. Hegel, Ranke, and Treitschke interpreted history in this way…. One experiences the uniquely Calvinistic when he raises up more strongly than the Germans the significance of the **great individual**, the hero called by God, who, as the instrument of God and proclaimer of a new order, has the inner right to carry through his will even with severity, because such severity is the true love for those who **are in need of** his leadership.[39]

---

[37] See the discussion in Assel, *Der andere Aufbruch*, 118–24.
[38] See the discussion in Assel, *Der andere Aufbruch*, 131.
[39] "In Deutschland bleibt als Erbe Luthers erhalten die Überzeugung von einem sittlichen Ziel der Geschichte, der Glaube an ein Unbedingtes, das auch auf Kosten des Glücks in ihr gewollt werden soll und in ihr sich durchsetzt, die Fähigkeit, selbst das Grausige und Abstoßende noch als ein Mittel zu begreifen, durch das der Sinn der Geschichte sich verwirklicht, und als Tiefstes die Einsicht, daß die Geschichte in Wahrheit nicht das Werk des Menschen, sondern der ihn lenkenden Macht ist. In diesem Stil haben ein Hegel, ein Ranke, ein Treitschke die Geschichte gedeutet…. Nur empfindet man

With Holl this connection of faith to action within the circumstances of the day remained somewhat murky. His own political leanings during and after the war were decisively to the nationalist right of the spectrum, though, as noted, his depiction of Luther avoids making him exclusively Germanic in his significance. But Holl clearly saw Luther's teachings as the key to understanding not simply one's relationship with God, but also how those who attain such a heroic faith might then work to translate that into action for the good of one's neighbor in the worldly sphere of power. It was suggestive, as well, of the anti-democratic dimensions of this teaching, as it highlighted the distinction between those, like Luther, who attain such heightened experience and insight into the nature of faith, and the great mass who do not. One can only speculate how Holl himself would have applied these concepts to the specific developments of the later 1920s and early 1930s, but he generated a wide following who worked out his ideas further, and lived through the upheaval that was to come. It is indicative of the open-endedness of his ideas that there are a variety of ways these ideas came to be worked through, such that the church struggles of the 1930s saw descendants of Holl on both sides.[40] In general, however, the Luther of Karl Holl's theology contributed to the development of ideas that leant credibility to radical racial/nationalist political forces that would come to successfully challenge the Weimar Republic, and lead to the establishment of an absolutist political order grounded in racial/nationalist principles and charismatic political leadership.[41]

What carried Holl's ideas forward was not only the broad influence of his Luther volume,[42] but his many influential students and their shaping presence in

---

das eigenartig Calvinische, wenn er starker als die Deutschen die Bedeutung des **großen Einzelnen**, des gottberufenen Helden, hervorhebt, der als Werkzeug Gottes und Künder einer neuen Ordnung das innere Recht hat, seinen Willen auch mit Härte durchzusetzen, weil solche Härte die wahre Liebe zu den seiner Leitung **Bedürftigen** ist. *Gesammelte III*, 528-9. It is notable that on this last point about the great individual, Holl refers to Calvin rather than Luther. As we saw with Berger, and will see repeatedly in later literature, this is a principle associated with Luther and his repeated speculations about divinely led *Wundermänner*. Holl, however, does not make reference to this idea as an aspect of Luther's thought either here or elsewhere.

[40] It is emblematic of the breadth of Holl's influence that he was an instrumental influence on a figure such as Emanuel Hirsch, as discussed below, who was a forthright advocate of the Nazi State and Hitler, and also Dietrich Bonheoffer, who studied under Holl in Berlin, and who was among the most heroic resisters of the Nazification of the German church and theology, a resistance grounded in his understanding of Luther.

[41] Holl's alienation from the Weimar Republic is typical of the great majority of theologians and laity who are active participants in the Protestant churches. See the discussion of Graf, *Der heilige Zeitgeist*, 6-8.

[42] One gets a sense of the impact of the volume from the following note in the 1922 edition of the *Lutherjahrbuch*. The editor, while noting that the publication has not yet achieved its goal of including a literature review, cannot let pass unmentioned Holl's new Luther volume: "Es ist darum nur eine Ausnahme, wenn ich trozdem hier auf den soeben bei J. C. B. Mohr, Tübingen, erschienenen ersten Band der Gesammelten Aufsätze von Prof. D. K. Holl, Berlin, unter dem Gesamttitel 'Luther', aufmerksam mache. Aber sie rechtfertigt sich durch das tiefe Gefühl der Dankbarkeit und Verehrung, das die ganze protestantische Welt seinem Verfasser schuldig ist. Denn die hier gebotenen Ausführungen...sind so aus dem Vollen schöpfend und tief schürfend, durchweg getragen durch eingehenden Quellenachweis und in lebendiger Auseinandersetzung mit dem Gegner durchgeführt,

the fields of church history and systematics in institutions across Germany from the late 1920s all the way up into the 1960s. It was a rare student in the first half of the 1920s who was not in one way or another influenced by his understanding of Luther. This is exemplified in the outpouring of publications that extended Holl's ideas already during his lifetime.[43] Two of the most immediately influential carriers of the ideas of Holl were Emanuel Hirsch (1888–1972) and Paul Althaus (1888–1966). Though both were deeply influenced by Holl, and carried forward his understanding of Luther, they were also original theologians in their own right, and major contributors to the dissemination of a Luther-grounded theology that was instrumental in making Protestantism susceptible to the appeal of the National Socialist movement.

Of all those who were profoundly impacted by Holl's work, it was Emanuel Hirsch who developed the concept of *Gewissensreligion* most expansively, creating a theological complex whose most striking consequence was to fully reconcile Christian identity with National Socialism, to connect the idea of conscience to a combative advocacy for Hitler and the Nazi regime. Hirsch has been described as a political theologian, and his political commitments indelibly color his work, though it has also been suggested he is better designated as a practitioner of "principled historicism."[44] Hirsch had a lifelong engagement with Luther, and

---

daß sie das Urteil über die Gedankenwelt des Reformators weithin auf ganz neue Grundlagen stellen, zugleich so klar und anschaulich herausgearbeitet, daß sie den Leser gar nicht wieder loslassen und auch den Nichttheologien aufs höchste fesseln" (It is consequently an exception when I nevertheless at this point make note of the appearance of the first volume of collected essays by Prof. D. K. Holl of Berlin, appearing under the collective title *Luther*. However, this is justified by the deep feeling of thankfulness and admiration that the entire Protestant world owes to the author. For the discussions offered here draw from such fullness, mine from such depths, ever supported with detailed primary source research and in living confrontation with the opponent, that they set the appraisal of the reformer's thought onto a completely new foundation; at the same time they are so clearly and transparently constructed that the reader can't put them down—they engage even the non-theologian at the highest level). *Lutherjahrbuch*, IV (1922): III–IV.

[43] See the discussion of Assel, *Der andere Aufbruch*, 22–33.

[44] "…gerade wegen des immerdar wachen Wissens um die historische Standpunktsbedingtheit seines eigenen wie alles theologischen Denkens ist es exakt zutreffend, wenn man Hirsch als Vertreter des 'Historismus aus Prinzip oder prinzipiellen Historismus' bezeichnet." (…precisely because of his ever-wakeful awareness of the historically conditioned viewpoint of his and all theological thinking, it is accurate to designate Hirsch as a practitioner of "principled historicism"). Martin Ohst, "Der I. Weltkrieg in der Perspektive Emanuel Hirschs." In *Evangelische Kirchenhistoriker im "Dritten Reich,"* ed. Thomas Kaufmann and Harry Oelke (Gütersloh: Chr. Kaiser Verlag, 2002): 64–121; 66–7. The comments of Klaus Scholder aptly describe the unique characteristics of Hirsch: "Zugleich aber war er ein leidenschaftlicher politischer Theologe, in allen Fragen, die Deutschlands Sendung und Schicksal betraffen von einer unbeirrbaren und hartnäckigen Beschränktheit, ein Parteigänger der völkischen Bewegung von Anfang an und glühender Verehrer Hitlers, dabei nie Parteimitglied und gewiß kein Opportunist—weder 1933 noch 1945. In mancher Hinsicht ist Hirsch, dessen persönlichem Schicksal ein Hauch von Tragik anhaftet, fast ein Symbol für den politischen Protestantismus in Deutschland, in dem sich Leidenschaft und Ahnungslosigkeit, hoher sittlicher Anspruch und krasses Versagen, geistige Weite und politische Enge so seltsam gemischt haben" (At the same time he was a passionately political theologian, in all questions concerning Germany's mission and fate limited by stiff-neckedness and a sense of infallibility, from the start onwards a partisan of the *völkisch* movement and passionate admirer of Hitler, though never a Party member and certainly no opportunist—not in 1933 nor 1945. In many ways Hirsch, to whose personal fate there attaches an aura of the tragic,

published extensively on various aspects of Luther's life and works.[45] As with Holl, Hirsch's experience of World War I was fundamental to the development of his thinking.[46] As with Holl, Hirsch brought to his reading of Luther already worked out concepts about the human self. Hirsch is a remarkably complex thinker, who deals at the level of highly abstract philosophical/theological definitions of the self in relation to the divine, but translates these into an intense engagement with the political events and movements of his time perceived and regulated through his abstractions. For Hirsch, Luther serves as the mediator between abstract principle and living faith in action.[47]

Hirsch as a theologian fully absorbed the implications of nineteenth-century philosophy and biblical criticism. He eschewed all forms of teleological thinking, as well as biblicism, an aspect of Luther he did not affirm. He built his theology off of the encounter of the self with its existence and the world around it. Philosophically he drew heavily from Fichte's understanding of the subjective self, but connected this over the longer term with the image of Luther drawn from Holl, though given Hirsch's own unique interpretation.[48] It is of note that Hirsch's first intense engagement with Luther takes place in the period 1918–20, at a time when Hirsch lost sight in one eye, was threatened with total blindness, and experienced the deep trauma of Germany's defeat and, as Hirsch saw it, immoral subjugation to the allied victors.[49] But the loss of the war was for Hirsch the necessary pretext for the creation of a new Germany, since, for Hirsch, suffering was the key

is almost a symbol for political Protestantism in Germany, in which we find a peculiar mixture of passion and cluelessness, high ethical demands and glaring failure, intellectual breadth and political narrowness). Klaus Scholder, *Die Kirchen und das Dritte Reich*, Vol. 1: *Vorgeschichte und Zeit der Illusionen 1918-1934* (Frankfurth a.M.: Ullstein, 1986): 128. Heinrich Assel in his article on political theology in the interwar era describes Hirsch as the quintessential political theologian. See Heinrich Assel. "Politische Theologie im Protestantismus 1914–1945." In *Politische Theologie: Formen und Funktionen im 20 Jahrhundert*, ed. Jürgen Brokoff and Jürgen Fohrmann (Paderborn: Ferdinand Schöningh, 2003): 67–80. Though these references might suggest a difference of viewpoint, fundamentally both Ohst and Scholder make the same point, which is that Hirsch was driven not by crass power politics, but by profound intellectual concerns, which drove him to support National Socialism to the bitter end.

[45] See the bibliography that is appended to Hirsch's publication of his *Luther Studien*; beginning in 1917, the list includes 81 separate publications up through 1954, which was the year the two-volume *Lutherstudien* was published. The first volume of the collection contains work on Luther's understanding of *Gewissen* that he wrote before the end of World War II, but never published, the second volume collects a number of the most substantial of his writings on Luther from the 1920s and '30s. He notes in the introduction his intention in his youth to publish a comprehensive portrayal of the theology of Luther, and adds that, despite not having completed such a work, he had expended enormous time and energy on it. That he didn't complete it he attributes to his conviction that others were there to pick up this labor—he mentions in this regard Erich Vogelsang, his student in the mid-1920s. Emanuel Hirsch, *Lutherstudien I* (Gütersloh: Bertelsmann, 1954): 7.

[46] Ohst, "Der I. Weltkrieg in der Perspektive Emanuel Hirschs," 67.

[47] For a thoughtful reflection on Hirsch's intellectual project and its connection to his politics, see Robert P. Ericksen, "Emanuel Hirsch—Intellectual Freedom and the Turn toward Hitler." *Kirchliche Zeitgeschichte/Contemporary Church History* 24 (2011): 74–91.

[48] See the comments of Assel, *Der andere Aufbruch*, 166–7.

[49] Assel, *Der andere Aufbruch*, 167–8.

element in the construction of the true, moral self. And in Luther's theology and experience Hirsch could model the movement of the self to its realization that paralleled the movement of spiritual rehabilitation in his own day that could overcome the crisis of Germany. As noted, Hirsch's theology is expansive, and was worked out over many years, with its full political implications becoming fully manifest with the National Socialist seizure of power in 1933 and following. It is in this context that a piece published in *Deutsche Theologie* (German Theology) in 1933, encapsulates best his worked-out use of Luther to model his spiritual ideal and profile its political actuation.[50]

Hirsch presented the article as a comparison between Luther's calling (*Berufung*) and that of the Apostle Paul. The comparison is for Hirsch especially germane, since it not only allows the exploration of Luther's unique spiritual journey, but allows a contrast between a quintessentially Jewish and German spiritual typology.[51] The Reformation breakthrough, argues Hirsch, is not just a repetition of Paul's spiritual breakthrough, but rather "the breakthrough of the Gospel to reality and form under a new historical context and new racial community (*Völkerkreis*)."[52]

> That this taking shape, this breakthrough among us Germans occurred in a German, that has grounded and secured anew for many centuries the supra-racial (*übervolich*) meaning and mission of Germanity in the history of the West.[53]

This quote epitomizes a number of dimensions of Hirsch's Luther interpretation. One, it highlights the scale of significance that is attributed to Luther's life, which enacts the racially determined and historically grounded working out of the divine within the *Volk* as a whole. Each age and each *völkisch* community has its own way of being, its own distinctive self, and within the parameters of time and *Volk* one can experience subjectively the activity of the divine within the saeculum.

---

[50] Emanuel Hirsch, "Luthers Berufung." *Deutsche Theologie* (1933): 24–34; republished in Emanuel Hirsch, *Lutherstudien II*, 68–79.

[51] See the discussion of the evolution of Hirsch's view of the Jews from the 1920s into the 1930s in Arnulf von Scheliha, "Das junge nationale Luthertum nach dem Ersten Weltkrieg und die Juden." In *Protestantismus, Antijudaismus, Antisemitismus*, ed. Dorothea Wendebourg et al. (Tübingen: Mohr Siebeck, 2017): 361–76.

[52] "Darin drückt sich nun gewiß Eines aus: daß die Reformation geschichtlich auch eine Seite hat, nach der sie etwas anderes ist als bloß erneuerter Paulinismus, nämlich eine neue geschichtliche Gestalt der Bestimmung des menschlichen Lebens durch das Evangelium, der Durchburch des Evangeliums zu Wirklichkeit und Form unter neuen geschichtlichen Verhätnissen in einem neuen Völkerkreise." Hirsch, *Lutherstudien II*, 68.

[53] "Daß diese Gestaltwerdung, dieser Durchbruch unter uns Deutschen an einem Deutschen geschehen ist, das hat für mehrere Jahrhunderte die übervolkliche Bedeutung und Sendung des Deutschtums in der abendländischen Geschichte neu begründet und gesichert." Hirsch, *Lutherstudien II*, 68. By 1933 Hirsch had absorbed the racialist ideals of National Socialism, and though he will resist grounding the identity of the *Volk* purely in biological factors, his use of the concept of *Volk* is as reductionist as that of the Nazis. See Jens Holger Schjørring, *Theologische Gewissensethik und politische Wirklichkeit: Das Beispiel Eduard Geismars und Emanuel Hirsch* (Göttingen: Vandenhoek & Ruprecht, 1979): 177–8.

Having framed a context for his treatment of Luther's conversion, he moves to a detailed consideration of the process that happened within Luther, where outward events are symbols of inner developments over time, a decade and a half "history of inner struggle and becoming…that inwardly as well as outwardly brings about the break with the papal church."[54]

For Hirsch it is Luther's inner experiences that are of significance, since they trace the movement of the self to its realization as a self, and exemplify the process of being that grounds his theory of experience. It starts with the primal experience of God in the fear of death encountered in the famous thunderstorm that drove Luther into the cloister. "Through this experience, in the way that he encountered and experienced it, did God become for him the Lord, whose words were the inescapable fate of his person from within, and who disposed over him in the power of his majesty."[55] This encounter with the God-who-is-other forms the basis for the movement of the self that will ensue over time. It leads Luther into his much analyzed "*Anfechtungen*" (temptations and trials) in the cloister, where he struggled to come to a full sense of his merit in the eyes of God. For Hirsch, this is the unavoidable outcome of an encounter of the self with the sovereign God, and such struggles are the necessary process for the realization of the moral self, since it is here the conscience works to shape our being.

It is in the desperation of the self as it encounters its insufficiency with God that the possibility of redemption emerges when one encounters the other aspect of God, which is his love and grace. "Then, a good decade later, is given to Luther in the midst of agonizing questioning that discovery of the Gospel in Romans 1:17, which overpowers him with the worshipful joy of God's wondrous mercy, and is sufficient to ignite his praise of God his whole life long."[56] But this wondrous salvation does not simply allow him to rest in the peaceful grace of divine favor; it exists in dialectical tension with the recognition of God in his awesome and terrifying majesty: "Accordingly his being before God is situated in the unrest and tensions of movement between the two poles of his experience of God."[57] It is in this state that Luther is called to realize his faith in action, to do battle against the false faith of the time:

---

[54] "Luthers Berufung zum Reformator umfaßt die lange, über zwei Jahrsiebente währende Geschichte inneren Kämpfens und Werdens vom Blitzschlag zu Stotternheim und dem Eintritt ins Kloster 1505 bis zu dem reichen Jahre 1520, das innerlich wie äußerlich den Bruch met der Papstkirche bringt." Hirsch, *Lutherstudien II*, 69.

[55] "Durch diese Erfahrung, so wie er sie nahm und empfing, ist Gott ihm der Herr geworden, dessen Rede das unentrinnliche Schicksal seines Menschen von innen her war, der über ihn verfügte in der Gewalt seiner Herrlichkeit." Hirsch, *Lutherstudien II*, 69.

[56] "Dann, ein gut Jahrsiebent später, ist Luther in sein angefochtenes Fragen hinein jene Entdeckung des Evangeliums über Röm I, 17 geschenkt worden, die ihn mit der anbetenden Freude an Gottes wunderrbarem Erbarmen überwältigte und reich genug gewesen ist, ihn zum Lobpreis Gottes zu entzünden sein ganzes Leben lang." Hirsch, *Lutherstudien II*, 69–70.

[57] "Darum ist sein Sein vor Gott in die Unruhe und Spannung einer Bewegung zwischen den beiden Polen seiner Gotteserfahrung gestellt." Hirsch, *Lutherstudien II*, 70.

His faith confesses itself in the risky act against the false belief, which comes not from his own resolution, but rather by being dragged step by step, to his own surprise, into the situation where it would be a betrayal not to draw all the consequences down to the last detail, and to stand by them before all the world. Thus he got to know God as the one who puts his suffering believers into a place of accountability for their own actions and decisions; and known as the one who makes one profusely free in the breaking of all bonds, even those that bind one from within. Thus the worshipful faith achieves its expression of reality, its actualized form (*Tatgestalt*).[58]

The stages of this movement of the self, from encounter with the sovereign God of judgment, then the breakthrough to knowing the God of love and grace, to the realization of both these images of God in oneself through the risky act of commitment to action, to realizing God's commands in the outer world of history, all this embodies the highest realization of the self, the self that has found itself and realized its meaning in action. Luther enacts in exemplary fashion what Hirsch had already defined philosophically in his encounter with the philosophy of Fichte, providing a portrayal of meaningful existence that serves as an ideal type for Germans in their immediate historical situation.

Hirsch moves from this discussion of Luther's conversion to consider that of Paul's, and to draw some sharp distinctions between the two, which for Hirsch represent the difference between the German conversion type of Luther and the Jewish conversion type of Paul. Hirsch does not negate the conversion of Paul as a real encounter with the divine, nor its historical significance. But because it takes place in a past context which no longer represents the current movement of providential history, and came out of the racial experience of a Jew, he sees it as subsumed in and superseded by Luther's Germanic conversion. Each experience responds to the circumstances of the day, but Luther's is now the one that for Germans holds great resonance. In the Germanic encounter with God, the divine is experienced in its dialectical tensions, and in that form one sees unveiled the lordly highness of the all-powerful. And this God of contrary, mysterious power is found nowhere in all his dimensions so clearly as in Luther's story of conversion, which highlights the boundaries of this experience in ways that define it for the German *Volkstum*:

> The Germanic boundary that is exploded in Luther is just this, that this whole type of encounter with God is sharply reflected as the unheard of miracle of

---

[58] "Sein Glaube bekennt sich in der wagenden Tat wider den Irrglauben, aber nicht aus eigenem Entschluß heraus, sondern so, daß er Schritt um Schritt zur eignen Überraschung in die Lage hineingerissen wird, in der es Verleugnung wäre, nicht all Folgen bis ins Letzte zu ziehen und zu ihnen zu stehen vor aller Welt. Da hat er Gott kennengelernt als den, der den ihn glaubend Erleidenden in die Verantwortung eignen Tuns und Entscheidens stellt, und kennengelernt als den, der überschwenglich frei macht im Zerbrechen aller Bande, auch der von innen her bindenden. So gewinnt der anbetende Glaube den Wirklichkeitsausdruck, die Tatgestalt." Hirsch, *Lutherstudien II*, 70–1.

God's deed in Christ that comes to us from without; this is precisely what gives the history of his calling its unfathomability; here the ultimate possibilities for the reception of God within our *Volksart* (type of racial community) are fulfilled for the first time. Only at the boundary, where there is the danger of being shattered, will the reception of the revelation of God come to fulfillment in a *Volkstum* in a way native to it (*in ihm eigne Weise*). About this ultimate dialectic, which indeed can be reflected upon only within the Christian-Germanic type, only those can rightly speak who are able to see that the specificity of the encounter with Christ according to the Christian-Germanic type makes Luther fit to be a messenger of God in a Christianity that encompasses the *Volkstum*, where what matters is being raised up and shaped into Christianity.[59]

This passage, which translates awkwardly into English, highlights a number of the unique assumptions with Hirsch's interpretation of Luther. In particular, he sees in Luther's inner conversion experience and its historical outward realization the enactment of the Germanic type of Christian religiosity. And it is those mighty spirits who are capable, like Luther, of enacting this in themselves who become then the ones who provide the model for the *Volk*, from whom the whole people can be instructed. Though Hirsch doesn't think that only Germans had the unique form of salvific relationship with God—hence his discussion of Paul—he does see its German form as exclusive to the Germans, and it is clear he valorizes it in comparison to other *Volk* types. By the 1930s, Hirsch will apply his dialectic of the self within history to the Nazi movement and Hitler, seeing in their seizure of power the outward manifestation of the divinely willed order for the Germans, whose new order will lead Germans to realize their God-ordained historical calling. As with Luther, the historical events that come into focus in 1933 are perceived by Hirsch as parallel to the events that Luther set in motion in his day, as an instance of the boundary (*Grenze*)[60] where the eternal is translated into history with the coming together of the *Volk*; the inner dialectic of the human self as experienced by Luther realizes its outward form in the dialectic of history, where the same God who can afflict the individual works out his wrath and grace in the outward order of peoples (*Völker*) and struggle. Like Luther, Hirsch believed that it was necessary to commit fully to a cause that one thought fulfilled the divine

---

[59] "Das die germanische Grenze in Luther Sprengende ist freilich dies, daß diese ganze Art der Gottesbegegnung scharf reflektiert ist als das unerhörte, von außen zu uns kommende Wunder der Gottestat in Christus; eben das gibt seiner Berufungsgeschichte die Unergründlichkeit, in der sich die letzten Möglichkeiten des Gott Empfangens innerhalb unsrer Volksart erst erfüllen. Nur an der Grenze, da es zersprengt zu werden droht, wird in einem Volkstum die ihm eigne Weise, die Offenbarung Gottes in Christus zu empfangen, vollendet. Von dieser letzten—ja nur innerhalb des Christlich-Germanischen überhaupt reflektierbaren—Dialektik kann indes nur der recht reden, der wiederum sieht: die Bestimmtheit der Gottesbegegnung in Christus nach christlich-germanischer Art macht Luther tüchtig zum Boten Gottes in einer das Volkstum umspannenden Christenheit, in der es auf das Hineinziehen, Hineinbilden ins Christentum ankommt." Hirsch, *Lutherstudien II*, 76–7.

[60] On Hirsch's use of this term see Schjørring, *Theologische Gewissensethik*, 202–3; 261–2.

purpose, to do so without reservation or apology. In this, Luther's inner struggle and outward challenge to the order of his day became a template within which the upheavals of Hirsch's day could be situated and encountered, and with which Hirsch could justify his own passionate commitment to National Socialism.[61]

Hirsch's extracts from Luther a model of piety the implications of which go well beyond the particulars of his life and theology. In fact, to the extent that Luther built his theology out of an encounter with scripture, he was not of especial significance for Hirsch, who disdained biblicism.[62] For Hirsch the starting point for interpreting Luther lay in his existential reality, the encounter with God inside himself, and then the action that he took to translate that outwardly. From there he could connect Luther to his own understanding of the subjective self, and the challenge of the German *Volk* in the 1920s and '30s. In this he took the idea of Luther's *Gewissensreligion* much further than Holl had himself, and in directions that are in many ways unique. While many will build forward their understanding of Luther with a primary emphasis on *völkisch* identity, none will take the existential model of the conscience-driven self that wagers everything in realizing its inner calling in outward commitment quite as far as Emanuel Hirsch, who was one of the most uncompromising supporters and promoters of National Socialism in the 1930s and '40s, and who would never publicly disavow that commitment after the utter collapse of the Nazi regime.

When compared to Hirsch, Paul Althaus appears a much more moderate and conventional theologian and interpreter of Luther, yet his long engagement with Luther, his influential place within Lutheran theological circles in the 1920s and '30s, his long advocacy for a theology of creation in which the *Volk* took a central place within the divine plan, make him more seminal in his influence, on the whole, than Hirsch. Holl's influence on Althaus was extensive: he studied with Holl in Tübingen at the beginning of his theological education,[63] and his own development of a Luther-grounded theology owes a great deal to Holl.[64] Althaus succeeded Holl as the head of the *Luther-Gesellschaft,* a position he held from 1926–64. And while on the surface Althaus' distinctive theological emphasis on the orders of creation (*Schöpfungsordnungen*) may seem tenuously connected to Holl's Luther, or Luther's writings themselves, in fact they highlight the plasticity and multivalence of Holl's Luther interpretation and its impact on the larger theological developments of the 1920s. Althaus' Luther, like Holl's and Hirsch's, is grounded in an understanding of Luther's religion as *Gewissensreligion*. Even more

---

[61] See Assel, *Der andere Aufbruch*, 275–6, for an discussion of how this dialectical understanding worked itself out in specific reference to the various acts of political violence by the Nazis—see in particular footnote 39.

[62] Schjørring, *Theologische Gewissensethik*, 290.

[63] Gerhard Jasper, *Paul Althaus (1888–1966): Professor, Prediger und Patriot in seiner Zeit* (Göttingen: Vandenhoeck & Ruprecht, 2013): 40.

[64] Walther von Loewenich, "Paul Althaus als Lutherforscher." *Lutherjahrbuch* 35 (1968): 9–47; 12.

than Holl and Hirsch, Althaus focuses a central part of his theology around connecting Lutheran religiosity to the *Volk*, which in the eyes of some scholars makes him especially responsible for the readiness of the church to greet National Socialism with enthusiasm.[65]

We have already encountered Althaus in Chapter 2 (p. 40ff.), with his contribution to the 1917 celebration in *Luther und die Deutschen*. In that early piece, he gave distinctive voice to the common portrayal of Luther as quintessentially Germanic in his character, as well as the spiritual significance of Luther as a living repository of Germanic virtue and inspiration. In the development of his theology of the 1920s, he will provide a much more sophisticated ideological matrix within which to connect Germanity to Christianity, one that is grounded in his understanding of Luther, but which builds an extensive edifice onto the base. An article published in the *Lutherjahrbuch* in 1925 exemplifies vividly the way Althaus' Luther grows out of Holl's representation of Luther's *Gewissensreligion*. The article, "Luthers Haltung im Bauernkriege" (Luther's conduct in the Peasants' War),[66] was written to acknowledge the four-hundredth anniversary of an event which had brought much criticism down upon Luther for his exhortation to the German princes to use deadly violence in dealing with the Peasants' revolt.[67] In framing his defense of Luther's behavior in the context of the Peasants' War, Althaus resorts to the model of *Gewissen* (conscience) that Holl had emphasized. In narrating his account of Luther's actions, Althaus highlights the intractable circumstances facing Luther, with a restless peasantry petitioning for recognition of their rights against noble rulers who, Luther admits, are frequently abusive in their treatment of their subjects. Althaus frames Luther as one called into the world of action through the grace that he encountered from the God who created, rules, and judges time and space, and hence is called to put faith into action in that creation. And here is a set-piece of just what confronts those who have encountered God's grace in its fullness. In Althaus' view, Luther carried out his calling from God with heroic obedience to the divine order in the world. With his initial tract,

---

[65] For an overview of the variety of scholarly viewpoints on how to judge Althaus' role in 1920s and '30s, see the discussion in Ryan Tafilowski, *"Dark, Depressing Riddle": Germans, Jews, and the Meaning of the Volk in the Theology of Paul Althaus* (Göttingen: Vandenhoeck & Ruprecht, 2019): 18–35.

[66] Paul Althaus, "Luthers Haltung im Bauernkrieg." *Luther Jahrbuch* 7 (1925): 1–39.

[67] Luther wrote a series of tracts that dealt with the events of the Peasants' rebellion, advising the peasants prior to the violence on the proper manner to pursue their grievances, then with the outbreak of the violence condemning them with his harsh tract "Wider die räuberischen und mördischen Rotten der Bauern" (against the robbing and murdering mob of peasants), where he exhorts the princes to meet violence with violence, and finally with his two tracts written afterwards on the judgment of Thomas Müntzer and his defense of his "hard" tract against the peasants. See *D. Martin Luthers Werke: Kritische Gesamtausgabe* 18 (Weimar: Hermann Bohlhaus Nachfolger, 1908): 279–334; 344–74; 362–74; 375–401. With his article, Althaus was, in part, responding to criticism of Luther's actions in the context of the Peasant's War in recent works by H. Barge, Friedrich Naumann, Ernst Troeltsch, G. Wünsch, Ernst Bloch, Hugo Ball, and Hartmann Grisar. See Althaus, "Luthers Haltung," 34, n. 1, where Althaus identifies the critical works to which he is responding.

while Luther exhibits sympathy for the legitimate grievances of the peasants, he admonishes them to obedience, since no matter what the comportment of the duly authorized rulers, Christians are called to suffer injustice in this world, if it comes to that, and all are commanded to obey legitimate authority, such that armed rebellion is never justified.

When the peasants then do turn to violence, Althaus praises Luther's rigorous admonition to the princes to slay the peasants as one would a mad dog that was running amok. In doing so, Luther was being deeply obedient to his conscience, and using his office to advise peasants and princes of their appropriate calling within the worldly order put in place by God. In particular he identifies the tract in which Luther encourages the princes to violence as a signal instance of Luther's conscientious obedience to God:

> It was a mighty, brave, manly deed when, as all those around him had lost their clear vision and right courage of conscience (*Gewissensmut*), Luther called to conscientiousness and duty. The Luther who here put everything on the line—his position among the *Volk*, indeed his life—for the sake of his conscience is of no less greatness than the Luther of Worms before the Kaiser and Empire.[68]

This evaluation of Luther's behavior fits with Holl's definition of *Gewissensreligion*, in that Luther, guided by his faith to action in the world, takes the risk of doing what his inner self tells him is right, despite all the outward incentives to hide, temporize, or play some sort of political game. Instead he calls others to take up their role in God's order, without consideration of the personal consequences. Moreover, in the midst of all this upheaval, he carries through with his already planned purpose of marriage:

> With such bitterness on all sides, he had to reckon with his imminent end. And so before it comes to that he wishes to avow himself to holy matrimony in very deed, as a true scandal for the pope and Satan, and, for the weak, as a living seal beneath his teachings. Truly a marriage under strange omens, but on the other hand an event of heroic dimensions in Luther's life![69]

---

[68] "Es war eine gewaltige, tapfere Mannestat, daß Luther, als alles um ihn herum das klare Auge und den rechten Gewissensmut verlor, mit seiner mächtigen Stimme zur Besinnung und zur Pflicht rief. Der Luther, der hier alles einsetzte, seine Stellung bei dem Volke, ja sein Leben, um des Gewissens willen, ist von nicht geringerer Größe als der Luther in Worms, vor Kaiser und Reich." Althaus, "Luthers Haltung," 18.

[69] "Bei solcher Erbitterung von allen Seiten mußte er mit seinem nahen Ende rechnen. Da will er sich vorher noch mit der Tat zum heiligen Ehestande bekennen, für die Päpstlichen und den Satan zu einem rechten Ärgernis, für die Schwachen als ein lebendiges Siegel unter seine Lehre. Wahrhaftig eine Hochzeit unter seltsame Zeichen, wiederum eine Epoche von heroischen Ausmaßen in Luthers Leben!" Althaus, "Luthers Haltung," 29.

All his actions bespeak one who is deeply obedient to his conscience:

> However earnestly all the general uproar led him to consider his death, the charges regarding his writing did not, as a whole, make any impression on him. He remained unshaken in his stance. With magnificent freedom and certainty of conscience he took on the charges. His conscience is 'secure in God.' That he caused offence actually pleased him. It would have been bad if he hadn't, since then he would have doubted if he were on the right path. Moreover, in the course of the years he had had to hear all sorts of things about and against himself—and with time all of it had come to naught.[70]

The image here of Luther configures nicely with that of Hirsch's, who emphasized the degree to which one's suffering for the sake of conscience affirmed the legitimacy of the commitment to conscience—it is with those actions that encounter the greatest condemnation that one's commitment to the risky business of obedience to the divine is tested. For Althaus, Luther's actions in the Peasants' War met such a standard. He reinforces this interpretation with his concluding observation:

> The year 1525 represents in many ways a highpoint of Luther's life. It was the year of the "Bondage of the Will," and the wonderful commentary on the Psalms of repentance. Should Luther's stance in the Peasants' War be viewed as an indelible black mark on this particular year of his life? Certainly it remains a painful year in German history, a fateful conjuncture in the Reformation in its connection to the life of the German *Volk*. It will always be easier to be enthused about the Luther of 1520 ("Letter to the Christian Nobility!") than for the Luther the Peasants' War tracts of 1525. Only the former Luther can be a populist (*volkstümlich*), not the latter. However, is that the decisive measure? The reformer was never more isolated than in May and June of 1525. It was not the isolation of guilt and unbridled contrariness, but of strict, unshakable obedience to the recognized truth. Whoever has understood this will no longer think Theodor Brieger's judgment peculiar concerning Luther in 1525: "he achieved the pinnacle of his greatness."[71]

---

[70] "Wie Ernst ihn aber auch die allgemeine Empörung an seinen Tod denken ließ—sachlichen Eindruck haben die Vorwürfe wegen seiner Schrift ihm insgesamt nicht gemacht. Er blieb in seiner Haltung unerschüttert. Mit großartiger Freiheit und Sicherheit des Gewissens nimmt er die Anklagen auf. Sein Gewissens ist 'für Gott sicher'. Daß er Anstoß gibt, freut ihn geradezu. Schlimm, wenn er keinen gegeben hätte, dann würde er irre werden, ob er auf dem rechten Wege sei. Im übrigen habe er im Laufe der Jahre schon allerlei sonst über und wider sich hören müssen—und mit der Zeit sei das alles von selbst zunichte und zuschanden geworden." Althaus, "Luthers Haltung," 30.

[71] "Das Jahr 1525 stellt in mehrfacher Hinsicht einen Höhepunkt in Luthers Leben dar. Es ist das Jahr von De servo arbitrio und der wundervollen Auslegung der Bußpsalmen in zweiter Bearbeitung. Sollte Luthers Haltung im Bauernkriege gerade diesem Jahre seines Lebens einen untilgbaren dunklen

In explicating how Luther understands the proper disposition of the princes and the peasants in their conflict, Althaus brings forward the teaching of Luther's that has been labeled the "Two-Kingdoms Theory" (*Zwei-Reich Lehre*). For Althaus, Luther's conduct in the Peasant's War is the best example of the application of this understanding of ethics:

> The tract against the peasants was not some monster born in a wild, undisciplined moment in the life of the reformer, but in all its rigor and passionate power nothing more than the clear and valiant expression of his ethical principles. The "scandal" of his stance stems above all from the paradox of his ethics of service. Everything that Luther has otherwise taught is presumed here: the state as the necessary precondition for the community of the kingdom of God in historical time, the unity of the Sermon of the Mount and the theory of the state within a delicate, yet manly understanding of love, which, though for itself without claims, rights, or force, nevertheless is sufficiently selfless not to refrain from hard actions and rigorous application of force in service to the community.[72]

For Althaus, Luther exemplified an understanding of ethics that legitimized the state as an order within which Christian love, which one receives with one's faith in God's grace, can be lived out in service to the community. On the one hand, God's love operates in the freely given grace of undeserved forgiveness of sin, and functions within the kingdom of God. But on the other hand, within the world of sin and the devil, love in service to a state may have to use force to maintain order and prevent the war of all against all. In that context, exhorting princes to do their duty in slaying the insurrectionist peasants can be understood as a fulfillment of one's moral obligations, directed by the conscience that is infused with Christian love. This reflects the two aspects of the divine, God as loving savior, and also as the hidden God of history whose purposes are hidden behind his

---

Flecken gegeben haben? Ein schmerzliches Jahr deutscher Geschichte bleibt es uns gewiß, eine Schicksalsstunde der Reformation in ihrem Verhältnis zum deutschen Volksleben. Es wird auch immerdar Leichter sein, sich für den Luther von 1520 (An den christlichen Adel!) zu begeistern als für den Luther der Bauernschriften von 1525. Volkstümlich kann wohl nur jener Luther, nicht dieser werden. Aber ist das der entscheidende Maßstab? Nie war der Reformator einsamer als im Mai und Juni 1525. Es war nicht die Einsamkeit der Schuld und des wilden Trotzes, sondern die des strengen, unverrückten Gehorsams gegen die erkannte Wahrheit. Wer das einmal gesehen hat, den wird Th. Briegers Urteil über Luther im Jahre 1525 nicht mehr seltsam dünken: 'Er erreicht den Gipfelpunkt seiner Größe.'" Althaus, "Luthers Haltung," 33–4.

[72] "Die Flugschrift wider die Bauern war wirklich nicht die Ausgeburt einer wilden, zuchtlosen Stunde des Reformators, sondern in aller ihrer Härte und stürmischen Gewalt nichts als der klare und tapfere Ausdruck seiner ethischen Grundgedanken. Das 'Ärgernis' seiner Haltung hängt an dem Paradoxon seiner Ethik des Dienstes überhaupt. Alles, was Luther sonst gelehrt hat, wird hier vorausgesetzt: der Staat als notwendige Vorbedingung für die Gemeinschaft des Reiches Gottes in der Geschichte, die Einheit von Bergpredigt und Staatsgedanken in dem zarten und doch männlichen Verständnis der Liebe, die, in eigener Sache ohne Anspruch, Recht und Gewalt, selbstlos genug ist, im Dienste an der Gemeinschaft auch harten Tuns und strenger Gewalt sich nicht zu weigern." Althaus, "Luthers Haltung," 20.

masks, and who sometimes places humans in situations where obedience to his order will necessitate affirmation of actions that might be viewed in the light of grace as immoral. As we will see, this perspective on the secular sphere will be deployed in the 1930s to affirm actions of National Socialism that used violence as a means to establish their authoritarian order.

One of the elements that underlays Althaus' explanation of Luther's actions in the Peasant's War is his understanding of the orders of creation, or *Schöpfungsordnungen*. This is a teaching that he will give the fullest explication to in his theological works that respond to the National Socialist seizure of power. The connection of this teaching to Luther is fairly tenuous. The concept itself does not stem directly from Luther, but rather developed within nineteenth-century Lutheran theology, in particular with theologians at Erlangen where Althaus spent the majority of his academic career. Indeed Luther did speak of the estates, such as marriage, the state, or the church, through which human community was structured, but did not work this out into any systematic orders-of-creation theology. And beyond lacking such a structure within his theology, he also did not consider the *Volk* as one of those orders, especially given that this concept did not exist in the intellectual universe inhabited by Luther. But, of course, by the later nineteenth-century notions of the *Volk* were ubiquitous in the concepts of ethnicity that were used to analyze the social world, and to define the nature of German identity. And Althaus is a main conduit to introduce a theological construction of the *Volk* into the mainstream of Lutheran theology and by implication give it the imprimatur of Luther, though he will only in the late 1930s seek to explicitly justify its use with reference to Luther.[73] But his initial development of the *Schöpfungstheologie* and of a robust concept of the *Volk* comes in the 1920s, exemplified vividly in his address given to the second German Evangelical Church Congress in 1927 in Königsberg.[74] As was discussed with Althaus' lecture on Luther in the context of the war in 1917, he considered Luther the ideal type of the German, and in this sense his understanding of the meaning of Luther was already embedded in a *völkisch* nationalism. In his address, he takes the idea that the *Volk* can be embodied in an individual and develops a conception of the *Volk* that is itself a vehicle through which the divine purpose is revealed in the context of history.

He begins his address by noting the spiritual sickness of the *Volk* in the current age, its "poverty and illness," but also how this crisis has led to a powerful revival of the *Volkstum*, such that from 1914 up to the time he is speaking he sees the possibility of a great revival of the *Volk*.[75] He defines the *Volk* not in material terms, or biologically, though he admits that has a shaping influence, but rather as

[73] See the discussion in Tafilowski, *"Dark, Depressing Riddle,"* 175–7.
[74] Published as Paul Althaus, *Kirche und Volkstum: der völkische Wille im Lichte des Evangeliums* (Gütersloh: Bertelsmann, 1928).
[75] Althaus, *Kirche und Volkstum*, 6.

a spiritual entity, a *Seelentum*, which all *Volksgenossen*, members of the *völkisch* community, experience inwardly with their emotions, values, desires, and thoughts: "the womb of their native spiritual/soul essence, an all-encompassing reality, given to all of us originally with our life, prior to our desires and decisions."[76] He goes to some length to emphasize that it is not merely the sum of material influences, but is a spiritual reality that exists beyond just material factors.

One feature of Althaus' definition of the *Volk* is both its embeddedness in the historical circumstances that give it shape, so that he admits that it is shaped by the blood, for instance, but also the insistence on its underlying spiritual structure. It is that spiritual ground for the *Volkstum* that gives it its larger religious significance as the arena wherein spiritual characteristics are translated into ethical actions: "For the life of the *Volk* is healthy when it is lived in *völkische* fidelity (*Treue*), in responsibility toward the higher inheritance, the image of the *Volk* which appears within it; when the ideas and forms are shaped out of deep sources of the *Volkgeist* (spirit of the *Volk*); when all life of the individual and the group is carried by the whole, who knows itself as a member of the whole, and serves it."[77] The problem of the present age, according to Althaus, is that the *Volk* has been degenerated (*entartet*), infected by a foreign spirit with foreign values, so that the values of individualism and the big city, forced upon Germany by their defeat in the war and inner corruption, now deracinate (*entwurzeln*) and send into exile (*entheimaten*) the German *Volkstum*. There are resonances in all this of anti-Semitism, which will become more specific in the second half of the talk where he speaks explicitly about the Jews as one of those foreign elements whose presence challenges the realization of the *Volkstum*'s spiritual values of community.[78] Given this dire state of affairs, it is a pressing obligation of the church to help the *Volk* return to itself, to become what it is intended to be as an order within which its divine purpose can be realized within history. And the church will do this by helping the *völkisch* movement find its connection (*Bindung*) to God.

What would that mean? In some sense it is the corporate version of the movement that Luther experienced within himself as he awoke to the reality of the God who judges, and found there the path forward to fulfillment of his being through God's grace. It works somewhat differently, as Althaus defines it,

---

[76] "Volkstum nennen wir das besondere, von anderem unterschiedenen Seelentum, das in aller einzelnen Volksgenossen Fühlen, Werten, Wollen, Denken als das Gemeinsame erscheint; den Mutterschoß arteigenen geistig-seelischen Wesens; eine übergreifende Wirklichkeit, ursprünglich für uns alle mit unserem Leben gegeben, vor unserem Entscheiden und Wollen." Althaus, *Kirche und Volkstum*, 6–7.

[77] "Dann ist das Volksleben gesund, wenn es in völkischer Treue gelebt wird, in Verantwortung gegen das hohe Erbe, gegen die Volksart, die in ihm erscheint; wenn das Denken und Gestalten aus den tiefen Quellen des Volksgeistes schöpft; wenn alles Leben der Einzelnen und der Gruppen gliedlich vom Ganzen getragen wird, sich als Glied am Ganzen weiß und ihm dient." Althaus, *Kirche und Volkstum*, 8.

[78] Althaus, *Kirche und Volkstum*, 8–9.

with the experience of the *Volk* with God. But the key is that the *Volk* recognizes its essence, its *Volkheit* in relation to God.

> And where is that recognized? We can only say, wherever in German history men have interpreted its being, its *Volkheit*, to our *Volk*, their conscience has stood before God. *Volkheit* is the will of God over a *Volk*. When a *Volk* ponders in the presence of the absolute holy Lord, then its *Volkheit* comes to light, its mission, its idea, as a synthesis of the eternal will of God over all humanity and their particular *Volk* type. Before God the *Volk* experiences inevitably the judgment about its prevailing reality, also about its past as well as, at the same time, its calling. Whoever would not want to face that truth, whoever would not be led by the question of German *Volkheit* before the eyes of God and under his sight and judgment, would necessarily come to adulterate the conscience; would deify the unsanctified *Volkstum*; would pass off what is earthly, flawed as something absolutely binding.[79]

What is particularly striking are the parallels between this description of the *Volk* coming to its consciousness in relationship to God, and the description of this process in Luther by the scholars of the Luther Renaissance. In this way, the life of the *Volk* takes on the same existential significance as a vehicle for spiritual generation as the movement of the individual soul in its relationship to God. It is critical for Althaus, as well, that the spiritual experience of God that is typologically appropriate (*artgemäß*) for the German *Volk* be Christianity.

This raises some sticky questions for Lutherans like Althaus who would situate the *Volk* as an order through which God realizes his purposes in relation to peoples. It was easy to argue that Christianity itself was a foreign introduction into the German self, given it emerged out of Judaism, which, as Althaus himself will argue in his address, is an especially problematic *völkisch* "other" in the midst of the Germans. Beyond that, Christianity first came to the Germans by way of the Catholic Church; within the world of Luther studies of the 1920s it was almost universally understood that Luther had not only restored the understanding of justification and salvation to its scriptural roots, but that he had done so by throwing off the foreign yoke of the "*welsch*" church of Rome. The connection to

---

[79] "Wo wird sie erkannt? Wir können nur sagen: wo immer in der deutschen Geschichte Männer unserem Volke sein 'Wesen', seine Volkheit gedeutet haben, da hatte ihr Gewissen vor Gott gestanden. Volkheit ist der Wille Gottes über ein Volk. Wenn ein Volk sich vor dem unbedingten heiligen Herrn besinnt, dann leuchtet ihm seine Volkheit auf, seine Sendung, seine Idee, als Synthesis des ewigen Gotteswillens über allem Menschentum und der besonderen Volksart. Vor Gott erlebt das Volk unweigerlich das Gericht über seine jeweilige Wirklichkeit, auch über seine Vergangenheit, aber doch zugleich Berufung. Wer das nicht wahr haben wollte, wen die Frage nach der deutschen Volkheit nicht vor Gottes Auge führte, unter sein Sichten und Richten, der käme notwendig zu einer Verfälschung des Gewissens: er vergöttliche das ungeheiligte Volkstum; er gäbe ein Irdisches, Fehlsames als unbedingt bindend aus" (13–14). Althaus, *Kirche und Volkstum*, 13.

Luther was in this regard critical, since he was the one who within his spiritual struggles had rendered Christianity Germanic:

> Certainly the Gospel was brought to our *Volk* from without, connected to a foreign, Roman culture, and with that at first it was like a foreign law. However look at how the German *Volkstum* seized the Gospel in freedom! It brought forth what was most noble and beautiful, and thereby understood itself out of the Gospel and understood the Gospel anew: leadership, allegiance, free dedication, trust, the entire personal path of the Germanic order of life. Emerging out of its most distinctive self, the result of a God-given elective affinity, the German *Volkstum* was able to grasp the Gospel in its depths, from *Heliand*[80] up to Luther.[81]

And it is specifically Luther's version of Christian understanding that Althaus insists is of need for the *Volk*, over and against elements within the *völkisch* movement that were putting forward German mysticism and spiritualism as the truly Germanic form of Christian belief; Althaus asks provocatively, "Is Sebastian Franck truly more German than Martin Luther?," clearly assuming the question answers itself.[82]

He summarizes his argument as follows:

> The *Volkstum* needs the Gospel in order to understand its mission, to purify its will, and to be born again out of love. The churches are called to be the instrument of this service of the Gospel to the *Volk*. The *Volkstum* needs a church that has the courage to stand in the midst of the needs of the *Volk*, to explain to it [the *Volk*] its mission, to call it [the *Volk*] again and again to the judgment of God and to the source of true community (*Gemeinschaft*).[83]

One can see here that for Althaus the church's service to the *Volk*, to the racially homogenous German people, has created a new dimension within which the

---

[80] An epic of the ninth century written in Old Saxon recounting the life of Jesus.
[81] "Gewiß, das Evangelium ist unserem Volke von außen her gebracht, verbunden mit einer fremden, der römischen Kultur, und dadurch zuerst wie ein fremdes Gesetz. Aber wie hat deutsches Volkstum dann das Evangelium in Freiheit ergriffen! Sein Edelstes und Schönstes hat es herzugebracht, um von ihm aus das Evangelium und es vom Evangelium aus neu zu verstehen: Führertum, Gefolgschaft, freie Hingabe, Vertrauen, den ganzen persönlichen Zug der germanischen Lebensordnung. Aus seinem Eigensten heraus, kraft einer gottgeschenkten Wahlverwandtschaft hat deutsches Volkstum das Evangelium ganz tief erfassen dürfen, vom Heliand an zu Luther hin." Althaus, *Kirche und Volkstum*, 18–19.
[82] "Ist Sebastian Franck wirklich deutscher als Martin Luther?," Althaus, *Kirche und Volkstum*, 19.
[83] "Wir fassen zusammen: Das Volkstum bedarf des Evangeliums, um seine Sendung zu verstehen, am Willen gereinigt und aus der Liebe widergeboren zu werden. Die Kirchen aber sind dazu gerufen, diesem Dienste des Evangeliums am Volkstum Werkzeug zu werden. Das Volkstum bedarf einer Kirche, die den Mut hat, mitten in der Not unseres Volkes zu stehen, ihm seine Sendung zu deuten, es immer wieder unter das Gericht Gottes und zu dem Quell wirklicher Gemeinschaft zu rufen." Althaus, *Kirche und Volkstum*, 27.

church works, not simply calling sinful humanity to repentance, or offering the individual the grace of God, but serving a whole defined by race, shared culture, and a mystical sense of shared identity. It will be this aspect of his understanding of the implications of Luther's teaching and the nature of God's work within historical time which will then regulate his response to National Socialism when it emerges from the *völkisch* movement to gain a hold on all of Germany. From this side of the historical divide it is easy to see the fateful consequences of Althaus' understanding of Lutheran religiosity, but in his own mind this commitment to the *Volk* was utterly compelling, promising as it did a deep connection to all Germans, a revived church that could recover from the erosion of its influence within German culture, and a service to the people to bring about a national revival. Though he is aware that the *Volk*, as with all the orders of creation, has the potential to be used for demonic purposes, this does not play a regulating role in his perception of racial nationalism within Germany, at least not until it was far too late. In the meantime, he would become a passionate advocate for the new, reborn German society of the 1930s as a vehicle of spiritual renewal.

By the end of the 1920s, Luther had been reborn as not simply a symbol of German identity, but as a living embodiment of the German *Volksgeist*, the intangible model for the German *Volkstum*. On the one hand, he harkened back to an older world of traditional virtue, of household and domesticity, of obedience to authority and duty, of doing what is right rather than expedient. For traditionalists yearning for a return to moral order in the face of a new Republic grounded, it was claimed, in profane, degenerate, and alien values, Luther represented the reestablishment of tradition and rectitude. With the reborn Luther of the Luther Renaissance, however, there was a new dynamism about his image. He wasn't simply a figure of the past, but a living spirit, who embodied the existential struggle for meaning in a world of crisis and collapse, as well the possibility of authentic action and redemption. This Luther had resources for the revival of the nation not simply as restoration, but as an agent for a new dialectical turn of the *Volkgeist*. In his encounter with the eternal God who moved history, the God of judgment and wrath, from which he was able to grasp a God of grace, he created the basis for his actions in reconfiguring the order of his day. This Luther could serve as the inspiration for the present, to suggest the wells of spiritual renewal for the German *Volk* out of which they too could reconfigure the order of the present. In the eyes of those who expounded or consumed this view of Luther, the racial nationalist "movement" of the 1920s appeared as a possible ally, where the church in service to its *Volk* might live out its living faith, and achieve both a restoration of its place within the nation and *Volk*, and create a dynamic new basis for realizing God's will in the world. As we will see, the coming of National Socialism was greeted as just this sort of opportunity.

The Luther Myth: The Image of Martin Luther from Religious Reformer to Völkisch *Icon*. Patrick Hayden-Roy, Oxford University Press. © Patrick Hayden-Roy 2024. DOI: 10.1093/9780198930297.003.0004

4
Luther's "German Hour"

Between 1927 and 1933 Germany experienced another revolution, though of an entirely different character from the one that came at the end of World War I. The Weimar Republic that resulted from the revolution of 1918 enjoyed its greatest period of stability in the middle years of the 1920s. Though the forces of radical opposition did not become more moderate—in fact it was in these years that the National Socialists built their national party structure and strategy—the economic and diplomatic circumstances became more favorable, the crisis mentality that afflicted the earlier years of the decade abated. Fatefully, those circumstances did not last, and the global economic crisis that first emerged in 1929, then deepened over the following years, threw the Weimar constitution into an even more profound crisis. One fundamental problem for the Republic was the readiness of those like Paul Althaus, who supported the conservative nationalism of the German National People's Party (DNVP = *Deutsche Nationalvolkspartei*), to see the radical racial nationalism of the National Socialists as a vehicle to realize their own vision of the church. While conscious that aspects of the National Socialist program drew from explicitly non-Christian, or even anti-Christian ideals and sources, there was a readiness to believe that the *Volksbewegung*, the *völkisch* "movement" could be bridled, that Hitler was sincere in his profession of "positive Christianity," which was left entirely undefined so that it could be shaped to fulfill the sensibilities of various audiences.[1] Althaus' address on "Kirche und Volkstum" from 1927 is a good example of the mentality within the church and the DNVP that looked to the National Socialists as a potential vehicle and ally in achieving a fundamental revision of the Weimar constitution and the German state to achieve nationalist goals—the abrogation of the Versailles Treaty, the return to a traditional moral order, the end to "parliamentarianism" and the creation of an authoritarian system of rule that fulfilled the "German" type of state formation.

Even before the collapse of the international economy in the Fall of 1929 the DNVP had joined forces with the National Socialists in promoting a referendum campaign against the Young Plan to refinance Germany's reparation obligations, and this sort of alliance building of a "respectable" political party associated with business and religious leaders provided new legitimacy for Hitler and the

---

[1] Frank Becker, "Protestantische Euphorien: 1870/71, 1914 und 1933." In *Nationalprotestantische Mentalitäten: Konturen, Entwicklungslinien und Umbrüche eines Weltbildes*, ed. Manfred Gailus and Hartmut Lehmann (Göttingen: Vandenhoeck & Ruprecht, 2005): 19–44; 37–8.

National Socialists at precisely a point where the conditions providing stability for the Weimar state broke down. In the following years, the forces that fundamentally rejected the Weimar Republic—the German Communist Party and the National Socialists—would claim so many seats in the *Reichstag* as to make the state ungovernable through the normal constitutional avenues. In this context, the ability of the state to respond to the economic crisis was severely compromised, and only the use of emergency provisions in the Weimar constitution that provided for the use of Presidential decree allowed any sort of legislation to be enacted. It was this context of economic and political crisis that eventually led to the appointment of Hitler as Chancellor in late January 1933, another instance of the "respectable" right seeking to bridle the mass popularity of National Socialism to achieve their aims. The results of that effort were of fatal consequence.[2]

It was clear even before the advent of Hitler to the Chancellorship that Protestant Germany was far more electorally supportive of National Socialism than any other segment of German society. Protestant areas voted in much higher proportions for the Nazis than Catholic areas.[3] Local party units took care to style their appeal in Protestant areas to the mindset of Protestant voters, and mute some of the more radical elements of party ideology. In the multiple elections of 1932 Protestant voters consistently voted for National Socialist candidates in high numbers, and at the local level Nazi Party members had already claimed positions of authority. The campaigns at the local level would frequently feature Protestant pastors who supported the idea that the Nazi movement was grounded in "positive Christianity." Given the way that Martin Luther had been styled as a *völkisch* hero, this openness to the rhetoric of National Socialism is hardly surprising.

Once in power, this affinity among many of those who grounded their religiosity in Luther would become even more pronounced. One gets a sense of this from the introductory comments included in the edition of the *Lutherjahrbuch* from 1933. In the final paragraph of the *"Zur Geleit,"* the editor, Theodore Knolle, had this to say:

> The new awakening of the German nation has brought about a new receptivity for a "Reformation order" of life, the state, and the church. For this reason the

---

[2] On the political machinations of the DNVP and the erosion of parliamentary democracy, see Heinrich August Winkler, *Weimar 1918-1933: Die Geschichte der ersten deutschen Demokratie* (Munich: C. H. Beck, 1993): esp. chs. 12-18.

[3] See the article by Hartmut Lehmann, "Hitlers evangelische Wähler." In *Protestantische Weltsichten*, ed. Hartmut Lehmann (Göttingen: Vandenhoeck & Ruprecht, 1998): 130-52. Lehmann notes the unanimity of the literature on voting patterns in the early 1930s that Protestant voters were almost twice as likely to vote for Hitler or the National Socialists as were Catholics—see 130-2. He has some highly suggestive comments about the role the image of Luther had to play in this greater attraction to Hitler and the Nazis—see 143-5.

Luther-Society will have the task of testifying to the promise of its legacy and mission for the German future with new joyousness.[4]

This burst of enthusiasm for and testimony to the benefits of the new regime was generally reflected in the work generated by Protestant scholars and church leaders. Once again, a work of Paul Althaus' provides a striking example of the logic and ideological mindset of those within the mainstream of the church who looked to the new regime for a national revival of the *Volk*.

Althaus' work was titled *Die deutsche Stunde der Kirchen* (The German hour of the Church), and appeared in October of the year of the seizure of power, 1933. Althaus' writings during the 1920s left no doubt he considered the Weimar Republic a foreign imposition, an instance of God's judgment on the German *Volk*, and that he was receptive to the advent of a new regime that would fulfill what Althaus conceived as the moral duties of the state and its *völkisch* destiny. The new publication affirmed that he considered the new turn of events to have the promise of fulfilling such duties and destiny: the first section is titled "the yes of the church to the German turn-about (*Wende*)," and the first sentence announces that "our evangelical churches have greeted the German *Wende* of 1933 as a gift and miracle of God."[5] And while Althaus could embrace the change that had overtaken the state in Germany, and see it as an instance of a revival of the *Volk*, it came with complications. The proportion of the embrace that the church should afford the new regime brought division within the church. The German Christian movement within the church (*Deutsche Christen* = DC) in its most radical form sought to have the church remade in the image of the state, with the territorial churches being dissolved into an overarching, "Arianized" *Reichskirche* (imperial church) with a bishop *Führer* who would ultimately answer to Hitler and the party.[6] Such a constellation was anathema to many in the church, including Althaus, and tempered to some degree his enthusiasm for the new regime. But Althaus also hoped to channel the energies of the new movement by coopting the DC for his idea of the *Volkskirche*. The 1933 tract was written as an attempt to embrace the movement while framing it appropriately within his understanding

---

[4] "Der Neuaufbruch deutscher Nation hat eine neue Empfänglichkeit für die reformatorische Ordnung des Lebens, des Staates, der Kirche gezeitigt. Die Luther-Gesellschaft wird von daher die Aufgabe haben, die Verheißung ihres Erbes und Auftrages für die deutsche Zukunft mit neuer Freudigkeit zu bezeugen." "Zum Geleit." *Lutherjahrbuch* 15 (1933): v.

[5] "Das Ja der Kirche zur deutschen Wende"; "Unsere evangelischen Kirchen haben die deutsche Wende von 1933 als ein Geschenk und Wunder Gottes begrüßt." Paul Althaus, *Die Deutsche Stunde der Kirche*. 3rd ed. (Göttingen: Vandenhoeck & Ruprecht, 1934): 5. The third edition was unchanged from the original edition.

[6] For the history of the German Christian movement, see Doris L. Bergen, *Twisted Cross: The German Christian Movement in the Third Reich* (Chapel Hill: University of North Carolina Press, 1996); ch. 1 discusses the aspirations of the movement for the church in relationship to the state.

of *Schöpfungstheologie* (creation theology).[7] In what in retrospect seems a wildly misjudged assessment, Althaus quotes from an announcement read from the pulpit of all the Lutheran churches in Bavaria on Easter Sunday, 1933, praising the new regime for having done away with the misguided Weimar Republic and implementing a regime that fulfills the appropriate duties of the state:

> A state that begins again to rule according to the laws of God may, with this accomplishment, reckon not only with applause, but also with the joyful and active assistance of the church. With thanks and joy the church acknowledges the way the new state defends against blasphemy, tackles immorality, establishes discipline and order with a strong hand, how it calls for the fear of God, desires that marriage be kept holy, the young raised as Christians, how it brings back to honor the accomplishments of the forefathers, and no longer bans fervent love of the *Volk* and fatherland but rather inflames it in a thousand hearts.[8]

This emphasis on the correspondence between Christian moral virtues and the actions of the new regime reflect Althaus' anticipation that the new regime represents the proper configuration of the *völkisch* orders of creation as intended by God. He argues passionately in the tract that a proper understanding of Luther, who affirmed the goodness of creation, supports the affirmation of this new order for the *Volkstum*.[9] He calls for a theology that attends to the action of God in time: "our proclamation and theology—exactly where it is at its best and deepest—has too often ignored the testimony to the reality of God in the reality of our historical life and has had too little sense and place also for the natural as well as the *völkisch* ethos."[10] "The knocking of the 'experience of National Socialism' on the door of the church poses to it a theological question and responsibility."[11] He references the older tradition of the *vocatio generalis* that allowed for this theological reading of God's action in time, which the newer theologies have discarded, and which now it is a pressing practical issue. He notes that among the German

---

[7] See the discussion of Althaus' complicated motives with the publication of the work in Jasper, *Paul Althaus*, 224–41.

[8] "Ein Staat, der wieder anfängt, nach Gottes Gebot zu regieren, darf in diesem Tun nicht nur des Beifalls, sondern auch der freudigen und tätigen mitarbeit der Kirche sicher sein. Mit Dank und Freude nimmt die Kirche wahr, wie der neue Staat der Gotteslästerung wehrt, der Unsittlichkeit zu Liebe geht, Zucht und Ordnung mit starker Hand aufrichtet, wie er zur Gottesfurcht ruft, die Ehe heilig gehalten und die Jugend christlich erzogen wissen will, wie er der Väter Tat wieder zu Ehren bringt und heiße Liebe zu Volk und Vaterland nicht mehr verfehmt, sondern in tausend Herzen entzündet." Althaus, *Deutsche Stunde*, 5.

[9] Althaus, *Deutsche Stunde*, 7–8.

[10] "Unsere Verkündigung und Theologie-gerade wo sie am besten und tiefsten waren-haben die Bezeugung der Wirklichkeit Gottes in der Wirklichkeit unseres geschichtlichen Lebens zu sehr außer Acht gelassen und haben für das natürliche, also auch das völkische Ethos zu wenig Sinn und Platz gehabt." Althaus, *Deutsche Stunde*, 9.

[11] "Das Anpochen der Frömmigkeit des 'nationalsozialistischen Erlebnisses' an die Tore der Kirche stellt ihr eine theologische Frage und Aufgabe." Althaus, *Deutsche Stunde*, 9.

Volk in the period since 1914 there has arisen an experience among those of no faith of a national "movement" (*Bewegung*), who are gripped, as they experience the historical turns of recent times, by the power of sacrifice that gives life joy and meaning:

> It is simply the case, that German men who no longer knew anything of faith or devotion in their life have experienced, in the relationship to the leader (*Führer*), in being exhorted to sacrifice, in sensing the call of the hour, a reality that can only be termed "religious."[12]

For Althaus the experience by the *Volk* of defeat in the war, the travails of the 1920s, and the passions evoked by the Nazis represent a religiously significant experience, an awakening, and that this hard experience, an experience that has within it the traces of God's action within the consciousness of the *Volkstum*, constitutes a reality that the church must address. His interpretation sees a pre-revelation experience of God—he calls it an *Uroffenbarung* (primal revelation)—which impacts the conscience of the *Volk*, in the same fashion Luther experienced something of God's awesome wrathful and judging reality before he ever experienced God's grace. Given this premise, Althaus asks the question:

> What do we, the theologians, the pastors, have to say to this? Should we announce to the people that everything that they've experienced has nothing to do with the living God and his instruction, that God never speaks to us anywhere but in the biblical witness of Jesus Christ? Do we want to make suspect as heathen for our *Volksgenossen* (people's comrades) the 'religious' promptings of their experience, and call them back from their supposed experience of God to the divine witness of the Bible? We can't do that and we don't need to do that.[13]

In the "primal revelation" that takes place in the orders of creation (*Schöpfungsordungen*), in those structures that God has provided for the ordering of life, there is an experience and understanding of God that happens in time even for those who do not know God. This is particularly relevant in the structures of the state and the *Volk*. He notes:

---

[12] "Es ist einfach so, daß deutsche Männer, die von Glaube und Hingabe des Lebens nicht mehr wußten, in dem Verhältnis zu dem Führer, in dem Angefordertsein zum Opfer, in dem Spüren des Rufes der Stunde, der Verantwortung zum Gehorsam gegen diesen Ruf eine Wirklichkeit erlebt haben, von der sie nur 'religiös' reden können." Althaus, *Deutsche Stunde*, 10.

[13] "Was haben wir, die Theologen, die Pfarrer, dazu zu sagen? Sollen wir den Menschen erklären, das alles, was sie erlebten, mit dem lebendigen Gotte und seiner Weisung nichts zu tun habe, daß Gott zu uns nirgends anders spreche als in dem biblishen Zeugnis von Jesus Christus? Wollen wir unseren Volksgenossen die 'religiöse' Deutung ihrer Erfahrung als Heidentum verdächtigen und sie von ihrer angeblichen Gotteserfahrung einfach fortrufen zu dem Gotteszeugnis der Bibel? Wir können das nicht und brauchen das nicht." Althaus, *Deutsche Stunde*, 10.

> When the historical order of the *Volkstum* or the power of the state wins over our hearts with the demand and joy of devotion up to the sacrifice of life, then we experience in earnest and immediately what a war volunteer from 1914 said for many: 'God calls us.' And when, through the demands of a *Führer*, the calling of our *Volk* to true and worthy life in an age of delusion and forgetting becomes anew the law for them, then they have in truth heard more than a human voice.[14]

Althaus is quick to add that this experience is itself not the suffering of Christ, which has an entirely different quality, and which is the pathway for salvation. Still, he wishes to use this sensibility and these experiences, which he sees as a possible pathway for the church to bring the *Volk* to the church, to make relevant the message of the church, without capitulating and simply affirming the experience as in itself of no eternal significance. The church must risk creating a theology of the historical experience that can give meaning to what is being experienced in this "German hour" or risk having others twist it to profane purposes.

But how to do this? He points to the experience of Israel in the Old Testament as a parallel on which one can draw, not that it is the same, since they had a larger significance in the history of salvation, but as an example of how God does work in time: "God enters concretely into the history of a *Volk*, interacts with it, calls and bestows gifts on it, draws it to responsibility, judges, shatters *völkische* usurpations, pardons, and raises it up to a new life."[15] He advocates the use of the Old Testament as the means through which to relate the working of God with a *Volk* as one addresses the circumstances of the present. One has to address not just the individual but also the *Volk*, and history cannot only be the history of judgment, but also the action of God with and for the *Volk*. He doesn't shy away from providing a concrete example of addressing the historical issues of the moment both in judgment and in affirmation. He cites his own denunciation of the betrayals at the end of the war when political forces signed a treaty that assigned guilt to the German *Volk* for the war, which was in Althaus' eyes not simply a political act, but a judgment of the *Volk*. Likewise, the most recent destruction of the "parliamentarianism" that had brought the German *Volk* into the abyss, as was accomplished by the National Socialists in the spring and summer of 1933, was more than just a profane revolutionary event, but had ethical depths

---

[14] "Wenn die geschichtliche Ordnung des Volkstums oder des Staates Gewalt über unser Herz gewinnt mit der Forderung und Freude der Hingabe bis zum Opfer des Lebens, dann erfahren wir im Ernste und unmittelbar, was ein Kriegsfreiwilliger von 1914 für die vielen aussprach: 'Uns ruft Gott.' Und wenn die Bestimmung unseres Volkes zum wahrhaften und würdigen Leben in Zeiten des Wahns und des Vergessens durch eines Führers Forderungen den vielen neu zum Gesetz wird, dann haben sie in Wahrheit mehr als eines Menschen Stimme gehört." Althaus, *Deutsche Stunde*, 11–12.

[15] "Gott geht in eines Volkes Geschichte konkret ein, handelt mit ihm, ruft und begabt es, zieht es zur Verantwortung, richtet, zerschlägt völkische Anmaßung, begnadigt, richtet auf zu neuem Leben." Althaus, *Deutsche Stunde*, 16.

and force—"the 'crisis' of parliamentarianism was judgment, true judgment which the church is called to address."[16]

This leads him to consider the whole arc of German history and its *Volk* as an example of the dealings of God—"do we really want to distance ourselves theologically when our *Volk* speak about their shakers and leaders as tools of God's grace?"[17] He considers various stages in the history of German *Volk* as part of the history that begins with the *Volk* of Israel:

> However when we hear as the **German** *Volk* "I am the Lord your God," the God of the Old and New covenant, then that means for us something more: the one who mysteriously called you to become a *Volk* in ancient times, who richly endowed you, who sent you the messengers of the Gospel and built his church in you; who made your path difficult and burdensome; who awakened Martin Luther in you, and powerfully testified to his faith; who called you back from self-alienation through prophets and heroes; such that your forefathers risked themselves in the War of Liberation; who gave you freedom from your enemies; who built for you the house of Empire, which often deeply humbled you and then miraculously again exalted you; who gave you responsibility and service above and beyond your boundaries—I am the Lord, your God!"[18]

This ascent of the German *Volk* through the action of God demonstrates the degree to which Althaus vests the historical with the divine, and also how Luther stands in the center of this drama, the one who made the Gospel into something that was German, and whose experience highlights this action of God in the individual spirit who is also a microcosm of the German, the *völkisch*, self, one of the prophets and heroes of the *Volk*.

In end, Althaus represents a significant constituency within the church that wishes to embrace the Third Reich as part of this historical movement of God's divine order within the German *Volk*, so that, despite the fact he is fully aware that no historical event or development brings about the eternal kingdom of God, that all peoples and states will pass away, and that salvation is not ultimately a

---

[16] "Die 'Krisis' des Parlamentarismus war Gericht, echtes Gericht. Davon zu reden ist die Kirche auch berufen." Althaus, *Deutsche Stunde*, 19.

[17] "Wollen wir wirklich theologischen Abstand nehmen, wenn unser Volk von seinem Aufrüttler und Führer als von dem Wekzeug göttlicher Gnade für uns redet?" Althaus, *Deutsche Stunde*, 20.

[18] "Aber wenn wir es als **deutsches** Volk hören: 'Ich bin der Herr dein Gott,' der Gott des Alten und Neuen Bundes, dann heißt es für uns weiter: der dich geheimnisvoll zu Volke rief in der Vorzeit, der dich reich begabte, der dir die Boten des Evangeliums sandte und seine Kirche in dir baute; der deinen Weg schwer und mühsam machte; der in dir Martin Luther erweckte und seinem Glauben sich gewaltig bezeugte; der dich aus der Selbstentfremdung zurückrief durch Propheten und Helden; auf den deine Väter es wagten in dem Freiheitskriege; der dir Freiheit von deinen Feinden schenkte; der dir das Haus des Reiches errichtete, der dich oft tief gedemütigt und dann wieder wunderbar erhöht hat; der dir Verantwortung und Dienst gab weit über deine Grenzen hinaus—ich bin der Herr, dein Gott!" Althaus, *Deutsche Stunde*, 20.

völkisch, corporate phenomenon, still he wishes to first address the current situation with affirmation. For him, it fulfills deeply rooted desires for retribution for the events that ended World War I, as well as his own naïve desire to return the basis of state and society back to the model of the Second Reich. If the church can just coopt the *völkisch* movement, draw the German Christians away from their radical form, back to the Lutheranism as understood by Althaus and those around him, then this Third Reich can be a true renewal of the German *Volk*, in the same way that in Luther's time the Gospel emerged from a movement of the *Volk*. It is not the case that Althaus, or most Lutheran theologians of his circle, were convinced Nazis, though this was the case for Emanuel Hirsch and not a few members of the German Christian movement, as we will discuss further on. But their readiness to embrace the movement as a vehicle for restoration of an order that conformed to their understanding of the *Volk* and its appropriate historical formation powerfully legitimated the actions of Hitler and National Socialism, and sapped the capacity of the church to resist when the regime became incrementally more radical in its policies.

Other less scholarly voices of the church also spoke loudly in support of the regime in 1933 through the platform of the four-hundred-fiftieth anniversary celebration of the birth of Martin Luther. As in 1883, though in this instance with an even more opportune convergence of dates, the church used Luther's birthday celebration fully to demonstrate its endorsement of the changes taking place in German society, which, in this instance, included valorizing the character of the leader of the new German state. That the celebration of Luther in 1933 would highlight the affirmation of the new regime was not in question, but the nature of that embrace was. The German Christians (DC), whose influence in the church had been growing since 1932, and whose activities and influence escalated in 1933, looked to use the celebration of Luther's birthday to highlight their own highly nazified understanding of Christianity, emphasizing a *völkisch* "German" Christianity where all foreign, that is to say Jewish, elements were purged. Though somewhat fractured in their organization and thinking, in general the DC promoted a subordination of the church under the leadership of the new National Socialist state. Both in terms of their program to "Arianize" Christianity, and concede the independence of the church's administration, the DC were at odds with much of the mainstream though conservative leadership within the church—as mentioned, Althaus wrote *Die deutsche Stunde der Kirche* in an attempt to coopt moderate elements of the DC for this "mainstream" conservative Protestantism. This division made itself felt in the planning and festivities surrounding Luther's four-hundred-fiftieth birthday.[19] While on the whole the tensions were not profiled

---

[19] See Björn Küllmer, *Die Inszenierung der Protestantischen Volksgemeinschaft* (Berlin: Logos Verlag, 2012): 53–78.

in the celebration itself, they certainly were perceptible in the different representations of Luther by contributors.

Given that the planning for the festivities had begun in 1932 or even earlier, the changes that came during 1933 meant a shift in emphasis. Once the church in March 1933 indicated its willingness to work with the regime (as indicated in the Easter announcement quoted by Althaus above), the door was open for restyling the official program for the day. Though the DC worked hard to gain control of such planning as a means to expand their influence both within the church and with the regime, in the end more mainstream conservative elements gained the oversight.[20] At no point was the regime itself the driver for the planning of the festivities, and, given the proportion of the *Volk* who were Catholic, there were in fact reasons that the new regime wished to modulate the idea of a strong connection between the new state itself and traditional Protestantism. In addition, the church itself represented a power center within society that in time the regime wished to weaken and coopt, but on its own terms. In the meantime, it was willing to work to overcome the historic divisions among the regional churches and implement a more centralized institutional structure. It is indicative of the regime's distanced regard for the Luther celebration that participation of the most prominent members of the party was limited, and Hitler himself was too preoccupied to appear at all. And to make the low priority of the celebration clear, the regime scheduled a plebiscite vote in conflict with the traditional celebration date of November 10, which scrambled much of the planning, and forced a good portion of the local celebrations to be rescheduled for over a week later on November 19—to make matters even worse, a Germany-wide action of the Hitler Youth was scheduled on that date.[21] Despite all these conflicts and setbacks, Luther's birth was celebrated nationwide in the late summer and fall of 1933, and highlighted the way the nationalistic Luther was now to be restyled for this new "German" hour.

The overall character of the celebration was keyed to the events of the moment. One sees this vividly exemplified in the work of Florentine Gebhardt, a popular author of curricula and novels for young people, who developed a format for the celebration that was published for use in churches and schools in 1933, "Luther, the German Man and Champion of God: three Luther celebrations for the congregations and schools of the Third Reich on Reformation Day."[22] Her introduction gives an excellent sense of the overall framing of Luther for the times:

---

[20] Kulmer, *Die Inszenierung*, 73–4.   [21] Kulmer, *Die Inszenierung*, 74–5.
[22] Florentine Gebhardt, *Luther, der deutsche Mann und Streiter Gottes: Drei Lutherfeiern in Gemeinde und Schule des 3. Reiches zum Reformationstag, inbesondere auch zur 450. Wiederkehr des Geburtstages Dr. Martin Luthers. Mit Ansprachen, Gedichtvorträgen, Gesängen usw. zusemmengestellt von F. Gebhardt* (Berlin: N.B. Buchvertrieb, 1933). Included were three celebrations: one for church congregations, and two for schools with more or less advanced students.

We prepare ourselves to celebrate the four-hundred-fiftieth birthday of a man who belongs among the greatest Germans of all time, the Reformer, the Bible Translator and creator of the New High German literary language, the fighter for and leader of the German *Volkstum*—Dr. Martin Luther. It was a November day which bestowed on us this man.... A November day admittedly like the one now more than fifteen years past that confronted the German *Volk* with bitter shame and oppression [the reference here is the convergence of Luther's birthdate with the Armistice of 1918 that signaled Germany's defeat].

Hail to us that today, where we prepare ourselves to celebrate the festival of the German *Volk* in commemoration of Martin Luther, this last memory has lost its most terrible sting, now that in our time was awoken a man who leads the German *Volk's* ascent again to freedom and justice. This is also Luther's work—the creation of a **German Christendom**, which up to this day hadn't yet found its embodiment, but seemed threatened through inner and outer fragmentation, now finally every effort is being made to bring it to its realization! Again, just as in Luther's day we are allowed in our own to experience that man's extremity is God's opportunity, that at the right time the right man was awoken for our *Volk*. Just like the *Führer* today, Adolf Hitler, Martin Luther was indeed a son of the *Volk*, a student of hard necessities, steeled by inner and outward struggle, rock-solid in his will, fearless and unafraid of sacrifice, purposeful, and cut from the most authentic German cloth (*von echtester deutscher Art*). Nobody would have greeted the current national movement more jubilantly and thankfully than Martin Luther. Consequently, he is situated inwardly very close to Germans of today. On this festive day of remembrance of him may his image be doubly precious to every German and become the model toward which the German youth should strive.[23]

---

[23] "Wir schicken uns an, den 450. Geburtstag eines Mannes festlich zu begehen, der zu den größten Deutschen aller Zeiten gehört, des Reformators, des Bibelübersetzers und Schöpfers der neuhochdeutschen Schriftsprache, des Kämpfers und Führers für und zum deutschen Volkstum—Dr. Martin Luther. Ein Novembertag war es, er uns diesen Mann geschenkt.... Ein Novembertag, wie freilich auch der, in welchem bitterste Schmach und Erniedrigung das deutsche Volk vor nunmehr 15 Jahren traf. Heil uns, daß heute, da wir den Festtag des deutschen Volkes im Gedenken an Martin Luther zu feiern uns anschicken, jene letzte Erinnerung ihren schlimmsten Stachel verloren hat, daß unserer Zeit ein Mann erweckt wurde, der das deutsche Volk aus der Tiefe wieder emporführt zu Freiheit und Recht. Der auch Luthers Werk—die Schaffung eines **deutschen Christentums**, das bis auf unsere Tage noch nicht die Ausgestaltung gefunden hatte, sondern bedroht schien durch innere und äußere Zersplitterung, nun endgültig zu seiner Vollendung zu bringen bestrebt ist! Wieder wie in Luthers Tagen durften wir es in unseren erleben, daß Gottes Hilfe am nächsten, wenn die Not am größten ist, daß zur rechten Stunde der rechte Mann unserm Volke erweckt ward. Wie der Führer von heute, Adolf Hitler, war Martin Luther ja ein Sohn des Volks, ein Schüler der harten Not, gestählt in inneren und äußeren Kämpfen, felsenfest im Willen, furchtlos und opfermutig, zielbewußt und von echtester deutscher Art. Keiner würde die heutige nationale Bewegung jauchzender und dankbarer begrüßen, als Martin Luther. Und deshalb steht er dem Deutschen von heute innerlich wieder ganz nahe. Der festliche Tag des Gedenkens an ihn möge sein Bild jedem Deutschen doppelt teuer werden und zum Vorbild erwachsen lassen, dem die deutsche Jugend nachstreben soll—Der Verfasser." Gebhardt, *Luther, der deutsche Mann*, 3.

A number of the notes here struck will resonate across most of the celebrations. For one the emphasis on the *völkisch* Luther will be almost universal, but framed within the context now of National Socialism. While there will be differences of emphasis between hardcore DC versions of Luther's *völkisch* calling, and those of more moderate nationalists, such as Althaus, almost all will strike this note. Further, the comparisons between Hitler and Luther will be persistent, not just as both being great men or great leaders, but as providential leaders who accomplished and are still accomplishing the divinely ordained construction of the German *Volk*. Of course, this being intended in part for an audience of students, the emphasis on the imitation of the great man's virtues and ideals is not surprising, the idea of setting the image of Luther into one's self highlights the *völkisch* ideal of Luther's living spirit as a resource for conformity to the national/ racial order.

From this opening frame, the prescribed festivities were to include a mixture of poetry, singing, "historical" reenactment, and exhortatory addresses. The providential theme is repeatedly emphasized, as well as Luther's deep connection to the common *Volk* of Germany; in one dramatic reenactment, he is depicted giving a sermon under the lindens to the trusting common people, his words resonating in their souls until the voice of a half-blind elderly man whispers "now will I go in peace as my eyes have now seen him,"[24] echoing the words of Simeon in Luke 2:29–30 and reinforcing the providentially ordained order of Luther's life.[25] But this ideal of the spiritual man of God is counterposed with the representation of him as the fulfillment of masculine, "Germanic" virtue:

Before the priests and throne of the Emperor/ in Worms the miner's son spoke simply/ 'here I stand as a German man/ I spoke because I can do no other/ I spoke in the name of God--/ so help me God! Amen!'--/

That was a truly manly word/ through the ages it resonates/ and in the face of the man who boldly spoke it/ the enemy's scorn and derision were smashed/ he fought in the name of God/ and therefore he remained the victor! Amen![26]

His powerful, masculine virtue is contrasted with that of Katherina von Bora, who, reminiscent of Treitschke's address fifty years prior, makes a guest appearance as the one whose soothing hand and domesticity makes possible the labors of her

---

[24] "Einer der Alten, schon halb erblindet, / Flüstert: Jetzt will ich in Frieden gehn, / Da meine Augen ihn noch gesehn—." Gebhardt, *Luther, der deutsche Mann*, 16.

[25] As was reflected in the work of Karl König dealt with in Chapter 2 (pp. 35-9), giving Luther a messianic dimension comes forward regularly in *völkisch* images of Luther.

[26] "1. Vor Priesterschaft und Kaiserthron / Zu Worms sprach schlicht der Bergmannssohn: / 'Hier stehe ich als deutscher Mann, / 'Ich sprach, weil ich nicht anders kann, / 'Ich sprach in gottes Namen— / 'so helfe Gott mir! Amen!—' 2. Das war ein rechtes Manneswort, / Durch manch Jahrhundert klingt es fort, / Und vor dem Mann, der kühn es sprach, / Der Feinde hohn und Drohn zerbrach. / Er stritt in Gottes namen, / Drum blieb er Sieger!—Amen!" Gebhardt, *Luther, der deutsche Mann*, 16.

husband through the consolation of the household and her healing touch.[27] Mostly, however, the emphasis is on the active struggle that he exemplified, and the degree to which it represents the spirit that through the ages has driven forward the construction of the German *Volk*.

Much is made of the challenges in the days ahead; how the spirit of Luther, who stands highest in a lineage of great men that comes down from his day to Hitler, and a series of armed struggles similar to those that brought German's their freedom, will carry things forward:

> Authentically German is the death-defying brave conviction with which he steps out against the enemy—a living admonition for every German now and in the coming days. For we stand on the brink of a hard time of struggle, where it will be on us to assert our right to life in the face of a hostile world. Luther's words and Luther's songs, Luther's power and Luther's brave spirit, Luther's faith and Luther's obedience to the Most High, they all can help us in the coming struggle to emerge triumphant. There have been hard times enough for Germany since the time of Luther. Always again and again Luther's image and Luther's instruction have helped us overcome them. And now we will and must succeed again, and proud and joyfully hopeful we will continually declare it, conscious of our task and our great *Führer*, just as an old song from 100 years ago put it, whose exhortation once again resonates for us today.[28]

---

[27] "Luthers Käthe. 1. Er war der Held, der die Waffen schwang, / Sieghaft wider der Lüge Macht. / Du aber botest den Labetrank / Müdem Kämpfer nach schwerer Schlacht! 2. Haß und Undank und Mißverstand / Schufen ihm schweren Wundenschmerz. / Du aber legtest die tröstende Hand / Leis und lind ihm auf haupt und Herz! / 3. Schattende Wolken scheuchtest du, / Räumtest die Steine vom Alltagspfad; / Brachtest Grollen und Grimm zur Ruh, / Schenktest Kraft ihm zu frischer Tat! / 4. Stark—wohl war er es ohne dich— / Daß er es bleib an Seele und Leib, / Daß seine Härte der Milde wich, / War dein wirken, liebendes Weib! 5. Daß er vollendet, was er begann, / Deutschen Glaubens stolzen Bau — / Danken wir's ihm, dem deutschen Mann, / Danken auch dir wir's, deutsche Frau" (Luther's Kate: 1. He was the hero who wielded the weapons / victorious against the lies of the powerful. / You however offered the restorative drink / to the tired warrior after the difficult battle! 2. Hate and ungratefulness and misunderstandings / caused for him severe and painful wounds. / You however laid your soothing hand / light and mild on his head and heart! 3. You chased away the dark shadows / cleared the stones from the daily path / brought thunder and fury to rest / and provided energy to him for new deeds! 4. Strong, he would have been that without you— / that he remained sound in soul and body / that his hardness was made soft / that was your accomplishment loving wife! 5. That he brought to closure what he started / German Faith's proud house— / we give thanks to him the German man / but we give thanks to you also, German woman!). Gebhardt, *Luther, der deutsche Mann*, 17.

[28] "Echt deutsche ist der todestrotzende Überzeugungsmut, mit dem er den Feinden entgegentritt— eine lebendig Mahnung für jeden Deutschen unserer wie der kommenden Tage. Denn noch stehen uns harte Kampfzeiten bevor, in denen es an uns sein wird, unser Lebensrecht gegen eine feindliche Welt zu behaupten. Lutherwort und Lutherlied, Lutherkraft und Luthermut, Lutherglaube und Luthergehorsam gegen den Höchsten, sie allein können uns helfen, die kommenden Kämpfe sieghaft zu bestehen. Schwere Zeiten genug sind seit Luthers Tagen über Deutschland dahingeschritten. Immer wieder half uns Luthers Bild und Lehre, sie zu überwinden. Auch jetzt wird und muß uns das gelingen, und stolz, hoffnungsfreudig werden wir es, unserer Aufgabe und unserer großen Führer bewußt, allzeit aussprechen, wie ein altes Lied aus der Zeit vor 100 Jahren es ausdrückt, dessen Mahnung auch uns heute wieder entgegenklingt." Gebhardt, *Luther, der deutsche Mann*, 26.

With that they sang "Deutschland, Deutschland, über Alles."

The closing words of the celebration bring this missionary sense forward one last time, this time highlighting the connection quite explicitly to Hitler:

"If Luther were to come today…"

Just as Luther was the man in his own day who was sent by God "in the fullness of time" on which history turned, so we see also how, as we again are living through such a historical turn, another man has arisen, called by the ruler of the world to be our *Führer* on the path through the confusions and needs of our time of change. A man filled with the fiery will of Luther, radiating Luther's power, with an affinity of being in many ways to the great Reformer, above all in iron-clad diligence, a clear purposefulness, and the devotion to the freely elected duty of the recognized mission, and German in his most inner core. If Martin Luther arose here today after four-hundred-fifty years, he would joyously affirm what our *Volk* has recognized as the duty of our age and actively taken on under Hitler's leadership. He would extend to him his right hand, happy and thankful that he has begun to build up again what over the centuries seemed to have become broken and eroded of Luther's work, bringing it under the protective roof of unity what had been for so long constructed of individual pillars and chapels; that Adolf Hitler has brought the German Evangelical Church, whose cornerstone and foundation Luther constructed, to this unified completion.[29]

This full-throated support for the unification of German Protestantism reflects the degree to which the politization of Luther's image to affirm the Hitlerian state was written into what was being presented both to school-age audiences and the German public at large.

As a national celebration of Luther, 1933 proved less potent than had been anticipated.[30] As noted, the actual date of Luther's birth, November 10, was

---

[29] "Wenn Luther heute käme — Wie Luther in seinen Tagen der Mann gewesen ist, von Gott gesandt, da 'die Zeit erfüllet,' eine Weltenwende gekommen war, so sehen auch wir, die wir wieder solche 'Weltenwende' durchleben, unter uns den Mann erstanden, vom Weltenlenker berufen, auf dem Pfade durch die Wirren und Nöte dieser Wendezeit uns Führer zu sein. Einen Mann, erfüllt von feurigem Lutherwillen, durchglüht von Lutherkraft, dem großen Reformator in vielem wesensverwandt, vor allem in ehernem Fleiß, klarem Zielbewußtsein und der Hingabe an die als Sendung erkannte, selbserwählte Pflicht, und Deutsch bis in den innersten Kern. Stünde Dr. Martinus Luther heute nach 450 Jahren auf, so würde er jauchzend das, was unser Volk als Aufgabe der Zeit erkannt und unter eines Hitler Führung in Angriff genommen hat, bejahen. Er würde diesem die Rechte reichen, froh und dankbar, daß er begann, wieder aufzubauen, was in Jahrhunderten vom Lutherwerk abgebröckelt und brüchig geworden schien, unter das schirmende Dach der Einheitlichkeit bringend, was solange noch in einzelnen Pfeilern und Kapellen geragt; Daß Adolf Hitler die deutsche evangelische Kirche deren Grundstein und Grundmauern Luther aufgerichtet, nun zu dieser einheitliche Vollendung gebracht." Gebhardt, *Luther, der deutsche Mann*, 29.

[30] There is no one study that fully encompasses the various elements of the Luther celebrations of 1933. See Björn Küllmer, *Die Inszenierung der Protestantischen Volksgemeinschaft*, cited above, as well as Nicola Willenberg, "'Mit Luther und Hitler für Glauben und Volkstum: Der Luthertag 1933 in Dresden." In *Spurenlese: Reformationsvergegenwärtigung als Standortbestimmung (1717–1983)*, ed.

preempted by the regime, which proved generally uninterested in promoting or facilitating the event. In part this may have resulted from the inability of the church and its groupings to work together—the growing alienation of the DC from more traditional elements in the church made it difficult to come to a unified understanding of what the celebration was meant to accomplish. One suspects, as well, that Hitler himself would not be enamored of the comparisons of himself to Luther; in some of the materials of the celebration, Luther is given precedence over Hitler as the greatest German.[31] By the end of 1933 the Protestant church was proving a disappointment as a vehicle to build the kind of indisputable legitimacy to which the regime aspired. While the church may have anticipated enthusiasm for the regime would translate into some sort of symbiosis between church and state, in fact that was not to be the case. Hitler and the party were looking to coopt on their own terms the legitimizing institutions of German culture and society, and while other elements, such as labor and the unions, political parties and local governments, schools and universities, clubs and private associations all proved unable to resist the regimes process of *Gleichschaltung* (coordination), the churches proved more intractable, though not because they intentionally were seeking to contest the legitimacy of the regime, or, at least on the Protestant side, weren't eager to find an active accommodation with the regime. But because the churches aspired to maintain their traditional privileges as spiritual guides for the larger society, even a *völkisch* Protestantism fell short of what National Socialism was looking to accomplish. The endless valorizing of Luther as the epitome of the *völkisch* hero highlighted the entanglement of religiosity and national identity and made Protestant religiosity difficult to fully coopt. And by the end of 1933 it became clear that the sharp differences that divided Protestants theologically and in their disposition toward the policies of the regime

---

Klaus Tanner and Jörg Ulrich (Leipig: Evangelische Verlagsanstalt, 2012): 195–238. More generally see Manfred Gailus, *Gläubige Zeiten: Religiosität im Dritten Reich* (Freiburg: Herder, 2021): esp. ch. 1.

[31] "Luther als Vorbild der Deutschen." "Unter den hervorragenden Menschen, die aus dem deutschen Volke hervorgingen, und wie sie eben einzig diesem deutschen Volke entwachsen konnten um die alle anderen Kulturvölker uns heiß beneiden, wie z. B. einen Goethe, Wagner, Bismarck, Adolf Hitler—nimmt Dr. Martin Luther, der große Reformator und Bibelübersetzer, die erste Stelle ein, auch heute noch, da überall in evangelischen Landen die 450. Wiederkehr seines Geburtstag festlich begangen wird. Er gehört zu den vorbildlichen Gestalten aller Zeiten—vorbildlich durch Wesen und Wirken, nicht nur für die Menschen der Vergangenheit, sondern gerade für uns Kinder des Heute, für die kommenden Geschlechter. Und nicht nur die Anhänger der evangelischen Lehre, jeder Deutsche darf und soll in Martin Luther seinen ersten geistigen Führer erkennen" (Luther as role model for the Germans. Among the outstanding men who arose out of the German *Volk*, who indeed alone could grow out of the German *Volk* to the envy of all the other *Kulturvölker* (cultural *Völker*), such as Goethe, Wagner, Bismarck, Adolf Hitler, it is Dr. Martin Luther, the great Reformer and Bible Translator, takes pride of place even today still, where everywhere in the evangelical territories the four-hundred-fiftieth anniversary of his birth will be celebrated. He belongs to the most exemplary personages of all time—exemplary in essence and action, not only for past generations, but directly for children of today, and for the coming generation. And not only for the followers of the evangelical teachings, but every German may and should recognize Martin Luther as his primary spiritual *Führer*). Gebhart, *Luther, der deutsche Mann*, 22.

were growing more intractable.[32] These divisions would express themselves in a number of ways in the struggle over Luther's image.

What became known as the "church struggle" (*Kirchenkampf*) was rapidly emerging in the last half of 1933, and played itself out in part in a struggle over Luther's meaning and legacy. While the nationalist, *völkisch* image of Luther had made deep inroads both theologically and in the popularized celebration of his birthday, dissenting voices that sought to wrest the understanding of his legacy from *völkisch* populism and creation theology emerged. These were directed both at the DC and its distinctive theological preoccupations, as well as the formal theological arguments of Althaus and those like him who would use creation theology as a vehicle to reconcile traditional Lutheran theology with a nationalistic religion of the *Volk*. Two publications of 1933 highlight this resistance to the predominating image of Luther, one from the pen of Karl Barth, and the other from the authors of the Bethel Confession.

Barth was one of the most influential figures in the field of theology in the 1920s and beyond, and a figure who was also highly polarizing. Much of the work of Paul Althaus, among others, was aimed at counteracting what he saw as the bane influence of Barth's "Theology of the Word."[33] Barth himself was a bit of an odd-man-out in the theological circles of post-war Germany, in that he came out of the Reformed tradition and was Swiss by background and citizenship. His experience of the German church world of the 1920s, and his theological battles, inoculated him against the stereotyped Luther image that was so readily absorbed by German theologians who lived through World War I and experienced the nationalist Luther orgy of 1917. His connection to Luther, while of some significance, was always distanced and critical.[34] One of the few individual works that Barth devoted to Luther emerged in the midst of the events of the summer and fall of 1933, with the celebrations of Luther's birth coupled with the increasing assault of the DC on the independence of the German Protestant church and the disposition of Jewish Christians within it. Barth's work, which was published as an immediate response to the events surrounding the *Sportpalast* scandal of

---

[32] The best discussion of the general situation of the Protestant church as a whole during the period of the seizure of power remains Klaus Scholder, *Die Kirchen und das Dritte Reich*, Vol. 1: *Vorgeschichte und Zeit der Illusionen 1918–1934* (Frankfurth a.M.: Ullstein, 1986). See in particular part II, chs. 12 and 13, for the conflicts in the second half of 1933.

[33] On the history of interchange and conflicts between Althaus and Barth, see Jasper, *Paul Althaus*, esp. 165–77, 230–2, and 257–61.

[34] For a thorough overview of Barth's conflicted relationship with Luther, see two works of Gerhard Ebeling, "Karl Barths Ringen mit Luther." In *Lutherstudien*, Vol. 3: *Begriffsuntersuchungen, Textinterpretationen, Wirkungsgeschichtliches* (Tübingen: J. C. B. Mohr (Paul Siebeck), 1985): 428–573; and "Über die Reformation hinaus? Zur Luther-Kritik Karl Barths." In *Zeitschrift für Theologie und Kirche*, Beiheft 6: *Zur Theologie Karl Barths: Beiträge aus Anlaß seines 100. Geburtstags*, ed. Eberhard Jüngel (Tübingen: J. C. B. Mohr (Paul Siebeck), 1986): 33–75.

November 1933,[35] is titled *Lutherfeier 1933*. In it, he seeks to refocus the lens through which Luther would be viewed, and move the focus away from Luther to larger theological concerns. His modulated approach to Luther forms a unique contribution to the literature of 1933, though one that remained without extensive resonance.

He begins not with the Luther celebration itself, but the threat coming from the DC, highlighted by the events of the moment, and the insufficiency of the approach being taken by the "Young Lutherans" who were seeking to resist. He sees in their readiness to negotiate, or find a modus vivendi with the DC, a greater threat than the one represented by the DC itself, since they will create a compromised middle ground from which to be rendered impotent. With his typical combative style, he seeks to use the commemoration of Luther's birth to call them to a reckoning with the heritage of the Reformation.[36] This carries over into his discussion of Luther in the first part of the work:

> The man whose memory should be celebrated on November 10th is more difficult to understand and less accessible than what one wants to be hearing these days. The warning is in place, that one shouldn't confuse him with the symbolic figure that is currently being made visible in the churches and on the streets. A serious commemoration of Luther would above all pass right by the Luther of most of the Luther celebrations.[37]

He questions the uniformity of the image that is being presented, and suggests that if one does want to present a uniform image of Luther it would start with him as a listener, as someone who listened to the Gospel, and thus directing one away from Luther himself. Barth seeks to move Luther from the center, and notes that while Luther seems so certain and sound in himself and his judgments, he is always plagued by doubts and temptations (*Anfechtungen*), and notes how "unsound" that all seems: "Contradiction? No, precisely that is Luther's healthiness, that he suffers from this sickness unto death!"[38] He notes as well that for all of Luther's ability to formulate his teachings in straightforward ways, such as with the Small Catechism, he was more subtle and took on more complex issues than the clever Melanchthon, was more differentiated and obscure than Thomas

---

[35] See the discussion in Scholder, *Die Kirchen und das Dritte Reich*, vol. 1, 701–10, as well as the treatment in Chapter 7 (184–5).

[36] Karl Barth, *Lutherfeier 1933* (Munich: Chr. Kaiser Verlag, 1933): 3–7.

[37] "Der Mann, dessen Gedächtnis am 10. November gefeiert werden soll, ist schwerer verständlich und Wenigeren zugänglich, als man es in diesen Tagen Wort haben wollen wird. Die Warnung ist am Platze, daß man ihn mit der symbolischen Gestalt, die jetzt in den Kirchen und auf dem Markt festlich sichtbar werden wird, nicht verwechseln soll. Ein ernstes Luthergedächtnis würde sich wohl vor allem an dem Luther der meisten Lutherfeiern vorbei freie Bahn brechen müssen." Barth, *Lutherfeier*, 8.

[38] "Widersprüche? Nein, das eben ist Luthers Gesundheit, daß er an dieser Krankheit zum Tode leidet!" Barth, *Lutherfeier 1933*, 9.

Aquinas or Schleiermacher. "Is it a coincidence, that perhaps in no area of church history are the exegetical possibilities and possibilities for error (even with good will and great ability) so many as in the area of Luther research?...And one falsifies Luther when on portrays him an anti-intellectual man of the *Volk* and man of action."[39] He consistently seeks to confound the image of Luther as it was popularly being conceived, noting that those who seek to glorify Luther's Worms heroics misunderstand the true spiritual struggle that stands behind it, and that over time there have been so many images of Luther, that each age assumed the right to remake him in their own image, including the current age with their "German Luther." "But whether they have in doing this captured him correctly is another question."[40] Which leads him to a concluding thought for this first section:

> I wouldn't know how I could come to terms with the allusive puzzles hinting at Luther's real image (*Gestalt*), and finally I also wouldn't know what to do with this completely strange man, if I wanted to understand and honor him other than as "the Evangelist" he preferred to call himself. Grasp this, those who are able: among all the categories by which one can understand "great men," there is also this one, whose property, however, is to abolish completely the very notion of the "Great Man."[41]

This section brilliantly undermines the various attempts to portray Luther as anything other than a student of and listener to the scripture, and in this way connecting Luther's image directly with Barth's theology of the Word.

He reinforces this emphasis with the second part of the tract, titled "Luther's Science" (*Wissenschaft*). This allows Barth to reframe the way of knowing that marked Luther's theology from that associated with the Protestantism that developed in the following centuries. He begins by defining Luther's "*Wissenschaft*" as the "*Dransein des Menschen*," an expression difficult to render in English, but which suggests that this science, this way of understanding, is what happens when one responds to God's Word. He elaborates as follows: "It starts fundamentally when humans realize the following: that they do not stand above themselves, thus they cannot contemplate themselves; they cannot speak about themselves,

---

[39] "Ist es ein Zufall, daß vielleicht auf keinem Gebiet der Kirchengeschichte der Auslegungs- und auch der Irrtumsmöglichikeiten (selbst bei gutem Willen und großer Kunst) so viele sind wie auf dem Gebiet der Luther Forschung?...Und man fälscht Luther, wenn man ihn als antiintellektualistischen Volksmann und Tatmenschen darstellt...." Barth, *Lutherfeier 1933*, 9–10.

[40] "Ob sie das Recht haben, indem sie es sich nehmen, ist eine andere Frage." Barth, *Lutherfeier 1933*, 11.

[41] "Ich wüßte nicht, wie ich mit den angedeuteten Rätseln der wirklichen Gestalt Luthers einigermaßen fertig werden und ich wüßte schließlich auch nicht, was ich mit dem ganzen merkwürdigen Mann anfangen wollte, wenn ich ihn anders verstehen und ehren wollte den als den 'Evangelisten,' als den er sich selber gerne bezeichnet hat. Fasse es, wer es fassen kann: daß es neben all den Kategorien, unter denen man, 'große Männer' verstehen kann, auch diese gibt, die nun freilich die Eigenschaft hat, den Begriff des 'großen Mannes' aufs gründlichste aufzuheben." Barth, *Lutherfeier 1933*, 11–12.

they can only confess (*aussprechen*) themselves."[42] He wishes to undermine, again, the view of Luther as someone who in himself, as a "great man" (or "great German"), spoke his truth in a fashion that would be reconstructed from his works. Rather, Luther pointed to scripture, aware that what came from within himself was undermined by the insufficiency of the inner self to come to an understanding God, such that one was thrown back upon what God had to say to humanity in the Word. Barth's anthropology of Luther the man seeks directly to confront the Luther of Karl Holl, or Emanuel Hirsch especially, with their definition of Luther's *Gewissensreligion*. Barth says that the word Luther has to speak is the word of prayer, of confession, and it is in this that one can have confidence. Not, however, he emphasizes, as a risk or wager (*Wagnis*), as with Hirsch's Luther; one turns to God because God has already turned to oneself. Though the self remains afflicted, one hears God's Word and it is a comfort and a help, so that the "no" that one finds within oneself, though deeply rooted, encounters an even more deeply rooted but fundamental "yes," one lives in a deeply hidden but joyful hope:

> How should the humanity to whom God has spoken, and who has heard God, otherwise respond than by lifting the word of their self-defense – their prayer – in simple adoration of the one who is not only their eternal, divine counterpart, the creator of all things and father of all humanity, but also the one who in his Word is eternally God for us and in his Holy Spirit eternally God with us?[43]

Luther's science is the action of prayer and confession, open to the Word, and focused on the salvation that comes to all through the Word. Barth clearly wishes to change the frame within which Luther is viewed away from the Luther who battled, or made heroic stands, to the one who pointed away from himself to scripture. Toward the end of the piece Barth says that what he has said in the brief piece was drawn from considering Luther's hymn "Out of the depths I cry to you," which he notes was based on Psalm 130, and exemplifies both Luther's disposition and his resort to scripture: "one would misunderstand Luther most egregiously…as philosophy or a worldview, that is, as an outline of human self-understanding."[44] He continues:

---

[42] "Man kann Luthers Wissenschaft—unverbindlich aber gemeinverständlich—als eine besondere Wissenschaft von Dransein des Menschen verstehen. Sie fängt grundlegend damit an, daß der Mensch einsieht: er ist sich selbst nicht überlegen; er kann sich selbst also nicht betrachten; er kann nicht über sich selbst reden, er kann sich nur aussprechen." Barth, *Lutherfeier 1933*, 13.

[43] "Wie soll der Mensch zu dem Gott gesprochen , der Gott gehört hat, anders dran sein als so, daß das Wort seiner Notwehr, sein Gebet aufsteigen muß zur einfachen Verehrung dessen, der nicht nur sein ewiges göttliches Gegenüber, der Schöpfer aller Dinge und Vater aller Menschen, sondern der in seinem Wort auch ewig Gott für uns und in seinem heiligen Geist auch ewig Gott bei uns ist?" Barth, *Lutherfeier 1933*, 15.

[44] "Der würde Luther am schlimmsten mißverstehen…der ihn als eine Philosophie oder Weltanschauung, das heißt als einen Entwurf menschlichen Selbstverständnis auffassen wollte." Barth, *Lutherfeier 1933*, 15.

Luther has shown with his science which is read, spoken, and written out of the Bible what theology is: under all circumstances science is that which God has had to say to humans about himself. The Luther Festival 1933 should not pass by without at least a couple of people maybe asking themselves in this Germany so occupied with an entirely different sort of science, whether Luther should have shown that to our generation in vain.[45]

Barth concludes the short book with a section in which he highlights with what other sorts of *"Wissenschaft"* the German church was preoccupied. He reprints theses that were sent to all the pastoral education schools in the Rhineland, and which put forward DC inspired propositions about revelation, Christendom, the Gospel coming to Germans with the Reformation, which was the form intended for the German race, as well as the appositeness of National Socialism for both faith and the *Volkstum*. Barth provides a pithy and stinging rebuttal that echoes much of what he just had to say in his discussion over Luther. In all, Barth's piece highlights the theological counterpoint that some were seeking to establish concerning Luther at the start of the Third Reich. Another instance of such resistance to the theology of the German Luther is provided by the Bethel Confession, though its fate highlights, as well, the enormous difficulty in establishing a sharp and decisive counterpoint in the midst, as Barth notes, of a Protestant Germany that was deeply immersed in the mindset of *völkisch* nationalism.

The Bethel Confession was initiated in August of 1933 when a few theologians were invited by Friedrich von Bodelschwingh to gather in Bethel to draft a statement to counter the teachings of the DC.[46] The invitation was prompted by the success of the DC in the church elections of that summer that had greatly expanded their influence. Dietrich Bonhoeffer would be the primary author of the first drafts, along with Hermann Sasse and Georg Merz, the results of which produced a succinct and pointed rejection of the theology and rhetoric which marked much of the Luther celebration of 1933 as well as the attempts to use creation theology to reconcile the church with the new regime.[47] The draft

---

[45] "Luther hat uns mit seiner aus der Bibel abgelesenen, nachgeredeten, nachgeschriebenen Wissenschaft vorgemacht was Theologie ist: unter allen Umständen Wissenschaft von dem, was Gott dem Menschen über ihn selbst zu sagen hat. Die Lutherfeier 1933 sollte nicht vorübergehen, ohne daß ein paar Menschen in dem mit so ganz anderer Wissenschaft beschäftigten Deutschland sich fragen möchten, ob Luther das unserem Geschlecht etwa umsonst vorgemacht haben sollte." Barth, *Lutherfeier 1933*, 16.

[46] Bodelschwingh was the director of Bethel, an institution of the church that ministered to people with handicaps. He was at the center of affairs within the Protestant church during the summer of 1933 as efforts to hinder the plans of the DC for the church were organized; he was put forward as an alternate candidate for *Reichsbischof* to Ludwig Müller, Hitler's chosen man to lead a unified Protestant church structure. His orchestration of the Bethel Confession highlights his efforts to develop a unifying theological basis for opposing the DC and their influence in the church.

[47] For the events surrounding the development of the *Betheler Bekenntnis* and its textual development see Christine-Ruth Müller, *Bekenntnis und Bekennen: Dietrich Bonhoeffer in Bethel (1933), ein lutherischer Versuch* (Munich: Chr. Kaiser Verlag, 1989). For the text of the first draft see Dietrich Bonhoeffer, *Gesammelte Schriften*. Vol. II, ed. Eberhard Bethge (Munich: Christian Kaiser Verlag,

exemplifies the early acumen of Bonhoeffer, who "poured heart and soul" into the early drafts,[48] in identifying the fatal flaws of racial nationalist theology, whether in its moderate Althausian form, or the more radical rhetoric and action of the DC. The Bethel Confession takes especial aim at certain themes that have been prominent in the literature concerning Luther in the 1920s and early '30s, especially the arguments that equate Luther's significance with his *völkisch* Germanness, or establish Luther-grounded orders of creation that feed into *völkisch*-nationalist German identity and state formation and provide theological justification for the new regime.

The Confession begins by establishing scripture as the sole avenue of revelation: "The Holy Scripture alone is the testimonial of God's revelation. This occurred in history once and for all, is unrepeatable and complete.... Only in the exegesis of Scripture is the church able to proclaim the revelation of God."[49] This basic principle is carried over and applied in much of what follows. When discussing "what is the Reformation?," they emphasize the following:

> [The church of the Reformation], as the congregation of Jesus Christ, is and remains just as essentially the church, for this reason separates itself from a Protestantism which equates the church with a national, cultural, religious movement. The Reformation is in its essence reflection on Holy Scripture, subjection to Holy Scripture. For [the church of the Reformation] Martin Luther is the teacher of Holy Scripture, obedient to the Word. To understand his accomplishment as the breakthrough of the Germanic Spirit, or the origin of the modern feeling of freedom, or as the institution of a new religion, contradicts his own words. He fought against the blind overestimation of human reason and

---

1959): 90–119. An English translation of the early drafts is provided in *Dietrich Bonhoeffer Works*, Vol. 12: *Berlin 1932–1933* (Minneapolis: Fortress Press, 2009): 374–424. Klaus Scholder, *Die Kirchen und das Dritte Reich*, vol. 1, 579, has the following to say about the significance of the first draft of the *Bekenntnis*: "Gleichwohl bleibt das Betheler Bekenntnis in seiner Erstfassung—gerade auch im Blick auf den großen deutschchristlichen Aufbruch der deutschen Theologie in dieser Zeit—ein glänzendes, scharfes und eindrückliches Zeugnis für das, was theologische Arbeit im Sommer 1933 nun doch auch zu leisten vermochte. In der Form zwar schwerfällig, befrachtet mit zahlreichen Belegen aus der Bibel, aus Luther und vor allem aus den Bekenntnisschriften, war dieses Bekenntnis doch an manchen Stellen theologisch und politisch klarer und genauer als die berühmte Barmer Erklärung vom Mai 1934" (At the same time the Bethel Confession in its first draft remains—exactly in light of the great German-Christian emergence of German theology at this time—a shining, sharp, and impressive testimonial of what theological work in the summer of 1933 was able to accomplish. Awkward in form, freighted with numerous passages out of the Bible, from Luther, and above all from the Lutheran Confessional writings, nevertheless this confession was in many places theologically and politically clearer and more exact than the famous Barmen Declaration from May of 1934).

[48] "...und dem ich wirklich leidenschaftlich mitgearbeitet hatte." Bonhoeffer, *Gesammelte Schriften*, vol. II, 132.

[49] "Die Heilige Schrift allein ist das Zeugnis der göttlichen Offenbarung. Diese hat sich in einer einmaligen unwiederholbaren und abgeschlossenen Geschichte ereignet.... Nur in der Auslegung der Schrift vermag die Kirche die Offenbarung Gottes zu verkündigen." Bonhoeffer, *Gesammelte Schriften*, II, 91, 92.

rejected as a diabolical seduction the human delusion of coming to God out of one's own spirit, apart from the Word of God. While he understood himself to have been sent to help the German nation, to improve their Christian station, at the same time he served then, and still serves today, all *Völker* in the office of one Gospel.[50]

This cuts across much of what was being said about Luther during the 1933 celebration, and precludes the sort of sacred significance that was being claimed for the turn of affairs in 1933; the Confession will focus again and again on this issue. This is especially pointed in the section "On Creation and Sin" (*Von Schöpfung und Sünde*):

> We discern the creator only through obedience to the Word of God, and not through any interpretation of occurrences in the world. We reject as heresy that God speaks to us immediately from a particular "historical hour" and reveals himself in an unmediated action within creation, for that is fanaticism (*Schwärmerei*), wanting to hear God's will without the "outer Word" of the Holy Scripture, to which God has bound himself.... We reject as heresy, as fanatical exegesis of history, that the *Volk*'s voice is the voice of God.[51]

The reference to a "historical hour" anticipates Althaus' use of the term in the title of his work, which had not yet appeared, and the references to "*Schwärmer*," roughly translated as "fanatics," picks up on Luther's use of the term, which had been highlighted in one of the articles by Karl Holl in his 1921 collection, associating this form of thinking with the radical elements of the Reformation, against whom Luther had fought.

---

[50] "Als Gemeinde Jesu Christi ist sie und bleibt sie ebenso wesentlich Kirche und scheidet sich darum von jedem Protestantismus, der die Kirche gleichsetzt mit einer nationalen, kulturellen, religiösen Bewegung. Die Reformation ist in ihrem Wesen Besinnung auf die Heilige Schrift, Beugung unter die Heilige Schrift. Martin Luther ist ihr der dem Worte gehorsame Lehrer der Heiligen Schrift. Seine Tat als Durchbruch des germanischen Geistes oder als Ursprung des modernen Freiheitsgefühls oder als Stiftung einer neuen Religion zu verstehen, verstößt gegen sein eigenes Wort. Er kämpfte gegen die verblendete Überschätzung der menschlichen Vernunft und verwarf den Wahn des Menschen, ohne das göttliche Wort aus eigenem Geiste zu Gott zu kommen, als teuflische Verführung. Wie er sich aber gesandt wußte, der deutschen Nation zur Besserung ihres christlichen Standes zu helfen, so diente er zugleich und dient noch heute allen Völkern im Amte eines Evangeliums." Bonhoeffer, *Gesammelte Schriften*, II, 95.

[51] "IV. Von Schöpfung und Sünde 1. Schöpfungsglaube und natürliche Erkenntnis/ Allein aus dem Gehorsam gegen das Wort Gottes aus der Schrift erkennen wir den Schöpfer, nicht aus irgendeiner Deutung des Geschehens in der Welt.... Wir verwerfen die Irrlehre, daß Gott aus einer bestimmten 'geschichtlichen Stunde' unmittelbar zu uns rede und sich in einem unmittelbaren Handeln in der Schöpfung offenbare, denn es ist Schwärmerei, den Willen Gottes ohne das 'äußerliche Wort' der Heilgen Schrift, an das Gott sich gebunden hat, vernehmen zu wollen.... Wir verwerfen die Irrlehre, daß des Volkes Stimme Gottes Stimme sei, als schwärmerische Geschichtsdeutung." Bonhoeffer, *Gesammelte Schriften*, II, 97, 98–9.

Althaus' theology of "*Schöpfungsordnungen*" is more explicitly targeted in the section that follows, where the authors emphasize the *Ordnungen* as *Erhaltungordnungen*, "orders of preservation," which are created by God as a result of sin and the fall, not as orders that antedate the cursing of creation: "we reject as heresy [the teaching] that there could be in the fallen world some sort of ultimate orders which aren't placed as a result of the Fall under the curse of God, that can be recognized and affirmed as a unbroken order of creation in their original form." The authors follow with a more specific rejection of the association of these orders with orders of society: "We reject as heresy that a particular social order could be designated an order of God's creation. Human society is, according to Luther, indeed ordered, but just so that the same person belongs at the same time to different orders or estates of society (the order of marriage, of politics, of the church). It would be a backslide into Catholic social teaching to ground a historical form of societal order in natural law and as a result present it as ultimate."[52] The authors seek with this section to stand on the authority of Luther, and to situate the teachings that find revelation within historical events and orders of creation as errors against which Luther struggled, both with the Reformation "radicals" as well as with the Catholic Church.

Further on in a section on "Church and *Volk*" they take on the sort of *völkisch* idea of the church purveyed by Althaus and the DC:

> The message of the Gospel is equally available or unavailable to all *Völker*. For God's Holy Spirit alone is able to effect faith in humanity and awaken the consensus of the true confession. The community of the confessing church goes far beyond the boundaries of the *Volk*. The boundaries of the *Volk* and the church never coincide. The Church of Christ never hovers above the *Volk*. It lives in the *Volk*, and indeed since the resurrection of Jesus Christ never in one [*Volk*] alone. The church lives in every *Völk* to whom the message of the church has come. The *Volk* is not the church; however humans who belong to both are connected to each in inseparable solidarity. They carry the guilt of their *Volk*. They are at the same time members of the people of God [*Gottesvolk*], whose citizenship is in heaven.[53]

---

[52] "Wir verwerfen die Irrlehre, daß es in der gefallenen Welt irgendwelche endgültigen Ordnungen gäbe, die nicht durch den Fall unter den Fluch Gottes gestellt sind und die als ungebrochene Schöpfungsordnungen in ihrer Ursprünglichkeit erkannt und bejaht werden können. Denn hier wäre dem Menschen der Ruckzug in eine sündlose Welt ermöglicht und damit der Kreuzestod Christi überflüssig gemacht." "Wir verwerfen die Irrlehre, daß eine bestimmte ständische Ordnung als Gottes Schöpfungsordnung bezeichnet werden könne. Die menschliche Gesellschaft ist nach Luthers Lehre zwar geordnet, doch so, daß derselbe Mensch den verschiedenen Ordnungen oder Ständen (ordo oeconomicus, politicus, ecclesiasticus) zugleich angehört. Es wäre ein Rückfall in die katholische Soziallehre, eine geschichtliche Gestalt der gesellschaftlichen Ordnung als im Naturrecht begründet und darum endgültig auszugeben." Bonhoeffer, *Gesammelte Schriften*, II, 100, 101.

[53] "4. Kirche und Volk." "Die Botschaft des Evangeliums ist allen Völkern gleich zugänglich oder gleich unzugänglich. Denn Gottes Heiliger Geist allein kann in Menschen den Glauben wirken und

This issue is addressed in an even more pointed fashion in a section on "The Church and the Jews": "The community of those who belong to the Church is not determined by blood and therefore also not by race." The draft goes on to explain exactly the implications of this for the issue that was facing the church concerning the status of "non-Aryan" Christians:

> We set ourselves against the venture to transform the German Evangelical Church into an Imperial church of Christians of Aryan race and thus deprive it of its promise. That would construct a racial law at the entrance of the Church, and such a church would become itself a Jewish/Christian legalistic congregation.... Consequently, because Jewish Christians are not in any sort of legal fashion specially situated in the church, there is in them a living memorial to God's faithfulness and therefore a sign that the barrier between Jews and gentiles is undone and that faith in Christ may not be adulterated in the direction of a national religion or a racially typologized Christianity.[54]

The authors address the issue of anti-Jewish legislation, which was being used to purge the civil service of Jewish presence, only in the context of Jewish Christian presence in the church, and not the larger issue of Jewish persecution overall. As with earlier sections, they seek to situate the condemned viewpoints confessionally, by designating them as a form of Judaized Christianity, and a departure from Lutheran confessional teaching. Though Luther will be drawn upon, as will be discussed in a later chapter, in support of anti-Jewish policies both within church and state in the 1930s, the points made here could have been supported by reference to philo-Jewish elements of his work, though the authors choose not to make any such explicit connection.

---

den consensus des rechten Bekennens wecken. Die Gemeinschaft der bekennenden Kirche geht über die Volksgrenzen hinaus. Niemals decken sich die Grenzen des Volkes und die der Kirche. Die Kirche Christi schwebt niemals über den Völkern. Sie lebt in den Völkern, und zwar seit der Auferstehung Jesu Christi niemals in einem allein. In Jedem Volk, zu dem die Botschaft der Kirche gekommen ist, lebt die Kirche. Das Volk ist nicht die Kirche; aber die Menschen, die zu beiden gehören, sind in unlösbarer Solidarität mit beiden verbunden. Sie tragen mit an der Schuld ihres Volkes. Sie sind zugleich Glieder des Gottesvolkes, dessen Bürgerschaft im Himmel ist." Bonhoeffer, *Gesammelte Schriften*, II, 112–13.

[54] "6. Die Kirche und die Juden." "Die Gemeinschaft der zur Kirche Gehörigen wird nicht durch das Blut und also auch nicht durch die Rasse, sondern durch den Heiligen Geist und die Taufe bestimmt" (116). "Wir wenden uns gegen das Unternehmen, die deutsche evangelische Kirche durch den Versuch, sie umzuwandeln in eine Reichskirche der Christen arischer Rasse ihrer Verheißung zu berauben. Dann damit würde ein Rassengesetz vor dem Eingang zur Kirche aufgerichtet und wäre eine solche Kirche selbst zur judenchristlich gesetzlichen Gemeinde geworden.... Dadurch, daß der Judenchrist gerade nicht in irgendeiner gesetzlichen Weise besonders gestellt wird in der Kirche, ist er in ihr ein lebendiges Denkmal der Treue Gottes und ein Zeichen dafür, daß der Zaun zwischen Juden und Heiden niedergelegt ist und der Christusglaube nicht in der Richtung auf eine Nationalreligion oder auf ein artgemäßes Christentum verfälscht werden darf." Bonhoeffer, *Gesammelte Schriften*, II, 116, 117.

The authors also take on the issue of church and state by explicitly rejecting the assignment of a providential significance to Hitler or the Third Reich:

> We reject as heresy any form of the Christian state. Authority among the heathens or Christians performs its office rightly when it uses the sword rightly and remains within its boundaries. "To the Word may be given no Emperor, no judge, nor any protector, but only God himself." (WA 17,2 S. 108)[55] They can therefore not presume to provide salvation for humanity. They cannot misuse the church as their ethical/religious foundation. It is a heresy [to say] that the church is only the soul or conscience of the state.[56]

Again, they make direct reference to Luther in establishing the basis of resistance to the attempts by the state to draw the church into constructing some sort of providentially ordained Reich that achieves a divinely ordained outcome. This point is explicitly articulated with the conclusion of the Confession:

> We reject as heresy that there is a gradual this-worldly development toward the world to come. Even the most noble things of this world must end in the grave. Christ must end up on the cross. Even the most pious will be judged. For us Christ was cursed by God on the cross. About the outcome of this judgment there can be no doctrine, neither a doctrine of the restitution of the whole world nor the other doctrine of the eternal rejection. The outcome of this judgment can only be spoken about prayerfully.
>
> We reject a version of the doctrine of the thousand-year Empire that would unambiguously recognize in particular historical events the beginning of the visible rule of Christ on earth.[57]

---

[55] The authors actually change the Luther text by using "Kaiser" instead of the original "meyster." This has the effect of strengthening Luther's admonition and targeting more directly the aspirations of those constructing a "Third Reich" or "Empire."

[56] "Wir verwerfen die Irrlehre vom christlichen Staat in jeder Form. Obrigkeit unter Heiden oder Christen versieht ihr Amt allein darin recht, daß die ihr Schwert recht führt und in ihren Grenzen bleibt. 'Dem Worte mag kein Kaiser noch Richter als auch kein Schutzherr gegeben werden denn Gott selber' (W.A. 17, 2, S. 108). Sie kann sich darum nicht anmaßen, dem Menschen das Heil zu schaffen. Sie kann die Kirche nicht als ihr sittlich religiöses Fundament mißbrauchen. Es ist Irrlehre, daß die Kirche nur Seele oder Gewissen des Staates sei." Bonhoeffer, *Gesammelte Schriften*, II, 114–15.

[57] "Wir verwerfen die Irrlehre, daß es eine allmähliche innerweltliche Entwicklung zur neuen Welt gebe. Auch das Edelste in dieser Welt muß in den Tod. Christus mußte an das Kreuz. Auch der Frömmste muß ins Gericht. Christus ist für uns von Gott am Kreuz verflucht. Vom Ausgang dieses Gerichtes kann keine Lehre gegeben werden, weder die eine Lehre von der Wiederherstellung der ganzen Welt noch die andere Lehre von der ewigen Verwerfung. Vom Ausgang dieses Gerichtes kann nur betend gesprochen werden. Wir verwerfen eine Auffassung der Lehre vom tausendjährigen Reich, die in bestimmten geschichtlichen Ereignissen den Beginn der sichtbaren Herrschaft Christi auf Erden eindeutig erkennen will." Bonhoeffer, *Gesammelte Schriften*, II, 119.

The first draft of the Bethel Confession demonstrates the resources within German Lutheranism that existed to reject the claims of the Third Reich to fulfill some sort of providential destiny for the German *Volk*. The cooptation of Luther for German nationalist political purposes was a result of the image of Luther that developed in the nineteenth century and was amplified by the events of World War I and following. We can see particularly with the career of Dietrich Bonhoeffer, whose fingerprints are all over the Bethel Confession, the possibility of resistance that grows out of an engagement with Luther, though this remains latent in much of what transpires during the 1930s.[58]

The fate of this draft of the Bethel Confession highlights the difficulty of developing a unified stance of resistance to the growing attempts to coopt the church for service to the new regime. Bodelschwingh circulated the early drafts composed by Bonhoeffer, Sasse, and Merz to a circle of twenty theologians, seeking feedback, among whom were Althaus and his older mentor Adolf Schlatter. Not surprisingly, deep reservations were expressed by a number of those who replied, and significant amendments were made to the text, to the extent that in the end Bonhoeffer refused to have his name associated with the published version.[59] Even Karl Barth, who was sympathetic to the arguments made in the text, found it too Lutheran, and wondered if what was needed was a confession grounded more broadly in the theologies of the German Protestant church in all its elements. In the end, the sharpness of the theological critique was diminished, and the publication was delayed until the end of December 1933, when the landscape had changed sufficiently that the work itself made very little public impact. And in the course of the 1930s in general, the public profile of Martin Luther would be insistently drawn by those who saw in him a cornerstone for the new regime, as had been so rabidly asserted in the majority of the celebrations of his birthday, and in the systematic theologies that affirmed a *völkisch* church. The most widespread representation of Luther in the first year of the new regime was of a figure who, were he alive today, would have dressed in brown and lent his fighting spirit to the construction of the earthly empire of the providentially ordained *Volkstum* and its *Führer*.

The Luther Myth: The Image of Martin Luther from Religious Reformer to Völkisch *Icon.* Patrick Hayden-Roy, Oxford University Press. © Patrick Hayden-Roy 2024. DOI: 10.1093/9780198930297.003.0005

---

[58] See in this regard the work of Michael DeJonge, *Bonhoeffer's Reception of Luther* (Oxford: Oxford University Press, 2017), who demonstrates compellingly the degree that Bonhoeffer's theology was drawn out of his intense and lifelong engagement with Luther, from his studies with Karl Holl, whose *Gewissensreligion* understanding of Luther he came to reject, to his work in the 1930s and '40s in resisting the Third Reich.

[59] See the succinct summary of events in Scholder, *Die Kirche und das Dritte Reich*, I, 579–82.

5
Luther, the National Socialist

The events of 1933–4 brought into being the Nazi state. From the initial foot in the door, Hitler and the National Socialists quickly used a combination of brutality, propaganda, populist politics, and economic revival to consolidate their authority, until after the summer of 1934 there remained almost no element of German society and culture that had not been coordinated with the order of the new state. In this context, Hitler emerged as the focal point for all state processes, and the legitimacy of the political order was grounded in his personal, charismatic authority. So thorough was the preemption of all other sources of cultural identity that individuals and institutions were confronted with stark choices: resistance with the certainty of fierce persecution and repression, exile, whether physical or spiritual, or thorough conformity. Within the history of the German church of the 1930s all these possibilities express themselves, though the dominant tendency was relatively willing accommodation. It is the case that even among the German Christians there was a resistance to abandoning Christian language and symbolism, even among the most rabidly nazified of their members. And within the Confessing Church there were grades of resistance, and sharp disagreements about how far resistance should extend. It is representative of the flexible boundaries of the Confessing Church that Paul Althaus aligned himself after 1934 with this movement, while still maintaining his previously established theological positions.[1] There is no simple typification of the response of German Protestantism to the onset of the National Socialist regime. However, in general there was a strong desire to represent the church as a willing participant in the revival of Germany: the economic recovery, the reestablishment of an assertive and powerful Germany in world affairs, and the sense of corporate identity that was built around the figure of Adolf Hitler.[2] And Luther proved a useful vehicle for building this sense of relationship between the "positive" features and

---

[1] See the discussion in Jasper, *Paul Althaus*, 277–97.
[2] Manfred Gailus, *Gläubige Zeiten*, 10, makes the following observations: "Ein prägendes Epochenphänomen war folglich nicht allein der Gegensatz von Christentum und NS-Weltanschauung, den es zweifellos gab und der eine gewichtige Rolle spielte, sondern zugleich die ebenso religiöse wie politische Kompatibilität beider Glaubenspositionen bei vielen Zeitgnossen. Es ist vor allem dieses Phänomen, das bei einer kultur- und religionsgeschichtlichen Neudeutung der Epoche in das Zentrum der Aufmerksamekeit zu rücken hat" (A distinctive phenomenon of the epoch was consequently not only the contrasts between Christianity and the worldview of the Nazis, which without doubt existed and played an important role, but at the same time the just as much religious as political compatibility of both positions of belief for many people of the time. It is above all this phenomenon that has to move to the center for there to be a new reckoning of the cultural and religious history of the era)."

accomplishments of the regime and the identity and ethos of the Protestant Church. Luther, as he was presented in a flood of works in the period from 1933 to 1939, was clothed in the ideas and language of National Socialism, realizing the aspirations projected in the effervescent rhetoric of the 1933 Luther celebration.

The seemingly endless flexibility of Luther's image in the early years of the Nazi regime is a result of a number of features of his image that had built up to this point. First, the emphasis on Luther as the embodiment of the German "spirit" (*Geist*) meant that whatever was construed to constitute this spirit was read back into Luther, using highly subjective terms, such as *Treue* (loyalty) or *Vertrauen* (trust), which then would lead to a search through his life and writings to demonstrate that he fulfilled these virtues. This could then be the basis for a demonstration that Luther, were he witness to the events of the present day, would support that movement that itself represented these virtues. Hans Preuß's 1934 work "Luther the German"[3] provides an extended exercise in this sort of process of image-making and interpretation. Preuß was a church historian at Erlangen, and had a long history of publishing on Luther; his tract on Luther written for the 1917 celebration of the Reformation was a best-seller.[4] Eventually Preuß's 1934 work would join three other Luther works of his to form a quartet.[5] In his 1934 work, he justifies its purpose as follows:

> Just as with all that is alive, so Luther stands also today again between two fronts: to the other Christian confessions in Germany he shows how one can (and should) fully and truly unite the authentic Gospel with authentic Germanity, and he shows the neo-Romantic German mythology how on the other hand one can and should fully and truly unite an authentic Germanity with the authentic Gospel. The purpose of this book is to present the historical records supporting this fact.[6]

Preuß represented a fairly common mentality among those who took up the treatment of Luther in this period in that he wished to use Luther to carve out a position in a debate about the proper relationship of Protestant Christian belief to

---

[3] Hans Preuß, *Luther der Deutsche* (Gütersloh: Bertelsmann, 1934).
[4] Hans Preuß, *Unser Luther* (Leipzig: Deichert, 1917).
[5] Hans Preuß, *Martin Luther. Der Prophet* (Gütersloh: Bertelsmann, 1933); *Martin Luther: Der Künstler* (Gütersloh, Bertelsmann, 1931); *Martin Luther, der Deutsche und Christ* (Leipzig: Bertelsmann, 1940). For a sharply critical view of Preuß as a church historian, see Hans Christof Brennecke, "Zwischen Luthertum und Nationalismus: Kirchengeschichte in Erlangen." In *Geschichtswissenschaft in Erlangen*, ed. Helmut Neuhaus (Erlangen: Palm & Enke, 2000): 227–68; on Preuß, 261–6.
[6] "Wie alles Lebendige, so steht Luther auch heute wieder gegenüber zwei Fronten: Den anderen christlichen Konfessionen in Deutschland zeigt er, wie man das echte Evangelium mit echtem Deutschtum völlig und wahrhaftig vereinen kann—und soll, und der neuromantischen Germanomytholigie zeigt er, wie man umgekehrt echtes Deutschtum mit dem echten Evangelium völlig und wahrhaftig vereinen kann und soll. Für diese Tatsache die historischen Unterlangen aufzuweisen, ist die Absicht dieses Buches." Preuß, *Luther der Deutsche*, V.

other competing religiosities, Christian and otherwise, and in doing so to demonstrate the aptness of his own view of Christianity for the new order in Germany.

He begins his discussion by defining what is meant by Germanity, or *Deutschtum*. Though he makes a point to assert that it is not just racial, noting that *Boden* (earth, i.e. physical environment) and history also shape the *Volk*, the distinction is mostly nominal, since the definition is very much shaped by birth, or blood. Not surprisingly, he identifies *Treue*, loyalty, as the distinguishing characteristic of the German being.[7] This leads him into a discussion of Luther's origins, which relies on racial science to determine the characteristics of Luther within the Aryan type. Though Luther, according to Preuß, has some characteristics that are not classically Aryan—so there was a little mixing of blood somewhere—he insists that there was no Slavic blood, and that a little intermingling actually is often associated with extraordinary geniuses.[8] Having established the racial soundness of Luther—"the housing is indeed German"[9]—he moves to consider whether his inner essence was typologically German. "The result? Everywhere we looked there grows up out of Luther's deepest foundation loyalty and trust as pillars of his entire being."[10] And though, he hurries to assure the reader, Luther's Germanity is the source of his sensibility whereby he is able to recover the Gospel, this doesn't mean the Gospel is specifically German…though he cannot help but add that "the German grasped this message most congenially just because of his character of trust."[11] He finds these virtues expressed in every aspect of Luther's career, and he adds some qualities that mark these characteristics, stressing especially masculinity:

> Luther's trust is always manly, and never goes over into pietistic confidentiality (*Vertraulichkeit*). It is friendship, not loving tenderness. Luther doesn't feel himself as the bridal soul—that's Roman/Western—but as a follower (*Gefolgsmann*) of his Lord Jesus Christ. That is once again authentically German.[12]

---

[7] "In der Regel wird als hauptzug nordische-germanischen und damit auch deutschen Wesens die Treue angeführt" (As a rule, faithfulness will be named as the chief element of the Nordic-Germanic and consequently the German essence). Preuß, *Luther der Deutsche*, 2.

[8] "Die Mischung ist also offenbar der Boden der genialisten Männer…Luther ist eins der hervorragensten Beispiele dafür." Preuß, *Luther der Deutsche*, 23. It was no doubt also in Preuß's mind that Hitler also was often accused of having some "non-Aryan" features. As we shall see, when Preuß considered Luther, Hitler was never far from his mind.

[9] "Das Gehäuse ist also deutsch." Preuß, *Luther der Deutsche*, 24.

[10] "Das Ergebnis? Überall, wohin wir schauen, wachsen aus tiefstem Grunde bei Luther Vertrauen und Treue auf als Säulen seines ganzen Wesen." Preuß, *Luther der Deutsche*, 24.

[11] "…wobei freilich das deutsche diese Botschaft am kongenialsten erfaßte—eben wegen seines Vertrauenscharakters." Preuß, *Luther der Deutsche*, 24–5.

[12] "Luthers Vertrauen ist immer männlich und geht nie in pietistische Vertraulichkeit über. Es ist Freundschaft, nicht Liebeszärtlichkeit. Luther fühlt sich nicht als Brautseele—das ist romanisch-westisch—, sondern als Gefolgsmann seines Herrn Christus. Das ist wieder urdeutsch." Preuß, *Luther der Deutsche*, 26.

The term "*Gefolgsmann*" resonates with the ethos of National Socialism—SA men were *Gefolgsmänner*. He plays on this connection even further, asserting that the Christ of the Middle Ages was feminine, while with Luther "Christ is not the bride of the spirit but the Field Commander, the feudal lord."[13] Again, the terminology echoes the mentality of the SA and its cult of militarized masculinity.

He finds further suggestive connections between Luther's understanding of faith and the ethos of the day. He emphasizes that though Luther's faith is often connected to German mysticism, it is not mystical, which is international and not specifically German; Luther's faith is grounded in his understanding of freedom, which is not that of Western democracy, but rather a freedom that freely chooses its loyalty and trust, and would rather die than to be a slave—the German idea of freedom. It does not have any mediator with its lord, but is grounded in the immediate relationship.[14] This would seem to suggest a disposition fitting to the new political realities of Germany with its oaths of personal loyalty to the *Führer*. He connects this idea of freedom to conscience: "It is clear that this is just about the same as what we call conscience (*Gewissen*). Again we encounter a typically German and Lutheran ethical stance."[15] This leads him to a list of highlights from Luther's life that exemplify this sensibility, all of which echo Holl, Hirsch, and Althaus.[16] He notes this disposition in his relationship to Emperor Charles V: "a striking instance of this German sincerity and openness is Luther's childlike attitude.... And how did he overestimate, in his childlike innocence, his great enemy Emperor Charles V! But certainly here, too, his German heart expresses his respect for the chosen leader (*Führer*) of the nation"[17] This aside would seem to suggest a disposition highly relevant to the public life of Preuß's own day and the demands for obedience towards the current regime, in this case legitimated even further since the leadership was Germanic.

He moves on from this consideration of Luther's *Treue*, connecting it to another characteristic that is a staple of the Germanic Luther, his fighting spirit (*Kampfgeist*). "German openness shows itself with Luther especially in the form of his struggle.

---

[13] "—Für ihn ist Christus nicht der Seelenbräutigam, sondern der Feldherr, der Lehensherr." Preuß, *Luther der Deutsche*, 28.

[14] "Sie ist nichts anderes als Freiheit des Christenmenschen, der nichts zwischen sich und seinem Herrn duldet, keine Priestervermittliung, keinen Mittelsmann irgendwelcher Art, keinen Zwischenhändler" (It is nothing other than the freedom of the Christian, which suffers nothing between it and its lord, no mediation of priest, no middle-man of any sort, no mediator). Preuß, *Luther der Deutsche*, 31.

[15] "Es ist klar, daß das fast schon dasselbe ist, was wir Gewissen nennen. Wieder stoßen wir auf eine typisch deutsche und lutherische sittliche Haltung." Preuß, *Luther der Deutsche*, 33.

[16] In this part of the book Preuß references frequently Althaus' 1917 tract discussed in Chapter 2 (pp. 40–3), *Luther und das Deutschtum*.

[17] "Eine besondere Prägung dieser deutschen Ehrlichkeit und Offenheit ist der kindliche Sinn Luthers.... Und wie hat er seinen großen Feind, den Kaiser Karl V., in seiner kindlichen Harmlosigkeit grenzenlos überschätzt! Doch spricht hier sicher auch das deutsche Herz mit seiner Achtung vor dem erwählten Führer der Nation." Preuß, *Luther der Deutsche*, 38.

Namely, it eschews all cunning. He goes directly to the point. He wears no masks. And he also has joy in the fight."[18] He continues:

> However, one must remember that Luther's fighting impulse never goes over into blind rage. It remains in a certain sense sober, in contrast to the fanaticism of primitive *Völker* or also Roman and Celtic instances. Also, there is nothing of the crusading fanaticism of Bernhard of Clairvaux or the destructive fervor of Mohammad or the visionary ecstasy of Savonarola or the shaking and quaking of George Fox, also nothing of the sadistic hate of the French or of the Jews. He never fights for the extermination of his enemy, but only for his freedom. However, for this with endless joy![19]

He also notes that he was no revolutionary like the Romans, the Slavs, or the Jews, but always had a positive "fatherland-directed, Christian goal. For at its base the German in Luther is conservative."[20] This excursus on Luther's fighting spirit betrays Preuß's own sensibilities, and his fundamentally mistaken reading of the National Socialist movement, which was in its core revolutionary and fanatical, committed, time would demonstrate, to a radical solution to Germany's putative problems. Preuß, like many who sidled up to the Nazi movement from the church, was looking for restoration, not upheaval and a new millennium. Though sharing the racist/nationalist assumptions of the regime, and willing to hand unlimited power over to a charismatic leader, they overlooked the basically biological and pagan bases of the movement, trying to find a definition of Lutheran religiosity that would be true to its roots but accommodate the powerful *völkisch* impulse of the new order. The lack of resonance that his, and others', vision of Luther would have for party ideologues is rooted in this fundamental misunderstanding of the regime and its "positive Christianity."

He spends quite a bit of time focusing on Luther's relationship with nature, another staple of this literature. This theme is another way to connect Luther's religiosity to the order of the material world, which, Preuß emphasizes, is in synch with the new order—"a German primal feeling that in our day once again

---

[18] "Deutsche Offenheit zeigt sich bei Luther ganz besonders in der Art seines Kampfes. Der entbehrt nämlich aller List. Er geht gerade drauflos. Er nimmt keine Maske vor. Und er hat auch Freude am Kampf." Preuß, *Luther der Deutsche*, 39.

[19] "Dabei ist aber zu beachten, daß Luthers Kampflust nie übergeht in blinde Wut. Sie bleibt in gewissem Sinne nüchtern, im Unterschied zum Fanatismus primitiver Völker oder auch romanischer und keltischer Erscheinungen. Nichts auch von dem Kreuzzugsfanatismus Bernhards von Clairvaux oder der zerstörenden Glut Mohammeds oder der visionären Ekstase Savonarolas oder dem Zittern und Zucken bei George Fox, auch nichts von dem sadistischen Haß der Franzosen oder der Juden. Er kämpft nie um die Vernichtung des Gegners, sondern nur um seine Freiheit. Für diese aber mit tausend Freuden!" Preuß, *Luther der Deutsche*, 40.

[20] "Aber all diese deutsche Kampfeslust will nicht zerstören, ist nicht revolutionär im Sinn der Romanen, Slawen oder Juden, sondern hat positive vaterländische, christliche Zwecke. Denn im Grund ist der Deutsche in Luther konservativ." Preuß, *Luther der Deutsche*, 40.

has been shown to full advantage under Adolf Hitler."[21] This connection to nature allows Luther to experience the divine in the material, unlike the sensibilities of the ancients or of Calvin. For Luther, God is experienced in the natural order, and this also relates to his sense of Christ's ubiquity, again as compared to Calvin or Zwingli; for Luther Christians are everywhere, as compared to the exclusivist priesthood of the Roman church. He labels this Luther's "Nordic sense of space."[22] He concludes the section with a remarkable comparison of Luther to the Nordic gods:

> I find that Luther's German being, when one seeks after a typical figure, finds itself most strikingly and comprehensively portrayed in Donar-Thor, who far more than Wodan is the true mirror-image of the old Germanic character: he is good-natured, awkward, but, when stirred up, full of fervent wrath. He smashed the giants in the thunderstorm, his hammer slicing through the turbulent air. He purged them of musty vapors with his refreshing rain that allows the fruit to ripen, destroying and refreshing at the same time, like a thunderstorm. His sons are Magoni and Modi, that is Power and Ferocity, his daughter Thruar, that is Strength. He takes joy in eating and drinking, has a loyal heart, is open and honorable, a friend of the family and its cozy hearth—all in all your German peasant type and... Martin Luther! Again is revealed—here in the mirror image of a German original—Luther's life connection with his *Volk* and its essence.[23]

One surmises that by connecting Luther to a pagan Germanic deity, using the stereotyped images of Germanic *gemütlichkeit*, Preuß imagined this styled Luther in a fashion endearing to the sensibilities of the new order—Luther the Thor-like German peasant would bridge the gap between pagan and Christian Germanity.

The chapters that follow show Luther's cultural significance for the German *Volk*, and his deep understanding of them in his own works. Inevitably he glorifies Luther's single-handed creation of German as a common language, noting that Luther didn't really separate Germans with his rebellion against Rome—it was

---

[21] "—ein deutsches Urgefühl, das in unsren Tagen erst wieder unter Adolf Hitler recht zur Geltung gekommen ist." Preuß, *Luther der Deutsche*, 42.

[22] "nordisches Raumgefühl." Preuß, *Luther der Deutsche*, 46. The whole discussion is found on pages 42–9.

[23] "Ich finde, daß Luthers deutsches Wesen, wenn man nach einer typischen Figur sucht, sich am umfassendsten und treffendsten im Donar-Thor vorgebildet findet, der weit mehr als Wodan das eigentliche Spiegelbild des altgermanischen Charakters ist: Der ist gutmütig, plump, aber, wenn gereizt, voll glühenden Zorns. Er zerschmettert die Riesen im Gewitter, seinen Hammer schleudernd durch die erregten Lüfte. Er reinigt sie von dumpfen Schwaden mit seinem erquickenden Regen der die Früchte schwellen läßt, zerstörend und erquickend zugleich wie ein Gewitter. Seine Söhne sind Magoni und Modi, d.h. Kraft und Heftigkeit, seine Tochter Thruar, d.h. Stärke. Eß- und trinkfreudig ist er, treuherzig, offen und ehrlich, Freund der Familie und ihres gemütlichen Herdes—alles in allem: dein deutscher Bauer und—Martin Luther! Wieder ergibt sich—hier im Spiegelbilde eines deutschen Urtums—Luthers Lebensverbundenheit mit seinem Volke und dessen Wesen." Preuß, *Luther der Deutsche*, 50–1.

the Roman church that divided Germans—but rather he brought them together with language in a most profound fashion.[24] He notes, as well, that Luther knew that the Germans were a race, though without that specific word: "He knew that the Germans belonged to a particular race, though naturally that word was unknown to him. He dubbed them the descendants of Japhet and meant the same thing that we today understand with the membership in the Aryan race."[25] With this Preuß solved a vexing problem for those who wished to argue for the relevance of Luther in the new order, since his lack of racial consciousness would seem to make him a relic of the past in the eyes of true National Socialists, though, as we'll see, others found even more creative ways to solve this issue. And Luther, Preuß continues, was sensitive to the special place the Germans occupied in the divine plan; having listed a number of passages through which German's unique history progressed, he notes: "this suggests that God once wanted to look upon this nation with mercy and honor it in unique fashion, just as history witnesses that the German nation has always been the most praised. If we ventured to say something like this today, we would harvest severe reprimands as nationalists from outside Germany and also from some on the German side."[26] This sense of justifiable yet aggrieved national pride, affirmed by Luther, captures nicely the tenor of discourse in Germany at the time. It was no accident that the rediscovery of the Gospel comes from Germany; Luther himself, Preuß argues, was aware of this providential connection of God's purposes with the German *Volk*: "This seems like the dark foretellings of a prophet, the German prophet: Germany, the exceptional *Volk*, still has a special mission for itself!"[27] This love of Germany and its mission in the world connects with his rediscovery of the Gospel, which Preuß says was specifically directed to the German people, and this love was combined with wrath (*Zorn*) against the corrupting foreigners who oppressed the Germans. In this sense, Luther's movement was a national revival responding to the needs of the oppressed *Volk*.[28] This nationalist sense of grievance is followed by Preuß's inventory of Luther's statements about other peoples, and in particular the Jews, where he notes that even though Luther's judgments were rooted in religion, that in many places he sounds like a modern racial nationalist in what he has to say.[29]

---

[24] Preuß, *Luther der Deutsche*, 60.
[25] "Er weiß, daß die Deutschen zu einer besonderen Rasse gehören, wenn ihm das Wort natürlich auch unbekannt ist. Er nennt sie Nachkommen Japhets und meint damit dasselbe, was wir heute unter der Zugehörigkeit zur arischen Rasse verstehen." Preuß, *Luther der Deutsche*, 62.
[26] "Es sei damit angedeutet, daß Gott einmal diese Nation barmherzig ansehen und in einzigartiger Weise geehrt haben wollte, wie denn auch die Geschichte bezeuge, daß die deutsche Nation immer die gelobteste gewesen ist. Wenn wir heute so etwas zu sagen wagten, würden wir von außerdeutscher und auch gewisser deutscher Seite schweren Tadel als Nationalisten ernten." Preuß, *Luther der Deutsche*, 62.
[27] "Das mutet an wie die dunkle Weissagung eines Propheten, des Deutschen Propheten: Deutschland, das Ausnahmevolk, hat auch eine besondere Sendung noch für sich!" Preuß, *Luther der Deutsche*, 73.
[28] Preuß, *Luther der Deutsche*, 74–80.
[29] "—Es ist nicht bloß christliche, sondern unmittelbar vaterländische Empörung, wenn ihm aus der Feder fließt...." Preuß, *Luther der Deutsche*, 85; "Er erinnert unmittelbar an moderne deutschantisemitische Klänge...." Preuß, *Luther der Deutsche*, 86.

Altogether, these chapters portray a Luther who is not only very much the German hero who was responsible for the revival of his *Volk* in his own time, but a prophet whose visionary actions and foresight provide full affirmation for the order and actions of the new Germany and its leader, implicitly anticipating it. And Preuß continues, he wasn't just a prophet, but the model of the "Nordic Leader":

> Luther's status as a German prophet can be understood in yet a broader perspective, that of the Nordic leader (*Führer*). Certainly, as we have seen in chapter 2, Luther is racially no pure Nordic product. He is, as all great German men, a synthesis of the Nordic race with one or many others of the Nordic family of races. But the Nordic predominates without doubt in his blood as much as in his being. This is also evident in the resounding nature of his leadership (*Führertum*).[30]

His historical role leading the German people provides the model for leadership that can be then transferred to the one who holds that title so prominently in Preuß's present historical moment; as we'll see in Chapter 6, this is a connection to which Preuß will dedicate an entire publication.

He concludes the volume with evaluations of Luther through the years, mostly showing how they affirm his status as the great German: he raises up Heine's judgment in a way that both affirms his point while profiling Preuß's racist bona fides: "Even out of the unclean mouth of Heine came this affirmation: 'Luther was not merely the greatest, but the most German man of our (?!) history.'"[31] This concern with the judgment of posterity becomes particularly pointed when he arrives at the opinions of contemporary authors. He spends a good deal of time refuting the negative judgments of recent Catholic historiography on Luther, but even more fraught are the anti-Christian views expressed by Alfred Rosenberg and other official organs of party opinion-making. Preuß has this to say in response:

> But this is in no way the official stance of the National-Socialist movement. It is well known that the 24th paragraph of the irrevocable Party Program professes positive Christianity, and the Evangelical representatives of the movement have

---

[30] "Luthers deutsches Prophetentum läßt sich noch in einem weiteren Rahmen verstehen: in dem des nordischen Führers. Gewiß, Luther ist, wie wir im 2. Kapitel gesehen haben, rassisch kein nordisches Reinprodukt. Er ist, wie alle großen deutschen Männer, eine Synthese der nordischen Rasse mit einer oder mehreren anderen, der nordischen verwandten Rassen. Allein das Nordische überwiegt zweifellos wie in seinem Blut, so in seinem Wesen. Das zeigt sich auch in der vorklingenden Art seines Führertums." Preuß, *Luther der Deutsche*, 101.

[31] "Sogar aus dem unsauberen Munde Heines kam die Überzeugung: 'Luther war nicht bloß der größte, sondern der deutscheste Mann unserer (?!) Geschichte'" Preuß, *Luther der Deutsche*, 108. Clearly Preuß intends to highlight and cast aspersions upon Heine's status as a Jewish convert and his claim to "our" history.

already frequently professed Martin Luther to be the German Reformer par excellence (for instance, Wilhelm Frick at the Eisleben Luther celebration of July 31st, and the one in Wittenberg on September 10th 1933).[32]

As we will see below, Preuß touches here on what is a particularly problematic issue for those like him who would seek to insinuate Luther into the heart of National Socialism; namely, within the party itself there was little inclination to pay much attention to their version of Luther. In the conclusion of the book the problem is highlighted by Preuß's own contorted attempts, having spent an entire book arguing the racially determined significance of Luther's person and message for the German *Volk*, to assert the essential universality of Luther's message concerning the Gospel, and the limits of viewing it as simply German. The passage that closes the book is emblematic:

> All peoples of the earth should, like the Wise Men at the manger, open their treasure that they have from God for Christ the Lord, each according to their type. The Germans lay their loyal allegiance at his feet. Thus alone they are able to give him honor from the bottom of their hearts—as men of the Duke, who are connected to him with loyalty and trustworthiness eternally. In no other historical figure has this singularly authentic German Christianity acquired a more complete form than with Martin Luther. For he was called to proclaim to his *Volk* the Gospel—not a German Gospel, but the Gospel in German.[33]

Preuß's book is a revealing artifact of the era in which it was written. As an academic writer, he aspires to exhibit scholarly rigor, but he also wishes to achieve a popular voice, to demonstrate the connectedness of the subject he is exploring to the *Volk*. This gives the work its stylistic awkwardness. What makes it an exemplary artifact of its time is how vividly it defines the contradictions of the Luther image of the Nazi era, and, by extension, the unwieldiness of the efforts by various factions of Protestant Christianity to reconcile fully with National Socialism. Preuß's work stands somewhere in the middle of the range of possible solutions, still seeking to maintain the independence of the Gospel as a universal message

---

[32] "Doch ist das keineswegs die offizielle Auffassung der nationalsozialistischen Bewegung. Bekanntlich bekennt sich der §24 des unabänderlichen Parteiprogramms zum positiven Christentum, und die evangelischen Vertreter der Bewegung haban sich schon des öfteren zu Martin Luther bekennt als dem deutschen Reformator schlechthin (z.B. Wilhelm Frick auf der Eislebener Luthertagung 31. Juli und Wittenberg 10. September 1933)." Preuß, *Luther der Deutsche*, 120.

[33] "Alle Völker der Erde sollen, wie die Weisen an der Krippe, ihre ihnen von Gott verliehenen Schätze Christus dem Herrn auftun, ein jegliches nach seiner Art. Die Deutschen legten ihm ihre Gefolgschaft zu Füßen. So allein vermochten sie ihm aus Herzensgrund die Ehre zu geben—als Mannen des Herzogs, dem sie in Vertrauen und Treue verbunden sind ewiglich. In keiner anderen geschichtlichen Figur aber hat dieses allein ganz echte deutsche Christentum vollkommenere Gestalt gewonnen als in Martin Luther. Denn er war berufen, seinem Volk das Evangelium zu verkünden— nicht ein deutsche Evangelium, aber das Evangelium deutsch." Preuß, *Luther der Deutsche*, 131–2.

beyond culture and race, the Gospel that Luther "recovered," with the notion that Luther is defined by, and defines in himself, Germanity in all that he said and did. As we have seen, some like Barth or Bonhoeffer will simply jettison nation and race as categories with meaning for understanding Christian faith. On the other hand, others will go well beyond Hans Preuß in remaking Luther in the guise of National Socialism.

As noted above, Preuß takes issue in passing with recent publications of Alfred Rosenberg. While Preuß does not engage extensively with Rosenberg, one can see the influence of Rosenberg all over his and other authors efforts to situate Luther and Protestant Christianity as the native religiosity of the Germans. This is a result of Rosenberg's religious viewpoints, his influence in the party and state apparatus, and his own attempts to use Luther as a foil for dechristianizing Germanic religion. Rosenberg joined the Nazi Party (then the German Workers Party) in January 1919, eight months before Hitler, and played a long-term role within the party. He was best known for his anti-Bolshevism and concern for issues of ideology, particularly for his promotion of a Germanic religion that was typologically suited to the German *Volk*, in contradistinction to Christianity with its "foreign" Jewish roots and long association with Rome. His publication in 1930 of *The Myth of the Twentieth Century*[34] became, after *Mein Kampf*, the largest selling National Socialist work. Rosenberg was decisively anti-Christian, and his best-selling works highlighted this aggressively. The popularity of *The Myth* grew in 1933 as the church struggle evolved and expanded and, in 1934, when Rosenberg was for a time given oversight of religious affairs in the Third Reich.[35] In the aftermath of the events of 1933, and the failure to create an integrated Protestant *Reichskirche*, Hitler had become increasingly less interested in pursuing unity in the church, and it came to be understood in the churches that the party's and state's stance toward religion in general would be strictly impartial. This, along with the seeming ascent of Rosenberg to even greater influence, led both the Protestant and Catholic leadership to assume the Rosenberg's version of a Germanic, pagan religiosity might potentially become the prescribed religious "confession" within the Third Reich. This led to a corresponding outpouring of critical responses from both confessions. In fact, though Rosenberg exercised a great deal of influence on popular opinion, Hitler really was not at this point interested in provoking the Christian churches with a prescribed turn to some sort of National Socialist church.[36] But even when Rosenberg was not named directly, the broad effort to use Luther to argue for the *völkisch* Germanness of

---

[34] Alfred Rosenberg, *Der Mythus des zwanzigsten Jahrhunderts* (Munich: Hoheneichen, 1930).
[35] For an overview of Rosenberg's involvement in the church struggle, see Ernst Piper, *Alfred Rosenberg, Hitlers Chefideologe* (Munich: Karl Blessing Verlag, 2005): 399–423. Piper notes that Rosenberg's writings attacking the churches were all bestsellers, with *Der Mythus* selling over 900,000 copies. See page 409.
[36] See the discussion in Scholder, *Die Kirchen*, I, 240-1, 570-7, 704-11; Scholder, *Die Kirchen*, II, 134-7.

Christianity is in part a response to Rosenberg's own efforts to present Luther as a cornerstone for his attack on Protestantism.

In some sense Rosenberg's use of Luther draws little from Luther himself, though as we have seen, that is not uncommon even in literature with more pious aspirations than Rosenberg's. Rosenberg's use of Luther first comes forward in *The Myth of the Twentieth Century*, but it is a publication of 1937, *Protestantische Rompilger: Der Verrat an Luther und der Mythus des 20. Jahrhunderts* (Protestant pilgrims to Rome: the betrayal of Luther and the myth of the twentieth century), which, as the title suggests, provides an explication of arguments first broached in the earlier book. Like *The Myth of the Twentieth Century*, the new title was a best-seller,[37] and elicited furious rebuttals from Protestant church leaders and theologians. Rosenberg begins his polemic by noting the church's passivity in the face of the godless Marxism of the Weimar Republic as compared to their attacks on the current regime and their endless struggles among themselves. As is a stock image of much Luther literature of this era, he imagines Luther returning and expressing outrage at the failure of the church to aid the state in its defense of the German *Volk* against the primal threat of the Bolsheviks. Rather than aiding the National Socialists, this was accomplished by the *Volk* despite the flaccid indifference of the church.[38] Given that Rosenberg makes no distinctions between DC church factions and others, this attack aims at the legitimacy of the church overall. One of Rosenberg's especial nemeses is the Catholic Church, and he draws this into his attack on the Protestants. Having established the short-circuiting of the Reformation's progress in Germany with the retention of many traditional practices and doctrines, he adds:

> And from this stance resulted the monstrous fact that the straight line of the Reformation, first begun by Martin Luther as a German [movement], became tangled, drawing, unmistakably, ever closer to the Church of St. Peter in Rome. The law, revelation, the Church, the creed stand today dogmatically once again above all the life necessities, both inner and outer, of the struggling German *Volk*. In this way the obscurantists (*Dunkelmänner*) in service to Roman principle have found new allies, and Martin Luther's reformation and revolution now are increasingly being handed over, both spiritually and politically, by his official, bureaucratic successors, to those against whom he had set a great, heroic life.[39]

---

[37] Piper, *Alfred Rosenberg*, cites 620,000 copies sold; 409.
[38] Alfred Rosenberg, *Protestantische Rompilger: Der Verrat an Luther und der Mythus des 20. Jahrhunderts*. 4th ed. (Munich: Hoheneichen Verlag, 1937): 7–9.
[39] "Und aus dieser Haltung ergab sich die ungeheuerliche Tatsache, daß die Linie der einst deutsch begonnenen Reformation Martin Luthers in krausen Formen, aber in ihrer Richtung doch eindeutig sich der Peterskirche in Rom näherte. Das Gesetz, die Offenbarung, die Kirche, das Kredo stehen

This idea of an incomplete Reformation, which he styles as a revolution, forms the basis for his further prescriptions, where only a complete abandonment of anything specifically Christian will address his accusation that Protestantism is a slave to its Roman roots. (Rosenberg is aware that among some Confessing Church Protestants there had been some discussion of the need to make common front with the Catholic Church against the greater threat of Rosenberg, hence his accusations about a "pilgrimage to Rome.")

He builds on this idea of betrayal and the need to finally fulfill the true spirit of Luther through the thorough purging of Lutheran religiosity of all non-Germanic aspects. He starts his second chapter, "Does Luther even mean anything still for Protestantism?,"[40] with this observation: "…and the rejection of the monkish way of being, the entire depravity of the Church didn't originate from dogmatics or metaphysics, but was born in the **heart** of an inwardly truthful man. And that is the most decisive element of his entire being."[41] He expands upon this point, noting Luther's comment on Copernicus' work, that if it were true then the Bible is false; Rosenberg claims this as an endorsement by Luther of the falsity of the biblical faith—were Luther alive today, he wouldn't be a Christian![42]

> And now the "Apologetics Central" of the Evangelical Church of Germany is characterized by its defense of an indefensible thing. Luther the German disappears; Luther the truthful man is reshaped as a preserver of dogma, and from the Protestant freedom of conscience grows…the ecclesiastical infantilism of Karl Barth.[43]

This sense of truthfulness, and the willingness to do for the sake of conscience whatever radical steps need to be taken Rosenberg assigns to Luther's "Nordic blood," exemplified in his burning of papal bulls and his radical attacks on the

---

heute dogmatisch wieder über allen Lebensnotwendigkeiten des nach innerer und äußerer Freiheit ringenden deutschen Volkes. Damit haben die Dunkelmänner im Dienste des römischen Prinzips neue Bundesgenossen gefunden, und die Reformation und Revolution Martin Luthers wird nunmehr fortschreitend von seinen heute maßgebenden beamteten Nachfolgern jenen geistig und damit machtpolitisch wieder ausgeliefert, gegen die er ein großes heldisches Leben gesetzt hatte." Rosenberg, *Protestantische Rompilger*, 10.

[40] "Bedeutet Luther noch etwas für den Protestantismus?" Rosenberg, *Protestantische Rompilger*, 17 and following.

[41] "…und die Ablehnung des mönchischen Wesens, der ganzen kirchlichen Verwahrlosung nahm nicht vom Dogmatisch-Metaphysischen ihren Ausgang, sondern wurde aus dem **Gemüt** eines innerlich Wahrhaftigen heraus geboren. Und dies ist das Entscheidende seines ganzen Wesens." Rosenberg, *Protestantische Rompilger*, 17.

[42] Rosenberg, *Protestantische Rompilger*, 17–18.

[43] "Und nun steht die 'Apologetische Zentrale' der evangelischen Kirche Deutschlands in Zeichen einer Verteidigung nicht zu verteidigender Dinge. Luther, Der Deutsche, verschwindet; Luther, der Wahrhaftige, wird zu einem starren Dogmenbewahrer gemodelt, und aus der protestantischen Gewissensfreiheit erwächst—der kirchliche Infantilismus Karl Barths…." Rosenberg, *Protestantische Rompilger*, 18.

papacy, which are expressions of his "Germanic outrage."[44] The Protestants today have Luther completely reversed:

> What was medieval and timebound with Luther they **celebrate** today as representing a revelation; what for Germans possesses eternal value in Luther's Germanic acts, those they try to diminish as side issues, as entirely inessential. If Dr. Martin Luther stood here today, he would box these men's ears with their measly tracts and, just as boldly as before, declare to the entire Germanic world an unbroken protest against Rome and Jerusalem, just as he did four hundred years ago.[45]

Though he spends some time taunting the Protestants for their Catholicism, as the preceding quote indicates, he does not forget to include the Jews in this formula, accusing the church of idolizing the Jews, and noting the much more reasonable position of Luther as revealed in his tract "The Jews and their Lies," which provides him an opportunity to polemicize against the Old Testament and its figures.[46] Not surprisingly, anything associated with ecumenism is condemned as another betrayal of Luther, as is any suggestion of pacifism.[47] As a whole, the tract exhibits no interest in the actual teachings of Luther, since they represent the husks of a withered Christianity. Rather, he finds an opening with the idea of a religion of conscience to focus exclusively on Luther's actions, which can be deployed to call for radical change in the face of a corrupted and outmoded set of beliefs and institutions. Quite a few of the most prominent themes that have marked the literature on the "German Luther" come forward in a frontal assault on all Christian institutions and any form of theological discourse reliant on the biblical text or the traditions of faith. Luther, it would seem, would be marching lock step with the SA.

Rosenberg's works and influence posed a perplexing challenge to all elements of Protestantism. Obviously the Confessing Church faction would see the work as completely untenable, and there were numerous publications from their ranks taking on the provocative claims of Rosenberg. Even here, however, the landscape was difficult to traverse smoothly, since one did not necessarily want to seem to be attacking the party or the state itself, but rather the ideas of this not-so-private

---

[44] Rosenberg, *Protestantische Rompilger*, 19.

[45] "Was mittelalterlich, zeitbedingt an Luther war, das **feiern** sie heute als Darstellung einer 'Offenbarung'; was für Deutsche Ewigkeitswert besitzt an Luthers germanischer Tat, das versuchen sie zu verkleinern, als Randerscheinungen, als gänzlich unwesentlich hinzustellen. Stünde der Dr. Martin Luther heute auf, er würde den Herren ihre Traktätchen um die Ohren schlagen und ebenso kühn wie früher den ungebrochenen Protest der ganzen germanischen Welt gegen Rom und Jerusalem anmelden wie einst vor 400 Jahren." Rosenberg, *Protestantische Rompilger*, 21.

[46] Rosenberg, *Protestantische Rompilger*, 33–4.

[47] He devotes a long section to both ecumenism involving the larger Protestant world beyond Germany, as well as anything related to finding reconciliation with the Catholic Church. Rosenberg, *Protestantische Rompilger*, 62–77.

individual.[48] Among the DC, the issue was how to style their support for Rosenberg-type ideas without abandoning the structure of the church entirely. Part of the problem facing the DC, who were in general enthusiastic followers of the regime and could for the most part agree with the prescriptions of Rosenberg, was that they did not grasp that the party and state were uninterested in their support, except to the extent it divided and weakened the church and its desire to resist the dictates of the regime. No level of conformity short of complete capitulation could satisfy the desire of the party to have no existing alternative institutions to those of the party and the state. Nevertheless, the DC theologians went to great lengths to fashion a *völkisch* Luther who would fit well with the profile of party.

One of the most noteworthy examples of this sort of Luther projection is a work by Wolf Meyer-Erlach,[49] *Verrat an Luther* (betrayal of Luther). Published in 1936, Meyer-Erlach's work echoes in many ways Rosenburg's claims, though it is clear, unlike Rosenberg, he wrote his book with the intention of preserving a church that he identifies as truly Christian. Though he does not mention Rosenberg in his arguments, he surely was cognizant of his views, and the book can be viewed as part of a continuing attempt to demonstrate to Rosenberg and those similarly minded that the Christian faith, properly understood, fulfilled their aspirations for a Germanic system of belief. This is clear with the introduction of

---

[48] Though Rosenberg said himself in his publications that he spoke as a private person with the viewpoints he put forward, thus not abrogating the party's insistence that it was impartial when it came to issues of belief, obviously his status as an upper-echelon member of the party with extensive responsibilities in the area of ideology would make one think twice. In addition, the "freedom" of religion was circumscribed, since it was free "so long as it didn't endanger the security of the state, or contravene the ethical or moral sensibilities of the German race," as paragraph 24 of the party program in force in the 1930s read. Given the haphazard fashion judicial processes in the Third Reich were carried out, the possibilities for prosecuting servants of the churches were open-ended, and lower-level members of the party, especially in the provinces, often took their lead from Rosenberg, and Catholic and Protestant clerics frequently were subject to persecution. See Piper, *Alfred Rosenberg*, 399–401.

[49] Meyer-Erlach (originally Wolf Meyer; he added "Erlach" in an attempt to counter associations of his name with possible Jewish ancestry) is one of the more striking and pugnacious figures within the DC universe. Like many, his experience of World War I left behind a deep impression, and attracted him in the early 1920s to radical racial nationalism. He eventually acquired a theological degree and an appointment in the Protestant church in Bavaria, from whence he developed a reputation as an effective voice for *völkisch* Christianity. The seizure of power in 1933 brought him wholeheartedly into the ranks of National Socialism, and eventually an appointment in Practical Theology at the University of Jena, whose theological faculty was being remodeled as a strong-hold of German Christian movement in Thuringia. It is in this role that Meyer-Erlach published numerous works advocating the sort of Christianity represented in *Verrat an Luther*. See the following for aspects of his history: André Postert, "'Lieber fahre ich mit meinem Volk in die Hölle als ohne mein Volk in Deinen Himmel': Wolf Meyer-Erlach und der Antiintellektualismus." In *Für ein artgemäßes Christentum der Tat: Völkische Theologen im "Dritten Reich,"* ed. Manfred Gilus and Clemans Vollnhals (Göttingen: Vandenhoeck & Ruprecht, 2016): 219–38; Klaus Raschzok, "Wolf Meyer-Erlach und Hans Asmussen." In *Zwischen Volk und Bekenntnis: Praktische Theologie im Dritten Reich*, ed. Klaus Raschzok (Leipzig: Evangelische Verlagsanstalt, 2000): 167–202; on the theological context of the German Christians in Thuringia, see Hans-Joachim Sonne, *Die politische Theologie der Deutschen Christen* (Göttingen: Vandenhoeck & Ruprecht, 1982); and for a broader overview of the German Christians in the church in Thuringia see Susanne Böhm, *Deutsche Christen in der Thüringer evangelischen Kirche (1927–1945)* (Leipzig: Evangelische Verlagsanstalt, 2008).

the book, where, after a fairly typically enthused celebration of the accomplishments of the regime, he turns to consider how well the church has fit into this new dispensation:

> When we see this breakthrough of the spirit, the victory of belief and the triumph of the will becoming active in all areas of our life, we sense in the so-called ecclesiastical space the age-old deadly spirit of the scribes and Pharisees. The ghost of the priest, who, in every age strangled God and the life that God has awoken, goes about seeking his victim. Our *Volk* was awakened by the words and actions of seers and heroes. In the church, which purports to possess the spirit of God, the spirit of freedom, an intellectual and spiritual attitude predominates among men, who, instead of eliminating formulas by the authority of this spirit, seek in fear and hatred to imprison the miracles of God in the suffocating formulas of the past. We experience the spectacle that the prophet mocked: the childish belief of ladling out the sea with cupped hands, and the depths and riches of the Godhead with their dogma.[50]

It is this anti-intellectual formula, this concept of a living spirit that flows through the new regime to which the church needs to open itself, that he will now legitimate by reference to the ideas and especially the actions and person of Luther. "Just as in the days of oversubtle, decaying orthodoxy, today Luther, the German prophet, is distorted into a scribe who brought nothing more than the pure teachings of Karl Barth or the Confessing Church."[51]

> We want the fighter, who, from his lonely wrestling with God, out of the depths of the eternal Word and akin to the great messengers of truth, burst open the church from within, leading entire generations out of the desert of theological speculation and enslavement to the priests into the freedom of the children of God. We want the whole Luther, who consciously as a German went about on

---

[50] "Wenn wir diesen Durchbruch des Geistes, den Sieg des Glaubens und den Triumpf des Willens auf allen Gebieten unseres Lebens wirksam sehen, spüren wir in dem sogenannten Raume der Kirche uralten tödlichen Geist der Schriftgelehrten und Pharisäer. Das Gespenst des Priesters, der zu allen Zeiten Gott und das Leben, das Gott geweckt hat, erwürgte, geht um und sucht sein Opfer. Unser Volk ist aufgewacht unter dem Wort und dem Werke von Sehern und Helden. In der Kirche, die vorgibt, den Geist Gottes, den Geist der Freiheit zu besitzen, herrscht weithin die geistige und seelische Haltung von Männern, die, statt in der Vollmacht dieses Geistes Formeln zu verschlingen, voll Angst und Haß versuchen, das Wunderwerk Gottes in den erstickenden Formeln von Gestern zu fangen. Wir erleben das Schauspiel, über das der Profet spottet: kindlische glauben, das Meer mit der hohlen Hand, die Tiefe und den Reichtum der Gottheit mit ihren Lehrsätzen ausschöpfen zu können." Wolf Meyer-Erlach, *Verrat an Luther* (Weimar: D.C. Verlag, [1937]): 5.

[51] "Wie einst in den tagen der überspitzten, dem Zusammenbruch verfallenen Orthodoxie wird Luther, der deutsche Profet, heute zu einem Schriftgelehrten verzerrt, der angeblich nichts weiter gebracht hat als die reine Lehre Karl Barths oder der Bruderräte." Meyer-Erlach, *Verrat*, 6.

earth, and who, because he was born a German, wanted also to serve his *Volk* with all his powers.[52]

The true fighters for truth today will be those like Luther who break free from the old formulas, who are led by the spirit of God, which is active among the *Volk*, as Luther knew and upon which he acted. Today the learned of the church are like the scribes of old, and those in the Nazi movement are like the Samaritan heathen, and it is from there that will flow the realization of a new church for a new age.[53] From here he dives into the body of his work, where he'll consider three aspects of Luther's legacy: the Bible, calling (*Beruf*), and authority (*Obrigkeit*).

Concerning the Bible, he seeks to demonstrate that Luther treated the Bible as a witness to the Word of God, and that the literal words of the Bible were to be evaluated based on this living Word. Luther himself, he notes, rejected those parts of the Old Testament that did not witness to Christ, and criticized aspects of the New Testament, such as the book of James, or Revelation. "And yet it is exactly Luther who most powerfully burst open the Bible's constricting binding, for he knows better than anyone else that this book, the Scripture, is a work of expediency. For him the Word of God is an actually spoken, not a written, Word, the Gospel in reality a living voice."[54] He applies this creatively to reimagine Luther's time in the Wartburg and Coburg Castle, when he most famously was translating the New Testament into German, or working on the Augsburg Confession:

> We need once again this Lutheran expansiveness, this prophetic eye and apostolic ear. Then we'll experience what Luther experienced in the Wartburg and at Coburg, in the midst of the most severe troubles of his life. The suffering drove him to the word, into Scripture. However in this suffering he found comfort and healing, when he saw the glorious, thick smoke rising out of the Thuringian forest, covering the heavens for a moment; look, there rises a gust of wind and the smoke is torn apart. Not only the letter of scripture spoke to him, but also tree and bush, bird and animal, weather and wind, preaching God's grace and his compassion. If we have both this breadth and depth, then we hear today from the great wondrous works of the history of our *Volk*, out of the incredible events of the last few years, God himself speak to us. For if the coming of nature's

---

[52] "Wir wollen den Kämpfer, der aus der ringenden Einsamkeit mit Gott, aus den Tiefen des ewigen Wortes, den großen Boten der Wahrheit verwandt die Kirche von innen sprengte und ein ganzes Volk, ganze Geschlechter aus der Wüste der theologischen Spekulation, aus der Priesterknechtschaft in die Freiheit der Kinder Gottes führte. Wir wollen den ganzen Luther, der bewußt als Deutscher über die Erde ging und der, weil er als Deutscher geboren wurde, auch seinem Volke mit allen Kräften dienen wollte." Meyer-Erlach, *Verrat*, 7.
[53] Meyer-Erlach, *Verrat*, 8–9.
[54] "Und doch ist es gerade Luther, der die Enge der Buchdeckel am gewaltigsten sprengt, denn er weiß wie kein anderer, daß dies Buch, die Schrift, ein Notwerk ist. Ihm ist das Wort Gottes wirklich gesprochenes, nicht geschriebenes Wort, das Evangeluium tatsächlich eine lebendige Stimme." Meyer-Erlach, *Verrat*, 21.

springtime is a word of God and a sermon to humanity, then how much more must that be the case for the springtime and the resurrection of a *Volk*.[55]

Meyer-Erlach, using the approach pioneered in the work of Holl and Hirsch where one reads the life events of Luther theologically, has expanded its reach; drawing from anecdotal descriptions of significant events in Luther's life he is able to turn Luther's scripture principle into a full embrace of the National Socialist state and its actions.

He carries this thought over into his next chapter that treats Luther's concept of calling:

> We have seen how Luther in his relationship to the Bible united boundness and freedom at once. Luther was able to do this, because for him the Bible was not a book of oracles, still less a treasure trove containing as many passages as possible in service to a system. He wasn't driven by some sort of speculative interest; rather an existential interest drove him to question and dig and bore: the need within his soul, the hunger for freedom, for power, for self-assurance in the face of God, the world and the devil. He found all of this in the prophetic-apostolic message of the power of faith. In faith he got control over his tumultuous soul, in faith he overcame the sinister anxiety of humanity and fate, which so dreadfully attacks the earnest and profound people in all millennia of human history. In faith he became free from himself, free for service to God in this world, in his *Volk*. Luther's faith, Luther's knowledge of God shines with worldliness.[56]

---

[55] "Wir brauchen wieder diese lutherische Weite, dieses profetische Auge und apostolische Ohr. Dann erfahren wir, was Luther erfuhr auf der Wartburg und auf der Koburg mitten in den schwersten Bedrängnissen seines Lebens. Die Anfechtung trieb ihn in das Wort, in die Schrift. Aber in dieser Anfechtung fand er auch Trost und Heilung, wenn er den breitprächtigen Rauch aus den Thüringer Waldtälern aufsteigen sah, um den Himmel zu bedecken für einen Augenblick. Siehe, da erhob sich ein Windstoß, und der Rauch zerriß. Zu ihm redete nicht nur der Buchstabe zu ihm redete Baum und Strauch, Vogel und Tier, Wetter und Wind und predigte Gottes Gnade und sein Erbarmen. Haben wir diese Weite und Tiefe zugleich, dann hören wir Heutigen aus den großen Wunderwerken der Geschichte unseres Volkes, aus dem ungeheuren Geschehen der letzten Jahre Gott selbst zu uns reden. Denn wenn der Frühling in der Natur ein Wort Gottes und eine Predigt an den Menschen ist, dann muß es der Frühling und die Wiederauferstehung eines Volkes noch viel mehr sein." Meyer-Erlach, *Verrat*, 22.

[56] "Wir haben gesehen, wie Luther in seiner Stellung zur Bibel Gebundenheit und Freiheit zugleich vereinigt. Er konnte das, weil ihm die Bibel nicht irgendein Orakelbuch war, noch viel weniger eine Fundgrube von möglichst vielen Stellen für ein System. Ihn trieb da nicht irgendein spekulatives, sondern ein existenzielles Interesse zum Fragen und Graben und Bohren: die Not seiner Seele, der Hunger nach Frieden, nach Kraft, nach Selbstsicherheit Gott, der Welt und dem Teufel gegenüber. Dies alles fand er in der profetisch-apostolischen Botschaft von der Macht des Glaubens. Im Glauben wurde er seiner stürmischen Seele mächtig, im Glauben überwand er die unheimliche Menschheits- und Schicksalsangst, die gerade die Ernsten und Teifen in allen Jahrtausenden der Menschheitsgeschichte so furchtbar überfällt. Im Glauben wurde er frei von sich, frei für den Dienst Gottes in dieser Welt, in seinem Volk. Luthers Glaube, Luthers Gotteserkenntnis strahlt von Weltlichkeit." Meyer-Erlach, *Verrat*, 23.

Lutheran calling, in this sense, is fully superimposed onto the world created by the history of one's *Volk*, again affirming the full participation in the new state as a religious act. He rejects all criticism of this position, once again relying on his understanding of the faith of Luther. Replying to criticism of the Thuringian DC by a church commission, he states: "Indeed these heresy hunters didn't even need to know that, according to Luther's *Freedom of a Christian*, the Christian ascends in faith up to heaven and to God, and descends in love back down to his neighbor. That means, then, that he allows the power of faith to stream into the orders (*Ordnungen*), in which he is situated, in the family, the state, in his *Volk* and fatherland." Here Meyer-Erlach quotes the motto of the DC: "Christ is our power, Germany is our duty."[57] He contrasts the structures and formal theology of the institutional church with the model of Luther's, where faith is realized in action in society. The following passage is representative of this direction:

> This faith has no confessing bishop above it and no Imperial Church Committee with its tame expert opinions. It has above it only one thing: the living God, who with the power of his word, with the force of his spirit, breaks into our heart and lifts us up above all churchdoms and Christendoms, above all high priests and scribes, and transforms us into lords of all things. And he has beneath him not the physical spaces of the church, not so much sectarianism, group think, and clubbiness, but the orders, into which he has placed us in our calling as father and mother, as farmer, craftsman, salesman, soldier, SA man, politician, and scholar. He bursts open today, just as he did before, the narrow spaces of the church and tears us out of the jurisdiction of the scribes into the everyday world, into our *Volk*. We want this heretical faith, even if all correct theories, all well-circumscribed doctrines are ripped to shreds like spiderwebs before it. For with Luther we want to be powerful in the world, never ever fleeing the world with the scribes.[58]

---

[57] "Diese Ketzermeister brauchen für ihre Gutachten ja gar nicht zu wissen, daß nach Luthers Freiheit eines Christenmenschen, der Christ fährt im Glauben in den Himmel zu Gott und dann wieder in der Liebe unter sich zu dem Nachsten! Das heißt aber, daß er die Kraft des Glaubens hineinströmen läßt in die Ordnungen, in die er gestellt ist, in die Familie, in den Staat, in sein Volk und Vaterland." Meyer-Erlach, *Verrat*, 25.
"Christus ist unsere Kraft, Deutschland ist unsere Aufgabe." Meyer-Erlach, *Verrat*, 25.

[58] "Dieser Glaube hat keinen Bekennerbischof über sich und keinen Reichskirchenausschuß mit seinen willfährigen Gutachtern. Er hat über sich nur eines: den lebendigen Gott, der mit der Kraft seines Wortes, mit der Gewalt seines Geistes in unser Herz bricht und uns über alle Kirchen- und Christentümer, über alle Hohenpriester und Schriftgelehrten hinaushebt und wandelt zu Herren aller Dinge. Und er hat unter sich nicht den Raum der Kirche, nicht diese ganze Sektiererei, Rotterei und Vereinsseligkeit, sondern die Ordnungen, in die uns Gott gestellt hat in unserm Beruf als Vater und Mutter, als Bauer, Handwerker, Kaufmann, Soldat, SA-Mann, Politiker und Gelehrter. Er zersprengt heute noch genau so den engen Raum der Kirche wie einst und reißt uns aus dem Herrschaftsbereich der Schriftgelehrten in die Welt des Alltages, in unser Volk. Diesen Ketzerglauben wollen wir, und wenn vor ihm alle korrekten Theorien, alle wohlabgezirkelten Lehrsätze wie die Spinnweben zerreißen. Denn wir wollen mit Luther weltmächtig, nie und nimmer aber mit den Schriftgelehrten weltflüchtig werden." Meyer-Erlach, *Verrat*, 28.

His sustained polemic against learnedness, somewhat unexpected in someone who at the time was serving as rector of a University, breaks down the church as a separate entity and superimposes on to it the larger world of the *Volk*, which itself is equated with the National Socialist state; where Althaus sought to circumscribe the breadth of significance of the orders of creation, insisting on the universality of Gospel above and beyond the material world, Meyer-Erlach makes no distinction. He punctuates this point with his conclusion to the chapter, anticipating the direction he will take in the following chapter on authority:

> Here all those find justification who, with a gun in hand, once set themselves against the threat of Bolshevism. Here lies the justification for the men who were persecuted by betrayers of the *Volk* as politically-motivated killers. against whom a whole pack of so-called Scriptural theologians flung charges. But then those men, who, in the time of our *Volk*'s deepest need, set themselves as followers of the Führer against the great flood coming out of the East, paying for their mission with their blood—those, too, must be considered true men of God, even if bishops and priests denied them a so-called Christian burial. Whoever fell in this battle truly became a martyr. Their 'fist was God's fist, their spear God's spear.'[59]

The section on authority that follows expands upon this idea, showing that service to the movement is in fact profound obedience to the divine will.

He opens the next section by noting Luther's admonition that because the Gospel can only be preached if there is order, those who serve the purposes of imposing order have a high calling, one that Meyer-Erlach highlights emphatically:

> One can only speak correctly about authority, the *Führer* and his work, when one pronounces the true Lutheran understanding against the sectarian theology of our day. **For Luther, God himself stood behind authority. Authority, the Führer, they are the revelation of the grace of God.** They are, as Luther said, "God's masks," in which the Almighty himself deals with us, indeed they are all, despite accusations of heresy, according to Luther saviors and even Gods.[60]

---

[59] "Hier erfahren alle die eine Rechtfertigung, die einst dem drohenden Bolschewismus sich engegenstellten mit dem Gewehr in der Hand. Hier liegt die Rechtfertigung für die Männer, die von Volksverrätern als Fememörder verfolgt wurden, und gegen die eine ganze Meute sogenannter Schrifttheologen den Bannbruch schleuderte. Das macht aber auch die Männer, die in der schwersten Notzeit unseres Volkes als die Gefolgsleute des Führers sich der Sintflut aus dem Osten entgegenstemmten und ihren Einsatz mit dem Blute bezahlten, zu rechten Männern Gottes, wenn auch Bischöfe und Priester ihnen das sogenannte christliche Begräbnis verweigerten. Wer in diesem Kampf gefallen ist, der ist wahrlich ein rechter Märtyrer gewesen. Ihre 'Faust war Gottes Faust und Spieß Gottes Spieß.'" Meyer-Erlach, *Verrat*, 44–5.

[60] "Man kann nur recht reden von der Obrigkeit, vom Führer und seinem Werke, wenn man wider alle Sektentheologie der Gegenwart die wirklichen lutherischen Erkenntnisse verkündet. **Hinter der Obrigkeit steht für Luther Gott selber. Die Obrigkeit, der Führer, sie sind Offenbarungen der**

He reinforces this point for a number of pages, drawing numerous passages from Luther that highlight the divinely sanctioned authority of the ruler, consistently punctuating the point with highlights and large type, and emphasizing the degree to which the learned have condemned this Luther-sanctioned truth as heresy. He raises again the specter of Bolshevism, noting, "had Luther experienced first our collapse and the atrocity of Bolshevism and the resurrection, he would not ever have grown tired of preaching about the honor and duty of the ruler. His church would have become the most powerful messenger of the *Führer* and his works, ignoring the fact that some would have accused it, as the Reformer himself was accused, of idolizing the Third Reich."[61] He emphasizes Luther's encouragement of violence in his response to the Peasants' War, and highlights for his day the holy calling of the SA man, the soldier, and those who serve in the military apparatus that was being built up by Hitler at the time.[62] Toward the end his voice takes on something of an apocalyptic urgency as he considers the dangers of the time and the unwillingness of church to heed Luther's call to unqualified obedience to the divinely ordained political order:

> The dispute about doctrine then becomes insanity, the struggle about the right Christology becomes criminal, when the issue is God himself, the existence or non-existence of Christendom. But Christendom is precisely what is at stake today. If the *Führer* hadn't come, then there would no longer be a church, or worship services or theologians. For us the *Führer* has become what Luther said about the ruler: a helper, savior. Millions see in him what Luther saw in the true prince: the Savior (*Heiland*), who saved us from doom. And when Luther says that the authorities are God's governors, indeed that they are even the embodiment of God, then we need not think or speak any less of the man who today is the only wall standing against the downfall of the West. Because we're Lutherans, we see appearances in their full depths, we see the work of the *Führer* as God's work.[63]

Gnade Gottes. Sie sind, wie Luther sagt: 'Gottes Larven', in denen der Allmächtige selbst mit uns handelt, ja sie sind allem Verketzerungsgerede zum Trotz nach Luther Heilande und sogar Götter." Meyer-Erlach, *Verrat*, 48.

[61] "Hätte Luther erst unseren Zusammenbruch erlebt und die Greuel des Bolschewismus und den Wiederaufstieg, er wäre nicht müde geworden, von der Ehre und den Pflichten der Obrigkeit zu predigen. Seine Kirche wäre die gewaltigste Verkünderin des Führers und seines Werkes geworden, ohne Rücksicht darauf, daß man ihr, wie einst dem Reformator selbst 'Vergötzung des Dritten Reiches' vorgeworfen hätte." Meyer-Erlach, *Verrat*, 53.

[62] Meyer-Erlach, *Verrat*, 53–5.

[63] "Der Streit um die Gotteslehre wird dann zum Irrsinn, der Kampf um die rechte Christologie zum Verbrechen, wenn es um Gott selbst, um Sein oder Nichtsein des Christentums überhaupt geht. Um das Christentum geht es aber heute schlechthin. Wäre der Führer nicht gekommen, in Deutschland gäbe es heute keine Kirche mehr und keinen Gottesdienst und keine Theologen. Uns ist der Führer das geworden, was Luther von der Obrigkeit sagt: Helfer, Retter. Millionen sehen in ihm, was Luther in dem rechten Fürsten sah, den Heiland, der uns vor dem Verderben bewahrte. Und wenn Luther von der Obrigkeit sagte, daß sie Statthalter Gottes, ja sogar der verkörperte Gott sei, dann brauchen wir nicht geringer zu reden und zu denken von dem Manne, der heute als die einzige Mauer

This personalizing of one's duty to God as duty to the *Führer* is reiterated in a number of ways as he brings the work to its close, leavened with a somewhat more optimistic perspective on the joys that attend such a life, and closing with the final pious observation, "since however our entire life should be a service to God, so service to the *Volk* and obedience to the *Führer* shall have no end except in death."[64]

Meyer-Erlach represents an extreme version of a theme that stretches across much of the literature about Luther in the 1930s, seeing in the return of a strong charismatic leader the fulfillment of the state ideal that Luther himself espoused. Meyer-Erlach is exceptional in the degree that he denies any sort of possible conflict between service to the new regime and Christian morality. His complete rejection of scholarly expertise, his valorizing of action as embodied in the fanatical devotion of SA men to service to the regime, his subsuming of the church entirely into the *Volk*, leaves little room for any source of resistance to the dictates of the regime. In Meyer-Erlach's mind, Luther would undoubtedly have worn a brown shirt and said "Heil Hitler" as fanatically as anyone, and to suggest otherwise is both a betrayal of one's Lutheran identity and of God as embodied by Adolf Hitler. It is somewhat ironic, then, to consider the Meyer-Erlach, despite his ingratiating theology of action, ended up on the wrong side of the regime. Beginning in 1938 he first lost his rector position, and, for a time, had a speaking and travel ban placed upon him, even though there was nothing in particular that had changed about his disposition to the regime, but simply because at least some factions of the regime were seeking not a Nazi movement endorsed by the church, but a Nazi movement that preempted the authority of the church. While Meyer-Erlach was entirely subservient to the needs of the regime for obedience, he did so from within the legitimating framework of the church, and that legitimacy in itself was coming into question.[65] By posing Luther as the legitimating voice to pronounce the providential bona fides of the *Führer*, Meyer-Erlach by implication was suggesting that the legitimacy of the *Führer* might rest on such authority. Just as ecclesiastical anointing of secular rulers in the Middle Ages provided leverage to the church, so Luther's imprimatur might suggest some area of cultural power that lay outside the prerogatives of the National Socialist state, a challenge also suggested by the very existence of the church, and something figures like Rosenberg and his circle aimed over time to eliminate.

---

wider den Untergang des Abendlandes steht. Weil wir Lutheraner sind, sehen wir die ganze Tiefe der Erscheinungen, sehen wir das Werk des Führers als Gottes Werk." Meyer-Erlach, *Verrat*, 70.

[64] "Da aber unser ganzes Leben ein Gottesdienst sein soll, so gibt es für den Dienst am Volke, für den Gehorsam gegen den Führer auch kein ende bis zum Tode." Meyer-Erlach, *Verrat*, 70-1.

[65] See Postert, "'Lieber fahre ich,'" 229-30.

Meyer-Erlach's book represented one extreme within the spectrum of DC positions in relationship to the issues raised in Rosenberg's *Mythus*.[66] Other DC authors who responded directly to Rosenberg's *Verrat an Luther* took a somewhat more measured, though decisively *völkisch* approach to Luther's accomplishments. Representative of this type of response would be Siegfried Scharfe, *Verrat an Luther?*, published in response to Rosenberg in 1937.[67] Where Meyer-Erlach represents the characteristics of the Thuringian DC to more or less conform their view of Luther and the church to the perceived needs and expectations of the new regime, Scharfe is more representative of the "moderate" DC, where the primacy of scripture and personal salvation exist in the midst of a *völkisch* Christianity and church. In most ways Scharfe has nothing particularly striking to say about Luther; his work repeats fairly conventional observations about his Germanness, his *völkisch* authenticity, his fighting spirit, and his having made the Gospel fit with a Germanic-type faith. But he accuses Rosenberg of presenting only one side of Luther, not the full Luther. Having described also Luther's more traditionally Christian characteristics, Scharfe states emphatically:

> The one picture corresponds to reality, the other no less: Luther was both **fighter and attacker, prayerful and a Christian**. Whoever tears apart the unity is guilty of an offense; the one, who wants to allow only Luther's Germanic way of thinking and withhold the Bible, and the other who would detach Luther's faith in Christ from its connection to the *Volk*. May God **preserve for us the entire Luther, the brave, defiant-in-faith, German Hero and the disciple of Jesus Christ, the prophet of divine truth.**[68]

He wishes to concede that Rosenberg raised legitimate issues concerning the need for a deep and searching renewal in the spirit of Luther,[69] and he sees this as

---

[66] On the spectrum of responses to Roserberg's *Rompilger*, see Raimund Baumgärtner, *Weltanschauungskampf im Dritten Reich: Die Auseinandersetzung der Kirchen mit Alfred Rosenberg* (Mainz: Matthais-Grünewald-Verlag, 1977): 231–50.

[67] Siegfried Scharfe, *Verrat an Luther? Erwiderung auf A. Rosenbergs "Protestantische Rompilger"* (Halle: Deutschen Bibeltag, 1938). Baumgärtner, *Weltanschauungskampf*, 233, designates Scharfe as "die Nachhut der Deutsch-christlichen Rosenbergdiskussion (the rear-guard of the German-Christian Rosenberg discussion)."

[68] "Das eine Bild entspricht der Wirklichkeit, das andere nicht minder. Luther war beides: **Kämpfer und Stürmer, Beter und Christ**. Wer die Einheit auseinanderreißt, macht sich schuldig: die einen, die nur Luthers germanische Denkart gelten lassen wollen und die Bibel unterschlagen, und die anderen, die Luthers Christenglauben herauslösen aus seinen volkhaften Bindungen. Gott **erhalte uns den ganzen Luther: den mutigen glaubenstrotzigen deutschen Held und den Jünger Jesu Christi, den Propheten göttlicher Wahrheit!**" Scharfe, *Verrat*, 23.

[69] "Wir fassen zusammen: Rosenbergs 'Rompilger' zeigen ein Gefühl für die Frage, vor die heute der gesamte deutsche Protestantismus gestellt ist. Es geht um eine tiefgreifende **Erneuerung im Geiste Luthers**" (To summarize, Rosenberg's *Rompilger* demonstrates a feel for the question that today is placed in front of the entirety of German Protestantism. It involves a deep and penetrating renewal in the spirit of Luther). Scharfe, *Verrat*, 24.

an issue of *völkisch* renewal. However, he sees Rosenberg as having shut off connections to the church that were previously open, and that he is now not working toward a "positive Christianity," but rather has emboldened a pagan, Germanic-faith movement that stands in opposition to the Christian church. One could speculate, Scharfe muses, that the accusations in Rosenberg's book has nothing to do with the DC, since they "have a sound sense for what fundamentally gives their lives its meaning, worth and purpose. It doesn't occur to them to close themselves off from new knowedge, they embrace without reservation National Socialism, and desire that the church and the *Volk* not be set against one another, but complement one another. The are no betrayers of Luther, but his true followers (*Gefolgsmannen*)."[70] In this way, Scharfe affirms all that the regime is doing, and acknowledges the need to conform the church to the needs of the regime; however, at the same time he wishes to hold onto a dimension of Christianity that can exist beyond simply the material life of the *Volk*:

> It's no different with **truth** than with life. The question is whether organic/natural existence and growth may claim to be true in and of itself, or whether truth points beyond the boundaries and possibilities of organic activity and development of life, even if it may be embedded in them, and whether it is capable of bursting these boundaries and possibilities. Rosenberg is clearly of the former opinion, Luther without doubt of the latter.[71]

On the one hand, Scharfe wants to stand with Rosenberg to use Luther as a weapon against the theologians and theologies of the Confessing Church and Barth:

> It may be that Luther, as Rosenberg put it, would box the ears of many current theologians who write in Luther's name using their own theological tracts, because while they are Lutheran in their rhetoric, in their religious and spiritual stance they are anything but, still it remains an open question how he would deal with those who propagandize for Germanic character values.[72]

---

[70] "...haben aber ein gesundes Gefühl für das, was ihrem Leben im letzten Grunde, Inhalt, Wert und Ziel gibt. Sie denken nicht daran sich gegen neue Erkenntnisse zu sperren, bejahen ohne Vorbehalt den Nationalsozialismus und wollen, daß Kirche und Volk nicht gegeneinander gestellt werden, sondern miteinander gehen. Sie sind keine Verrätter Luthers, sondern seine getreuen Gefolgsmannen." Scharfe, *Verrat*, 28.

[71] "Mit der **Wahrheit** ist es nicht anders wie mit dem Leben. Es ist die Frage, ob organisch-natürliches Dasein und Wachstum den Anspruch erheben darf, aus sich selbst und in sich selbst wahr zu sein, oder ob die Wahrheit über die Grenzen und Möglichkeiten organischer Lebensbetätigung und -entfaltung, wenngleich sie darin eingebettet sein mag, hinausweist und diese Grenzen und Möglichkeiten zu sprengen vermag. Rosenberg ist offenbar der einen Meinung, Luther ganz zweifellos der anderen." Scharfe, *Verrat*, 30.

[72] "Es mag sein, daß Luther, wie Rosenberg es andeutet, manchen der heutigen Theologen, die sich nach ihm nennen, ihre theologischen Flugschriften um die Ohren schlagen würde, weil sie wohl in der Wortprägung lutherisch, in der religiösen und geistigen Haltung aber alles andere als dies sind, es

Yet, as the closing thought reveals, he wants to resist Luther being completely absorbed into the ideology of a Germanic religion which would coopt Christianity entirely: "the evangelical Church is in its essence always been a *Volkskirche* and as a result is ready to integrate into the great front of the *völkisch* marchers; it wants to give to the *Volk* what belongs to the *Volk*, at the same time it wants to remain completely true to its spiritual vocation and 'give to God what belongs to God.'"[73] But it is this latter thought that demonstrates that Scharfe has not reckoned with what is possible under Nazism. His conclusion highlights this issue starkly:

> In his *Mythus* Alfred Rosenberg called Martin Luther "the greatest savior of the West,' and said that he has become **'the axis of a new development of the world'.** And Rosenberg knows what powers would rule today in Western cultural affairs if Luther had not come. Martin Luther will decisively determine the further development of evangelical churchdom in the future. We will have him to hold on to when we want to avoid false paths, we'll take our advice from him when we lack an answer to this or that individual question, and not least, we will trust that we will find our way with our Lutheran attitude and Lutheran stance, when questions are put to us that we must answer independently. That the interpretation of Luther as put forward by Rosenberg can help us, given all of what can be read about Luther in the *Rompilgern*, is seriously doubtful. The Luther of the *Mythus* and the *Rompilger* is a Luther for the particular objectives of the author of the book. It is not the true and actual 'Prophet of the Germans' who was led by his own inner self to dismantle the world of his own time, and **whose duty it is today and will remain in the future to show his German *Volk* with the Bible the way to the Lord Jesus Christ.**[74]

---

bleibt die Frage offen, wie er mit religiösen Propagandisten für germanische Charakterwerte verfahren würde." Scharfe, *Verrat*, 30.

[73] "Die evangelische Kirche ist ihrem Wesen nach von jeher Volkskirche gewesen und deshalb bereit, sich in die große Front der völkischen Marchierer einzuordnen, sie will dem Volk geben, was des Volkes ist, sie will allerdings zugleich ihrer geistlichen Bestimmung ganz treu bleiben und 'Got geben, was Gottes ist'." Scharfe, *Verrat*, 31.

[74] "Alfred Rosenberg hat Martin Luther in seinem 'Mythus' 'den größten Retter des Abendlandes' genannt und von ihm gesagt, er sei zur **'Achse einer neuen Weltentwicklung'** geworden. Und Rosenberg weiß auch, welche Gewalten heute das abendländische Kulturgeschehen beherrschen würden, wenn Luther nicht gekommen wäre. Martin Luther wird für die Zukunft die Weiterentwicklung evangelischen Kirchentums entscheidend bestimmen. Wir werden uns an ihn zu halten haben, wenn wir Irrwege vermeiden wollen, werden bei ihm uns Rat holen, wenn wir in dieser oder jener Einzelfrage keine Antwort wissen, und werden nicht zuletzt darauf vertrauen, daß wir in lutherische Gesinnung und lutherischer Haltung uns zurechtfinden, wenn wir selbstverantwortlich vor Entscheidungen gestellt sind. Daß uns die Lutherdeutung, so wie Rosenberg gibt, dabei helfen kann, muß nach allem, was in den 'Rompilgern' über Luther zu lesen ist, ernstlich bezweifelt werden. Der Luther des 'Mythus' und der 'Rompilger' ist ein für die besonderen Zwecke des Verfassers dieser Bücher zurechtgemachter Luther, aber nicht der wahre und wirkliche 'Prophet der Deutschen', der vom Innersten her dazu geführt wurde, die Welt seiner eigenen Zeit aus den Angeln zu heben, und **dessen Aufgabe es heute ist und in Zukunft bleiben wird, seinem deutschen Volk mit der Bibel den Weg zum Herrn Christus zu weisen.**" Scharfe, *Verrat*, 30–1.

This decisive conclusion to the work both sets a clear boundary, but also shows the weakness of those who wish to affirm the *völkisch* Luther and retain some unique space for an inner spiritual life that is not under the authority of the regime. Undoubtedly Scharfe intended to provide a principle that seemed to grant the *völkisch* state its legitimate rights while asserting the legitimacy of the church, but it had no hope of winning over with figures such as Rosenberg.

The rivalries and divisions within German Protestantism in the 1930s debilitated all factions in their efforts to carve out a space for a religiosity not simply subsumed into the ideology and practice of National Socialism. This is clear in the differences of view in Meyer-Erlach's definition of a Christianity faithful to Luther and that of Scharfe; like all aspects of Protestant belief and practice, there was no unanimity among the German Christians. But one area did bring the German Christians together, and that was the vehement rejection of the Confessing Church, both its theological bases and its ecclesiology. Though Scharfe is more moderate in expressing his rejection, he, like Meyer-Erlach, can affirm Rosenberg to the extent that Rosenberg is seeking to negate the arguments of the Confessing Church and its rejection of a *Volkskirche*. For Meyer-Erlach, his explicit target was the Confessing Church, which he attacks ad hominem for its betrayal of the German *Volk*. Supporters of the Confessing Church were not lacking in response to Rosenberg's work (or to Meyer-Erlach's), but, as with the German Christians, this was not a unified response.[75] But some works that came out of the Confessing Church did take a firm stance against Rosenberg's portrayal of Luther, such as Düsseldorf pastor Joachim Beckman's *Verrat an Luther?*, published by the Confessing Synod in the Rheinland.[76] Beckmann starts by noting the outrageous falsities that were put forward in Rosenberg's publication, but eschews taking them all on in serial fashion. Instead he defines four areas he wishes to use to show both the falsity of Rosenberg's argument, and what it would mean to be faithful to the teachings of Luther. Given Rosenberg's basic indifference to theology or the actual record of Luther's ideas, it proves fairly easy for Beckmann to

---

[75] On the variety of responses to Rosenberg's *Mythus*, see Baumgärtner, *Weltanschauungskrieg*, 206–27. See in particular 226–7, where he provides an overview of the different responses to the political challenge raised by critiques of Rosenberg's work which avoid questioning basic tenets of the regime, especially as regards race. Some, and Beckmann's work is an example of this, do not address at all how race figures into their response, and simply reply to theological issues raised by the work. Others, and Baumgärtner sees these as more numerous, give extensive attention to the issue, and concede significant legitimacy to the idea of race as an order within which God materially provides for his *Volk*, and through which he creates order; Baumgärtner notes that some go so far that the reader might become confused to what degree they are even dissenting from Rosenberg's arguments. He notes, as well, the extensive response of Walter Künneth, *Anwort auf den Mythus: Die Entscheidung zwischen dem nordischen Mythus und dem biblischen Christus* (Berlin, 1935), which attained something of the status of an official response. Many of these works don't actually address the representation of Luther in Rosenberg, being much more concerned with the issues surrounding the status of the Bible and the understanding of Christ.
[76] Joachim Beckmann, *Verrat an Luther?* ([Barmen]: Theologisches Amt der evang. Bekenntnissynode im Rheinland, [1937?]).

show the degree to which he has himself betrayed Luther's historical faith. The four areas of focus are the question of the authority of scripture, of original sin, of revelation of God through Christ Jesus, and place of the church.[77] As is typical of much of the Confessing Church literature concerning Luther, the interest is not so much Luther's actions as what Luther had to say about doctrine and how that doctrine was reflected in the Lutheran confessional literature. He rejects out of hand Rosenberg's contention that were Luther alive today, his revolutionary character would lead him to reject the Bible and Christianity as worn out, and embrace a truly Germanic religion. As Beckmann points out, Luther was a doctor of the Bible, and Rosenberg's attacks on his biblical faith are just another version of the Enlightenment attack on religion:

> Luther's way to the Reformation was indeed not the "revolutionary protest of a Germanic character" as Rosenberg would have it, but the way of the Doctor of Holy Scripture, that is to say the way of a man who through study and exegesis of the Holy Scripture became a reformer.[78]

He then quotes at length from Luther's introduction to the Old Testament, which, of course, sees Luther affirm unreservedly the status of the Old Testament as God's Word. He parries the claim by Rosenberg about the Bible as having been superseded as true as a result of the changed cosmological views of the present by noting that Luther did not see the cosmos as heaven above, hell below, but saw God's truth as transcendent of all physical constraints.[79] With the issues of original sin and Christ as the revealed truth of God, he makes relatively short work, quoting extensively from the Schmalkaldic Articles and from Luther's Small Catechism, and emphasizing the historically determined nature of orthodox teaching over against what he continually designates Rosenberg's rationalistic and Enlightenment-like arguments. Though he repeatedly challenges Rosenberg's accusation of betrayal by asking who actually has betrayed the faith of Luther, mostly the tract works as a refresher course in certain aspects of orthodox Lutheran teachings.[80] In the end, Beckmann's tract doesn't really take on the speculative stylings of Luther's image, or address the arguments about his "Germanic" mission, but asserts, rather, the universality of his message about sin and salvation. For the most part, Beckmann represents the attempt by the Confessing Church to defend traditional Lutheran religiosity while finding some modus vivendi with the National Socialist state. For that effort, the theological legacy of Luther was

---

[77] Beckmann, *Verrat*, 4.
[78] "Luthers Weg zur Reformation war ja nicht der Weg des 'revolutionären germanischen Charakterprotestes,' wie es Rosenberg wahr haben möchte, sondern der Weg des Doktors der Heiligen Schrift, d.h. der Weg eines Mannes, der durch Studium und Auslegung der Heiligen Schrift zum Reformator wurde." Beckmann, *Verrat*, 7.
[79] Beckmann, *Verrat*, 8–9. [80] Beckmann, *Verrat*, 14–23.

essential, the widely disseminated "Germanic" Luther inconvenient. It is no accident that Beckmann brings in the confessional literature to argue his case, rather than the broader corpus of Luther's writings, since the confessional literature provides settled interpretations of the meaning of Luther's Reformation teachings; the broader corpus was typically used by those who wished to craft a Luther more useful for the modern-day needs, and in tension with the settled legacy.

To the degree that Luther represented a principle of struggle, or revolt, or an existential wrestling for a meaningful God, he could be disentangled from his actual teachings, and used to argue for a new departure, a further Reformation, which might reject a number of the cornerstones of the historical Lutheran Confessions. The seemingly endless flexibility of such an approach is well demonstrated by Hans Preuß's treatment of Luther, where the Reformer is seemingly comfortably aligned with the tenets of the new age as a result of his exemplary Germanity, his sense of racial consciousness (despite lacking the vocabulary to articulate it clearly), his faith whose values fit so comfortably with the values of the new regime, and his theological affirmation of a created order permeable to the work of providence in the historical journey of the *Volk*. The somewhat contorted nature of his argumentation, seeking to preserve a space for salvation beyond the experience of the *Volk*, reveals both the desire to preserve something specifically Christian beyond the reach of the new age, and the intellectual flaccidity of the results. This is even more manifest in the work of Meyer-Erlach, where there is little separation between the Germanic Luther and the prototypical SA man. Luther's teachings are creatively shaped to fit the ideal of a church that is completely embedded within the *Volk*, to the extent that it is unclear how such a religiosity differs in kind from whatever spiritual ideal might be projected from within National Socialism. Rosenberg might have reasonably expected his own argument about Luther to have taken hold within circles of the church, given perspectives such as Meyer-Erlach. And in fact, for many Christians they did not see anything contradictory about being both within the church and a member of the party. In that regard, responses like Beckmann's, that sought to reclaim Luther for a traditional confessional Lutheran religiosity, were not typical, even within the Confessing Church. In general, the styling of Luther in the garb of the *Volk* created a powerful legitimating image for the regime, both by affirming a racially defined German *Volk*, and by making a large subset of the church susceptible to the claim of the regime that they were sincerely committed to establishing "Positive Christianity" at the center of the state, despite the publications of Rosenberg, or the continuing harassment of the church at the local party level. But this styling of Luther in the image of National Socialism was only one dimension of his rebranding; as we will see, he also served as a powerful affirmation for the leadership principle at the center of the Nazi state.

The Luther Myth: The Image of Martin Luther from Religious Reformer to Völkisch Icon. Patrick Hayden-Roy, Oxford University Press. © Patrick Hayden-Roy 2024. DOI: 10.1093/9780198930297.003.0006

6
Luther [and] *der Führer*

One unique feature of German political thought and rhetoric beginning in the late nineteenth century, and becoming more prominent after World War I, was the emphasis on charismatic leadership as the political form most congenial to the German racial type. This ideal of not just authoritarian but organically racial and charismatic leadership (*Führertum*) came to make a deep imprint on the development of German political culture. In this way of thinking, democratic forms of government as practiced in the West were rejected as foreign to Germans, and morally debilitating because they played on individual selfishness, which then expressed itself in partisan party building and political action, dividing and weakening the whole. Germans found their form of representation in the person of an individual who through their experience and exemplary inner being represented in themselves the character of the racial/spiritual *Volk*. This way of thinking anticipated the coming of a charismatic leader to save the nation. It is clear the development of German politics in the 1920s was deeply impacted by this ideal. It was of great influence on the ideology of National Socialism before Hitler joined the Party, and only gradually came to be associated with him.[1] Eventually the status of Hitler as the *Führer* became a centerpiece of National Socialist ideology, shaping the whole structure of authority in the Third Reich and Hitler's understanding of himself. Such ideas were influential among Protestant Nationalists, as well, where the concept came to be applied not only to Hitler but also to Luther. What made such ideas even more compelling was the fact that Luther himself developed an understanding of the "miracle man" (*Wundermann, vir heroica*) who, blessed by God, comes to lead a people and reset the trajectory of history.[2]

---

[1] See Ian Kershaw, *The Hitler Myth* (Oxford: Oxford University Press, 1987): ch. 1. Early on Dietrich Eckart, one of the founding ideological influences on the early Nazi Party, and mentor to Hitler and Alfred Rosenberg, expressed such ideas in articles published in *Auf Gut Deutsch*, the periodical he founded in the aftermath of World War I to agitate for the revival of Germany. See Barbara Miller Lane and Leila J. Rupp, eds., *Nazi Ideology before 1933: A Documentation* (Austin, 1978): esp. 3–9.

[2] Patrick Hayden-Roy, "Unmasking the Hidden God: Luther's *Wundermänner*." *Lutherjahrbuch* 82 (2015): 66–105. There is a passage in *Mein Kampf* that suggests Hitler was influenced by Luther's perspective in developing his own understanding of heroic leadership: "Denn je größer die Werke eines Menschen für die Zukunft sind, um so weniger vermag sie die Gegenwart zu erfassen, um so schwerer aber ist mithin auch der Kampf und um so seltener der Erfolg. Gelingt dies aber dennoch in Jahrhunderten Einem, dann kann ihn vielleicht in seinen späten Tagen schon ein leiser Schimmer des kommenden Ruhmes umstrahlen. Freilich sind diese Großen nur die Marathonläufer der Geschichte; der Lorbeerkranz der Gegenwert berührt schon nur mehr die Schläfen des sterbenden Helden. Zu ihnen aber sind sie zu rechnen die großen Kämpfer auf dieser Welt die, von der Gegenwart nicht

As we have already observed in the Luther celebrations of 1933, many assigned to Luther the status of *Führer*, and projected that status onto Hitler, either by comparison to Luther, or as another obvious instance of God raising up a great man to save the people from oppression and realize their destiny. Two works published in the 1930s are exemplary in this regard, having as their main purpose the direct comparison of Luther with Adolf Hitler; one by Hans Preuß in 1933, whose *Luther der Deutsche* was discussed in Chapter 5 (p. 105ff), and the other by Hermann Werdermann in 1935. In both instances, the authors develop a point-by-point comparison, the implications of which demonstrate the providential nature of Hitler's ascension to power while at the same time affirming Luther's remarkable status as himself a comparable chosen vessel of God. And since Luther is still spiritually present to endow Germans with his inspirational influence, he, too, could be assigned the status of *Führer*.

Preuß's work was published in the *Allgemeinen Lutherischen Kirchenzeitung* in 1933, a time when Preuß was especially active in promoting the fortunes of the new regime.[3] To begin, Preuß notes that the comparison of Luther to Hitler has been made by others, and his work will demonstrate how apt that comparison is. He concedes that there are obvious differences, since one was a reformer, the other a politician—Hitler admitted he wasn't a reformer. "So he [Hitler] distinguishes most clearly the two leadership types. Nevertheless, Luther and Hitler are

---

verstanden, dennoch den Streit um ihre Ideen und Ideale durchzufechten bereit sind. Sie sind diejenigen, die einst am meisten dem Herzen des Volkes nahestehen werden; es scheint fast so, als fühlte jeder einzelne dann die Pflicht, nun in der Vergangenheit gut zu machen, was die Gegenwart einst an den Großen gesündigt hatte. Ihr Leben und Wirken wird in rührend dankbarer Bewunderung verfolgt und vermag dann besonders in trüben Tagen gebrochene Herzen und verzweifelnde Seelen wieder zu erheben. Dies sind aber nicht nur die wirklich großen Staatsmänner, sondern auch alle sonstigen großen Reformatoren. Neben einem Friedrich der Großen steht hier ein Martin Luther sowohl wie ein Richard Wagner" (For the greater the works of a person are for the future, the less likely is the present able to comprehend them, but also the more difficult the struggle will be, and the rarer the success. But if, in the course of centuries, one man should achieve success, then in his later years a faint shimmer of coming glory can perhaps shine upon him. Of course, these great ones are the marathon runners of history; the laurel wreath of the present only touches the temples of the dying hero. Among them are counted the great fighters of this world who, though not understood by the present, nevertheless are ready to fight through to the end for their ideas and ideals. They are those who one day will stand closest to the hearts of the *Volk*; it's almost as if everyone felt the duty to make right in the past whatever sins the present had committed against the great ones. Their life and works are followed with touchingly thankful admiration, and are able, especially in troubled times, to lift up again broken hearts and despairing spirits. Among these are not only the truly great statesmen, but also all the other great reformers. Alongside a Frederick the Great stands here a Martin Luther as well as a Richard Wagner). *Hitler, Mein Kampf. Eine kritische Edition*. Vol. 1, ed. Christian Hartmann et al. (Munich/Berlin: Institut für Zeitgeschichte, 2016): 573. *Mein Kampf* was written while Hitler was imprisoned in 1923–4, a period, Ian Kershaw suggests, that was especially important for the development of Hitler's ideas about charismatic leadership. See *Hitler, 1889–1936: Hubris* (London: Penguin Press, 1998): ch. 7.

[3] The piece was also published separately as a tract, *Luther und Hitler* (Erlangen: Freimund Verlag, 1933). In addition to his two Luther publications of 1933 and 1934, Preuß also actively aided the burning of the books in Erlangen, helping identify suspect publications held in the University library, which were then, on May 10, 1933, incinerated publicly on campus. See Hartmut Lehmann, "Hans Preuß 1933 über 'Luther und Hitler.'" *Kirchliche Zeitgeschichte* 12 (1999): 287–96, esp. 289.

one in that they are **German** leaders, who both know they were called to save their *Volk*. And there are not only truly **fundamental** parallels, but also remarkable correspondences in what can be **derived** and is seemingly **accidental**."[4] Throughout the work he accentuates the sense that the striking parallels, even when they seem strained, are indicative of the divine plan at work, a messianic purposefulness which might suggest in the mind of the reader another parallel, that to Jesus; it can be no accident that both appeared, he says, when the cry had gone forth from the people for a great man, "a savior."[5] He reminds his reader of Luther's prophetic calling, coming from humble roots to bring a new order; his audience needs no reminder of that with Hitler, since they are experiencing this remarkable realization. He follows with an account of the striking parallels in their life courses— peasant roots, accused of Czech (i.e. foreign, Slavic!) roots, experiencing the misery of their times, and then, in their thirties, stepping forward out of nowhere to become people of power, only to be brought down after three-plus years and incarcerated, where they brought forth great works, then returned to the public sphere with great jubilation for their followers and vexation for their enemies. From there they brought their movements of liberation to fruition, each using a new technology to aid their cause—printing for Luther and the radio for Hitler.[6]

Of course each loved his fatherland, was deeply connected to it, knew it in the most profound sense, being connected to the land and also to the tribulations that came through commercial exploitation, against which both of them stood.[7] He notes that each had a sublime appreciation for nature and creatures, and found there the traces of the divine. Both advocated that women should find their honor in the home, in child bearing and rearing.[8] Both were artists, loved history, and recognized its practical worth.[9] Both believed in struggle, and fought through difficulties, even when their supporters turned against them—he sees the truly heroic in this aspect of each.[10] Each embodies the "Nordic" style of leadership (*nordischer Führer*), exercising leadership through their blunt way of stating the case, and drawing others to them based on their response. Both were against parliamentarianism, and affirmed authoritarian leadership.[11] Both seized power through legal, public, constitutional means, proceeding in a "German" manner, not through organizations or laws but through leadership, attracting good people who would be the basis for their movement.[12]

Finally, having established the deeply ethical means through which they achieved leadership, he closes by emphasizing that the most important aspect of

---

[4] "Er unterscheidet also aufs allerdeutlichste jene beiden Führerarten. Aber darin sind doch Luther und Hitler eins daß sie **deutsche** Führer sind, daß sich beide zur Errettung ihres Volkes berufen wissen. Und das gibt nicht bloß rein **grundsätzliche** parallelen, sondern auch merkwürdige Uebereinstimmungen im **Abgeleiteten** und scheinbar **Zufälligen**." Preuß, *Luther und Hitler*, 3.
[5] "…der Rettung." Preuß, *Luther und Hitler*, 3.   [6] Preuß, *Luther und Hitler*, 3–5.
[7] Preuß, *Luther und Hitler*, 5.   [8] Preuß, *Luther und Hitler*, 6.
[9] Preuß, *Luther und Hitler*, 6–7.   [10] Preuß, *Luther und Hitler*, 7–8.
[11] Preuß, *Luther und Hitler*, 8–9.   [12] Preuß, *Luther und Hitler*, 9–10.

their leadership was their deep connection to God: "First it is clear to him that great decisive leaders of humanity don't come from their own power and mission. While Luther says 'it depends not on books, but on the fact that **God** send people to earth' (1527), so Hitler said in a speech from May 4, 1923, 'Is the suitable *Führer*-personality at hand? Our duty is not to seek after a person. They are either sent by heaven or they are not.'"[13] Hitler, Preuß assures his readers, was profoundly aware that all he had was from God, allegedly telling Bishop Ludwig Müller, "when I now look at everything, how it happened and came to be, for me it is a miracle of God."[14] He picks up on this with his conclusion, noting how providentially ordained the work of each great man has been:

> And again there appears here another fundamental parallel: both their accomplishments are the salvation from German need. Luther cleared away the boulders that the centuries had rolled over the source of the Gospel of Christ, and washed the German soul clean again in this water from heaven. He pulled the wagon of the church of Christ back at the last moment as it was just about to fall into the looming chasm of the ancient heathen being. Hitler also pulled our *Volk* back at the last minute from the uttermost collapse of body and soul, and has started to place our *Volk* again back on a purer and sounder foundation, chasing off all that is rotten, harmful, unhealthy.[15]

To finish he places Hitler in the pantheon of the German heroes, with Charlemagne, Frederick the Great, and, of course, Luther.[16]

Though today one stands back agape at a work like this, at the time it would have not raised many eyebrows, since unbridled Hitler encomia were legion in 1933, building such a chorus that Hitler himself, who was surely witness to and active participant in the propagandistic artifice that lay behind such rhetoric, was increasingly internalizing this idea as part of his core image.[17] And compared

---

[13] "Zunächst ist ihm klar, daß große entscheidende Führer der Menschheit nicht aus eigener Kraft und Sendung kommen. Wenn Luther sagt: Es liegt nicht an Büchern, sondern daran, daß **Gott** Leute auf Erde schickt (1527), so sagte Hitler in einer Rede vom 4. Mai 1923: 'Ist die geeignete Führerpersönlichkeit da? Unsere Aufgabe ist es nicht, nach der Person zu suchen. Die ist entweder vom Himmel gegeben oder ist nicht gegeben.'" Preuß, *Luther und Hitler*, 10.

[14] "Wenn ich das alles jetzt sehe, wie das geworden ist und wie es kam, ist es für mich ein Wunder Gottes." Preuß, *Luther und Hitler*, 13.

[15] "Aber doch besteht auch hier eine grundlegende Parallele: ihre Werke sind beidemal Errettung aus deutscher Not. Luther räumte das Geröll hinweg, das Jahrhunderte über die Quelle des Evangeliums von Christus gewälzt hatten, und badete die deutsche Seele wieder rein in diesem lauteren Himmelswasser. Er riß den Wagen der Kirche Christi im letzten Augenblick zurück, als er gerade in den jähen Abgrund antikisch-heidnischen Wesens stürzen wollte. Auch Hitler hat unser Volk in letzter Minute zurückgerissen vor dem äußersten Sturz Leibes und der Seele und begonnen, unser Volk wieder auf reinere und gesündere Grundlagen zu stellen, alles Faulige, Schädliche, Ungesunde verjagend"; 13.

[16] Preuß, *Luther und Hitler*, 14.

[17] Ian Kershaw in his Hitler biography sees the internalizing of this myth constructed and projected by Goebbels and others as one of the most significant developments of this period, so that at a

to the second Luther/Hitler comparison of this era by Hermann Werdermann (1888-1954), Preuß's work seems somewhat sober and restrained. In many ways Werdermann simply echoes Preuß's comparison, acknowledging and apparently copying the earlier work, and laying out the same basic narrative. However, Werdermann is much more aggressive in providing Hitler with the explicit imprimatur of Luther, quoting from Luther himself about the *Wundermänner* of history, and applying this to Hitler, and then imagining Luther and Hitler finding one another and as a team bringing Germany to its world historical destiny:

> Luther knew what a great political leader meant for a *Volk*. He said: "when God wished to help a *Volk* he didn't do it with books, but rather he sent out a man or maybe two; and he ruled better than all writings and laws." He had to lament of his own times: "Germany is like a right beautiful stallion that has food and everything else it needs. What is missing is the rider. Just like a strong horse without a rider to guide it will now and again go astray, so Germany is also mighty enough with its strength and people; what it lacks however is a good head and regent." How joyful Luther would be today to see that Germany has such a leader! And if Luther could say, when looking at the first great German *Volk* hero, Arminius the Cherusker, "If I were a poet, I would want to celebrate him. He is dear to my heart. If I had now an Arminius and he a Dr. Martin, together we would seek out the Turks," so we could continue in Luther's vein and have him say: "because in time of greatest need God has gifted the German *Volk* with such a *Führer*, he is dear to my heart. For such a *Führer* can fend off the Bolsheviks and give to our Germany the place in the world that it deserves." And if in his time Luther could long for an Arminius, so we would not be mistaken to imagine our *Führer* sometimes wishing in his heart, in the quiet hours: "If only I had a Martin Luther! Then Germany could fulfill its world historical mission both outwardly and inwardly."[18]

certain point Hitler was entirely incapable of thinking outside its framework. See Ian Kershaw, *Hitler, 1889–1936: Hubris* (London: Penguin Press, 1998): esp. chs. 12 and 13.

[18] "Luther weiß, was ein großer politischer Führer für sein Volk bedeutet. Er sagt: 'Wenn Gott einem Volk hat wollen helfen, dann hat er's nicht mit Büchern getan, sondern nicht anders, denn daß er einen Mann oder zwei hat aufgeworfen: der regiert besser denn alle Schrift und Gesetze'. Er mußte in seiner Zeit klagen: 'Deutschland ist wie ein schöner weidlicher Hengst, der Futter und alles genug hat, was er bedarf. Es fehlt ihm aber an einem Reiter. Gleichwie nun ein stark Pferd ohn einen Reiter, der es regiere, hin und wieder in der Irre läuft, also ist auch Deutschland mächtig genug von Stärcke und Leuten; es mangelt ihm aber an einem guten Haupt und Regenten.' Wie freudig würde Luther heute wohl feststellen, daß Deutschland solchen Führer hat! Und wenn Luther im Blick auf den ersten großen deutschen Volkshelden, Hermann den Cherusker, sagt: 'Wenn ich ein Poet wäre, so wollt ich den zelebrieren. Ich habe ihn von Herzen lieb! Wenn ich jetzung einen Arminium hätte und er einen D. Martinum, so wollten wir den Türken suchen', so könnten wir in Luthers Sinn wohl fortfahren, daß er heute sprechen würde: Wo Gott nach schwerer Not dem deutschen Volk einen solchen Führer beschert hat, den habe ich von Herzen lieb; denn ein solcher Führer kann den Bolschewismus abwehren und unserm Deutschland die Stellung in der Welt schaffen, die ihm gebührt. Und wenn Luther sich damals nach einem Arminius sehnte, so gehen wir wohl nicht fehl, wenn unser Führer in der Stille es sich manchmal von Herzen wünscht: Wenn ich einen Martin Luther hätte! Dann könnte

This specious claim of a fundamental elective affinity between the two highlights the unbounded affirmation that flowed outward from the image of Luther to the new *Führer* of the German *Volk*. Going beyond Preuß's work into even more disturbing territory, Werdermann highlights Luther's anti-Jewish writing, and uses that connection to extend the sense of common purpose between the two:

> It is surprising that the **Jews and Jewishness** were seen not only by Hitler but also by Luther as his and the German *Volk*'s especially terrible **enemy**. Regarding the viewpoint of our *Führer* nothing more needs to be said here. Everyone knows how necessary for life was and is the purification of German blood and German economic and spiritual life from adulterated (*artfremden*) influences. However far too little is known about how powerfully Luther struggled against the Jews.[19]

He quotes at some length from Luther's 1543 tract "The Jews and their Lies," and then notes that if one understands Luther correctly, no conflicts could arise in an evangelical Lutheran *Volkskirche* against the racial lawmaking of the state, but quite to the contrary, "**Adolf Hitler in his treatment and solution to the Jewish question has become the perpetuator and perfecter of Luther.**"[20] In a note he thanks the National Socialists for making the church aware of the order of race when considering God's orders of creation. Werdermann composed his work in 1935, and it was republished a number of times up to the outbreak of the war, at a time when the severity of the measures against the Jews was becoming increasingly clear, and when, as we shall see, Luther was increasingly being used to legitimate the harshness of the measures; in this sense, his emphasis on Luther's anti-Semitism, which he saw as underappreciated at the time, fits with the increasing instrumentalization of Luther as an advocate for racial cleansing.

Deutschland seine Weltsendung nach innen und außen ganz erfüllen!" Hermann Werdermann, *Martin Luther und Adolf Hitler: Ein geschichtliche Vergleich.* 3rd ed. (Gnadenfrei in Schlesien: Gustav Winter Verlag, 1938): 5–6. The text was first delivered as a lecture at the *Hochschule für Lehrerbildung* (College for Teacher Education) in Dortmund on Reformation Day 1935, where Werdermann was a professor, and then first published in 1936 as volume 5 of *Aufbau im "Positiven Christentum"!*, a periodical series of the Deutsche Christen.

[19] "Überraschend ist es, daß von Hitler nicht nur, sondern auch schon von Luther als sein und des Deutschen Volkes besonders schlimmer **Gegner der Jude und das Judentum** angesehen wurde. Über die Einstellung unseres Führers hierzu braucht nichts Näheres gesagt zu werden. Jeder weiß, wie lebensnotwendig die Reinigung des deutschen Blutes, des deutschen Wirtschafts- und Geisteslebens von artfremden Einflüssen war und ist. Aber viel zu wenig bekannt ist, wie gewaltig Luther gegen die Juden gekämpft hat...." Werdermann, *Martin Luther und Adolf Hitler*, 8.

[20] "Man sieht schon an diesen Proben, daß, wenn Luther auch noch die rassischen Fragen, die heute so akut geworden sind, fern gelegen haben, von dem recht verstandenen Luther her in einer evangelisch-lutherischen Volkskirche Gegensätze gegen die Rassengesetzgebung des Staates nicht entstehen können, daß im Gegenteil **Adolf Hitler in der Behandlung und Lösung der Judenfrage der Fortsetzer und Vollender Luthers geworden ist**"; Werdermann, *Martin Luther und Adolf Hitler*, 8–9.

In general, these two works are transparent attempts to ingratiate the Protestant church with the regime, infinitely eager to prove through Luther a boundless loyalty and sense of common purpose. Toward the end of Werdermann's comparison, he turns to the question of religion and politics, and repeats some of the common arguments about how much Luther elevated and honored the authority of the ruler, and also how much Hitler respects the church and will give it its due. He emphasizes the common notion that National Socialism promoted and would protect "positive Christianity,"[21] and that both Hitler and Luther were advocates of a "practical" Christianity that honored good works. On Luther's side he quotes passages where Luther highlights that faith leads to good works, and then turns to note all the signs of economic revival under the Nazis, a favorite talking point of the regime, and lauds as true Christianity all the good that the regime has done for the German *Volk*. They don't just preach and read, but they act, which is infinitely closer to the essence of the savior. "Our reformer would, had he experienced all this, find a deep joy in this, even if he must recognize that in many places a clear Christian understanding was not the driving force, but rather an unconscious Christianity. However 'by their fruits you shall know them'; Luther and Hitler are in agreement about Jesus meaning!"[22] Both Preuß and Werdermann represent the deepest sort of susceptibility of those within the church to the notion that National Socialism in its essence was an attempt to restore Christianity to its rightful place among the German *Volk* and state, though also revealing in their overeager rhetoric a sense of uncertainty about the true intentions of the regime, as if they were trying to convince themselves as well as National Socialists that this is really what defines the new order. Werdermann concludes his tract with a string of quotes from Hitler's speeches in 1933 which make reference to God, and affirm his own sense of respect for divine providence.[23] While one surmises it was Werdermann's intent to somehow contain Hitler by superimposing Luther on to his image, the effect of the work, as well as Preuß's, was to impose Hitler onto Luther, such that what was distinctive about Luther, which was his understanding of faith with its deep sense of human insufficiency apart from the saving grace of Christ, was entirely obscured. Instead, we get a Luther who unreservedly affirms all the measures taken by the regime, and walks in lock-step with the "movement." Further, both Preuß and Werdermann end up attributing to Luther and Hitler messianic characteristics and motives, the inevitable comparison point for which is Jesus Christ. In that sense, these works, at least in any conventional understanding of Lutheran religiosity, demonstrate how far the image of

---

[21] Werdermann, *Martin Luther und Adolf Hitler*, 16.
[22] "Unser Reformator würde, wenn er das miterlebte, eine tiefe Freude daran haben, selbst wenn er feststellen müßte, daß an manchen Stellen nicht klare christlich Erkenntnis, aber unbewußtes Christentum die Triebkraft gewesen ist. Aber 'an ihren Früchten sollt ihre sie erkennen'; darin stimmen im Sinne Jesu Luther und Hitler überein!" Werdermann, *Martin Luther und Adolf Hitler*, 17.
[23] Werdermann, *Martin Luther und Adolf Hitler*, 19.

Luther has strayed at this point from its traditional associations, despite coming from authors with impeccable Lutheran credentials.

The associations suggested in Preuß's and Werdermann's brief works lack any real intellectual heft, but are rhetorical exercises meant to impress a lay public, ingratiate the church with the party, and perhaps sell some product. But the sort of associations they portray were affirmed in more scholarly addresses and works by some of the leading theological figures of the 1930s, beginning with the addresses that were delivered in the Luther observations of 1933, and a host of works published in the years to follow. Perhaps most exemplary of these arguments for both Luther as *Führer* and for the application of his notion of charismatic, authoritarian leadership in the contemporary setting is an address delivered by Erich Seeberg (1888–1945) in 1933 and published in the *Zeitschrift für Kirchengeschichte*, one of the leading German scholarly journals of church history.[24] Seeberg held a chair on the theological faculty in Berlin, was the son of the eminent theologian Reinhard Seeberg, and one of the most vociferous supporters of the new regime.[25] Seeberg begins his address by stressing that Luther was no mere churchman, but something more: "Luther was neither pastor nor professor—although he was both, but who would want to set himself alongside this 'colleague?'—but he was a great prophet and *Führer*, as seldom enough emerges...among the German *Volk*."[26] "He is the 'eternal German,' who has for the first time embodied in himself the consciousness of the *Volk*; in him is revealed the riches of the German spirit (*Geist*): the profundity and willpower, the world dominance and diligence, the reaching for the stars and the obedience to the demands of the times."[27]

> Luther, however, did not just look on and think, but while doing so believed and experienced. He also belonged to those who believe what they think, and live what they believe. The great *Führer* doesn't just know, but his thoughts arise immediately out of his being; that is, he believes. Thus Luther truly made the great walk with God and experienced the distant and hidden as near and present. As with all great ones, the deepest aspect of his soul is religion, the submission to God.... That is Luther's faith, the sense for the unseen and the obedience in the face of what is contrary to reason; behind the unsolvable problem of life he sees the reality of God, which gives him certainty in life and the

---

[24] Erich Seeberg, "Martin Luther," *Zeitschrift für Kirchengeschichte* 52 (1933): 525–44.
[25] On the Seebergs, see the article by Thomas Kaufmann, "Die Harnacks und die Seeburgs—'Nationalprotestantische Mentalitäten'." In Thomas Kaufmann, *Aneignungen Luthers und der Reformation: Wissenschaftsgeschichtliche Beiträge zum 19.-21. Jahrhundert* (Tübingen: Mohr Siebeck, 2022): 119–70.
[26] "Luther ist weder Pfarrer noch Professor—obwohl er beides war, aber wer wollte sich neben diesen 'Kollegen' stellen?—sondern er ist einer der großen Propheten und Führer, wie sie selten genug im deutschen Volk hervorgehen." Seeberg, "Martin Luther," 525.
[27] "Er ist der 'ewige Deutsche', der das Bewußtsein unseres Volkes zum erstenmal in sich verkörpert hat; und in ihm offenbart sich der Reichtum des deutschen Geistes, der Tiefsinn und die Willenskraft, die Weltüberlegenheit und die Tüchtigkeit, das Suchen nach den ewigen Sternen und der Gehorsam gegenüber der Forderung des Tages." Seeberg, "Martin Luther," 527.

humble/proud self-confidence that belongs to the essential features of the religion of all heroes. "God has guided me like a workhorse whose eyes are blinded so that it doesn't see what is rushing toward it."

Thus was Luther the miracle man (*Wundermann*) of God; no harmless superintendent who keeps watch over right teaching, and no expostulating professor, who always arrives too late, because the story is over by the time they have understood it. Rather he was a prophet, one of the few uncanny geniuses of world history, who take into themselves all the deepest powers of their time and in their own soul make something new out of them.[28]

He continues with this emphasis on the way God's hidden will is worked out in the acts and accomplishments of the great *Wundermänner*, exemplified in Luther's life and recognized by him as a principle of history. "...it is a crude misunderstanding of Luther when one designates his sense of history as senseless and its events ungodly. History is 'God's carnival play' and God's 'hind quarters'; and the idea of incarnation, which is the key to Luther's theology, leads beyond this to the notion that the hidden life of God unfolds in history; history is not God, but in it and only in it, in its events and words, unfolds the paradox and contradictions of God's power."[29] Ultimately one has to learn through both Luther's example and his teaching how to read the meaning of the world:

> In this sense Luther remains for us at once a legacy and a duty. It is highly symbolic, that in this Luther year the German *Volk*, having been shaken awake by its great *Führer*, is proceeding to shake off the Western and Eastern restrictions that were imprisoning its being, and to restore the balance between reality and spirit

---

[28] "Aber...Luther hat nicht bloß geschaut und gedacht, sondern er hat dabei geglaubt und erlebt. Auch er gehört zu denen, die glauben, was die denken, und die leben, was sie glauben. Der große Führer weiß nicht bloß, sondern seine Gedanken steigen unmittelbar aus seinem Sein empor, d.h. er glaubt. So hat Luther wirklich den großen Gang mit Gott getan und den Fernen und Verborgenen als den Nahen und Gegenwärtigen gehabt. Wie bei allen Großen ist das Tiefste in seiner Seele die Beugung unter Gott, die Religion.... Das ist Luthers Glaube, der Sinn für das Unsichtbare und der Gehorsam gegenüber dem Widervernünftigen; hinter dem Leben, das nicht aufgeht, sieht er die Wirklichkeit Gottes; das gibt ihm die Sicherheit im Leben und das demütig-stolze Selbstbewußsein, das zu den Grundzügen in der Religion aller Heroen gehört. 'Gott hat mich hinangeführt wie einen Gaul, dem die Augen geblendet sind, daß er die nicht sehe, so ihm zurennen.' So war Luther, der Wundermann Gottes; kein harmloser Superintendent, der über die rechte Lehre wacht, und kein räsonnierender Professor, der immer zu spät kommt, weil die Geschichte getan ist, wenn sie begriffen wird; sondern ein Prophet, eins der wenigen unheimlichen Genies der Weltgeschichte, welche die tiefsten Kräfte ihrer Zeit in sich aufnehmen, um in der Kraft ihrer Seele etwas Neues daraus zu machen." Seeberg, "Martin Luther," 528–9.

[29] "Auch von hier aus ergibt es sich, daß es ein grobes Mißverständnis Luthers ist, wenn man in seinem Sinn die Geschichte als sinnlos und ihre Hervorbringungen als widergöttlich bezeichnet. Die Geschichte ist 'Gottes Fastnachtspiel' und Gottes 'Rücken'; und der Gedanke der Menschwerdung, der der Schlüssel zu Luthers Theologie ist, führt über diesen Ausspruch hinaus: in der Geschichte entfaltet sich verborgen das Leben Gottes; sie ist nicht Gott. Aber in ihr und nur in ihr, in ihren Geschehnissen und Worten, entfaltet sich paradox und im Widerspiel Gottes Kraft." Seeberg, "Martin Luther," 543.

that had been lost after the Great War. And in this sense, what I have portrayed today is not dead occurrences, but is, especially today, living history. Luther is the present, and the strength of his faith, the depth of his thought and the free power of his personality will grasp our heart and stir our spirit for as long as the German spirit remains capable of the power of its own being and the profundity of Christianity.[30]

Seeberg's address provides a theological matrix within which to consider Luther and Hitler, and define the nature of the *Führer*, the miraculous leader who drives forward the divine plan within the material sphere. By expanding the space for the "hidden" God to operate within Luther's theology, Seeberg provides a justification for equating the historical figures of Luther and Hitler with the providentially ordained divine actors of Luther's *Wundermänner*. In this, he anticipates many others who in the 1930s will build upon this aspect of Luther's theology to affirm the revolution in German public life, and the status of Hitler as unquestioned ruler.

In the unusual universe of Luther interpretation in Germany in the 1930s, Seeberg, for all his radical remodeling of Luther's faith to embrace the events of the day, represents something of a moderate when compared to other commentators who wrote in the years to follow. One striking example of this is an article published in 1934 by Theodor Pauls (1885–1962), "Martin Luthers Geschichtsauffassung" (Martin Luther's concept of history).[31] Writing in a publication designed for educators, with his article Pauls ostensibly provides for teachers a practical guide to Luther's use of history. He summarizes Luther's view as follows: "The active God of history is for many people a hidden God. They don't recognize God, and therefore they don't pay attention to him. However history is nothing less than a special type of the Word of God."[32] He justifies this with reference to the notion that the history of your *Volk* with all its ups and downs is a piece of creation, the memory and representation of which shows God at work: "Historical meaning belongs to the first article of our faith: I believe that God the father, the

---

[30] "In diesem Sinn bleibt Luther uns Vermächtnis und Aufgabe zugleich. Es ist von symbolischer Kraft, daß dasjenige Jahr ein Lutherjahr ist, in dem das deutsche Volk, wachgerüttelt von seinem großen Führer, daran geht, die westlichen und östlichen Verstrickungen, in denen sein Wesen gefangen war, abzuschütteln und das Gleichmaß von Wirklichkeit und Geist wiederherzustellen, das in Deutschland nach dem großen Krieg verloren gegangen war. Auch in dieser Hinsicht ist das, was ich heute geschildert habe, nicht gestorbenes Geschehen, sondern es ist gerade heute lebendige Geschichte. Luther ist Gegenwart; und die Kraft seines Glaubens, die Tiefe seines Denkens und die freie Macht seiner Persönlichkeit werden so lange unsere Herzen ergreifen und unsern Geist aufwühlen, als der deutsche Geist der Kraft seines eigenen Wesens und der Tiefe des Christentums fähig bleibt." Seeberg, "Martin Luther," 543–4.

[31] Theodor Pauls, "Martin Luthers Geschichtsauffassung." *Deutsche Evangelische Erziehung* 45 (1934): 264–71.

[32] "Der wirkende Gott der Geschichte ist für viele Leute ein verborgener Gott. Sie erkennen Gott nicht, und darum achten sie ihn nicht. Aber die Geschichte ist nichts Geringeres als eine besondere Art von Wort Gottes." Pauls, "Martin Luthers Geschichtsauffassung," 265.

almighty creator has created us in the natural world and—in history—yet still maintains us."³³ This recourse to the first article of the Small Catechism is a common strategy to find a theology of creation in Luther, and Pauls pushes his argument forward from here. "How Luther understood this faith in creation and his confession of the creator God in connection with the great historical figures is indeed best known from his exegesis of Psalm 101 from 1534/5. Heroes make history and are God's miracle people (*Wunder Leute*)."³⁴ He opens up the implications of this understanding for the current context:

> We feel powerfully today the truth of this view of history, as well as the calling to which we, the "others, who aren't *Wunderleute*," have been called. The obedience of those who "follow", who crawl behind, and remain students, who are to adhere to the commandment and example as well as they are able, is obedience to God.³⁵

He emphasizes repeatedly how history throws up such guiding lights and how they represent the hidden providence of God, his working through his masks and larvae, God's providential hand lying hidden behind the heroes and mighty ones. Though he doesn't bring Hitler in specifically, he clearly considers the current context as an exemplary instance of the phenomenon to which he refers, and emphasizes that for Luther and for the *Wundermann* the defining feature is *Kampf*, "struggle" or "battle." C. J. Franke, in an address at the Luther commemoration in Eisleben defined this formula much more overtly:

> We see in Luther a fighter, *Führer* and Reformer. The recognition impresses itself into our heart and sensibilities with elementary force; we must see in the National Socialist movement a second Reformation in the sense of a renewal of Germany, whose realization a great fighter and *Führer* is bestowing upon us—Adolf Hitler!…What a powerful, strong yet fine and tender tone: "Luther and Hitler!" Powerful and strong in action and striving for Germanity, fine and tender in grasping the German soul…. Luther and Hitler: paving the way for

---

[33] "Geschichtlicher Sinn gehört zum ersten Artikel unseres Glaubens: Ich glaube, daß Gott der Vater, der allmächtige Schöpfer, uns Menschen in die Natur hineingeschaffen hat und—in der Geschichte—noch erhält." Pauls, "Martin Luthers Geschichtsauffassung," 266-7.

[34] "Wie Luther diesen Schöpfungsglauben und sein Bekenntnis zum Schöpfergott in bezug auf die großen geschichtlichen Gestalten verstanden hat, ist wohl am bekanntesten aus seiner Auslegung des 101. Psalms von 1534/35. Helden machen Geschichte, und sie sind Gottes Wunderleute." Pauls, "Martin Luthers Geschichtsauffassung," 267.

[35] "Wir spüren heute die Wahrheit dieser Geschichtsauffassung überwältigend, zugleich aber auch den Beruf, in den wir 'andern, die nicht Wunderleute sind', hineingerufen werden. Der Gehorsam derer, die 'nachfolgen', 'hinnach kriechen', 'Schüler bleiben', die sich an Gebot und Beispiel zu halten und es so gut wie möglich zu machen haben, ist Gehorsam gegen Gott." Pauls, "Martin Luthers Geschichtsauffassung," 268.

Germanity, model for all Germans, saviors from need and torment!—Luther the reformer, Hitler the renewer, creator of the Third Reich![36]

Though more crudely framed, the address highlights how the formula reduces down to a basic equation that puts the two inextricably together.

A 1934 article by Walter Grundmann (1906-1976) in *Deutsche Theologie*[37] translates Franke's sentiment into a new charge for German theology:

> Perhaps one might say the following: Just as once the reformer of the church, Martin Luther, journeyed during twelve years of wrestling with God in the quiet of the cloister to a new, living faith in Christ, which enabled him to become a reformer, so for fourteen years the Christian message was newly clarified for our *Volk* through a comparable new consideration of its theology, which our *Volk* needs in its present historical hour, where the future of our *Volk*, and also that of the West, will be decided. This new consideration of theology is also at the same time a reconsideration of Luther and a new discovery of the Reformation message.[38]

And what might this new consciousness look like?

> On this front Adolf Hitler says that here Germany stands. The development of German history has shown that the hope placed on Adolf Hitler has not deceived, that he truly is the *Führer* who was called to pave the way for his *Volk* into a new future. Through him and his movement our *Volk* has been wrested from its despair and at the last minute pulled back from the abyss. A new will to live and for the future fills our *Volk*. In this event in the history of our *Volk* we

---

[36] "Wir sehen Luther als Kämpfer, Führer und Reformator. Da drängt sich uns mit elementarer Wucht die Erkenntnis in Herz und Gemüt, daß wir in der nationalsozialistischen Bewegung eine zweite Reformation im Sinne der erneuerung des Deutschtums zu erblicken haben, deren Verwirklichung uns wieder ein großer Kämpfer und Führer beschert-Adolf Hitlers!" "Welcher gewaltige, starke und doch feine, zarte Zweiklang; 'Luther und Hitler!' Gewaltig und Stark im Handel und Streben für das Deutschtum, fein und zart in der Erfassung der deutschen Seele.... Luther und Hitler: Wegbereiter des Deutschtums, Vorbilder für alle Deutschen, Retter aus Not und Qual!—Luther der Reformator, Hitler der Erneuerer, Schöpfer des Dritten Reiches!" Siegfried Bräuer, "Die Lutherfestwoche vom 19. bis 27. 1933 in Eisleben." In *Lutherinszenierung und Reformationserinnerung*, ed. Stefan Laube und Karl-Heinz Fix (Leipzig: Evangelische Verlagsanstalt, 2002): 391-451: 424.

[37] Walter Grundmann, "Die Neubesinnung der Theologie und der Aufbruch der Nation." *Deutsche Theologie* 1 (1934): 39-46.

[38] "Vielleicht darf man einmal so sagen: Wie einst der Reformator der Kirche, Martin Luther, in zwölf Jahren klösterlicher Stille im Ringen um Gott heranreiste zu einem neuen lebendigen Christusglauben, der ihn zu einem Reformator werden ließ, so ist unserem Volke in einer stellvertretenden Neubesinnung seiner Theologie durch 14 Jahre hindurch die christliche Verkündigung von neuem klargestellt worden, die unser Volk in seiner geschichtlichen Stunde der Gegenwart, in der die Entscheidung über die Zukunft unseres Volkes und darüber hinaus die des Abendlandes fällt, braucht. Diese Neubesinnung der Theologie ist aber zugleich eine Widerbesinnung auf Luther und Neuentdeckung der reformatorischen Botschaft." Grundmann, "Die Neubesinnung," 41-2.

hear God's footsteps and hear him speaking. In this historical hour it will all depend on the new consideration of theology leading to a proclamation that places our *Volk* beneath the God's lordship, which is the source of life and the future. The new consideration of theology and the arising of the nation (understood as God's action among our *Volk*) are dependent on one another and belong together. That is indeed the theological/*völkisch* mission of this hour.[39]

And what would be the political translation of this theological mission that would pave the way for a new future? Many scholars developed a clear interpretation of how the church, understood as the *Volk*, should situate itself in relation to the ruling authority. One exemplary interpretation was put forward by Helmuth Kittel (1902–1984), student of Karl Holl, professor of the New Testament and Religious Pedagogy, and advisor to Hanns Kerrl, who held various posts within the regime related to church policy. Kittel's 1938 work, *Religion als Geschichtsmacht* (religion as a historical force), crafts an argument justifying the full subordination of the church to the state using Luther as his primary point of reference. He notes, as had Rosenberg, that the Reformation remained incomplete: "Only in one point did the Germans of the ensuing centuries shrink back from the call to decisive new deeds which lay in Luther's message, [the area of] political action and the formation of the life of the state. To carry out the inheritance of the Reformation in this area seems to be left for our generation, therefore what Luther had to say on this theme must be especially be thought through here."[40] He explains the key principle for understanding what Luther intended in the sphere of politics:

> The secret of Luther's teaching about the state lies in the fact that he found an overarching religious concept that allowed him to ascribe to the state the same

---

[39] "Von dieser Front sagte Adolf Hitler, daß hier Deutschland stehe. Die Entwicklung der deutschen Geschichte hat gezeigt, daß die auf Adolf Hitler gesetzte Hoffnung nicht trügt, daß er tatsächlich der Führer ist, der berufen ist, seinem Volk den Weg zu bahnen zu einer neuen Zukunft. Durch ihn und seine Bewegung wurde unser Volk aus der Verzweiflung herausgerissen und in letzter Stunde vom Abgrund zurückgeholt. Ein neuer Wille zum Leben und zur Zukunft erfüllt unser Volk. In diesem Geschehen in der Geschichte unseres Volks hören wir Gottes Schritt und vernehmen wir seine Sprache. **In dieser geschichtlichen Stunde nun wird alles darauf ankommen, daß die Neubesinnung der Theologie zu einer Verkündigung führt, die unser Volk unter die Herrschaft Gottes stellt, aus der Leben und Zukunft kommt. Die Neubesinnung der Theologie und der Aufbruch der Nation als Handeln Gottes an unserem Volke sind aufeinander angelegt und gehören zusammen. Das ist aber die theologisch-völkische Aufgabe der Stunde.**" Grundmann, "Die Neubesinnung," 42.

[40] "Nur in einem Punkt sind die Deutschen der folgenden Jahrhunderte vor dem Aufruf zu entscheidenden neuen Taten zurückgeschreckt, der in Luthers Botschaft lag, beim politischen Handel und in der Gestaltung des Staatlichen Lebens. Das Erbe der Reformation auf diesem Gebiet zu vollstrecken, scheint unserer Generation vorbehalten zu sein, und deshalb muß das, was Luther zu diesem Thema zu sagen hatte, hier noch besonders durchdacht werden." Helmuth Kittel, *Religion als Geschichtsmacht* (Leipzig: B. G. Teubner, 1938): 34.

religious importance as the church. It is the Kingdom of God. Augustine divided the church and state into the city of God and the city of the devil; for Luther the church is God's Kingdom on his right hand, the state God's Kingdom on his left. Pastor and statesman both serve God.[41]

But God intends the ruler to rule apart from the ideals and influence of the church. He turns to Luther's *Wundermänner* to set within the political sphere a divinely inspired understanding appropriate to its purposes. "The ruler administers his office with a God-given reason, and as such one can learn nothing from the Bible appropriate for politics."[42] Extrapolating freely from Luther's writings, he frees the ruler from the usual constraints of the law. "Written laws are meant for the *Volk* and the common man. But high, natural understanding belongs to the special miracle people (*Wunderleuten*)."[43] Though he is eliding a significant qualification that Luther made about the status of the "miracle people," namely that they are rare, undoubtedly Kittel felt the applicability of this idea to the current setting justified his rather free application of the theory.

And what would this faculty of reason or understanding, unbound by the written law, allow the miraculous leader to do?

> He weaves together the various classes into one interest and accustoms them to serve God, to honor virtue, to hold to traditional morals, to raise up the youth, to protect respectable people and to hold evil in check. Such a ruler is God's likeness on earth, and his bodyguard does not consist of the disloyal masses... but of the very servants of the Most High, the angels.[44]

While, he notes, this way of viewing the power of the ruler may seem radical, it is in fact in keeping with the Reformation, which was a revolution that awakened a *völkisch* movement. He adds an anti-intellectual note, decrying the way the Reformation was captive to the static sensibilities of the learned, when it was a movement of that took place in the streets and was driven by the passions of *Volk*,

---

[41] "Das Geheimnis der Staatslehre Luthers liegt darin, daß er einen übergreifenden religiösen Begriff findet, der es ihm erlaubt, dem Staat die gleiche religiöse Würde zuzuschreiben wie der Kirche. Es ist der des Reiches Gottes. Augustin schied Kirche und Staat als *civitas dei* und *civitas diaboli*, Luther: Die Kirche ist Gottes Reich zur Rechten, der Staat Gottes Reich zur Linken. Pfarrer und Staatsmann dienen beide Gott." Kittel, *Religion als Geschichtsmacht*, 35.

[42] Die Obrigkeit führt ihr Amt aus der gottgegebenen Vernunft, in der Bibel als solcher kann man für die Politik nichts lernen." Kittel, *Religion als Geschichtsmacht*, 35.

[43] "Beschriebene Gesetze gehören für das Volk und den gemeinen Mann. Der hohe natürliche Verstand aber steht sonderlichen Wunderleuten zu." Kittel, *Religion als Geschichtsmacht*, 37.

[44] "Er verflicht die verschiedenen Klassen in ein Interesse und gewöhnt sie, Gott zu dienen, die Tugend zu verehren, Sittenzucht zu halten, die Jugend zu bilden, den anständigen Mann zu schützen, die Bösen im Zaun zu halten. Ein solcher Herrscher ist Gottes Ebenbild auf Erden, und seinen Leibgarde besteht nicht aus dem ungetreuen Haufen, der sich sonst um Fürsten drängt, sondern aus des Allerhöchsten eigenen Dienern, aus den Engeln." Kittel, *Religion als Geschichtsmacht*, 37–8.

not speaking with the forked tongues of the learned but with the voice of the *Volk*.[45] "Past generations bear a very heavy guilt, which has avenged itself bitterly on them, for styling Luther and the Reformation movement so that it was bearable for the mental capacity and the moral prudery of the educated burgher. Even in the purely scholarly literature there are few works which portray Luther and his movement as it really was."[46] These sensitivities prevented a true understanding of Luther, who was part of a "joyously barbaric" century.[47] He closes out his indictment of the scholarly interpreters of Luther by noting, "and isn't it the case that Luther's writings on the Jewish question were practically suppressed because they named the thing by name all too indelicately?"[48] He notes that this understanding of Luther is dangerous, and that may explain why Luther himself put such emphasis on the Bible as the source of understanding, wishing to have some sort of anchor in the stormy seas that came with the encounter with the dynamic God of history.[49] Kittel suggests that Luther would advocate the full empowerment of the current regime, and endorse even those areas where it seems to shock traditional sensibilities, or take measures that destroy the world of the past in order to achieve the divinely ordained world of the future, which is very much how the actions of the regime were justified within the ideology of the party.

An only slightly different way of looking at this is provided by Rudolf Thiel (1899–1981), a popular author of the era who became enamored of Luther and wrote a well-received two volume biography of the Reformer; he presented Luther's theory of the unbridled *Führer* in even starker terms in an article he published in 1935.[50] Having demonstrated that Luther intended the power of the state to prevail over all aspects of society, he adds:

> It self-evident that [Luther] never gave the slightest consideration to democratic or parliamentary forms of rule. "If a land only had one splendidly gifted man, then all advice and laws would move along much better. But where there is no such man, then everything gets bogged down, even if there are many who advise and rule." That is a *Führer*-principle (*Führerprinzip*), clearly stated. And to believe

---

[45] "...sie [spielte] sich nicht ausschließlich in Studierstuben, Disputationssälen und auf Kathedern, auch nicht auf Reichstagen abspielte, sondern ebenso in Kirchen und auf Märkten, in Bürger- und Bauernhäusern. Deshalb hat in ihr auch nicht bloß ein theologisch wissenschaftliches Bemühen gewaltet, sondern sie wird von Volksleidenschaften getragen. Und nicht bloß die spitze Zunge der Gelehrten redet, sondern der Mund des Volkes." Kittel, *Religion als Geschichtsmacht*, 38.

[46] "Es ist eine ganz schwere Schuld vergangener Generationem, die sich an ihnen selbst bitter gerächt hat, Luther und die reformatorische Bewegung so stilisiert zu haben, daß sie dem seelischen Fassungsvermögen und der moralischen Prüderie des gebildeten Bürgertums gerade noch erträglich war. Es gibt sogar in der rein wissenschaftlichen Literatur nur wenige Werke, die Luther und seine Bewegung so gefährlich zeigen, wie sie war." Kittel, *Religion als Geschichtsmacht*, 38.

[47] "...diesem so erfreulich barbarischen Jahrhundert." Kittel, *Religion als Geschichtsmacht*, 38.

[48] "Und ist es nicht wirklich so, daß Luthers Schriften zur Judenfrage praktisch unterschlagen wurden, weil sie allzu unfein die Dinge beim Namen nannten?" Kittel, *Religion als Geschichtsmacht*, 38.

[49] Kittel, *Religion als Geschichtsmacht*, 39.

[50] Rudolf Thiel, "Staat und Kirche bei Luther." *Glaube und Volk in der Entscheidung* 4 (1935): 161–77.

that with this splendidly gifted man Luther had only a hereditary ruler in mind would be a gross error. When Luther speaks about the *Führer* of the nation, he names them with truly special names. He speaks of created, not self-made men, of God's miracle people (*Wunderleuten*), of the healthy heroes.[51]

Having established that Luther was the advocate of this *Führerprinzip*, he goes forward to describe the sort of obedience that would be owed by all to this *Führer*, whom providence would have ordained to rule, noting that the understanding among Christians of the true authority of the ruler makes them some of the most loyal and duty-conscious among the *Volksgenossen*.[52] He summarizes at the end as follows:

> With this we've arrived at our departure point, Martin Luther's deep and unshakable respect for the *Führer* of his *Volk*. When the *Führer* only wants to be the loyal servant of God, then the Reformers reverent heart knows no longer any distinction between his worldly and his spiritual duties and rights. Then he praises him with unqualified, overflowing enthusiasm.[53]

Thiel is a bit more careful in noting the signs that legitimate one's status as the *Wundermann*, but the description he provides clearly is keyed to the public presentation of Hitler and his accomplishments. As he notes in closing his piece, for Luther everything comes down to the personality and his qualities, and if those are present, he would throw himself into the struggle.[54] Luther's concept of the *Wundermann* repeatedly provided the theoretical foundation for affirmation of

---

[51] "Es versteht sich ganz von selbst, daß er niemals etwas wissen will von demokratischen und parlamentarischen Regierungsformen. 'Wenn ein Land nur einen trefflichen geschickten Mann hätte, so gingen alle Ratschläge und Gesetze besser fort. Wo aber keiner ist, da gehet alles hinter sich, ob ihrer wohl viele sind., die da raten und regieren.' Das ist ein ausgesprochenes Führerprinzip. Und wenn man meint, daß Luther bei dem trefflichen geschickten Mann nur an den angestammten Herrscher gedacht habe, irrt man sich gewaltig. Wenn Luther von den Führern der Nation spricht, nennt er sie mit ganz besonderen Namen. Er spricht von geschaffenen, nicht gemachten Herren, von Gottes Wunderleuten, von gesunden Helden." Thiel, "Staat und Kirche bei Luther," 162–3.
[52] Thiel, "Staat und Kirche bei Luther," 166–71.
[53] "Damit sind wir bei unserem Ausgangspunkte angelangt, bei Martin Luthers tiefer und unzerstörbarer Achtung vor dem Führer seines Volkes. Wenn dieser Führer nur der treue Diener Gottes sein will, dann kennt des Reformators ehrfürchtiges Herz keinen Unterschied mehr zwischen seinen weltlichen und seinen geistlichen Verpflichtungen und Rechten. Dann preist er ihn mit einer rückhaltlosen, überströmenden Begeisterung." Thiel, "Staat und Kirche bei Luther," 177.
[54] "Und es gehört zu Luthers Größe, daß man sich nicht auf irgendeine seiner Außerungen stützen kann, um ein genehmes und bequemes Leitmotiv zu finden für die eigene Auffassung von Tagesfrage, oder gar, um sich selbst vor der persönlichen Entscheidung zu drücken. Luther stellt seine Christen, seine Kirche in den Kampf. Er gibt dem Staat das Seine und gibt Gott das Seine—alles übrige stellt er auf die Persönlichkeit" (And it is part of Luther's greatness, that one can't rely on any one statement of his in order to to find a convenient or comfortable argument concerning the questions of the day or even to avoid making one's own personal decision. Luther puts his Christians, his church, into the struggle. He gives the state what is the state's, and God what is God's—all the rest he bases on personality); Thiel, "Staat und Kirche bei Luther," 177.

Hitler's calling, and grounded an understanding of rule that advocated the obedient coordination of the *Volk* under the authority of this providentially called leader.[55]

One additional prominent vehicle for projecting this symbiotic image of Luther and Hitler are the numerous novelistic and dramatic representations in the years following the seizure of power of Luther's "heroic" acts. Some of these are written for a youthful audience, and tell the story of Luther while noting how it epitomizes the fashion in which God works in time through heroic leaders. Hermann Simon, school inspector in Erfurt, published in 1933 a work, *Luther der Deutsche Mann*, which exemplifies the application of the *Führerprinzip* to the sixteenth century. He starts with the "unrest in Germany," noting:

"The tremendous upheaval of the times" first presents itself clearly to later generations in hindsight. For this reason historians designate Luther's Reformation as the beginning of a new age of history. But the feeling of living in a time of change was widespread even at the beginning of the sixteenth century, just as it lives today among us. Such times of upheaval have their distinctive mark in unrest, the violent ferment in people's sensibilities, and in the general desire for change in the prevailing circumstances. New spirits rise up and threaten the old status quo. Until the leader (*Führer*) appears, the carrier of a great idea, that allows the old to be toppled and a better world to be built, until he plants his banner, gathers together the diverging spirits and leads them in magnificent struggle to victory.[56]

---

[55] Other works that echo the formula put forward by Kittel and Thiel include Ernst Kohlmeyer, *Gustav Adolf und die Staatsanschauung des Altluthertums* (Halle (Saale): Max Niemeyer Verlag, 1933), which was originally delivered as an address for the Luther celebration; see esp. 7–11; and Otto Rießmüller, *Martin Luther Ruf an die Deutsche Nation* (Berlin-Dahlem: Burckhardthaus-Verlag, 1933), first delivered as part of a series of sermons in the Fall of 1933; see esp. 19–20, 34–7. Paul Althaus published in 1935 a reply to the Thuringian DC, *Politisches Christentum. Ein Wort über die Thüringer "Deutschen Christen"* (Leipzig: A. Deichertsche Verlagsbuchhandlung, 1935), in which he sought to emphasize that Luther's theory of the *Wundermann* did not equate the work of such a ruler with the salvation of the soul that came through Christ: "'Von Gott getrieben' werden, wie Luther es an der angeführten Stelle von den Wunderrmännern aussagt, und von seinem heiligen Geiste bewegt werden, ist im Sinne Luthers zweierlei" ("to be driven by God," as Luther expresses it in the passage referenced about the *Wundermänner*, and to be moved by his Holy Spirit, are in Luther's sense two different things); 11. But, despite this distinction, he affirms the theory itself for understanding the nature of political leadership in this time of national renewal, as he would have it. One thing that is little seen in the literature affirming Hitler's status as fulfilling Luther's ideal of the *Wundermann* is any sense of qualification over time. One finds these claims being articulated in the late 1930s, during a time when all the churches in Germany were being put under increasing pressure, and the public violence against Jews in Germany was being exercised ever more overtly, such that these measures could be also viewed as the obedience to the unwritten law of the God of history.

[56] "Die Unruhe in Deutschland." "'Der Zeiten ungeheurer Bruch' stellt sich erst den späteren Geschlechtern rückschauend klar vor Augen. Darum hat die Geschichtsschreibung mit der Reformation Luthers den Beginn eines neuen Zeitalters der Geschichte angesetzt. Aber das Gefühl, in einer Zeitenwende zu stehen, war doch schon damals, zu Beginn des 16 Jahrhunderts, weit verbreitet, wie es ähnlich heute in uns lebt. Solche Zeiten des Umbruchs haben ihre Kennzeichen in der Unruhe, der heftigen Gärung in den Gemütern und in dem allgemeinen Verlangen nach Änderung der

148   THE LUTHER MYTH

Having established the general landscape of change, which signals the comparison of Luther's time with the current time of upheaval, he moves to describe the events surrounding the crisis of the sixteenth century, the emergence then of a *Führer*: "And who will break the path for this movement? That was the fateful question for the German *Volk*. It had to be a man whom the nation trusts and whom they joyously recognized as *Führer*."[57] Of course it had to be Luther, who drew his power from the unlikely source of the Bible. Nevertheless he was a great leader:

> So he became the ***Führer* of his nation.** Not from the authority of a Prince or of a majority of the *Volk*, but out of his own authority, no, more accurately from the authority and through the calling of the Most-High. For that is the mystery of true leadership (*Führerschaft*), that a person feels themselves pressed and forced by God and knows that he serves God when he is shaking up the whole world. It didn't take long for Luther to step forward before the world as the *Führer* of the nation. It occurred in the year 1520 in three powerful works that overshadowed all their predecessors.[58]

And Luther did what he did for the *Volk*, for the salvation both of their souls but also to wake up the nation and to move it forward. Luther does this with heroic self-sacrifice and as someone following the promptings of God.[59] Simon's representation lays down the basic script that is played out in a number of dramatic works that were published and staged in the period after 1933.

One such work was Kurt Eggers'[60] *Revolution um Luther. Ein Spiel* published in 1935. The play was a musical, and in it Eggers highlights the dramatic national setting within which Luther emerges through the song of a balladeer:

---

bestehenden Verhältnisse. Neue Geister drängen empor und bedrohen das Alte in seinem Bestand. Bis endlich der Führer erscheint, der Träger einer großen Idee, die das Alte zu stürzen und eine bessere Welt aufzubauen vermag, bis er sein Panier aufpflanzt, die auseinanderstrebenden Geister sammelt und in herrlichem Kampfe zum Siege führt." Hermann Simon, *Luther der Deutsche Mann* (Halle: Pädagogischer Verlag von Hermann Schroedel, 1933): 35.

[57] "Wer sollte dieser Bewegug die Bahn brechen? Das war die Schicksalsfrage des deutschen Volkes. Es mußte ein Mann sein der die Nation vertraute und den sie freudig als Führer anerkannt." Simon, *Luther der Deutsche Mann*, 36.

[58] "So wurde er der Führer seiner Nation. Nicht aus der Vollmacht eines Fürsten oder einer Volksmehrheit, sondern aus eigener Vollmacht, nein vielmehr aus Vollmacht und durch Berufung des Höchsten. Denn das ist das Geheimnis wahrer Führerschaft, daß ein Mensch sich gedrungen und gezwungen fühlt durch Gott und weiß, daß er Gott dient, wenn er die Welt aus den Angeln hebt.

Es währte nicht lange, da trat Luther als der Führer der Nation vor die Welt. Es geschah in drei gewaltigen Schriften, die alle bisherigen übertrafen, im Jahre 1520." Simon, *Luther der Deutsche Mann*, 36-7.

[59] Simon, *Luther der Deutsche Mann*, 38-47.

[60] Kurt Eggers, *Revolution um Luther. Ein Spiel* (Munich: Chr. Kaiser, 1935). Kurt Eggers (1905-43) had a long history of activity in extreme right-wing circles prior to the advent of the Third Reich. Though active in paramilitary organizations early on, he later gained a theological degree, and served as a pastor for a short time. Eventually he turned toward literary activity, in which role he produced during the Nazi era numerous works that were well received by the regime. His great historical hero

I know a land/like no other/a land between mountains and the sea. / But this land / is bewitched, / bewitched with foreign teachings. / The peasants sow / the seeds in the earth / and plow and labor day in and day out. / But the one who takes away the fruit / must always be a foreigner.[61]

He sings further of the soldiers who sharpen their swords, only to spill the blood of their friends, and everyone, the soldiers, the peasants and the women are all bewitched:

Yet someday / the hour shall be, / When to Germany, too, the man will come / that will be a day of sunshine, / when the man comes to Germany.
THE MERCENARY: when?
THE PEASANT: And the sun will shine.
SOME GUESTS: A man will come from among the *Volk* and go into the *Volk* and lead the *Volk*.
A VISIONARY: There will come a time of a prophet. As God dealt with the Israelites in the old covenant through prophets, so he will deal with Germany through a prophet whom he will awaken.[62]

We now switch to a scene with scholars speaking about Luther:

One scholar: remarkable how Dr. Luther reads his lectures. // Second scholar: He continually loses himself. When he speaks about creation, he ends up on Germany, when he reads from the Psalmist, he ends up on Germany. // Third scholar: And then his eyes begin to glow. Fourth scholar: Some even say that he is possessed. // First scholar: Just think about all the great ones of the Bible and history. They were all possessed in one way or another. If someone isn't possessed, they can't prevail in battle." Finally a speaker closes this passage by saying "Heretics—they were all heretics who were anything at all.[63]

---

was Ulrich von Hutten, whom he portrayed in his novel *Hutten. Roman eines Deutschen* (Berlin: Propyläen, 1934) in the colors of a National Socialist knight fighting to free Germany from its foreign oppressors, clearly paralleling Hutten's career with the actions of the SS. See Jay W. Baird, *Hitler's War Poets: Literature and Politics in the Third Reich* (Cambridge: Cambridge University Press, 2008): 208–53; on his Hutten novel, see 229–32.

[61] "Der Bänkelsänger: Nun gut, so gebt Acht: Ich weiß ein Land, / Das wie keines ist, / Ein land zwischen Bergen und Meeren. / Doch dieses Land / Verzaubert ist, / Verzaubert von fremden Lehren. / Der Bauer sät / Die Saat in die Erd / und pflügt und ackert tagaus, tagein. / Doch wer die Frucht/ Von dannen führt,— / Das muß ein Fremder stets sein." Eggers, *Revolution um Luther*, 27.

[62] "Doch einmal soll / Dann die Stunde sein, / Da auch Deutschland wird kommen der Mann. / Das wird ein Tag der Sonne sein, / Wenn Deutschland wird kommen der Mann. / Der Landsknecht: Wann? // Der Bauer: Und die Sonne wird scheinen. // Einige Gäste: Ein Mann wird kommen aus dem Volk und er wird ins Volk gehen und das Volk führen. // Ein Verzückter: Es wird kommen die Zeit eines Propheten. Wie Gott schon gehandelt hat an den Israeliten im alten Bunde durch die Propheten, so wird er handeln in Deutschland durch einen Propheten, den er erwecken wird." Eggers, *Revolution um Luther*, 27–8.

[63] "Ein Scholar: Merkwürdig, wie der Dr. Luther jetzt seine Kollegien liest. // 2. Scholar: Er verliert sich immer. Wenn er von der Schöpfung spricht, kommt er auf Deutschland, wenn er aus den Psalmen

This work captures the providential yet rebellious image of Luther that supported the idea of a movement of struggle to throw off the baleful limits of foreign occupation and exploitation; the parallels to Germany's current regime and its struggles against the chains of the Versailles Treaty would have been obvious to an audience.

Another musical theater piece from 1933, Otto Bruder's[64] *Luther der Kämpfer. Ein chorisches Feierspiel* (Luther the fighter: a choral celebration), captures in a different way the leadership profile of Luther. Luther himself is portrayed as a man of passion, prone to angry eruptions against the exploitation of the Church, denouncing indulgences as "the Devil's fruit" (*Teufelsfrucht*). His calling is for Germany and has been sent to fight for Germany, as the chorus highlights: "Blessed be you German land, / God has sent you a man, / a hero of faith, worthy to be a knight, / who with the sharp sword of the spirit / fights the good fight of faith."[65] Eventually his passions and faith lead him to his journey toward Worms, where the messianic comparisons to Hitler are unmistakable: "Narrator: in a victory parade through the German land / there comes a monk, banned by the Pope, / forth he rides in a little cart, / as if he were a Prince or the Emperor! // All the men speak: he is truly an Emperor strong and noble / who would have such power as he? // Narrator: In thousands they push forward cheering! / The hats and caps waving / and climbing up on the steep roofs // All the men and women together saying "Heil Luther / Heil to our Luther!"[66] It would be impossible for any contemporary viewer of this scene not to immediately hear the parallel to the public acclamations of Hitler. And Luther came by his power not as a result of manipulation or playing a political game, but through the integrity of his commitment to the *Volk*. Another play from 1933, Franz Kern, *Der Bergmann Gottes. Ein Lutherspiel* (the miner of God: a Luther drama), presents this vividly. Again, the setting is Worms, and Luther is being urged by Martin Bucer to step back, not confront the Emperor publicly, but play the game of diplomacy:

---

liest, kommt er auf Deutschland. // 3. Scholar: Und dann fangen seine Augen an zu glühen. // 4. Scholar: Manche sagen ja, er sei besessen. // 1. Scholar: Denkt doch nur an alle Großen der Bibel und der Geschichte. Irgendwie besessen waren sie alle. Wenn einer nicht besessen ist, dann kann er sich nicht durchkämpfen. // Ketzer—Ketzer waren alle, die etwas waren." Eggers, *Revolution um Luther*, 46-7.

[64] Otto Bruder (1889–1971), born Otto Salomon, was from a liberal Jewish family, converted in 1911 to Christianity, and wrote under the pseudonym Otto Bruder. He would later in the 1930s flee Germany for Switzerland. He was active as a publisher with the Christian Kaiser Verlag in Munich, publisher, among others, of Karl Barth.

[65] "Der Sprecher: Gesegnet sei, du deutsches Land, / Gott hat dir einen Mann gesandt, / den Glaubensheld, den Ritter wert, / der mit des Geistes scharfem Schwert / den guten Kampf des Glaubens ficht." Otto Bruder, *Luther der Kämpfer. Ein chorisches Feierspiel* (Munich: Chr. Kaiser Verlag, 1933): 7-8.

[66] "Der Sprecher: Im Siegeszug durchs deutsche Land / kommt da ein Mönch, vom Papst gebannt, / in einem Wäglein fährt er her, / als obs ein Fürst oder Kaiser wär! // Alle Männer sprechen: Ist auch ein Kaiser stark und hehr! / Wer hätte solche Macht wie er. / Der Sprecher: Wie tausendfach sich jauchzend drängt! / Die Mützen und die Hüte schwenkt! / Und klettert auf die Dächer steil! // Alle Männer und Frauen sprechen zusammen: Heil, Luther, unserm Luther Heil!" Bruder, *Luther der Kämpfer*, 20.

MARTIN: Behind closed doors? I will speak before all the *Volk*, and God's sun shall see my countenance.

BUCER: Your success will speak for you. The Emperor doesn't want to suppress your teaching, although some of it appears heretical to him.

MARTIN: Will he then allow my works to be burned?

BUCER: That will occur only to deceive the Roman party. The Emperor needs the Pope's help because he's arming himself against France. If you concede you will save the Empire.

MARTIN: And sacrifice the truth. Indeed the craft and power are great that they use to suppress the truth.

BUCER: The Emperor needs also the princes and lords.

MARTIN: Don't rely on princes; the Emperor should call upon the *Volk*. He should be a German king, not a Roman Emperor. Not the Roman crown, not the Spanish purple robe, nor the foreign tongue helps the Emperor; German loyalty alone secures the Empire.[67]

Further down Bucer appeals in a different way:

BUCER: But we stand without a *Führer*. Martin, save your work! I'll tell you straight up who has sent me. The noble knight Franz von Sickingen invites you to come to the Eberburg; there we'll negotiate with your opponents, and his knightly army and weapons will protect you so that not a hair on your head will be mussed.[68]

MARTIN: Give the knight my hearty thanks and tell him his friendship is like a drink from a fresh spring for me and I shake his loyal German hand. But yet I will stand before Emperor and Empire; I owe this to the Germans; I came from the *Volk*, and before the *Volk* I will remain.[69]

---

[67] "Martin: Hinter verschlossenen Türen? Ich will reden vor allem Volk, und Gottes Sonne soll mir ins Antlitz sehen. Butzer: Der Erfolg wird für dich zeugen. Der Kaiser will nicht, daß deine Lehre unterdrückt werde, wiewohl ihm manches ketzerisch erscheint. Martin: Läßt er darum meine Schriften verbrennen? Butzer: Geschieht es doch nur, um die Römlinge zu täuschen. Der Kaiser braucht des Papstes Hilfe; denn er rüstet gegen Frankreich. Gibst du nach, rettest du das Reich.— Martin: —und opfere die Wahrheit. Wie wenden sie doch groß Macht und viel List an, die Wahrheit zu unterdrücken. Butzer: Der Kaiser braucht auch die Fürsten und Herren. Martin: Verlasset euch nicht auf Fürsten; das Volk sollt' der Kaiser aufrufen. Deutscher König sollt' er sein, nicht römischer Kaiser. Nicht die römische Krone, nicht der spanische Purpurmantel, nicht die welsche Zunge hilft dem Kaiser, allein die deutsche Treue sichert das Reich." Franz Kern, *Der Bergmann Gottes. Ein Lutherspiel* (Eisleben: Ernst Schneider, 1933): 39.

[68] Though impossible to capture in English translation, the author is echoing Luther's "Ein Feste Burg" in this line, as he did above where Bucer speaks of the "craft and power" of the Roman church.

[69] "Butzer: Wir aber stehen ohne Führer. Martin, rette dein Werk! Ich will dir's sagen, wer mich schickt: Der edle Ritter Franz von Sickingen ladet dich ein, auf die Ebernburg zu kommen; da wollen wir verhandeln mit den Gegnern, und sein ritterlich Wehr und Waffen wird dich schützen, daß dir kein Härlein gekrümmt wird. Martin: Melde dem Ritter, ich sag ihm herzlich Dank, und seine Freundschaft ist mir wie ein Trunk aus frischem Quell, und ich drück ihm die treue deutsche Hand. Aber dennoch will ich stehen vor Kaiser und Reich; ich bin es den Deutschen schuldig; vom Volke kam ich, vor dem Volke will ich bestehen." Kern, *Der Bergmann Gottes*, 40.

Luther embodies the selflessness, the integrity, the loyalty, and the other authentic Germanic virtues that bespeak his *völkisch* calling. This was just the manner in which Hitler, also, was presented to the German *Volk* in the propaganda of Goebbels, and this passage of the play affirms the lineage of such qualities of leadership.

Another radio drama, Josef Buchhorn,[70] *Wende in Worms. Eine deutsche Freiheitsdichtung* (turning point in Worms: a German poem of freedom), also from 1933, plays heavily on the themes of foreign oppression, and the need for a leader to throw off the oppressive chains. Here the figure of Aleander, the papal *nuncio*, serves as the representative of foreign oppression, combining characteristics of the allied powers and Jewish oppressors, seeking to suppress Luther's national uprising. Here he talks with another cleric:

ALEANDER: ...If the Germans, I say in spite of Luther, want to shake off the yoke of Rome, then we will ensure that they mutually beat themselves to death, and wade in their blood. What's important is that Rome stands and endures.

GLAPION: Amen. And three times, Amen and in addition a blessing. Only—this Luther wants Germany...his Germany, as he says and writes...to live, and he is now the conscience of his land. Nine tenths of the nation and the stones are crying: that man Luther has power....

ALEANDER: Well he isn't going to be allowed to hold it, noble Father. And so once more I'll shout it in all the ears that aren't stopped up, Worms must be his court. Imperial ban, extradition to Rome, and then...then...then he shall see, how certain he is of his savior, this Luther.[71]

It goes on in this vein, and the parallels between Germany in the time of Luther and the time of Hitler are on the surface—he's woken the nation up to its outside oppression, he's stirred their blood, we oppressed them and bear the blame. Aleander is, of course, unrepentant, and insists on forcible suppression, but Glapion doubts it will be possible. Further scenes show Aleander increasingly frantic about the effects of Luther on the German *Volk* and what might come with his appearance before the Emperor:

---

[70] Josef Buchhorn (1875–1954) was a newspaper man who served during the Nazi era in the Kurmark in the office overseeing the press and cultural affairs.

[71] "Aleander:...wenn die Deutschen, sag' ich, trotz der Luther, das römische Joch abschütteln wollten, so werden wir dafür sorgen, daß sie sich gegenseitig totschlagen und in ihrem Blute waten. Wichtig ist, daß Rom besteht und bleibt. Glapion: Amen. Und dreifach: Amen und den Segen dazu. Nur—der Luther will daß Deutschland...sein Deutschland, wie er sagt und schreibt...lebt, und er ist itzt das Gewissen seines Landes. Neun Zehntel der Nation und die Steine schreien: Luther hat Macht der Mann.... Aleander: Darf sie aber nicht behalten, Herr Pater, Darum noch einmal, ich schreie es in alle Ohren, die nicht verstockt sind, muß Worms Gericht sein. Reichsacht, Auslieferung an Rom, und dann...dann...dann soll er sehen, wie er seines Heilands gewiß werde, der Luther." Josef Buchhorn, *Wende in Worms. Eine deutsche Freiheitsdichtung* (Cottbus: Verlag Albert Heine, 1937): 33 (first performed as a radio drama in November 1933).

ALEANDER: Today he is already mightier than you believe.... I'm speaking bluntly now. Tomorrow he'll become *Führer* and awaken a *Volk* united in spirit, who sees its mission only in work, duty, and faith.... Where is Rome in all this? That is the question, the only question.... Germany may not become alive, may not awaken to all its old power, as in the time of Barbarossa. It must remain bound, ruled by foreigners and under the spell of foreigners. Ruled... by Rome...Germany may not have a conscience. But this Luther is its conscience, therefore, away with him and—let him be assassinated!... Rome pardons and God will set Charles V above all Emperors.... For the last time, I swear to you—

[After a couple of interjections, he closes the conversation with the following]

Germany will live in Luther, and he will be Germany's *Führer*, if we don't wither his tongue before tomorrow.[72]

The passage resonates with all the nationalist anger expressed in National Socialist propaganda about the foreign exploitation and the need of Germany and the *Volk* to awaken and seize back their rightful freedom and power, all projected back onto Luther and the drama around Worms. The drama concludes with the classic set-piece before the Emperor and his Diet in Worms, with Luther giving his famous response. A tumultuous scene follows, with the Spanish calling for Luther to be executed, only to be overwhelmed by the shouts of the German crowd:

VOICES: Luther! Luther! Luther!...praise and honor him, Heil him, rich in grace!...Apostle of the Lord!...savior of German Christendom!...Brother Martin!...Luther! Luther! Luther! Heil him, the German man!...who saved the German *Volk*. Heil him! Heil! Heil![73]

They then break into singing "A Mighty Fortress," bringing the drama to a close. Buchhorn more than other dramas frames Luther as an Early Modern German incarnation of Hitler, and, while not completely shorn of his religiosity, he is framed mostly as a *völkisch Führer* who awakens the *Volk* to their oppression by

---

[72] "Aleander: Er ist schon heute mächtiger, als ihr glaubt.... Ich spreche jetzt ohne alle Floskeln. Morgen wird er Führer sein. Ein einig Volk des Geistes wecken, das allein in Arbeit, Pflicht und Glauben seine Sendung sieht.... Wo bleibt da Rom? Das ist die Frage, allein die Frage.... Deutschland darf nicht lebendig werden, nicht zu alter Kraft erwachen, wie zu Barbarossas Zeit. Es muß gebunden bleiben, beherrscht von Fremden und im Bann von Fremden. Beherrscht—von Rom...Deutschland darf kein Gewissen haben. Aber der Luther ist sein Gewissen und darum: weg mit ihm und—laßt ihn meucheln! Rom verzeiht und Gott wird Karl den Fünften über alle Kaiser setzen. Zum letzten Mal beschwör ich euch—" "Deutschland wird in dem Luther leben, und er wird Deutschlands Führer sein, wenn ihm vor morgen nicht die Zunge dorrt!" Buchhorn, *Wende in Worms*, 60–1.
[73] "Stimmen: Luther! Luther! Luther! // Lob ihm und Ehr'! // Heil ihm, dem Gnadenreichen! // Dem Apostel des Herrn! // Erlöser deutscher Christenheit! // Bruder Martinus! // Luther! Luther! Luther! // Heil ihm, dem deutschen Mann! // Der Deutsches Volk errettet! //.... Heil ihm! Heil!!! Heil!!!" Buchhorn, *Wende in Worms*, 67.

foreigners and ignites a rebellion that topples the power of Rome, which clearly stands in for oppressors of the modern day. These dramas come to an end, typically, with Worms, since what comes after doesn't plot as nicely onto the circumstances of 1933 and following; the sixteenth-century version of the Reformation remained incomplete, which allows the scene to shift to 1933 and the taking up the struggle once again.

Perhaps the best place to conclude the dramatic reenactment of Luther *der Führer* is with the words of the bishop of the Protestant church in Brandenburg, Joachim Hossenfelder (1899-1976), in his introduction to yet another dramatic recounting in 1933 of Luther's life by Wilhelm Fronemann:

> Luther is not dead! Luther lives! Luther's spirit, Luther's will, his heroic stance of faith arises again in a movement of belief sent to the German *Volk* by God. We German Christians profess Luther. For us he is the symbol of the German Christian. His faith, his humility, his reverence for God's order of creation, his magnificent irreverence before all pathetic, miserable humanity, his fearless struggle against every adversary of God, in glowing certainty of victory—through faith.... In the enormous upheaval of the times our *Volk* is stirred up to its innermost depths as only in the days of the Reformation.[74]

Hossenfelder's words highlight this sense of the indwelling presence of Luther as an incarnation of the ideal that inspired not a few Germans in their response to the Nazi movement. He embodied as a living symbol what they wanted to see in the new state and its *Führer*, the reenactment of the faith that Luther introduced to the Germans, that God in his providence would bless them with leadership that would bring renewal and the realization of their God-ordained destiny. While none of this had very much to do with the historical Luther—not even the endless references to his ideal of the *Wundermann* captures much that was authentic to Luther's ideational world—it provided a sense of continuity, of lineage, and sacral meaning to the events of the day. For many of those within the church who wrote these works, the expectation was undoubtedly that their enthusiasm for the regime as expressed through comparisons to their greatest hero would prove ingratiating, and create a point of connection. And while it does appear that Hitler did think of himself as fulfilling a providential role of

---

[74] "Luther ist nicht tot! Luther lebt! Luthers Geist, Luthers Wille, seine heldische Glaubenshaltung ersteht wieder in der dem deutschen Volk von Gott geschenkten Glaubensbewegung. Wir deutschen Christen bekennen uns zu Luther. Er ist für uns das Symbol des deutschen Christen. Sein Glaube, seine Demut, seine Ehrfurcht vor Gottes Schöpferordnung, seine prachtvolle Respektosligkeit vor allem kläglichen, erbärmlichen Menschentum, sein unerschrockenes Kämpfen wider jede Gottwidrigkeit, in strahlender Siegesgewißheit—aus dem Glauben.... In dem ungeheuren Umbruch der Zeit ist unser Volk aufgewühlt bis ins Innerste wie nur in den Tagen der Reformation." Wilhelm Fronemann, *Der deutsche Luther. Mit einem Vorwart von Joachim Hossenfelder, Bischof von Brandenburg* (Leipzig: Franz Schneider Verlag, 1933): introductory page.

greatness like that of Luther, such comparisons as we see in this literature can only have been obnoxious to his, and the regime's, desire to have him singular in his distinctive world historical achievements, and not sharing the stage with some religious icon. There is no evidence that all these attempts to affirm Hitler through Luther had any resonance with Hitler, or improved the Protestant church's fortunes in relation to the regime. This element of Luther's image simply wasn't attuned to the ideological realities of National Socialism, though the various dramatic representations suggest how widely disseminated this image of Luther was. However, whereas Luther's "heroic" actions may not have proved useful to the regime, there was another aspect of Luther that would hold promise to have more resonance and utility within the regime, namely Luther's own antipathy for the Jews.

The Luther Myth: The Image of Martin Luther from Religious Reformer to Völkisch *Icon.* Patrick Hayden-Roy, Oxford University Press. © Patrick Hayden-Roy 2024. DOI: 10.1093/9780198930297.003.0007

7
Luther the Anti-Semite (?)

Given the legacy of the Nazi era, today perhaps the most distressing element of Luther's enormous corpus of works is his writings about the Jews. This is reflected in the focus they have received in the last fifty years or so, part of the larger attempt to come to terms with the legacy of Christian and racial anti-Semitism. Beginning in the 1970s, and gaining momentum since the celebration of four-hundredth anniversary of Luther's birth in 1983, the vile anti-Jewish writings of his later years have drawn intense scholarly as well as general interest. This includes studies that look at those works both in their own context, as well as consider the reception and influence of those works, especially during the Wilhelmine era through to the 1930s and '40s.[1] The two works that provided the most material for the anti-Semitic movement that emerged in the 1870s and expanded its influence, especially after World War I, culminating in the policies of National Socialism, were *On the Jews and their Lies* and *On the Unknowable Name of God and the Generations of Christ*, both from 1543.[2] These works, along with other excerpts drawn from Luther's letters and Table Talk, provided a ready-made body of material with which to justify, based on the authority of the most German of all Germans, religious prejudice against the Jews, often adeptly translated into the new language of modern racial anti-Semitism. So it would seem as if the image of Luther as the

---

[1] A few of the more prominent titles: Johannes Brosseder, *Luthers Stellung zu den Juden im Spiegel seiner Interpreten* (Munich: Hueber, 1972); C. Bernd Sucher, *Luthers Stellung zu den Juden: ein Interpretation aus germanistischer Sicht* (Nieuwkoop: B. de Graaf, 1977); Heinz Kremers, ed., *Die Juden und Martin Luther: Martin Luther und die Juden: Geschichte, Wirkungsgeschichte, Herausforderung* (Neukirchen-Vluyn: Neukirchener Verlag, 1985); Peter von der Osten-Sacken, *Martin Luther und die Juden: neu untersucht anhand von Anton Margarithas "Der gantz Jüdisch glaub" (1530/31)* (Stuttgart: Kohlhammer, 2002); Thomas Kaufmann, *Luthers "Judenschriften"* (Tübingen: Mohr Siebeck, 2011); Johannes Wallmann, *Martin Luthers Juden Schriften*. 2nd ed. (Bielefeld: Luther Verlag, 2019). In addition, the full texts of the main works of Luther dealing with the Jews have been republished in new editions in order to make them more accessible. One three-volume edition puts the original texts next to modern German translations and provides a glossary of terms; Karl-Heinz Büchner et al., Vol. 1: *Martin Luther: Von den Juden und ihren Lügen* (Aschaffenburg: Alibri Press, 2016); Vol. 2: *Martin Luther: Judenfeindliche Schriften* (2017); Vol. 3: *Martin Luther: Judenfeindliche Schriften* (2018). Another three-volume set provides a full commentary: Vol. 1: Matthias Morgenstern, ed., *Martin Luther: Dass Jesus Christus ein geborener Jude sei und andere Judenschriften* (Berlin: Berlin University Press, 2019); Vol. 2: Matthias Morgenstern, ed., *Martin Luther: Von den Juden und ihren Lügen* (Berlin: Berlin University Press, 2016); Vol. 3: Matthias Morgenstern, ed., *Martin Luther und die Kabbala: Vom Schem Hamephorasch und vom Geschlecht Christi* (Berlin: Berlin University Press, 2019); this edition has a vol. 4; Dietz Bering, *War Luther Antisemit?: Das deutsch-jüdische Verhältnis als Tragödie der Nähe* (Berlin: Berlin University Press, 2015).

[2] *Von den Juden und ihren Lügen* and *Vom Schem Hamphoras und vom Geschlecht Christi*. See WA 53, 412–552, 573–648.

anti-Semite par excellence would comfortably fit with his other putative virtues and attributes as conceived in this era. And while certainly the image of him as the first and greatest of all enemies of the Jews was widely projected, what is more revealing was the difficulty in portraying this consistently, the complications that were attendant to such efforts, and the seemingly limited resonance that this image evoked. Posing Luther as an anti-Semite meant dealing with him historically in ways that weren't required with other aspects of his image, which were more imaginative constructions that didn't really rely on authentic features of his historical self. In addition, this image actually connected directly with a major priority of the party, a priority that impacted the church's own practice of faith, and reflected the deep divisions in the Protestant church. In the end, the anti-Semitic Luther lacked the broad appeal of other versions of his image, but also played a significant role in legitimizing measures against the Jews, and muting resistance by the church to the implementation of these measures. In that sense, this image, while not broadly consumed, had a more direct impact than any other.

As it relates to Luther's image in the Nazi era, initial interest in Luther's anti-Jewish writings, and his status as a possible witness against the Jews, developed first in the context of anti-Semitic movements of the Wilhelmine era. To begin, this came about slowly, since the writings themselves were not widely disseminated. It is striking that Heinrich von Treitschke in his famous Luther address of 1883 did not bring forward Luther's hard words against the Jews, despite the fact that in the previous few years he had been embroiled in the so-called "anti-Semitic dispute" that was generated from his article in the *Preußische Jahrbücher*, where he famously concluded that the Jews were Germany's misfortune.[3] And it was in this context that Adolf Stoecker, prominent court preacher of the Wilhelmine period, emerged as an influential voice within Protestantism, deploying anti-Jewish rhetoric as part of his Christian Socialist movement, though also with no recourse to Luther's writings.[4]

The development of greater public profile for Luther's anti-Jewish writings begins in the early 1880s with the publication of an anonymous work, *Dr. Martin*

---

[3] "Die Juden sind unser Unglück." Heinrich von Treitschke, "Unsere Aussichten." *Preußiche Jahrbücher* 44 (1879): 559–76; 575. See Andreas Stegmann, "Der Berliner Antisemitismusstreit 1879/80." In *Protestantismus, Antijudaismus, Antisemitismus*, ed. Dorothea Wendebourg et al. (Tübingen: Mohr Siebeck, 2017): 239–74. Stegmann points out that there is no evidence that Treitschke was familiar with Luther's anti-Jewish writings, and he does not ever resort to citing them in the course of the dispute, which would suggest that these writings, while certainly not unknown at that time, were not a focal point of his image in the period around 1880. It is suggestive of the seminal nature of the anti-Semitic controversy of the late 1870s that Julius Streicher would use Treitschke's statement "Die Juden sind unser Unglück" as the motto for his virulently anti-Semitic weekly *Der Stürmer*.

[4] See Martin Ohst, "Antisemitismus als Waffe im weltanschaulichen und politischen Kampf: Adolf Stoecker und Reinhold Seeberg." In *Protestantismus, Antijudaismus, Antisemitismus*, ed. Dorothea Wendebourg et al. (Tübingen: Mohr Siebeck, 2017): 275–308; 289. Ohst surmises that Stoecker must have been aware of Luther's writings, given some publicity about them in the aftermath of the Neustettin synagogue fire in 1880, which brought Luther's writings into the public debate about the causes of the event.

Luther und das Judenthum, attributed to one "Islebiensis."[5] This work first broaches many themes that will become part of the stock images of the anti-Semitic version of the reformer. For one, Islebiensis decries the unwillingness of the church to recognize the destructive influence of the Jews, calling upon Luther's Christian example: "Just how nonsensical this is will be demonstrated with the following selections from Luther's works." Luther, he touts, was the best and truest anti-Semite for which one could hope; those philo-Semites should recognize that this isn't just some stirring of the pot, but a matter of right and wrong.[6] He references the two Luther works of 1543 that call for synagogues and Jewish writings to be burned and the Jews to be expelled, criticizing other contemporary anti-Jewish voices, such as Adolf Stoecker's, whom the author accuses of holding onto the fantasy that the problem can be solved by conversion, against which he poses Luther's radical solution.[7] Using what will be a common motif of Luther literature, Islebiensis imagines Luther returning in the 1880s and seeing the power that the Jews have gathered to themselves: "how would it be if the right honorable German man who wrote our victorious Reformation battle cry 'A Mighty Fortress' and was first to take the field against the Jews, lived today and saw our beloved German fatherland in the claws of these 'damned Jews'!"[8] The answer is obvious to the author; he would thunder against all those places in German society where the Jews have grabbed power—the courts, newspapers, and all those who have given to the Jews their rights. "O wise Luther, righteous judge! You write as if you already knew back then our Jewish newspaper writers."[9] He quotes at length from Luther's call to the rulers to expel the Jews, burn their places of worship, or force them to do hard physical labor, emphasizing that Luther called for the expulsion of the Jews.[10] This leads him to conclude the work with the following incitement to action:

> "Out with them!" should be our call that we direct to all true Germans. Wake up, German *Volk*!—see how the Jews insult, cheat and suck you dry; grab your weapons worker and farmer, you who earn your money by the sweat of

---

[5] Jslebiensis, *Dr. Martin Luther und das Judenthum* (Berlin: Im Commissions-Verlag von Oscar Lorentz, [1882]).

[6] "Wie unsinnig das ist, sollen eben die folgenden Zeilen aus Luthers Werken beweisen." Jslebiensis, *Dr. Martin Luther*, 3.

[7] Jslebiensis, *Dr. Martin Luther*, 7.

[8] "Wie würde der ehrenfeste, deutsche Mann, der unser siegreiches, reformatorisches Schlachtlied 'Eine feste Burg' gedichtet, erst gegen das Judenthum zu Felde ziehen, wenn er heute lebte und unser liebes, deutsches Vaterland in den Klauen dieser 'verdampten Jüden' sähe!" Jslebiensis, *Dr. Martin Luther*, 10.

[9] "O weiser Luther, gerechter richter! Du sprichst, als ob Du damals schon unsere jüdischen Zeitdungschreiber—wollte sagen Zeitungsschreiber—gekannt hättest!" Jslebiensis, *Dr. Martin Luther*, 13. There's a word play that one can't capture in translation where the author imitates 16th-century orthography for the word "Zeitung," while at the same including within it the word for excrement—*Dung*. This sort of sneering approach is typical of the genre.

[10] Jslebiensis, *Dr. Martin Luther*, 15–16.

your brow in order to have it robbed by the Jews; grasp your weapons, true Christian, so that you protect your God from the attacks of the Jews; grasp your weapons German youth, let not your highest good, your honor, be maligned with impunity.[11]

There are a number of exemplary features to this first draft of the anti-Semitic Luther. For one, just as Luther was being remodeled in the late nineteenth century as a *völkisch* nationalist, which left aside what was distinctly Christian and religious in his message, effectively ignoring the most prominent features of his historical identity, so Islebiensis has remade Luther as a material anti-Semite who decries the Jews for the power they have claimed in the new Germany, exploiting the people. Of course, Luther did channel the traditional image of the Jews as supposed exploiters of Christians, so the author of this tract had good material with which to work, but by carefully excerpting Luther's writings[12] he could ignore the larger theological matrix within which Luther was working. And his hostile comments about religious anti-Semites such as Stoecker indicate that he is conscious of the difference between a perspective that vilifies the Jews based on religious ideology and one that is grounded, as is the case here, in a racial ideology.[13] He anticipates later authors by finding in Luther's skepticism about the possibility of Jewish conversion evidence that Luther understood the issue in the same way as modern racial anti-Semites.[14] Despite his emphatic affirmation of Luther as a racial anti-Semite, the issue of making Luther's anti-Jewish mentality fit with modern racialist concepts will remain a challenge, in this case solved by simply excerpting the "good" parts, and ignoring the great majority of his theological arguments.

---

[11] "'Hinaus mit ihnen!' soll auch unser Ruf sein, den wir an alle echten Deutschen richten. Wache auf, deutsches Volk!—siehe wie Dich die Juden lästern, betrügen und aussaugen, greift zur Wehre Arbeiter und Bauersmann, die ihr im Schweiße eures Angesichts euer Geld verdient, um es dann von Juden rauben zu lassen; greife zur Wehre, treuer Christ, damit Du Deinen Gott vor den Lästerungen der Juden schützest; greife zur Wehre, deutsche Jugend, laß Dir Dein höchstes Gut, Deine Ehre, nicht ungestraft schmähen." Jslebiensis, *Dr. Martin Luther*, 16.

[12] This type of excerpting was a primary avenue through which Luther's anti-Jewish works were made accessible and his image styled in the era from 1880 to 1940. See Thomas Kaufmann, "Antisemitische-Lutherflorilegien." In *Aneignungen Luthers und der Reformation: Wissenschaftsgeschichtliche Beiträge zum 19.-21. Jahrhundert* (Tübingen: Mohr Siebeck, 2022): 3–36, esp. 18–26.

[13] On the issue of specifically Christian anti-Semitism versus racial anti-Semitism, see the article by Johannes Wallmann, "Luthertum und Zionismus in der Zeit der Weimarer Republik." In *Protestantismus, Antijudaismus, Antisemitismus*, ed. Dorothea Wendebourg et al. (Tübingen: Mohr Siebeck, 2017): 377–406, esp. 399–406.

[14] "Trefflich und wohl zu beachten ist hierbei besonders seine Meinung von der 'Unbekehrbarkeit der Juden'; denn damit hat er vor über 300 Jahren schon dasselbe ausgesprochen, was Henrici wieder zuerst hervorhob und an was besonders die humanitätsdusseligen Herrn Fortschrittler immer noch nicht glauben wollen—'die Race ist Alles; die Judenfrage ist Racenfrage!'" (Striking and indeed noteworthy is especially his view on the 'inconvertibility of the Jews'; for with this he expressed three hundred years ago the same thing that Henrici first raised up again, and which in particular the idiotic humanistic Mr. Progressives don't ever want to admit—'Race is everything; the Jewish question is a race question!'). Jslebiensis, *Dr. Martin Luther*, 6.

Islebiensis' work anticipated another work of the 1880s, Theodor Fritsch's (1852–1933) *Anti-Semiten-Kathechismus*, which would also excerpt from Luther for the sake of gaining his imprimatur for modern anti-Semitic advocacy.[15] This handbook for anti-Semites contained a variety of materials; the first half was made up predominately of excerpts of writings mostly from famous authors that had something negative to say about the Jews, which is where Luther was drawn in. The rest of the work contained statistical information about the Jews in various facets of public life, as well as discussions of their presence in professions. At six hundred plus pages in its later editions it contained a wealth of fodder, and was consumed widely among radical racist circles in the 1920s, including Hitler.[16] Fritsch seems to have cooled in his enthusiasm for Luther across the many editions, as the amount of space devoted to him was somewhat reduced after the twenty-third edition.[17] Nevertheless, given the many editions and the volume of sales, Fritsch was a major source for the anti-Semitic Luther, and reflects some of the issues related to using Luther to promote a modern anti-Semitic agenda. In the 1919 edition, Fritsch begins by proclaiming his support for religious tolerance of a modern variety; "We are consequently extremely tolerant in issues of faith—as long as a teaching doesn't endanger the common good."[18] Of course it is the latter issue that he will proceed to explore in relation to the Jews.

The fundamental issue with the Jews is that they are a race, not a faith, so in that sense the ideal of religious tolerance does not apply to them. He speaks, he reassures his readers, with a "scientific" voice, and will simply present the evidence that there are different racial types, and they differ from one another fundamentally, having not just their own outward form, but differences that

[15] The work was first published in 1887 under the pseudonym Thomas Frey as the *Antisemiten-Katechismus: Eine Zusammenstellung des wichtigsten Materials zum Verständniß der Judenfrage* (Leipzig: Verlag von Theod. Fritsch, 1887), later under the author's real name, Theodor Fritsch. It went through 49 editions, the last published in 1944. After 1907 it was titled *Handbuch der Judenfrage* (handbook of the Jewish question). The author reedited it a number of times, making adjustments to the material to suit the contemporary context. The first edition began with an introduction explaining the pressing need for a work that provided all the necessary materials for propaganda against the Jews, and the promise to expand upon the current work over time. This edition had about 200 pages of material, configured somewhat differently than later editions, but with much the same emphasis on the need to oppose the Jews based on their racial disposition, and not their religion, and using quotes from eminent past authors to highlight the nefarious character of the Jews. In the first edition there were about three pages of quotes from Luther, with no additional commentary, but set off in a separate section. Later editions were constantly expanding, so that the later edition of 1940 was about three times as long as the original publication. On Fritsch, see Massimo Ferrari Zumbini, *Die Wurzeln des Bösen. Gründerjahre des Antisemitismus: Von der Bismarckzeit zu Hitler* (Frankfurt a.M.: Vittorio Klostermann, 2003): esp. 321–422, 449–62, and 605–34. Zumbini emphasizes the broad impact of Fritsch's literary and political activity over many decades in expanding the reach of anti-Semitism.
[16] Kaufmann, "Antisemitische-Lutherflorilegien," 22.
[17] Dorothea Wendebourg, "Die Bekanntheit von Luthers Judenschriften im 19. Und frühen 20. Jahrhunderts." In *Protestantismus, Antijudaismus, Antisemitismus*, ed. Dorothea Wendebourg et al. (Tübingen: Mohr Siebeck, 2017): 147–80; 172.
[18] "Wir sind darum äußerst duldsam in Glaubensdingen—solange eine Lehre nicht das Gesamtwohl gefährdet." Theodor Fritsch, *Handbuch der Judenfrage*. 28th ed. (Hamburg: Sleipner-Verlag, 1919): 6. This formulation actually tracks what was highlighted in party platform of the Nazis.

express themselves inwardly in "temperament, sensibilities, intellectual and moral disposition."[19] He emphasizes that these characteristics are hardwired and persistent, based as they are on "hereditary, inborn powers, which are not to be permanently erased through any external influence, and which are carried over from generation to generation, often reemerging after centuries once again unchanged."[20] But, he assures the reader, it is not based on a lack of brotherly love that he makes these comments; in fact "aside from the Germans there is not a *Volk* in the world who has taken the idea of fraternity seriously; all others are filled with ruthless national selfishness and are proud to label it *sacro egoism* (holy selfishness)."[21] But races can only flourish if they are true to their fundamental essence, and that means separation so as not to be morally degraded by the influence of a foreign type: "morality is basically a product of racial experience; it lays fast the foundation through which the flourishing of the racial type is conditioned."[22] Having established this principle, it follows that the Germans have abandoned proper racial conditioning by allowing the Jews in their midst, with predictable results: "they [the Germans] have betrayed their concepts of honor and virtue, of justice and duty, of decency and morals, and now endeavor to measure all matters of life only by the standard of the Hebrews."[23] The great ones of the past, among whom is Luther, warned about this, but their warnings have been suppressed, so the *Volk* don't know about them. The emancipation of the Jews was a fundamental error that has corrupted the Germans; it is all well and good to talk about the brotherhood of men, but this should mean "protecting the human community from the common enemy; it must not however lead to betraying the higher spiritual and moral criteria to please a special type, and invert the natural rank-ordering of the human race."[24] He goes on to describe the dire consequences that have arisen for the Germans by allowing the Jews to flourish among them, such that he wonders whether the German *Volk* will ever truly recover from the destructive effects of the Jews.

---

[19] "…nach Temperament, Gemütsart, intellekutueller und sittlicher Anlage." Fritsch, *Handbuch der Judenfrage*, 6.
[20] "…erblich eingeborene Kräfte, die durch keinerlei äußerliche Einflüsse dauernd zu verwischen sind, die von Geschlecht zu Geschlecht sich übertragen und oft nach Jahrhunderten unverwandelt wieder hervorbrechen." Fritsch, *Handbuch der Judenfrage*, 6–7.
[21] "Außer den Deutschen hat bisher kein Volk in der Welt es mit den Verbrüderungs-Gedanken erst genommen; alle sind sie von rücksichtsloser nationaler Selbstsucht erfüllt und bezeichnen sie stolz als *sacro egoism* (heilige Selbstsucht)." Fritsch, *Handbuch der Judenfrage*, 7.
[22] "…die Sittlichkeit ist in letzter Linie ein Ausfluß der Rassen-Erfahrung; sie legt die Grundlagen fest, durch die das Gedeihen der Art bedingt ist." Fritsch, *Handbuch der Judenfrage*, 10.
[23] "Er hat seine Begriffe von Ehre und Tugend, von Recht und Pflicht, von Anstand und Sitte preisgegeben und bemüht, alle Dinge des Lebens nur noch mit dem Maßstabe des Hebräers zu messen." Fritsch, *Handbuch der Judenfrage*, 11.
[24] "Allgemein-Menschliches gegen gemeinsame Feinde zu Verteidigen; sie darf aber nicht dazu führen, die höheren geistigen und sittlichen Maßstäbe zu verleugnen, einem besonderen Typus zu gefallen, und die natürliche Rang-Abstufung der Menschen-Geschlechter umzukehren." Fritsch, *Handbuch der Judenfrage*, 12.

But in case you might think this was just his own personal fixation, he wants to prove that from time immemorial the bane influence of the Jews has been recognized, which leads into a series of chapters where he quotes from unimpeachable sources from across the ages. This is where Luther is brought in to add his voice. He draws in about two pages of material, most of which was also quoted by Islebiensis, though he adds a few unique passages, all of which focus on the low moral character of the Jews, their exploitation of good Germans, and advocate for violence and expulsion to be visited upon them as a result. In a footnote he provides some historical context, noting Luther's initial more sympathetic observations on the Jews:

> In his younger days, when Luther didn't yet know the Jews, he spoke very respectfully about them (1523).[25] He advised that one should treat them fairly, since Jesus Christ was also born a Jew. He later recognized the twin error and corrected his views of the Jews, having been made wiser as a result of life experience. When, through his dealings with the *Volk* he learned about the unprecedented usury and dishonest nature of the Jews—when he saw how the Jews exercised their secret influence up into the circles of the princes and rulers, misusing it to plunder the *Volk*—when he learned the hidden sensibilities and laws of the Jews, which make a mockery of all morals and Christianity—he gave vent in bitter words to what was in his honorable heart, with the full passion of an authentic man, a great nature. He published in the year 1543 two books, "On the Jews and their Lies" and "On the unknowable name of God," in which he pronounced absolutely nothing short of devastating judgments regarding this degenerate *Volk*, which bears the curse of God. No modern opponent of the Jews has resorted to such sharp words as this God-fearing man; today no one would risk speaking and writing this way if he wanted to avoid being hauled into court. Consequently, we can't reproduce the strongest words of Luther.[26]

---

[25] He is here referencing the 1523 work *Dass Jesus Christus ein geborener Jude sei* (that Jesus Christ was born a Jew); WA 11, 307–36.

[26] "In seinen jungen Jahren, als Luther die Juden noch nicht kannte, hat er sich sehr respektvoll über sie geäußert (1523). Er riet, daß man sein säuberlich behandeln solle, da Jesus Christus doch auch ein gebornener Jude gewesen sei.—Den doppelten Irrtum, der hierin lag, hat er später wohl klar erkannt und seine Ansicht über das Judentum, durch Lebenserfahrung gewitzig, wesentlich berichtigt. Als er im Verkehr mit dem Volke den unerhörten Wucher und das heuchlerische Wesen der Juden kennen gelernt hatte—als er sah, wie das Judentum seinen heimlichen Einfluß bis in die Kreise der Fürsten und Regierungen ausübte und zur Plünderung des Volkes mißbrauchte—als er die verborgenen Gesinnungen und Gesetze der Juden kennen lernte, die gegen alle Sittlichkeit und Christlichkeit ein Hohn sind—das machte er seinem ehrlichen Herzen in bitteren Worten Luft—mit der ganzen Leidenschaft eines echten Mannes, einer großen Natur. Er ließ im Jahre 1543 zwei Bücher erscheinen: 'Von den Jüden und ihren Lügen' und 'Vom Schem Hamphoras', in denen er geradezu vernichtende Urteile über dieses verworfene, mit dem Fluche Gottes beladene Volk fällt. Keiner der heutigen Juden-Gegner hat zu so scharfen Worten seine Zuflucht genommen, wie dieser gottesfürchtige Mann; es dürfte auch heute keiner so zu sprechen und zu schreiben wagen, wenn er nicht den Gerichten verfallen wollte. Wir können deshalb die derbsten Worte Luthers gar nicht wiedergeben." Fritsch, *Handbuch der Judenfrage*, 46–7.

Fritsch brings forward in his commentary an issue that will be a constant source of contention for those who wish to reference Luther for the continuing debates about the "Jewish question," namely his early writings about the Jews, where he spoke in an entirely different voice, if not necessarily with a fundamentally different understanding, of the Jews as a people. Though modern scholars have noted that in essence the early Luther, similar to the later Luther, viewed the Jews through the lens of his Christian belief, and saw them both as an example of what happens to those who reject the offer of God's grace through Christ, falling under his wrath, and also as a people who were once a vehicle for God's work in time, remain so even under his wrath, and may yet have a future place in the divine plan of salvation.[27] The issue that will recycle throughout the inter-war period is how to connect this tract to the harsh later words he will throw at the Jews. Many, especially those who are like-minded to Fritsch, will parse this as he does, observing that the young Luther didn't really know the Jews, but that, once he did, he came to the same conclusion that modern anti-Semites do, which is that they are a social plague who can't be tolerated to pollute German society and so must be eliminated. In this perspective, the theological argument that the tracts of Luther's later years put forward concerning the status and understanding of the Old Testament is of little interest or use, and hence ignored. For their purposes, that Luther suggests the social separation from and punishment of the Jews provides ample connective tissue to their own political project. That Luther was, for Fritsch, particularly useful is suggested by the fact that he brings him back at the very end of the work, in his closing words, noting that "already Luther cried out with indignation, 'there the princes and authorities sit snoring away with open mouths, letting the Jews use the public purse and treasury to rob and steal.'"[28] His work was intended as a call to action, and in that regard the late Luther was well suited to his purposes.

Another work by Fritsch highlights the difficulty of bridling Luther for his anti-Semitic project. In this instance it was a work titled *Der Falsche Gott (Beweis-Material gegen Jahwe)* (the false God (evidence against Jahweh)) first published

---

[27] The issue of Luther's views on the possible conversion of the Jews, either individually or as a people is complicated, since he speaks somewhat differently at differently points in his career. In his 1523 writing, conversion is at the center of his concern, since he hopes that through treating the Jews decently, and engaging them reasonably with scripture, that at least some Jews may be drawn to convert. Later, in the 1543 writings, he seems to have rejected this optimism about Jewish conversion, and casts doubt on any true conversion of a Jew, though at the end of *On the Jews and their Lies* he does express the thought that they lie in the hands of God, and he may effect their conversion in his own time. How exactly to read Luther's viewpoint is subject to controversy, but it is clear that the issue for Luther is not the Jews' status as a race, but rather their rejection of God's grace, that leads them to their diabolical ways and their suffering. For an overview of Luther's views see Sucher, *Luthers Stellung zu den Juden*, 238–52.

[28] "Schon Luther ruft mit Entrüstung aus: 'Dazu sitzen die Fürsten und Oberkeit, schnarchen und haben das Maul offen, lassen die Juden aus ihrem offenen Beutel und Kasten stehlen und rauben." Fritsch, *Handbuch der Judenfrage*, 648.

in 1911 but republished in new editions after the war. In this work Fritsch uses Jewish scripture against the Jews, seeking to prove that *Jahwe*, and other Jewish names for God, demonstrate that this god was only a tribal god of the ancient Hebrews, and in no way is connected to the one true God of the Christians. This fits with one element of the anti-Semitic movement, one that would flourish in the 1930s, that sought to disentangle Christianity completely from Judaism, and to jettison the Old Testament and its god, equating him with Satan, over and against the God of the New Testament. In truth, for Fritsch this did not come, as it would for some later advocates of this view, from any particular commitment to Christianity as a religion, but because it allowed a powerful entry point into the sympathies of doctrinal Christians, at least in theory. But Fritsch identifies in the work one particular problem with this viewpoint, and that is that Martin Luther didn't endorse it. He notes in the course of his argument that Luther completely muddied the waters with regard to the identity of this foreign Jewish God when in his translation of the Old Testament he rendered Jahweh and all the other names for God as "Gott der Herr" (the Lord God), obscuring, as Fritsch would have it, that these were all just tribal Gods, and unconnected to the God that Christians worship.[29] Further on in the work he will claim that Jesus himself was not Jewish, and that his religion was particularly aimed against the Jews. He seeks to use Luther again in this work, quoting from "The Jews and their Lies," exactly in the same fashion and for the same reasons as was the case in his *Handbook*. And he leaves aside the issue of Luther's own view of the Old Testament or of Jesus, which clearly were at odds with the claims Fritsch was putting forward in this work. While Luther certainly came to advocate harsh measures against the Jews, his larger argument was that the God of the Old Testament was the very God of Christ, and that in the Old Testament one can decipher the larger plan of salvation that was to come through Christ; though his two works of 1543 were shot through with coarse and inflammatory language, much of the content was in fact pursuing such a theological argument. Even the violent prescriptions for their treatment was framed under the notion of a "scharfe Barmherzigkeit" or "severe mercy," posing God's treatment of the Jews, as expressed in historic persecutions and Luther's own call for contemporary violence against them, as a legitimate exercise of the law against those who have fallen under God's wrath. While such ideas can be remodeled, as Fritsch does in his work, to fit with the eliminationist ideal of modern anti-Semites, the radical attack on the Old Testament and the Jewishness of Jesus will create a challenge for tapping into Luther and creating a seamless façade for his anti-Semitic image.

---

[29] Theodor Fritsch, *Der Falsche Gott (Beweis-Material gegen Jahwe)*. 7th ed. (Leipzig: Hammer Verlag, 1920): 58–9. As we will see in other later works, the very fact that Luther translated the Old Testament into idiomatic German was itself a problem with which to wrestle when trying to claim his legacy.

Though Fritsch's ideas feed directly into the anti-Semitism of post-World War I political racial German nationalism, they also find resonance among anti-Semitic groups who are within the Protestant church, for whom coopting Luther's religious legacy was a more pressing concern. A work from 1917 highlights in exemplary fashion the issues involved in that effort. Published as part of the four-hundredth anniversary of the Ninety-Five Theses, it was titled *Deutschchristentum auf rein-evangelischer Grundlage. 95 Leitsätze zum Reformationsfest 1917* (German Christianity on a pure, evangelical foundation. 95 guiding principles for the Reformation celebration 1917) and authored by four eminent ecclesiastical and literary figures.[30] At first glance the work seems something like the typical encomium that was produced by the score in 1917, praising the "kerndeutsche Mann" (German-to-his-core man) Martin Luther, noting his masterful works, extolling him as a discoverer even greater than Columbus, who uncovered the person of the Savior, revealing the inner depths of the German *Volk* soul. The authors emphasize the Germanness of Luther's Gospel, how it reveals the elective affinity between the Gospel of Christ and the German *Volk*. But, they note, this symbiosis of Germanity and Christianity as exemplified in Luther's Gospel happened as the wheel of history turned and new growth occurred, and the process was not brought to full fruition. For that reason, they will offer ninety-five new theses for the present context, to finish what Luther started.[31]

The rest of the book lays out a plan of advancement for what Luther initiated. Thesis number four provides a frame for understanding why this is necessary: "With the Reformation Luther took the first mighty step to the freeing of the German *Volk* from the foreign spiritual spell; Bismarck took the second step, in that he brought it to political maturity; we must all take the third step through the Germanifying of Christianity in ourselves."[32] Why the time is ripe for a new step

---

[30] *Deutschchristentum auf rein-evangelischer Grundlage. 95 Leitsätze zum Reformationsfest 1917* von Hauptpastor Friedrich Andersen in Flensburg, Professor Adolf Bartels in Weimar, Kirchenrat D. Dr. Ernst Katzer in Oberlößnitz bei Dresden, Hans Paul Freiherrn von Wolzogen in Bayreuth (Leipzig: Theodor Weicher, 1917). Andersen, a veteran anti-Semite within the Protestant church, can be seen as the moving spirit behind the work, as it captured his own Christian racial nationalist sentiments. Even prior to the war, he had long been active in anti-Semitic circles, and he would remain active up into the 1930s, eventually joining the DC and the Nazi Party. Katzer was near the end of his long career, but added the endorsement of a significant church administrator. Bartels and Wolzogen were literary scholars of some significance, and Bartels in particular would go on to prominence during the Nazi era. Both were instrumental in connecting literary figures such as Schiller, and cultural figures such as Wagner, to the racial/nationalist cause. On Andersen see Gisela Siems, "Hauptpastor Friedrich Andersen, Bund für Deutschkirche—ein Wegbereiter des Nationalsozialismus in der Stadt Flensburg." In *Kirche und Nationalsozialismus. Beiträge zur Geschichte des Kirchenkampfes in den evangelischen Landeskirchen Schleswig-Holsteins*, ed. Klauspeter Reumann (Neumünster: Karl Wachholtz Verlag, 1988): 13–34.

[31] *Deutschchristentum auf rein-evangelischer Grundlage*, 3–4.

[32] "Luther hat mit der Reformation den ersten gewaltigen Schritt getan zur Befreiung des deutschen Volkes aus fremdem geistigen Bann; Bismarck den zweiten, indem er es politisch mündig machte; den dritten müssen wir alle selber tun durch Verdeutschung des Christentums in uns selbst." *Deutschchristentum auf rein-evangelischer Grundlage*, 5.

forward in this process of reform is made clear in thesis six: "The new research on race has finally opened our eyes to the destructive effects of blood mixing between Germanic and non-Germanic peoples (*Volksangehörigen*) and admonishes us to strive with all our might to preserve our *Volkstum*, keeping it as pure and as enclosed within itself as possible."[33] Religion, they assert in the next few theses, is essential to the inner power and vitality of a *Volk*, but is also especially vulnerable to disruptive effects when connected to alien influences. Thus it is essential now to move forward to complete the inner connection of Germanity to Christianity by dissolving the unnatural connection with the Jewish religion which has come down from the past.[34] This means two things, showing first that the Old Testament is in no way connected to Christianity, and second that the New Testament and Jesus come out of a completely different source of inspiration than the religion of the Old Testmaent. Unfortunately, as they recognize, Luther is not particularly useful for such a theological project, and they make almost no reference in what follows to anything he wrote. In fact, as in thesis seventeen, they take issue with him, noting how he remains entangled in a Jewish/medieval mentality when he advocates both fearing and loving God, since fear is a Jewish way of viewing God. They note that it was the late Luther who emphasized that formula, and they refer the reader back to his earlier writings and translation of the New Testament, where he laid claim to an authentic German Christianity.[35] This seems a bit confusing, since it was the early Luther who exhibited seemingly greater sympathy for the Jews, and the later Luther who turned so violently against them, but the authors don't mention any of Luther's writings about the Jews one way or another, leaving their argument undisturbed. And those mighty figures of the Old Testament whom Luther lauded as *Wundermänner*[36] the authors bring forward as the embodiment of the corrupt spirit of the so-called patriarchs, who clearly don't exemplify Christian/Germanic virtue or faith.[37] Thesis twenty-six seeks to tap into Luther for this point, noting that "Luther recognized that Christ alone may and can be the measure for this essence of the Christian religion. 'Moses has nothing to do with us Christians.'"[38]

Since among all the *Völker* Christianity is the most spiritually related to the Germans, it is consequently essential, as occurred in the Reformation, to bring the two together in an ever-closer relation, so that the Germans can become truly

---

[33] "Die neuere Rassenforschung endlich hat uns die Augen geöffnet für die verderblichen Wirkungen der Blutmischung zwischen germanischen und nicht-germanischen Volksangehörigen und mahnt uns, mit allen Kräften dahin zu streben unser Volkstum möglichts rein und in sich geschlossen zu erhalten." *Deutschchristentum auf rein-evangelischer Grundlage*, 6.
[34] *Deutschchristentum auf rein-evangelischer Grundlage*, 6.
[35] *Deutschchristentum auf rein-evangelischer Grundlage*, 10.
[36] See Hayden-Roy, "Unmasking the Hidden God," 78–95.
[37] *Deutschchristentum auf rein-evangelischer Grundlage*, 10–11.
[38] "Luther erkannte, daß Christus allein Maßstab für dieses Wesen der christlichen Religion sein kann und darf. 'Moses geht uns Christen nichts an.'" *Deutschchristentum auf rein-evangelischer Grundlage*, 13.

Christian, realizing their true self. "Thus emerges the mission of the German-Protestant church and theology, to gradually bring about the purity of Christendom and thereby make it discernable to all other *Völker*, and to make possible for them its full appropriation as a perfected religion."[39] The latter half of the theses expends great effort seeking to fully isolate Jesus from anything Jewish, proposing the possibility that he might in fact be of Aryan descent, something already suggested by the elective affinity between Germanity and Christianity. In thesis ninety-one, Luther's faith is equated with Kantian freedom, such that Kant's categorical imperative becomes the expression on which the entirety of Christianity rests, as it is understood by the German spirit.[40] In the end it becomes clear that the authors in fact are not really interested in Luther's understanding of faith, but wish to establish a "pure" Christianity that is separate from all Jewish connection, in spite of what Luther might have to say about that. There are a number of themes that are anticipatory of the tangents that members of the *Deutsche Christen* will take in the 1930s, a movement that Andersen will endorse and participate in. The formula of the new ninety-five thesis takes as axiomatic that someone as fully German as Luther, someone who is by 1917 almost universally acclaimed as the most German persona of all time, must certainly endorse the completion of the Reformation as a project of racial cleansing, whatever else might be suggested by his theological legacy. It is clear from this work that constructing a theological argument for the separation of the Old Testament and Judaism from Christianity does not find much of use in Luther's anti-Jewish writings, rooted as they are in a theology that apprehends the Old Testament as an essential witness to the truth of Christianity. That the Jews didn't recognize this truth was the source of Luther's massive assault on the Jews of his own time, but not because their very being poisoned the well of a Germanized Christian faith, a notion that had no meaning for Luther.

While Andersen et al., sought to construct a program for a racialized Christianity with little resort to Luther's actual writings, another work published shortly after the war took on that challenge. Alfred Falb (1864–1933), *Luther und die Juden*,[41] represents the first extended work that sought to present Luther straightforwardly as a true racial nationalist, taking on his writings and translating them into terms that suggested Luther himself shared a racial understanding from which emerged his hatred of the Jews. Falb was a publicist, not a theologian, but wrote with a seeming passion for convincing contemporary Protestantism that an anti-Semitic purging was in keeping with the spirit of the great hero of the Reformation.

---

[39] "Hieraus erwächst der deutsch-protestantischen Kirche und Theologie die Aufgabe, die Reinheit des Christentums allmählich herbeizuführen und es dadurch allen anderen Völkern erkennbar und ihnen seine volle Aneignung als die vollkommene Religion möglich zu machen." *Deutschchristentum auf rein-evangelischer Grundlage*, 17.
[40] *Deutschchristentum auf rein-evangelischer Grundlage*, 32.
[41] Alfred Falb, *Luther und die Juden* (Munich: Deutscher Volksverlag, D. E. Boepple, 1921).

He sets up his topic with great drama at the start, with a sweeping view of the events just prior to the Reformation, as the heathen/Jewish spirit of the Roman Church, combined with the money-lending of the Jews and the introduction of Roman law sought to complete the enserfment of the Germans:

> There emerged for the German world, in its most bitter need, the liberator in Luther's fighting heroics. Born of blood that was German to the core, in an impoverished hut, he carried the fate of Germany in his breast. What is happening today—he **foresaw** it; posterity did not heed his warning. Thus the coming age will first complete what he held fearfully in his breast... may this book be a harbinger.[42]

Having set the scene, he proceeds to recount the early, heroic actions of Luther in opposing the foreign oppressors with his theses, bull burning, dramatic oratory at Worms, and powerful bible translation, highlighting the Germanic characteristics of it all. What sets apart Falb's depiction of these oft-repeated scenes is his sensitivity to the supposed Jewishness of Luther's opponents, and the blood purity of the man who carried out these feats—he goes out of his way to assure his reader that Luther certainly was of pure blood against the libel that somehow Slavic blood might lie in his ancestry.[43] Falb wishes with his recreation to show that the events of Luther's time can be overlayed onto the contemporary scene, where betrayal by predatory Jews has brought the German people into bondage to those who are controlled by the Jews. The German people yearn to break their chains but need a leader who has seen through the machinations of the Jews. He repeatedly references a work of Friedrich Delitzsch's, *Die Große Tauschung* (the great deception) as a source that has seen through the work of the Jews, and Falb's work now will show that Luther's witness completely endorses Delitzsch's thesis.[44]

---

[42] "In einer Zeit, da heidnisch-jüdischer Geist in der Römischen Kirche das Abendland erobert hatte, als die jüdische 'Geldleihe über Europa hinging und langsam aus sich den Kapitalismus gebar' und schließlich...das Römische Recht in Deutschland...die völlige Unterjochung der deutschen Seele unter fremde Anmaßung und Heuchelei vollenden sollte—da erstand der germanischen Welt in bitterster Not der Befreier in Luthers kämpfendem Heldentum. Aus kerndeutschem Blut in ärmlicher Hütte geboren, trug er das Schicksal Deutschlands in seiner Brust. Aber—er hat es **vorausgesehen**; die Nachwelt hat seiner Warnungen nicht geachtet. So wird erst die kommende Zeit vollenden, was seine Seele schon bange barg.... Ein Fingerzeig sei dieses Buch." Falb, *Luther und die Juden*, 4.

[43] "Daß Luther, wie oft behauptet, auch slavisches Blut in den Adern gehabt, ist nicht nachzuweisen. Seine Ahnen sind deutsche Bauern aus seiner Gegend, in der von slavischen Siedlungen und slavischer Blutmischung bisher keine Spur gefunden worden. Boehmer S. 1-2" (That Luther, as is often asserted, also had Slavic blood in his veins cannot be demonstrated. His ancestors are German peasants of his area, in which there has been found no trace of Slavic settlements or Slavic mixing of blood. Boehmer, pp. 1-2). Falb, *Luther und die Juden*, 8. The reference is to Heinrich Boehmer, *Luther im Licht der neueren Forschung*, first published in 1910. Falb uses the 1918 edition.

[44] Falb, *Luther und die Juden*, 10. Delitzsch was a biblical scholar who published in 1920 the work cited by Falb wherein he argues for the complete separation of the Old Testament from Christianity based on his scholarship on the Old Testament. Delitzsch himself represented an older strain of

And Luther is an invaluable witness, since no one can accuse him of harboring unchristian sympathies.

Unlike earlier authors' treatment of Luther, Falb takes head on the issue of Luther's early, irenic writings about the Jews, "That Jesus Christ was born a Jew," and its implications. As he starts his discussion, however, he adds a conspiratorial note, accusing the editors of the Weimar edition of Luther's works of suppressing the publication of the later anti-Jewish writings, such that he will have to resort to the earlier Erlangen edition.[45] It is a peculiarity of Falb's narration that he takes long detours into the history of the world as it relates to the Jews, so that for his introduction of Luther's 1523 work he spends pages discussing all the various permutations of the history surrounding the events preceding that year, and finding in every exploitative or unjust action the sneaking hand of the Jews.[46] Falb will explain Luther's vexing unwillingness to blame the Jews for all the evil they were enacting as a result of his isolation in the monastery, his focus on the corruptions of the Church (without recognizing the degree to which it danced to the tune of the Jews), and his general honesty and sense of justice.[47] Falb spends the majority of his time when treating this early work showing how the Catholic practices Luther attacks as the source of Jewish alienation from Christianity were in fact exactly the same sorts of things the Jews themselves do even more egregiously.[48] He then spends many pages contesting the assertion made by Luther's title, showing how the latest research would suggest that Jesus was not born a Jew, bringing forward the views of Houston Stewart Chamberlain and Theodor Fritsch.[49] In the end Falb clearly doesn't quite know what to do with the work, which seems to contradict a number of basic assumptions of the contemporary anti-Semitic movement. In the end he can only affirm Luther's final statement, which expresses his intention to leave things where they are and see how events unfold. This provides Falb a transition point, noting that once Luther came to know the Jews his tone was utterly transformed, as he will now amply document.[50]

With the later works, Falb emphasizes that Luther now worked with a much fuller knowledge of the Jews, and what he has to say is based on direct experience. He notes that there are long passages of theological disputation, which are tiresome,

---

anti-Jewish thinking, rather than the sort of racial anti-Semitism advocated by Falb, though for Falb such distinctions are irrelevant when coopting the substance of Delitzsch's work.

[45] This accusation, which is echoed frequently by other authors, was in fact outdated, at least in regards to the Weimar edition, since volume 53 of the Weimarer Ausgabe with the late Jewish tracts had been published in early 1920. The idea that somehow there was a conspiracy to hide these writings would persist in anti-Semitic circles.

[46] Falb, *Luther und die Juden*, 10–17. An example of his technique is glimpsed as he describes Johann Tetzel selling his indulgences with his promise of forgiveness for all sins once payment is rendered as "echt Judisch! (authentically Jewish!)"; Falb, *Luther und die Juden*, 18.

[47] Falb, *Luther und die Juden*, 18.

[48] Falb spends five pages detailing Jewish usury practices that are specifically designed to exploit Christians, Falb, *Luther und die Juden*, 19–23.

[49] Falb, *Luther und die Juden*, 24–7.   [50] Falb, *Luther und die Juden*, 29.

and these he is going to leave aside in order to focus on the passages where Luther speaks of his experiences.[51] He then excerpts at length, adding commentary along the way, noting, for instance passages that would seem to affirm the views of Friedrich Delitzsch. Or, having excerpted a long passage where Luther decries how the Jews take advantage of princely tolerance to exploit the people, Falb expostulates: "How truly have these prophetic words been fulfilled today! The Jews have, in the World War and in the 'Revolution,'[52] basically behaved the same as in the combative times of Luther."[53] Other passages remind him of the Russian Revolution, which he views as another instance of Jewish manipulation.[54] He of course devotes many pages to excerpting passages about usury, and adding his own affirmation of what Luther has to say, and how much Luther, were he around in Falb's time, would affirm the work of anti-Semitic publicists.[55] To punctuate some points he creates a dialogue between Luther and modern researchers whose work highlights the banditry of the Jews in ancient times, providing passages from Luther's works that affirm these viewpoints.[56]

This introduces a long passage where Falb first provides some excerpts from Luther's works that comment on the God of Israel, and then follows by quizzing Luther—"what would you say Luther about this?"—concerning the ideas of current anti-Semitic literature which asserts that the gods of the ancient Israelites could not be the God of Jesus or the New Testament, but, in fact, a demonic god. Though he doesn't have Luther answer directly, he speculates about his response:

> I believe that this realization would have been a redemption for Luther in the deepest sense! He recounted in 1545 in the historical introduction to his collected works how he, in his terrible struggles of conscience of his youth, "truly hated **this God of wrath and judgment**, who had entangled humanity through the law of the old covenant!" Only now can we understand that in this 'God of the old covenant' he hated, and had to hate, not the God of Christian love, not the eternal father of heaven and earth, but the 'God of the Jews,' the *schaddaj*, the *sched*, **who incurred the outrage of his Germanic soul**, this "servant of all the devils," as he himself later called the God of the Jews. The living power of his heart recognized the truth instinctively ages ago, without his conscious

---

[51] Falb, *Luther und die Juden*, 32.

[52] He is referencing here the collapse of the Wilhelmine State at the end of the War and the establishment of the Weimar Republic.

[53] "Wahrlich, wie haben sich diese prophetischen Worte heute erfüllt! Die Juden haben im Weltkrieg und in der 'Revolution', im Grunde genommen, nicht anders gehandelt als in den kampferfüllten Tagen der Lutherzeit." Falb, *Luther und die Juden*, 35.

[54] Falb, *Luther und die Juden*, 36–7. It was an established fact among followers of the anti-Semitic right that the Russian Revolution was a Jewish conspiracy, carried out as another avenue to establish their world-wide hegemony, along with their control of market capitalism. Alfred Rosenberg, who was born in Tsarist Russia, gained some of his earliest notoriety writing tracts purportedly demonstrating the overwhelming Jewish character of Bolshevism.

[55] Falb, *Luther und die Juden*, 37–44.   [56] Falb, *Luther und die Juden*, 44–6.

understanding, hemmed in by the old conventional formula of education, being able to make sense of the horrible struggle of the soul! For Luther, in his life of many upheavals, didn't take this last step of understanding that the Old and New Testaments have **different** gods who rule (if one is allowed to say that!), that *Schaddaj, Jaho* or *Jahwe* are only the tribal gods of the Jews, not God the Father of Christ.[57]

With this transposition of Luther's understanding Falb is able to claim Luther's lineage for the modern project of purging Christianity of its Jewish roots. Falb suggests, as well, that Luther understood that what was of universal value in the Mosaic law, namely the decalogue, was natural law, which came through a general revelation. Luther recognized that such a revelation came through nature and history, and that the Jews probably plagiarized it from some more ancient source that has been lost.[58] He speaks with outrage about how the learned ones and church leaders have suppressed this legacy of Luther: "He [Luther] would certainly never have hesitated or vacillated to reveal every last falsehood of the Jews, had he had our knowledge of history and the discovery of cuneiform inscriptions!"[59]

Turning to the theme of converting the Jews, Falb believes he has found the clinching argument to convince all that Luther, centuries ago, saw the racially determined nature of the Jews evil. Falb cites a couple of passages out of context where Luther expresses some doubts about the Jews ever truly converting, then quotes Luther's interpretation of the 109th Psalm, where the words "blood," "nature," "life," and "flesh" come forward to typify the hardness of heart of those who reject God, unless God works some miracle; Falb pounces: "It has become for them [the Jews] their 'nature and life': yes, that's it!...And with this Luther—this shining sun in the night of medieval delusion, which also still afflicts us today!—by his own resources with the instinctive insight of genius

---

[57] "Ich glaube, daß diese Erkenntnis gerade für Luther ein Erlösung hätte im tiefsten Sinne! Erzählt er doch in seiner historischen Einleitung, die er zum 1. Band der Gesamtausgabe seiner Werke von 1545 noch selbst schrieb (5. März 1545), wie er in den furchtbaren Gewissensqualen seiner Jugend '**diesen Gott der Rache und des Gerichtes**, der die Menschen durch das Gesetz des Alten Bundes schon in allerlei Elend verstrickt habe, förmlich gehaßt habe'! Nun erst verstehen wir, daß er in diesem 'Gott des Alten Bundes' nicht den Gott christlicher Liebe, nicht den ewigen Vater Himmels und der Erde, sondern den 'Gott der Juden', den *schaddaj*, den *sched*, haßte und hassen mußte, dem die Empörung seiner **germanischen Seele** galt: dem 'Knecht aller Teufel', wie der den Gott der Juden später selber nennt. Die lebendige Kraft seines Gemütes hatte also längst das Richtige fühlend erkannt, ohne daß sein bewußter Verstand, eingezwängt in die althergebrachten Formeln der Erziehung, den ungeheueren Seelenkampf zu deuten wußte! Denn zu dem letzten Schritt der Erkenntnis, daß im Alten und im Neuen Testament **verschiedene** Götter—(wenn ich so sagen darf!)—herrschen, daß *Schaddaj, Jaho* oder *Jahwe* nur der Stammesgötze der Juden, niemals der Gottvater Christi ist—bis zu diesem letzten Schritte kam Luther in den Kämpfen seines vielbestürmten Lebens nicht!" Falb, *Luther und die Juden*, 51-2.
[58] Falb, *Luther und die Juden*, 52-3.
[59] "...er hätte gewiß nicht gezagt und gezaudert, auch den letzten falschen Schein des Judentums zu enthüllen, hätte er **unsere** Kenntnis des Geschichte und Keilinschriftfunde gehabt!" Falb, *Luther und die Juden*, 53.

(without modern racial and hereditary science!) himself directly hit upon what is really at stake in the most final and deepest ground of being!"[60] While Luther may still talk in places as if what matters is environment, he has intuited the true reason why peoples behave the way they do, which is the result of their inherited traits. This leads Falb to observe how working to convert peoples is like trying to convert infectious disease agents; no matter what you do, you can't change their basic function.[61] This thought then leads him to Luther's recommendations for what should be done, using excerpts from his writings that advocate expulsion of the Jews, separation from them, and other harsh prescriptions for their treatment. He devotes many pages of excerpts enumerating all of what Luther had to say on this topic.[62] The conclusion of the work brings Friedrich Delitzsch back into the dialogue, and develops a point-by-point demonstration of how well Luther's views track onto what Delitzsch also has argued concerning the Jews, and how Luther's witness refutes Delitzsch's opponents.[63]

Falb's work represents the most industrious attempt to remake Luther in the guise of a twentieth century anti-Semitic publicist. By strategically ignoring the theological arguments put forward in Luther's anti-Jewish writings, by assuming the arc of his arguments implied continuity with modern anti-Semitic understanding of the Jews, by finding language that could be appropriated as anticipations of modern racial consciousness, and situating them beside long excurses on related topics drawn from contemporary authors, Luther is given the appearance of relevance for post-War German debates on the "Jewish question." Looked at in retrospect it has little merit for understanding what motivated Luther, or how one should understand him, but for the world of the early 1920s the work was compelling if one shared Falb's basic sympathies. For one, it exposed extensive passages from Luther's anti-Jewish writings, more than had been the case in previous compendia. In addition, it made them accessible, and surrounded them with seemingly enlightening background about the Jews across the ages. His arguments for Luther's own recognition of racial ideology, based on Luther's supposed insightful genius and supported by careful proof-texting, is logically strained but enthusiastically promoted. In many ways Falb's work opens up a new pathway for Luther's image, and after his death the work was republished in 1936, where it is lauded as pathbreaking.[64] Indeed, Falb's work clearly influenced members of the

---

[60] "'Nature und Leben' ist's ihnen geworden: ja, das ist's!...Und damit ist Luther—diese Strahlensonne in der Nacht mittelalterlichen Wahns, an dem wir heut noch kranken!—aus sich selbst heraus mit dem Gefühlsblick des Genies (ohne moderne Rassen- oder Vererbungsforschung!) unmittelbar herangekommen an das, worum es geht im allerletzten, tiefsten Wesensgrunde!" Falb, *Luther und die Juden*, 54.
[61] Falb, *Luther und die Juden*, 56–7.   [62] Falb, *Luther und die Juden*, 61–73.
[63] Falb, *Luther und die Juden*, 74–6.
[64] The 1936 edition had an editorial introduction by Falb's brother, who noted Falb's passing, regretting he could not experience the great national revival that came with Hitler. The editor has the following to say about the work: "...das im Jahre 1921 erschien und in dem zum ersten Male, was man bisher verschwiegen hatte, ans Licht gebracht wurde: wie Luther sich vom Judenfreund zum Juden

Nazi Party, including Alfred Rosenberg and quite likely Hitler himself, and set the precedent for repeated accusations brought against the Protestant church that they had suppressed or betrayed Luther's anti-Semitic character and writings.

While Falb's work represents the more typical treatment of Luther's anti-Jewish writing during the Weimar era, there was one remarkable work of the 1920s that sought to frame his legacy in a starkly different light. *Evangelische Kirche und Judentum* (the evangelical church and Judaism) by Eduard Lamparter (1869–1945)[65] was written as a resource for members of the Protestant church in Germany to show the close ties that existed between Judaism and Christianity. Lamparter represents that element of the church that took a more positive approach to Jewish/Christian relations, though still with the ultimate goal of using such relations as a vehicle to attract Jewish converts. Nevertheless, Lamparter's work stands out for its rare appreciation of Jewish culture and religious traditions as having legitimacy in their own right. His approach to Luther is diametrically opposed to all the authors discussed above in that he takes as normative Luther's 1523 writing, and sees the later 1543 pieces as a backsliding into crude medieval anti-Jewish polemic. "The fair and truly evangelical position with respect to the Jewish question which Luther at first assumed as authentic Reformer but unfortunately subsequently abandoned, has been asserted only rarely by evangelical theologians."[66] He notes the contradictions that emerged in Luther's relationship to the Jews, seeing his early writings expressing the truly Gospel-based response to the Jews, with the later writings representing Luther giving into received prejudices and errors.[67] He quotes from a number of Luther's early writings where Luther repeatedly states that one cannot expect the Jews to be attracted to the Gospel or to the church if all they experience is mistreatment and rejection. He recognizes that for Luther it was an issue of the Jews' relationship to the Gospel and to Christ, and his desire to draw them in to Christian belief, but also highlights the way Luther frames the mistreatment they have experienced.[68] He notes, too, Luther's great love for the

---

feind wandelt, welche Bedeutung Luthers Tat für die arische Menschheit besitzt; ein erster Schritt zu einer deutschen Religion!…Luther ist der bedeutendste Vorläufer der völkisch religiösen Bewegung unserer Zeit, er ist es, der den Grundstein legte zum heutigen germanischen Reich! (This first appeared in 1921 and brought to light for the first time what has been silenced previously, how Luther evolved from a friend of the Jews to their enemy, and what significance Luther possesses for Aryan mankind: a first step to a Germanic religion!…Luther is the most significant forerunner of the *völkisch* religious movement of our time, he laid the foundation stone for the present Germanic Empire!)." Alfred Falb, *Luther und die Juden* (Munich: Deutscher Volksverlag, 1936): 6.

[65] Eduard Lamparter, *Evangelische Kirche und Judentum: Ein Beitrag zu christlichem Verständnis von Judentum und Antisemitismus* (Gotha?: Leopold Klotz?, 1928).

[66] "Die gerechte und wahrhaft evangelische Stellung zur Judenfrage, die Luther zuerst als echter Reformator eingenommen hatte, ist leider bald von ihm selbst preisgegeben und später nur selten von evangelischen Theologen behauptet worden." Lamparter, *Evangelische Kirche*, 5.

[67] Lamparter, *Evangelische Kirche*, 7.

[68] "Wir erkennen Luthers Größe an der Offenheit und Wahrhaftigkeit, mit welcher er wider das schwere bisher an den Juden begangene Unrecht der Christenheit gezeugt, an der Kühnheit, mit welcher er überkommenen Mißständen und Irrtümern auch auf diesem Gebiet den Kampf angesagt hat, und an dem starken Mitgefühl, das er in dem bisher von Kirche, Staat und Gesellschaft Mißhandelten

174 THE LUTHER MYTH

Old Testament, the care and effort he took in translating it into German, and his appreciation of the essential place of the Old Testament as a stage toward the revelation of the Gospel.[69] Once, however, Luther saw the Jews were not going to convert, he turned about in his view of them. He relates many of the hard sentences that Luther flung against the Jews, and then adds:

> It belongs to the most painful things that this greatest of Germans, who previously had found such warm words full of sympathy, justice, and love for the Jews, now worked himself up into such blind hatred against them that he no longer asked for proofs of their alleged atrocities.[70]

Lamparter notes the degree to which Luther has become the tool of modern anti-Semites:

> The Luther who wrote the two works "On the Jews and their Lies" and "On the Unspeakable Name and the generations of Christ" has become the key witness of modern anti-Semitism. We would rather linger with the Luther who, at the high point of his reforming work, stood up for **the oppressed, the reviled and exiled with such warm words**, and so warmly recomended love of neighbor to all Christians as their most noble duty, **including toward the Jews**.[71]

---

entgegengebracht hat. Er hat vermöge seines Gerechtigkeitsgefühls und seiner Nächstenliebe die damalige Lage der Juden als eine Schmach für die Christenheit empfunden. Aber der entscheidende Punkt für ihn war das Verhalten der Juden zum Evangelium. Er wirbt um ihre Seelen und möchte sie mit heißem Bemühen für Christum gewinnen. In der Predigt am Stephanstag 1521 sagt er: 'So ist es nun gewiß, daß die Juden noch sagen werden zu Christus; "Gelob sei, der da kommt im Namen des Herrn."' In der Schrift: 'Daß Jesus ein geborener Jude sei' hat er ihnen die Hand gedoboten, es heißt am Schluß: 'Hier will ich's diesmal lassen bleiben, bis ich sehe, was ich gewirkt habe'" (We recognize Luther's greatness in the openness and truthfulness with which he witnessed to the injustice that Christendom has up until now visited on the Jews, also in the boldness with which he set out to fight against the long-established abuses and errors in this area, and in the strong sympathy he displayed for those who up to now had been mistreated by the church, state, and society. He had, as a result of his sense of justice and love of neighbor, experienced the existing circumstances of the Jews as Christendom's shame. However the decisive point for him was the reaction of the Jews to the Gospel. He seeks their souls and with fervent effort he wishes to win them for Christ. In the sermon an St. Stephen's Day 1521 he says: 'It is now certain that the Jews will yet say to Christ; "blessed is he who comes in the name of the Lord." In the tract "that Jesus was born a Jew" he offered them his hand, and said at the end: "Here's where I'll leave it this time, until I see what I have accomplished"'). Lamparter, *Evangelische Kirche*, 10.

[69] Lamparter, *Evangelische Kirche*, 11–12.

[70] "Es gehört zum Schmerzlichsten, daß dieser größte Deutsche, der zuvor solch warme Worte voll Mitleid, Gerechtigkeit und Liebe für die Juden gefunden hatte, sich jetzt in einen solchen blinden Haß gegen sie hineinsteigerte, daß er gar nicht mehr nach Beweisen für ihre angeblichen Schandtaten fragte." Lamparter, *Evangelische Kirche*, 15.

[71] "Der Luther, welcher die zwei Schriften 'Von den Juden und ihren Lügen' und 'Vom Schem Hamphoras und dem Geschlecht Christi' niedergeschrieben hat, ist zum Kronzeugen des modernen Antisemitismus geworden. Wir aber verweilen Lieber bei dem Luther, der auf dem Höhepunkt seines reformatorischen Wirkens für **die Unterdrückten, Verachteten und Verfemten in so warmen Worten eingetreten ist** und der Christenheit die Nächstenliebe als die vernehmste Pflicht **auch gegen die Juden** so eindringlich ans Herz gelegt hat." Lamparter, *Evangelische Kirche*, 17.

Further on in the tract Lamparter looks to the Jews as dialogue partners for Christians, from whom one could learn. This is a unique perspective in the environment of the 1920s, and one of the few places where Luther's anti-Jewish writings are discussed in a work at all sympathetic to the plight of the Jews. It is the case that, just as the anti-Semites over-interpret the degree Luther's writings affirm their own ideological preoccupations, Lamparter has exaggerated the degree to which Luther's milder early writings corresponds to his own philo-Semitic stance. Though one can understand his eagerness to use Luther to counteract the anti-Semitic literature that had gained such a hearing in the church.[72]

Unfortunately Lamparter's views did not gain a foothold, and the turn of events of the early 1930s created an environment where the views of Fritsch and Falb became the basis for the expansion and elaboration of Luther's anti-Jewish writings and profile, though with a great deal of disjunction and controversy about their ultimate implications. In the end, however, Luther's views provided additional justification for the abuse and violence that was the answer to the "Jewish question."[73] The general direction of sentiment is well represented in a work, Erich Vogelsang's essay, *Luthers Kampf gegen die Juden* (Luther's struggle against the Jews),[74] published as part of Luther's four-hundred-fiftieth birthday celebration of 1933. Vogelsang's work follows in the wake of Falb in its representation of Luther, though it treats the subject with a good deal more scholarly rigor and knowledge of the sources.

Vogelsang wrote at a time when the first anti-Jewish measures by the National-Socialist regime were being implemented, measures that he explicitly endorses at the start of his study.[75] He notes that while before the War Luther's anti-Jewish views were considered an embarrassment, there has been a fundamental shift: "our time grasps these directly, irrespective of all theology, with passionate understanding, and in this we believe our time stands close to Luther, the German

---

[72] See Christian Wiese, "'Unheilsspuren': zur Rezeption von Martin Luthers 'Judenschriften' im Kontext antisemitischen Denkens in den Jahrzehnten vor der Schoah." In *Das mißbrauchte Evangelium: Studien zu Theologie und Praxis der Thüringer Deutschen Christen*, ed. Peter von der Osten-Sacken (Berlin: Inst. Kirche und Judentum, 2001): 91–135; 121–3.

[73] For a cogent analysis of the apprehension of Luther's anti-Jewish writings by the factions in the Protestant church of the 1930s, see Christopher Probst, *Demonizing the Jews. Luther and the Protestant Church in Nazi Germany*. (Bloomington: Indiana University Press, 2012). Probst looks in particular at how the specifically non-rational and irrational elements of Luther's writing became the focus of both academic theological treatment of Luther's works as well as their translation by pastors in the communication with the laity.

[74] Erich Vogelsang, *Luthers Kampf gegen die Juden* (Tübingen: J. C. B. Mohr (Paul Siebeck), 1933). Vogelsang was a student of Karl Holl, and wrote his dissertation under Emanuel Hirsch. He joined both the Nazi Party and the SA, though over time his scholarly work somewhat qualified his racial nationalist sentiments, at least as reflected in his work on Luther and mysticism. See Volker Leppin, "In Rosenbergs Schatten: zur Lutherdeutung Erich Vogelsangs." *Theologische Zeitung* 61 (2005): 132–42. For biographical details see the article by Jens Wolff in the *Biographisch-Bibliographischeslexikon* 17, Ergänzungen IV (Herzberg: Verlag Traugott Bautz, 2000): 1507–21. Wolff's article does not discuss Vogelsang's work on the Jews.

[75] Vogelsang, *Luthers Kampf*, 6–7.

176 THE LUTHER MYTH

Luther!"[76] Vogelsang rejects decisively the idea that Luther started as a philo-Semite and then ended up as an anti-Semite, but rather he sees continuity in his understanding of the Jews across his career. He introduces his essay by placing emphasis on the fact that *"for Luther the Jewish question is first and last the question of Christ,"*[77] i.e. a question of faith. Vogelsang quotes extensively from Luther's writings on the Jews to show that for Luther the Jews' fate is connected to their rejection of Christ as savior and participation in the crucifixion.[78] Having established this point, he observes:

> Every enlightened liberal who measures everything according to its rationality will reject this historical interpretation of the Jews' fate; that through an historical event, namely Jesus Christ, should be decided the fate of a *Volk*. But the reality of a *Volk* is constructed, after all, from its history and not out of pure reason. And only an enlightened Jewish people who had forgotten its history with God and his Christ would dare to attempt to conform themselves to a Christianity that itself had forgotten its history, in order to become similarly enlightened cosmopolitans with a universal religion of reason.[79]

This emphasis on history as the revealer of divine providence, and the dismissal of reason as a tool for understanding, bespeaks Vogelsang's scholarly origins in the Luther Renaissance; the Jews are here associated with an Enlightenment rationality that led them to conform to a Christianity that had become cosmopolitan and rational, a Christianity at odds with Luther's faith. This way of perceiving Luther integrates him into Holl and Hirsch's existential Luther of faith.

Vogelsang notes that throughout Luther's writings the Jews are woven as a red thread, as an existential threat and warning for humanity:

> Luther never believed in such a return of all of Israel in the course of world history. *The* Jews as an entirety and a *Volk*, as destiny, remain an open wound on the body of humanity unto the end of all things, remain the embodied scandal of the cross, remain as the visible hand of the God of wrath in human history.[80]

---

[76] "...gerade das greift unsere Zeit—abseits aller Theologie—mit leidenschaftlichem Verstehen auf, hier glaubt sie Luther, dem deutschen Luther nahe zu sein!" Vogelsang, *Luthers Kampf*, 5.

[77] "*Für Luther ist die Judenfrage zuerst und zuletzt die Christusfrage.*" Vogelsang, *Luthers Kampf*, 9.

[78] Vogelsang, *Luthers Kampf*, 9-10.

[79] "Jeder nach Vernünftigkeit messende aufgeklärte Liberalismus wird diese Geschichtsdeutung des jüdischen Schicksals als Unvernunft ablehnen: daß durch ein Geschichtsereignis, das da heißt Jesus Christus, ein Volksschicksal entschieden sein soll. Aber die Wirklichkeit eines Volkes baut sich nun einmal aus seiner Geschichte und nicht aus reiner Vernunft auf. Und nur ein seine Geschichte mit Gott und seinem Christus vergessendes, aufgeklärtes Judentum konnte den Versuch wagen, sich einer ebenfalls seine Geschichte vergessenden Christenheit anzugleichen zu einem gleichartigen aufgeklärten Weltbürgertum und zu einem allgemeinen Vernunftreligion." Vogelsang, *Luthers Kampf*, 10-11.

[80] "An solche Rückkehr von ganz Israel innerhalb dieses Weltlaufs hat Luther niemals geglaubt. *Das* Judentum als Ganzes, als Volk, als Schicksal bleibt die offene Wunde am Körper der Menschheit

In this sense, the Jews serve an admonitory function for other *Völker*, and their corporate suffering reveals the hidden judgment of God. Vogelsang chronicles from Luther's writings all the ways the Jews actions have brought this fate upon themselves, revealed as a people who think themselves chosen, who epitomize the self-satisfied, egotistical religiosity that is the obverse of Luther's understanding of justification. This leads them into their materialism, their predatory dealings, and their obliviousness to things of the spirit and the spiritual nature of faith in Christ. Having rejected Christ, and having rebelled against God, they now stand under the wrath of God, and suffer a savage justice, living as they do under the power of the devil.[81] He extols Luther's judgment over the Jews, his shock that they should stand under God's wrath as they do, such that Luther speaks of them as "cursed and damned Jews."[82] He again contrasts this with liberalism and its viewpoint:

> Liberals will relegate the connections between World Jewry and unseen power, money, blood and fate to the stuff of legends, and not grasp that with the Jewish question in the German revolution of 1933 a world-historical question that had been veiled for a hundred-and-fifty year once again has become visible.[83]

The treatment of the Jews as it is being administered by the new regime is simply the inevitable outcome of the longer tribulations of the Jews as articulated in Luther's writings; they stand under God's wrath, so their fate is the result of how their very essence interacts with the providential will of the God of history, who is also visible in Christ, as well.

It was an aspect of Luther's greatness that he perceived and articulated this, and made admirably well-judged recommendations for their treatment (though Vogelsang does acknowledge that for a time in the 1520s Luther took another approach):

> Luther's church-practical solution to the "Jewish question" is not by any means "understanding" or "assimilation," or friendly acknowledgement, "so the Jewish religion, *alongside* Christianity, is conferred (still today) a divine right to be, a special gift and mission in the spiritual life of humanity" (Lamparter, 2). For the church the only thing that counts is the acknowledgement of the synagogue's completely different ground of being, the separation of the two spirits, and the

---

bis zum Ende aller Dinge, bleibt das verkörperte Ärgernis am Kreuz, bleibt der sichtbare Gottesfinger des Zornes in der Menschheitsgeschichte." Vogelsang, *Luthers Kampf*, 20–1.
[81] Vogelsang, *Luthers Kampf*, 12–16.
[82] "verfluchten und verdammten Juden." Vogelsang, *Luthers Kampf*, 18.
[83] "Der liberale Mensch wird auch den unsichtbaren Macht- und Geld- und Bluts- und Schicksalszusammenhang des Weltjudentums in den Bereich der Legende verweisen und nicht begreifen, daß mit der Judenfrage in der deutschen Revolution 1933 eine hundertundfünfzig Jahre lang verschleierte welthistorische Frage wieder sichtbar geworden ist." Vogelsang, *Luthers Kampf*, 18.

resolute defensive battle against the degradation through the Jewish *völkisch* type, against all "Judaizing" and "things Jewish".[84]

His explicit rejection of Lamparter reflects the hopelessness of such views in the environment created now by the Nazi regime. Vogelsang argues that the measures recommended by Luther are a practical, political approach based on *Volk* and state.[85] The Jews should be put to work, and if they prove irredeemable, then physically punished, "in particular to protect the Christian understanding of life and thus the elementary conditions for guarenteeing the unity of the life of the *Volk* and driving out its enemies."[86] The practicality and contemporary relevance of Luther's recommendations in his late Jewish writings raise the question of whether Luther actually had an understanding of racial hygiene and the danger of foreign "types" imperiling the *Volk*. Vogelsang answers with a qualified "yes":

> ...with Luther it is much more the case, as with Hutten, that a characteristically *völkisch* attitude towards Rome, towards foreigners, and towards the Jews has awoken, which is, however, so strongly directed, held, purified, and shaped by his evangelical consciousness, that the boundaries between both can scarcely be distinguished in any particular statement. The inner unification and synthesis of Germanity and Christianity is indeed Luther's strength.[87]

Luther has intuited a racial understanding, and this is what allows him to synthesize an understanding of the Gospel with a racial, *völkisch* mindset, such that his ideas have a remarkable relevance for the current context. This is reflected, Vogelsang argues, also in Luther's dismissal of conversion, which he rejects as either a solution to the "Jewish question" or as the intended outcome of salvation history. Luther's view of the Jews, he stresses, is not fueled by animus, but is an objective decipherment of the larger question:

---

[84] "Luthers praktisch-kirchliche Lösung der 'Judenfrage' heißt also keineswegs 'Verständigung' oder Angleichung ('Assimilation') oder freundliche Anerkenntnis, 'daß auch der jüdischen Religion *neben* der christlichen ein göttliches Daseinsrecht, eine besondere Gabe und Aufgabe im Geistesleben der Menschheit (heute noch) verliehen ist' (Lamparter 2. 294). Für die Kirche gilt nur Anerkenntnis des gänzlich verschiedenen Wesensgrundes der Synagoge, Scheidung der Geister und entschiedener Abwehrkampf gegenüber der inneren Zersetzung durch jüdische Art, gegenuuber allem 'Judaisieren' und 'Judenzen.'" Vogelsang, *Luthers Kampf*, 25.
[85] "volkspolitische und staatspolitische." Vogelsang, *Luthers Kampf*, 28.
[86] "...im besondere die christliche Lebensauffassung zu schützen und so die elementaren Bedingungen des einheitlichen Volkslebens zu garantieren und seine Feinde zu vertreiben." Vogelsang, *Luthers Kampf*, 30.
[87] "...bei Luther ist es vielmehr so, daß bei ihm ähnlich wie bei Hutten ein eigentümliches völkisches Bewußtsein gegenüber Rom, gegenüber den Welschen und gegenüber den Juden erwacht ist, dies aber so stark von seinem evangelischen Bewußtsein ausgerichtet, gehalten, gereinigt und geformt ist, daß die Grenzen zwischen beiden an der einzelnen Aussage kaum erkennbar sind. Die innere Einigung und Durchformung von Deutschtum und Christentum ist eben Luthers Stärke." Vogelsang, *Luthers Kampf*, 32.

The Jewish question has become since Luther's time much more complex through the emancipation of the Jews, through assimilation, and increasing numbers of Jewish Christians. It is good that today we can't simply base our decisions on Luther without our own responsibility. However, from his energies, which are so close to the sources of life, and from the connection of his passions to what is essential, we can learn everything crucial, can grasp that the Jewish question is not something cultivated for the sake of agitation, nor is it a purely German-internal issue; it is a world-historical question that must be seen not individualistically, but with an eye to the *Volk*, state and church, not within the circumference of mere humanity, but under the perspective of the eternal, or, more precisely posed, in the presence of the cross of Christ.[88]

Vogelsang's article represents a sophisticated attempt to integrate Luther seamlessly within the ideals and policies of National Socialism, strategically conceding his lack of an explicit racial consciousness, but bringing it in through the back door with his *völkisch* sensibilities which imply an intuited sense of racial consciousness. On the one hand he is too aware of the specifically religious dimensions of Luther's view of the Jews to ignore them out of hand, but on the other he poses Luther's "solution" as a practical approach applicable to the specific circumstances of the present, at least in broad strokes. And, as the final comment demonstrates, he sees Luther's relevance not so much in specifics, but in the spirit with which he approaches the question, bringing it all to a close with reverence for the cross of Christ as the central feature of Luther's viewpoint, both in his own day and for the present. Vogelsang in 1933 was a decisive supporter of the Deutsche Christen, as well as a party member; this piece of writing is emblematic of the attempt within DC circles to portray Christianity convincingly as the racial/typological ideology for the new *völkisch* state. However, Vogelsang does not treat explicitly two issues related to the "Jewish question": whether baptized Jews can have any place within the German Protestant church (though his discussion implies a negative view), and whether the Old Testament, i.e. Jewish scripture, can have any place within Christian religiosity, with its related issue of how to treat the Jewish connections of Jesus and the New Testament. These two issues will tear apart the unity of German Protestantism beginning in 1933.

---

[88] "Die Judenfrage ist seit Luthers Zeiten durch die Judenemanzipation, durch Assimilation und vermehrtes Judenchristentum sehr viel differenzierter geworden. Es ist gut, daß wir unsere Enscheidungen heute nicht einfach ohne eigene Verantwortung aus Luther ablesen können. Aber aus der lebensnahen Energie seines Glaubens und aus der inneren, sachlichen Gebundenheit seiner Leidenschaft können wir alles Entscheidende lernen, können begreifen, daß die Judenfrage keine agitatorisch gezüchtete, auch keine nur innerdeutsche, sondern eine weltgeschichtliche Frage ist, die nicht individualistisch, sondern im Blick auf Volk, Staat und Kirche, nicht im Umkreis der reinen Humanität, sondern sub specie aeternitatis, genauer gesagt: im Angesicht des Kreuzes Christi gesehen werden muß." Vogelsang, *Luthers Kampf*, 34–5.

What comes into clear focus in the course of 1933 and following are the contradictions between Luther's understanding of salvation and the demands of the new regime for a racialized understanding of the German people and humanity as a whole, which is especially sharply reflected with the "Jewish question." Vogelsang makes clear in his essay that one can construct a decisively prejudicial view of Judaism and the Jews from Luther's theology, modulated by his understanding of justification and the place of the Jews in salvation history, and at the same time one can draw amply from his anti-Jewish tracts to affirm prejudicial and violent state measures against the Jews. Bringing these two things into coherent relationship with one another based on the racial/*völkisch* assumptions of National/Socialist ideology is not really possible without finding hidden "assumptions" in Luther's writings. The fundamental issue is that for Luther the drama of salvation is individual. All humanity is alienated from God, the sources of the human self having no capacity to conform to the divine will, and consequently all humanity stands under the wrath of God—Luther makes no distinctions between different orders or segments of humanity, and certainly had no concept of biological dispositions in this regard. God offers grace to all through Christ, and by trusting in this grace one is saved, despite the persistence of sin within the self. Luther's unbridled anger against the Jews is predicated on their rejection of Christ, and persistent resistance to the appeal of the Gospel, which makes them a visible and convenient exemplar of the wages of sin, and suggests some corporate guilt, though ultimately each individual Jew has the potential to trust in the proffered grace.[89]

The challenge for church historians and theologians of the 1930s was to figure out how to make Luther's understanding, which came out of a different mental universe, speak and conform to the dictates of a twentieth-century state that prescribed racialist thinking for all areas of culture, including the practices of the churches. Protestant Christians of 1933 responded in a number of ways. Most commonly they sought to split the difference, and not come clearly to terms with the contradictions, both in their view of Luther and in the way they related to the new authoritarian state. To the degree that the state allowed them to continue with their seminary training, preaching, and traditional church order, there was a broad willingness to endorse and celebrate a regime and especially its leader that seemed to embrace at least some of the traditional values of Protestant Christian Germany. But even with this malleable approach, difficulties arose. Part of the

---

[89] The issue of Jewish conversion is vexed in the sixteenth century. On the one hand, the hope that the recovery of the true message of grace would overcome Jewish resistance to accepting the Gospel lay behind Luther's early tract about Christ being born a Jew. Yet there was a prevailing deep suspicion about Jewish conversion, and to the extent that the Jews were seen as being particularly susceptible to diabolical influences, the sincerity of any conversion was always open to question, potentially ending up with a view, as Luther did in his later denunciatory writings, that casts doubt on the sincerity of any conversion.

problem stemmed from the fact that there was a movement within the church, the "German Christians" (*Deutsche Christen* = DC), who were ready to concede to the regime a great deal more, to purge those with Jewish "blood," to expunge the Old Testament from Christian scripture, either in part or in whole, to contest the Jewishness of Jesus, and even to reject Pauline Christianity as corrupted by Jewishness. Vogelsang represented a somewhat moderate version of this wing of the church, and we have met earlier on, and will encounter later in this chapter, others whose viewpoints are hard to differentiate from the views of Alfred Rosenberg. Finally, as events transpired in 1933, there emerged, as a response to the aggressiveness of the DC in pushing their agenda and the insistence of the regime on coordinating the churches and purging Jews from all aspects of public life, including within the clergy of the church, a movement to resist the attempts to coordinate the church and to define Christian identity in terms of racial typology. Even this last group, associated with the Confessing Church movement, rarely protested the measures being taken by the regime against the Jews in society at large, but nevertheless it was their response to Rosenberg and the DC movement that created the so-called "church struggle" (*Kirchenkampf*), which represented a modulated resistance to at least some aspects of the regime. And the image of Luther as an anti-Semite was caught up in the theological battles that emerged from this political, religious, and cultural environment.

The fact that the church felt compelled to respond to the new racial consciousness of the Third Reich is well represented in a *Lehrgang* (seminar series) held in June of 1933 at the University in Giessen for faculty and pastors, including DC clerics, within the Hessian Protestant Church, the results of which were published under the title *Volk, Staat, Kirche* (*Volk*, state, church).[90] The general theme was a "theological consideration of *Volk* and State,"[91] and it set as its mission to articulate a teaching that remained both true to the calling of the Word, but also fulfilled the duty to the *Volk* in an hour of radical change.[92] The proceedings were framed by the seminar session titled "Martin Luther's understanding of *Volk* and Race," conducted by the young Heinrich Bornkamm (1901–1977), at this point at the start of his long and productive career.[93] The session he delivered highlights the challenge of racializing Luther's consciousness, as represented in his initial framing of it:

---

[90] *Volk, Staat, Kirche: Ein Lehrgang der Theolog. Fakultät Giessen* (Giessen: Alfred Topelmann, 1933).
[91] "theologische Besinnung auf Volk und Staat." *Volk, Staat, Kirche*, 3.
[92] *Volk, Staat, Kirche*, 4.
[93] Bornkamm was associated with the DC in 1933, and would join the SA as well, but would later in 1933 distance himself from both. He is somewhat similar to Paul Althaus in his embrace of the fruits of National Socialist rule while also seeking to resist the more radical reconfigurations of doctrine. See Hartmut Lehmann, "Heinrich Bornkamm im Spiegel seiner Lutherstudium von 1933 und 1947." In Thomas Kaufmann and Harry Oelke, *Evangelische Kirchenhistoriker im "Dritten Reich"* (Gütersloh: Kaiser Verlag, 2002): 367–80.

The unity of the whole *Volkstum* also requires that the question be posed a bit differently than with other topics. Not only the historical/governmental, but also the natural/hereditary fundamental consciousness of the *Volk* unit must be viewed in light of the Gospel. To be sure the concept of '*Volk*' and 'race' don't mean the same thing within our topic as for us today. In the case of 'race', a concept that Luther naturally didn't know, this is obvious. But Luther's use of '*Volk*,' as shall be demonstrated, is also different [from ours today]. It is just as obvious, however, that the reality to which these concepts refer already existed back then. They must have somehow penetrated Luther's field of observation. We are concerned here with these realities, which perhaps were hidden for Luther beneath other concepts only to the extent that he was able to recognize them. Luther must have known something about the combined biological and historical unity of a state within the *Volkstum* of which he was a part, no matter how he expressed it or how limitedly he perceived it. What matters is how he perceived these realities and judged them, and particularly, of course, how he consequently perceived and assessed the German *Volkstum*.[94]

This somewhat tangled framing of the task profiles the general challenge of integrating Luther into the mindset of the 1930s. Reading between the lines, Bornkamm will find a racial consciousness for Luther from his somewhat disparate communications to the *Volk*. Bornkamm follows with a chain of assumptions: that while the Gospel is addressed to individuals, they are not isolated, abstract individuals, but they exist in a context, within a *Volk*, so it only makes sense to look at Luther addressing "German humanity"—each part of humanity is part of a *Volkstum*, and it is within that reality that the Gospel must speak.[95] Luther was alive and worked at a time when the German *Volkstum* was awakening, and while such a consciousness is not fixed and eternal, "it is much more a possession that was intensely fought for in the suffering and ups and downs of our history." This feeling of national identity was on the march in Luther's time, and when we see Luther addressing the "nation," Bornkamm suggests, it makes sense

---

[94] "Die Verbundenheit des gemeinsamen Volkstums erfordert zugleich, daß die Aufgabe ein wenig anders als in den übrigen Fragenkreisen gestellt wird. Nicht nur das geschichtlich-staatliche, sondern auch das natürlich-stammesmäßige Grundbewußtsein der Volkseinheit muß in das Licht des Evangeliums treten. Allerdings bedeuten die Begriffe 'Volk' und 'Rasse' in unserem Thema nicht dasselbe wie bei uns. Bei 'Rasse', einem Begriff, den Luther natürlich nicht gekannt hat, versteht sich das von selbst. Aber auch für 'Volk' wird ein anderer Sprachgebrauch bei Luther aufzuweisen sein. Ebenso selbstverständlich aber hat es die Wirklichkeiten, von denen die Begriffe sprechen, schon gegeben. Sie müssen irgendwie auch in das Beobachtungsfeld Luthers gedrungen sein. Es geht nur um diese Wirklichkeiten, die bei Luther vielleicht unter anderen Begriffen verborgen sind, so weit sie überhaupt schon für ihn erkennbar waren. Luther mußte etwas wissen von der zugleich biologischen und geschichtlichen Einheit eines Staates in dem ihn tragenden Volkstum, ganz gleich wie er sie ausdrückte und begrenzt sah.... Es kommt nur darauf an wie er diese Wirklichkeiten sah und beurteilte, im besonderen natürlich, wie er dabei das deutsche Volkstum sah und einschätzte." *Volk, Staat, Kirche*, 5–6.
[95] *Volk, Staat, Kirche*, 6–7.

to translate that in our minds as *"Volk."*[96] "For [Luther] nation is *Volk* constituted in a strong state structure. He expresses approximately what we today understand by *Volk* when we grasp the concept in its depths."[97] Given the prominence of race in his subject matter, he turns to see how this might ensue from his understanding of *Volk*.

At this point Bornkamm brings in the Jews, quoting at some length from "that great writing" *On the Jews and their Lies*.[98] Having recounted Luther's views for three pages, he closes this section by observing:

> As certainly as we can sense Luther's instinctive racial aversion to the Jews (and no less to the Wends and the *Welsch*, for whom since his trip to Rome he had little sympathy), nevertheless his incendiary call to fight against the Jews doesn't come out of racial differences. They rang out, rather, against a *Volk* who continually offended God through disbelief and blasphemy.[99]

With this ambiguous formula he drops the topic of race, with which, it is clear, he does not have much to work. Rather, he now turns to discuss the *Schöpfungsordnungen* (orders of creation), using them to demonstrate, as had Althaus, that the church resides within the context both of the *Volk*, an order that precedes the Fall, as well as the state, which was created as a consequence of the Fall. In both instances, the necessity of the church adapting itself to the order of *Volk* and state is clear. Which, undoubtedly, is why Heinrich Bornkamm, despite the lack of material, goes to such lengths to try to find in Luther something that can stand in for racial consciousness.[100] However, in training servants of the church to think in these terms, in celebrating Luther's birthday by dressing him in a brown shirt, the more

---

[96] "Es ist vielmehr ein in den Leiden und Wechselfällen unserer Geschichte schwer erkämpftes Gut." *Volk, Staat, Kirche*, 7.
[97] "Nation ist ihm das im festen Staatsgefüge verfaßte Volk. Er drückt also annähernd aus, was wir heute, wenn wir den Begriff in seiner Tiefe fassen, unter Volk verstehen." *Volk, Staat, Kirche*, 10.
[98] "…aus der großen Schrift." *Volk, Staat, Kirche*, 13.
[99] "So gewiß bei Luther eine instinktive rassenmäßige Abneigung gegen die Juden wie gegen die Wenden und die Welschen, denen er seit seiner Romreise wenig freundlich gesinnt war, deutlich zu fühlen ist, so sind doch gerade seine flammenden Kampfrufe gegen das Judentum nicht aus dem Rassegegensatz abzuleiten. Sie erklangen vielmehr wider ein Volk, das unausgesetzt Gott durch Unglauben und Lästerung beleidigte." *Volk, Staat, Kirche*, 16.
[100] One intriguing addendum to Bornkamm's article comes with his republication of it in significantly edited form in 1947, now rebranded as "Luther und der deutsche Geist" as part of a collection of his essays, *Luthers Geistige Welt* (Lüneburg, 1947). Harmut Lehmann has analyzed comparatively the two versions of the essay, and found that about 20 percent of the *Urtext* [original] was deleted, and about 15 percent of the republished essay is now new material. Not surprisingly, all mention of race is expunged, the sections dealing with the Jews significantly remodeled, though not eliminated, and the use of *Volk* in its various forms greatly reduced, though not entirely eliminated. The differences are a fascinating example of how the mentality of Luther research was consciously edited with the collapse of the regime, and also how artificially and opportunistically constructed this image of Luther was. See Hartmut Lehmann, "Heinrich Bornkamm im Spiegel seiner Lutherstudium von 1933 und 1947." In, *Evangelische Kirchenhistoriker im "Dritten Reich,"* ed. Thomas Kaufmann and Harry Oelke (Gütersloh: Kaiser Verlag, 2002): 367–80.

radical elements of the DC, an organization of which Bornkamm was a formal member at this juncture in June 1933, were emboldened to push an agenda that would go well beyond the lukewarm endorsement of Bornkamm or even Vogelsang for a full-throated attack upon Jewishness within the church.

The contradictions rooted in this racial/nationalist incarnation of Protestantism and Luther came to a head with the so-called "Sports Palace scandal" of November 1933. As previously noted, the *Deutsche Christen* saw as their mission bringing the revolution begun by Luther in the sixteenth century to full fruition in National-Socialist Germany, and they imagined that this meant, as had been articulated by people such as Theodor Fritsch and Alfred Falb, the thorough cleansing of the church of all Jewish influences, which also meant great sympathy for all that was going on against the Jews in 1933.[101] For much of 1933 the DC movement appeared ascendent within the Protestant church, having positioned one of their own to lead the newly created office of *Reichsbischof* (imperial bishop), having taken control of a number of state churches, and having expanded their influence in general. But the tensions within the movement, and between the movement and the larger church were latent yet significant. It was one of the most radical factions within the DC movement, centered in greater Berlin, that organized the Sports Palace event in Berlin for November 13, designed to get a jump on the celebration of Luther's anniversary ahead of the countrywide events set for November 19. At this juncture, one of the most aggravating issues for the more radical DC factions such as dominated in Berlin was the status of the Arian Paragraph within the church.[102] The meeting for the Berlin area DC was primed to express this frustration concerning the continued influence of Jews in the church.

On that evening 20,000 members gathered, filling the arena, opening with a chorus of "A Mighty Fortress," and then hearing various addresses, the keynote of which was delivered by Dr. Reinhold Krause (1893–1980), district *Führer* (*Gauführer*) and rabid anti-Semite, whose message, calling for a realization of the destiny that Luther had left behind, "the completion of the German Reformation in the Third Reich," was greeted over and over with thunderous applause.[103] Calling repeatedly on Luther's fiery and heroic piety, Krause envisioned a *Volkskirche* that would be the fulfillment of Luther's ideal. And what would this church look

---

[101] On the progression of measures carried out by the regime in 1933, see Saul Friedländer, *Nazi Germany and the Jews*, Vol. I: *The Years of Persecution, 1933–1939* (New York: Harper Collins, 1997): esp. chs. 1 and 2.

[102] "The law for the restoration of the Professional Civil Service" stipulated that civil servants with Jewish heritage were to be dismissed from their positions. This was brought into effect in April 1933 and immediately set off a debate within the churches on how it was to be carried out. It was around the so-called Arian Paragraph which defined this law that the origins of the Confessing Church can be found, whose questioning of its application within the church was countered by factions within the DC. See Klaus Scholder, *Die Kirchen und das Dritte Reich*, vol. 1, page 345ff. for a discussion of the initial reaction within the churches.

[103] "die Vollendung der deutschen Reformation im Dritten Reich." Scholder, *Die Kirchen*, vol. 1, 703.

like? For one, it would be driven by the healthy sentiments of the *Volk*, and not some outmoded structure of pastors and hierarchy. But more importantly, it would be a church purged of Jewish influences. If we're called not to buy products from Jews, Krause asks, why would we let them dictate the substance of our religion? Sounding strikingly similar to Alfred Rosenberg, Krause called for the elimination of the Old Testament and the inferiority complex of the Rabbi Paul, and the establishment of the teaching of the purified Jesus, drawing from the Gospel only what resonates with the German heart, such that what resulted would be pure, Germanic Christianity. That meant a diminishment of the centrality of the cross, since the *Reich* needed proud rather than slavish men. He closed his speech by emphasizing that with such a church would be experienced "the close kinship between the Nordic spirit with the heroic spirit of Jesus. Then will become manifest that the completion of the Reformation of Martin Luther means the final victory of the Nordic Spirit over oriental materialism. Heil!"[104] Transcripts from the speech emphasize the enormous enthusiasm of the 20,000 in the arena for his message, after which a six-point resolution was affirmed that more or less codified the substance of his message with virtually no dissent. The significance of the Sports Palace meeting was not the content of the address, which was nothing new, however extreme it sounds today, but the subsequent reaction to the press reports about the event. Mainstream leaders within the Protestant church responded with concern about such unconventional prescriptions, and were pressured by members of the incipient Confessing Church movement to take action. Figures such as Paul Althaus and Erich Vogelsang, who had some level of sympathy for *völkisch* Christianity, felt compelled to disassociate from the DC. In general the various reactions reveal the degree to which such views were not broadly popular. The aftermath fractured the DC movement into constituent parts, making it ineffectual as a vehicle for integrating the Protestant church around a radical, nazified Christianity. In addition, it brought together elements within the rest of the church who in one way or another had deep reservations about the theological and institutional ideas of the DC, and provided the basis for a common front, though, as was the case with the DC, this common front disguised what were deep divisions.[105] While much of the fallout fed into the struggles of the German Protestant church, it also is an essential backdrop for understanding the struggles around Luther's racial and anti-Jewish legacy from the end of 1933 forward.

The basic theme that Krause had deployed concerning Luther in his address came to be repeated endlessly in the struggles around Luther's anti-Semitic image, namely that the larger church had betrayed Luther by, among other issues,

---

[104] "...wie eng sich dann die Verwandtschaft des nordischen Geistes mit dem heldischen Jesusgeist zeigt. Es wird dann offenber werden, daß die Vollendung der Reformation Martin Luthers der endgültige Sieg des nordischen Geistes uber orientalischen Materialismus bedeutet. Heil!" Scholder, *Die Kirchen*, vol. 1, 705.
[105] See the discussion in Scholder, *Die Kirchen*, vol. 1, ch. 13.

suppressing his anti-Jewish writings in a conspiracy of silence in order to protect the Jews. Such accusations had been heard prior to the Nazi seizure of power; both Fritsch and Falb contended that Luther affirmed the racial cleansing of Christianity, and such accusations had been broached by Mathilde Ludendorff in publications of the late 1920s, as well as by Alfred Rosenberg in his *Mythus*.[106] As discussed in Chapter 5 (pp. 113–24), by the mid-1930s the idea of a betrayal of Luther by the Protestant church had become something of fixed idea both among the non-Christian Germanic belief movements and within DC circles. Though this supposed "betrayal" gained a great deal of attention, for the DC it was the racial cleansing of Christianity that loomed as the ultimate omega point in finishing Luther's revolutionary Reformation. As the 1930s went forward, and ever more extreme measures were taken against the Jews, each stage was greeted within broad sections of the DC with approval as an appropriate step toward a fulfillment of Luther's *völkisch* Christianity.

This phenomenon is exemplified in the wake of the Nuremberg Laws[107] in a 1937 piece titled "Von den Jüden [sic] und ihren Lügen," published in *Die Christus Bekennende Reichskirche* (the Christ-confessing imperial church), an organ of the Bishop of Breman, Heinrich Weidemann, one of the most aggressive DC supporters among the German bishops. The periodical was particularly devoted, as its title suggests, to publishing articles attacking the Confessing Church, and exemplifies the deep fissure between the DC and the Confessing Church during the 1930s. This particular article was authored by Gerhard Hahn (1901–1943), theologian and church administrator in Hannover and later in Thuringia. The piece begins with an emotion-laden confession of faith in Christ and National Socialism, and then provides a full-throated endorsement of the recently enacted Nuremberg Laws, quoting from Goebbels about the necessity of using a strong

---

[106] Mathilde Ludendorff was the second wife of Erich Ludendorff, World War I hero and early supporter of Hitler, though by the second half of the 1920s he had become estranged from Hitler. Mathilde Ludendorff was an active author who specialized beginning in the 1920s in conspiracy theories about the Jews, including those concerning Luther's anti-Jewish writings. Her ideas were prominent enough to engender a response by Hermann Steinlein, *Frau Dr. Ludendorffs Phantasien über Luther und die Reformation* (Leipzig: A. Deichertsche Verlagsbuchhandlung, 1932), where he demonstrated that her accusations of a churchwide conspiracy to suppress Luther's works were nonsensical, given the long record of their publication over the years. Steinlein represents the middle position within the church, attributing to Luther's anti-Jewish writings an important perspective while noting that it is not compulsory for the church to follow every one of his prescriptions (28). During the 1930s Steinlein, who was a pastor in Ansbach until his retirement in 1935, will publish a few other short pieces on the "Jewish question," taking an anti-racialist position regarding the treatment of the Jews within the church. Hermann Steinlein, "Luthers Stellung zur Frage der Judentaufe." *Die Junge Kirche* 3 (1935): 842–6; Hermann Steinlein, "Kennt Luther einen 'deutschen Glauben'?" *Luther* 21 (1939): 17–24.

[107] The Nuremberg Laws were passed in late 1935, though their enactment was delayed until after the Berlin Olympics in 1936. They stripped those defined racially as Jews of their citizenship, and prohibited marriage or sexual intercourse between "Germans" and "Jews," as these categories were now defined. They represented a ratcheting up of the pressure on Germany's Jewish population and the separation of Jews from the rest of German society. See Saul Friedländer, *Nazi Germany and the Jews*, vol. I, ch. 5.

dose of Lysol to kill off particularly malevolent germs, as well as noting a recent issue of *Der Stürmer*[108] about how the Jews use marriage as a means through which to subvert German blood, and how the church facilitates that by baptizing Jews. He expresses great frustration with those who want to claim the Jews as brothers in Christ, or who question the legitimacy of being a National Socialist and a Christian.[109]

With this as his preface, he moves into a polemic against the Confessing Church by deploying Luther, whom no one, he notes, could accuse of being a Nazi or betraying loyalty to the Lutheran Confessions. The piece will constantly play upon the word "confessing" as it targets the supposedly indefensible positions of the Confessing Church. He quotes long passages from Luther's 1543 work *On the Jews and their Lies*, and then provides his readers with their significance:

> When one reads these words of Luther's—and I would point out again emphatically that these radical demands about the Jews are not taken from *Der Stürmer*, but from the above-mentioned work of Luther!—then a serious Christian can hardly avoid the impression that a montrous, satanic danger coming from the Jews must indeed be threatening our German *Volk*; it was not for naught that Martin Luther was so agggressive in the advice he gave to to the lords and rulers. Luther saw the danger clearly and distinctly, and knew what it meant; consequently he stood up to give warning because he felt obligated to do so.[110]

He notes that Luther is equally sharp in reminding the rulers of their duties, given the gravity of the situation. And lest one think this comes out of anything but the most admirable of motives, he reassures his readers:

> Luther sees the great danger and he warns, not to be sure out of hatred for the Jews, but out of love for Christ and love for his German *Volk*. And by the way,

---

[108] *Der Stürmer* was a rabidly anti-Semitic weekly newspaper published by Julius Streicher, and was a mouthpiece for the most extreme anti-Semitic voices in the Third Reich. Streicher's development as an anti-Semite was heavily influenced by the writings of Theodor Fritsch. See Daniel Roos, *Julius Streicher und der Stürmer, 1923-1945* (Paderborn: Ferdinand Schöningh, 2014). The comparison of Jews to a biologically infectious agent has a long lineage in the rhetoric of the anti-Semitic right, and was used repeatedly by Hitler beginning in 1919 and following.

[109] Vortrag von Vizepräsident Hahn, Hannover [Gerhard Hahn], "Von den Jüden und ihren Lügen." *Die Christus Bekennende Reichskirche. Eine Schriftenreihe*, ed. Landesbischof Lic. Dr. Weidemann, Bremen (Bremen: Haushild) Heft 7, (1937): 1-16; 3. Hahn adopts both the title and the orthography of Luther's 1543 tract.

[110] "Wenn man diese Worte Luthers liest—und ich weise nochmals ausdrücklich daruauf hin, daß diese Radikalforderungen gegen die Juden nicht etwa dem 'Stürmer' entnommen sind, sondern der oben erwähnten Lutherschrift!—, dann kann sich ein ernster Christenmensch wohl kaum des Eindrucks erwehren, daß in der Tat unserem deutschen Volk von Seiten der Juden eine ungeheure, satanische Gefahr drohen muß; umsonst ist ein Mann wie D. Martin Luther nicht so scharf geworden in seinem Ratschlag, den er seinen Herren und Obrigkeiten gibt. Luther sah klar und deutlich die Gefahr er wußte, worum es ging, und darum steht er auf als Warner, weil er sich dazu verpflichtet fühlt." Hahn, "Von den Jüden und ihren Lügen," 9.

this deep and truly justified rationale for the struggle against the Jews has also been expressed by our *Führer* **Adolf Hitler**, who once said "we don't hate the Jews, but we love our German *Volk*." And that is also the position, grounded in the will of God (the law of love), of the National Socialists and Christians in their struggle with the Jews and the Jewish demon.[111]

It goes without saying, however, that the loving spirit of the struggle against the Jews does not preclude him from adding a list of vicious accusations against their intentional corruption of the German *Volk*:

If the Jews had come among our *Volk* in order to live among themselves in their families and clans, then scarcely anyone would object. When, however, the Jews come among our *Volk* in order to pollute and defile the German blood, as the Jews have done systematically for centuries, then the German Christian is obligated according to God's holy order of creation to take a stand and with all available power to ensure that the German blood given to us by the creator God not be defiled, but preserved in its purity. Whoever can't or won't do that is no German or Christian![112]

He closes by emphasizing how much Luther's prescriptions, though written four hundred years prior, fit with what is being carried out by the regime, and reminding his readers of Weimar and Bolshevism, both examples of what the Jews would do if they could. Though Hahn's piece is rhetorical in nature, and lacks scholarly rigor, it reflects well the logic of the DC position regarding the treatment of the Jews: that racial types are part of the God ordained ordering of creation, that the German *Volk* are one of those orders and especially holy given the special calling of Luther in bringing the Gospel, that Luther himself advocated the harsh treatment of the Jews, and that this is not some sort of blind pogrom driven by popular prejudice and hate, but a loving fulfillment of the obligation one has to God's well-ordered creation, which is under attack by the nefarious Jews. This sort of logic will allow the DC faction every step along the way to applaud, based on

---

[111] "Luther sieht die große Gefahr und warnt—nicht etwa aus Haß gegen die Juden, sondern aus Liebe zu Christus und aus Liebe zu seinem deutschen Volk. Diese tiefe und wahrhaft berechtigte Begründung des Kampfes gegen die Juden ist übrigens auch bei unserem Führer **Adolf Hitler** zu finden, der einmal gesagt hat: 'Wir hassen nicht den Juden, aber wir lieben unser deutsches Volk.' Und das ist auch die in Gottes Willen (Gebot der Liebe) begründete Stellung der Nationalsozialisten und Christen in ihrem Kampf gegen die Juden und gegen den jüdischen Ungeist." Hahn, "Von den Jüden und ihren Lügen," 10.

[112] "Wenn die Juden in unser Volk kämen, um hier unter sich in ihren Familien und Sippen zu leben, dann wird das wohl kaum jemand beanstanden. Wenn aber die Juden in unser Volk gekommen sind, um das deutsche Blut zu schänden und zu verseuchen, wie die Juden das systematisch jahrhundertelang getrieben haben, dann ist der deutsche **Christenmensch** nach Gottes heiliger Schöperordnung verpflichtet, dagegen Front zu machen und mit allen Kräften dafür zu sorgen, daß das uns vom Schöpfergott gegebene deutsche Blut nicht geschändet, sondern rein erhalten wird. Wer das nicht will noch kann, ist weder Deutscher noch Christ!" Hahn, "Von den Jüden und ihren Lügen," 11.

faithfulness to Luther and the Gospel, the work of the National Socialist state against the Jews.

This logic is highlighted even more starkly in a work of Wolf Meyer-Erlach's in 1938, a follow-up to his earlier *Verrat an Luther*, titled *Juden, Mönche, Luther* (Jews, monks, Luther). In this work, Meyer-Erlach frames Luther's harsh recommendations for the Jews in parallel to the measures being taken by the Nazis, framing it all as an apocalyptic struggle being played out for the survival of humanity. While the church has failed in its duty to carry on this struggle, now the state has carried it forward.[113] However, he begins by noting that the demands of Luther make the measures the state has taken so far seem moderate: "Luther in his work of judgment *On The Jews and their Lies* presented, as a Christian, as a path-blazer of the Reformation, as a torchbearer of a new world epoch, demands beside which the Nuremberg Laws for the regulation of the Jewish question in Germany appear coolly scientific, sober, and objective."[114] The heart of the book moves to explore these demands, laying them out in detailed fashion as prescriptions for dealing with the problems of the Jews. He enumerates each measure in turn: burning their synagogues and literature, attacking their houses, forcing them to remain at home, preventing them from lending money, forbidding the Rabbis to preach, and forcing the able-bodied to do productive labor.[115] It is this legacy that the church has turned away from, becoming as a result a protector of the Jews, instead of exhorting, as Luther did, the authorities to take up the struggle against the predatory menace, with predictable consequences:

We **became** jewified, until we heard the call of the awakened *Volk*, the death cry of the millions, until we awoke through the word of the Führer and those true to him, through those fighters, who devote an entire life in order to lead the *Volk* to the Luther in the time of his greatest maturity. They have preserved the legacy of the German Luther, Luther the guardian of the entire West, while the church betrayed it. They have saved Luther's struggle against the Jews from being buried by ecclesiastical, confessional habit. But the bishops of the Lutheran Council, the men of Oxford and their confessing brothers in Germany still dream on and on the Jewish dream.[116]

---

[113] Wolf Meyer-Erlach, *Juden, Mönche, Luther* (Weimar: Verlag Deutsche Christen, [1938]): 11–14.
[114] "Luther hat in seinem Gerichtswerk 'Von den Jüden und ihren Lügen' als Christ, als Bahnbrecher der Reformation, als Fackelträger einer neuen Weltepoche Forderungen aufgestellt, neben denen die Nürnberger Gesetze zur Regelung der Judenfrage in Deutschland wissenschaftlich kühl, sauber und sachlich erscheinen." Meyer-Erlach, *Juden, Mönche, Luther*, 39.
[115] Meyer-Erlach, *Juden, Mönche, Luther*, 47–8.
[116] "Wir **waren** verjudet, bis wir den Ruf des erwachten Volkes, den Todesschrei der Millionen hörten, bis wir aufwachten durch das Wort des Führers und seiner Getreuen, durch jene Kämpfer, die ein ganzes Leben dransetzten, um das Volk hinzuführen zu dem Luther in der Zeit seiner höchsten Reife. Sie haben das Erbe Luthers des Deutschen, Luthers des Wächters für das ganze Abendland gehütet, während die Kirche es verriet. Sie haben Luthers Kampf gegen die Juden vor der Verschüttung durch die kirchlichem bekenntnismäßige Gewohnheit gerettet. Aber die Bischöfe des lutherischen

What the pastors and church servants need to do now, however, is become advocates for this program of Luther's:

> In the struggle of Christian *Volk* who are hard-pressed by the Jews, the preachers should not be bystanders, much less confessors who confuse the conscience of the *Volk* with their fairy tales and theologies, but admonishers and voices crying out when the princes and rulers are lax in their fighting the Jewish danger. **From the protector of the Jews against the *Volk* emerged the protector of the *Volk* against the Jews and their comrades....**[117]

And what would that mean? He repeats once again even more extensively the list of Luther-endorsed measures he had earlier enumerated, noting how in nick of time the ravages of the Jews have been checked, no thanks to the church, and then reframing again the apocalyptic consequences of this struggle:

> Nevertheless the truth is victorious. In the stance and decisions of National Socialism against the Jews, Luther's desires are fulfilled after centuries. Today the Jewish question is no longer sentimentalized as individual fate but as the fate of the *Volk* which will decide the future of the West and the spirit and profile of the world in the coming centuries. It is precisely the leading men in the fight against the Jews, whose life work has been made possible by the Nuremberg Laws, who see, in contrast to the blind-leading-the-blind, the religious depths of the question, the eternal struggle of the Jews against everything divine, against the Divinity, against Christendom. They are fighting the *völkisch* and economic struggle, the decisive battle of Western, Christian humanity, of Western, Christian culture against the demonic wasteland of Judaism, the struggle of the *Völker* created by God against the trans-national, international work of degradation by the Jew.[118]

Rates, die Männer von Oxford und ihre bekennenden Brüder in Deutschland träumen noch immer den jüdischen Traum." Meyer-Erlach, *Juden, Mönche, Luther*, 51.

[117] "Bei dem Kampf des christlichen, von den Juden bedrängten Volkes sollen die Prediger nicht Zuschauer sein, noch viel weniger Bekenner, die das Gewissen des Volkes mit ihren Märlein und Theologien verwirren, sondern Mahner und Rufer, wenn Fürsten oder Herren lässig sind in der Bekämpfung der jüdischen Gefahr. **Aus dem Schutzherrn der Juden wider das Volk wurde der Schutzherr des Volkes wider die Juden und ihre Genossen...**" Meyer-Erlach, *Juden, Mönche, Luther*, 53.

[118] "Aber dennoch siegt die Wahrheit. In der Haltung und Entscheidung des Nationalsozialismus gegen das Judentum geht Luthers Wollen nach Jahrhunderten in Erfüllung. Heute wird die Judenfrage nicht mehr Sentimental als Einzelschicksal gesehen sondern als Volksschicksal, das über die Zukunft des Abendlandes, über Geist und Gesicht der Welt in den kommenden Jahrhunderten entscheiden wird. Gerade die führenden Männer im Kampfe wider die Juden, deren Lebensarbeit die Gesetze von Nürnberg möglich gemacht haben, sehen im Gegensatz zu den blinden Blindenleitern die religiose Tiefe der Frage, den ewigen Kampf des Juden gegen alles Göttliche, gegen den Göttlichen, gegen das Christentum. Sie kämpfen den völkischen und den wirtschaftlichen Kampf, die Entscheidungsschlacht der abendländisch-christlichen Menschheit, der abendländisch-christlichen Kultur wider die

This happy set of circumstances provides a new opportunity for the church to find its way back to become supporters of their true legacy, which the Nazi State has taken up on its own:

> Dead are the princes who at one time protected the Jews from the *Volk*, who let them suck the *Volk* dry. The will of the *Volk*, which the princes betrayed for centuries, has today become the law. We have the clean division between the Jews and non-Jews in Germany, and with it also between those Luther called murderers and desecraters of Christendom and the Christians. Out of the realm of the external and accidental, the struggle has been directed into the last depths of religion, the orders of creation, the order of the *Völker*, If at one time the great German prophet stood before the worldly lords and spiritual leaders as the watchman of the Christian West, calling them to battle against the Jews, so now today secular leaders stand before the church, before Christendom, and call them to their Christian, German, Western duty.[119]

Meyer-Erlach published this work in the course of 1938, and while he exhibits satisfaction at what the Nuremberg Laws have wrought, his repeated emphasis on the violent measures that populated *On the Jews and their Lies* left no doubt that such an attack on the Jews would be seen as obedience to the divinely ordained world-historical battle against the Jewish Moloch. Clearly such a frame suggests that the Nuremberg Laws did not finish the struggle, but was another station along the way, and would countenance even more dramatic interventions.

That this affirmation of "sharp" measures had few boundaries is made manifest in the response to the so-called "Night of Glass" (*Reichskristallnacht*) of November 9–10, 1938 (also the four-hundred-fifty-fifth anniversary of Luther's birthday), by Martin Sasse (1890–1942), Bishop of the Protestant church in Thuringia, a center for radical DC activism.[120] Titled *Martin Luther über die Juden: Weg mit ihnen!* (Martin Luther on the Jews: away with them!), it begins by celebrating the recent event:

Wüstendämonie des Judentums, dem Kampf gottgeschaffner Völker wider die überstaatliche, international Zersetzungsarbeit des Juden." Meyer-Erlach, *Juden, Mönche, Luther*, 60.

[119] "Tot sind die Fürsten, die einst die Juden wider das Volk schützten, die das Volk von ihnen aussaugen ließen. Der Wille des Volkes, den die Fürsten jahrhundertlange verrieten, ist heute zum Gesetz geworden. Wir haben die reinliche Trennung zwischen Juden und Nichtjuden in Deutschland, damit aber auch zwischen denen, die Luther Mörder und Schänder des Christentums nennt, und den Christen. Aus dem Äußerlichen, Zufälligen ist der Kampf hineingeführt worden in die letzte Tiefe der Religion, die Schöpfungsordnung, der Völkerordnung. Stand einst der große deutsche Profet als Wächter des christlichen Abendlandes vor den weltlichen Herren und geistlichen Führern und rief sie zum Kampfe auf wider die Juden, so stehen heute die weltlichen Führer vor den Kirchen, vor der Christenheit und rufen sie zu ihrer christlichen, deutschen, abendländischen Pflicht." Meyer-Erlach, *Juden, Mönche, Luther*, 60.

[120] It is apt that Meyer-Erlach had dedicated *Juden, Mönche, Luther* to Martin Sasse, "his comrade in arms for a German church" (...*dem Kampfgenossen für eine deutsche Kirche*): 5. Both Meyer-Erlach and Sasse were leading figures of the DC movement in Thuringia.

192 THE LUTHER MYTH

On November 10, Luther's birthday, the synagogues burned in Germany. The power of the Jews in the economic arena in the new Germany was finally broken by the German *Volk* as atonement for the murder of the ambassadorial councilor vom Rat at the hands of a Jew, and with this act is crowned the divinely blessed struggle of the *Führer* for the full liberation of our *Volk*. World Catholicism and Oxford-World Protestantism raise up their voices together with the Western democracies as protectors of the Jews against the Third Reich's opposition to the Jews. In this hour the voice of this man must be heard who began, as the German prophet of the sixteenth century, out of ignorance, as a friend of the Jews, but driven over time by his conscience, driven by experience and reality, became the greatest anti-Semite of his time, warning his *Volk* about the Jews. In this work Luther alone shall speak to us in his own words. Even today his voice is still more powerful than the paltry words of the international Jewish comrades and ivory-tower types, both estranged from God and *Volk*, who no longer know anything about Luther's works and will.[121]

There follows about sixteen pages of excerpts from Luther's two works of 1543, with little commentary other than his dramatic highlighting of especially "powerful" words. As with many works of the right, the excerpts treat only the harsh measures, and do not engage the larger theological arguments about the interpretation of the Old Testament. One hundred thousand copies of the tract were published for distribution in congregations. Clearly Sasse considered the words themselves to make the point. Though there is no clear coordination of the work of Meyer-Erlach and Sasse, the earlier work segues seamlessly with Sasse, the one framing the appropriate measures, the latter providing the post-mortem reaffirmation of the justness of what was carried out with the burning of synagogues and books, attacks on the businesses, and the mass incarceration of Jews, all of which could easily be posed as faithfulness to the work of the Reformation started in Luther's day.

---

[121] "Am 10. November, an Luthers Geburtstag, brennen in Deutschland die Synagogen. Vom deutschen Volke wird zur Sühne für die Ermordung des Gesandtschaftsrates vom Rath durch Judenhand die Macht der Juden auf wirtschaftlichem Gebiete im neuen Deutschland endgültig gebrochen und damit der gottgesegnete Kampf des Führers zur völligen Befreiung unseres Volkes gekrönt. Der Weltkatholizismus und der Oxford-Weltprotestantismus erheben zusammen mit den westlichen Demokratien ihre Stimmen als Judenschutzherren gegen die Judengegnerschaft des Dritten Reiches. In dieser Stunde muß die Stimme des Mannes gehört werden, der als der Deutschen Prophet im 16. Jahrhundert aus Unkenntnis einst als Freund der Juden begann, der, getrieben von seinem Gewissen, getrieben von den Erfahrungen und der Wirklichkeit, der größte Antisemit seiner Zeit geworden ist, der Warner seines Volkes wider die Juden. In dieser Schrift soll nur Luther mit seinen eigenen Worten zu uns reden. Seine Stimme ist auch heute noch gewaltiger als das armselige Wort gottferner und volksfremder internationaler Judengenossen und Schriftgelehrter, die nichts mehr wissen von Luthers Werk und Willen." Martin Sasse, *Martin Luther über die Juden: Weg mit ihnen!* (Freiburg i.B.: Sturmhut-Verlag, 1938): 1.

Unfortunately, the attempts to modulate Luther's words as they related to the circumstances of the Protestant church in the 1930s by those who opposed DC prescriptions for the church fell well short of decisively counteracting the forceful statements of DC supporters. Hansgeorg Schroth, *Luthers christlicher Antisemitismus heute* (Luther's Christian anti-Semitism today), published in 1937, is perhaps the best example of how a work that rejects racial anti-Semitism and the *völkisch* Christianity does not really call into question the measures being taken by the Nazi state. Schroth study was responding to the numerous works that extolled Luther's anti-Jewish writings for their harsh recommendations, suggesting thereby that Luther also advocated a racially motivated program of defense against the Jews. Schroth rejects out of hand such a reading of Luther, and seeks to center Luther's understanding on an exclusively Christian basis. For Schroth, this means understanding how Luther understood the Jews in the larger history of salvation:

> We are not church in order to act politically or by *völkisch* principles. With that, every misunderstanding regarding what it means to consider Luther's 'Christian anti-Semitism' must be precluded. Where the church as church answers, it answers based on salvation history. That alone is the appropriate place to discuss what Luther has said and meant, and to consider to what extent his statements and ideas are still binding for us today.[122]

He notes that during Luther's time the Jews had a political existence as a religious community, and were situated so that they could try to undermine Christian teachings, and that is, in part, what leads Luther to recommend such harsh measures, measures that Schroth quotes at some length. But, one cannot leave that as the base reason Luther speaks as he did: "what is decisive for Luther is not this judgment [against the Jews] alone; he inquires as to the reason why the Jews are this way, and why it is necessary to defend against them by every means, and to be free of them."[123] According to Schroth, for Luther the Jews of his day were like Mathilde Ludendorff or other Germanic Religion types of today who try to lure people away from their Christian faith. In that way, says Luther, they become instruments of the devil. To be Israel meant in the Old Testament to be the chosen people of God through a covenant, a covenant that with the New Testament came to be fulfilled in Christ. The Jewish people of today, Schroth argues by way

---

[122] "Wir sind nicht Kirche, um politisch, und völkisch zu handeln. Damit muß jedes Mißverständnis über den Sinn einer Besinnung auf Luthers 'christlichen Antisemitismus' ausgeschlossen sein. Wo aber Kirche als Kirche antwortet, antwortet sie heilsgeschichtlich. Allein dies ist der angemessene Ort einer Erörterung dessen, was Luther gesagt und gemeint hat, und inwieweit dieses sein Sagen und Meinen für uns heute noch verbindlich zu sein hat." Hansgeorg Schroth, *Luthers christlicher Antisemitismus heute* (Witten: Westdeutscher Lutherverlag, 1937): 6.

[123] "Das entscheidende für Luther ist aber nicht dieses Urteil allein; er fragt nach dem Grunde, warum die Juden so seien und warum es nötig ist, sich ihrer mit allen Mitteln zu erwehren und sie los zu werden." Schroth, *Luthers christlicher Antisemitismus*, 9.

of Luther, are not the same people, since they rejected Christ, and as a result stand under the wrath of God. This has nothing to do with blood or race, but faith. They are a sign of what happens when grace is rejected, something that can happen to any people, the Germans as much as the Jews—Schroth again notes that those who read faith in racial terms are a modern equivalent to the Jews. The Jews are a sign of God's wrath against sinful humanity, just as Christ is the sign of divine love and grace.[124]

Schroth does not have anything decisive to say about the measures being taken against the Jews as a community; he concedes that it lies within the power of the state to take such measures, and it can be, as in Luther's time, there are reasons the Jews actions might need to be interdicted, though as a "severe mercy" (*scharfe Barmhärzigkeit*).[125] But when it comes to the baptism of Jews, and their inclusion in the Christian community, or the pastorate, Schroth is decisive that they should be treated as any other people, since salvation is offered to each of us apart from any physical circumstance; salvation is not based on *Volk* or race. "Here it is indeed for the Jews as for the non-Jews about one and the same question of obedience. And with baptism it is about the obedience to the election of God— indeed, the election of God and not about political circumstances."[126] For Schroth Jewishness does not designate a people or historical religious group, but rather the absence of Christian faith. In this sense, racial/cultural "Jews" who confess Christ are not Jews, but Christians, and those "Christians" who confess faith in the Volk or the state, have become Jews:

> No, the Jewish question is not a question of 'Jew or German?'—that has been answered, but a question of 'Jew or Christian?' And as such a, no, the decisive question of every *Volk*: 'German without Christ?'—'German with Christ', that is to say, in Christ?' **Saying 'yes' to the former means falling into Jewishness, into *völkisch* death-- despite one's *völkisch* and political anti-Semitism; Saying "yes' to the latter question means not just being church, but also being and remaining *Volk* in perfected fashion.**[127]

---

[124] Schroth, *Luthers christlicher Antisemitismus*, 9–14.
[125] Schroth, *Luthers christlicher Antisemitismus*, 14–16.
[126] "Es geht hier sowohl für den Juden wie fur den Nichtjuden um ein und dieselbe Gehorsamsfrage. Und es geht bei der Taufe um den Gehorsam der Erwählung Gottes gegenüber; aber eben der Erwählung Gottes und nicht nach politischen Bedingungen." Schroth, *Luthers christlicher Antisemitismus*, 18–19.
[127] "Nein, die Judenfrage ist nicht eine Frage: 'Jude oder Deutscher?'—hier ist sie gelöst, sondern eine Frage: 'Jude oder Christ?'—und als solche eine, nein, die entscheidende Frage eines jeden Volkes: 'Deutscher ohne Christus?'—'Deutscher mit Christus, d.h. in Christus?' Das Ja dem ersten, heißt trotz eines völkisch-weltanschaulichen und politischen Antisemitismus dem Judentum verfallen, dem völkischen Tod. Das Ja dem zweiten, das heißt nicht nur Kirche sein, sondern eben auch in vollkommener Weise Volk sein und bleiben." Schroth, *Luthers christlicher Antisemitismus*, 22.

Returning to the question of Jewish baptism and membership in one church, he affirms this again, though gives credence to the idea that many Jews might do this just for its advantages, and not sincerely, so that they should be carefully monitored.[128]

In the end he comes back to his formula: any way of viewing the world, whether it be racial ideology or Bolshevism, which lays claim to the place of Christ in the salvation of humanity is equivalent to what Luther saw as the fatal error of Judaism and its rejection of Christ. On the one hand, Schroth's work is a bold rejection of the sort of racist religiosity that marked the DC understanding of Luther, but on the other hand offers no solace for Jews as Jews, who are seen as marked for rejecting Christ. Schroth does say that measures by a state should be justified based on actual wrong-doing, but he doesn't suggest the measures taken against the Jews as a community were necessarily wrong.[129] Yet it is the views of people like Schroth, who identify with the Confessing Church, who are the targets of massive anger from those within the DC. And while for someone like Schroth, Luther is decisively not an anti-Semite, his anti-Jewish religiosity only affirms Jews who would convert, at which point they would lose their culture and identity. This offers little beyond assimilation, which was not going to be countenanced by the Nazis in any case, who did not recognize such conversions as having any bearing on whether one was Jewish or not. In the end, the distinction between Luther the anti-Semite and Luther the anti-Jew held little consolation for the Jews of Germany, and exemplifies why Luther's anti-Jewish writings were so enabling for the measures being taken against the Jews, since it eroded any religiously motivated determination to resist such persecution.[130]

In the end, the question remains to what degree Luther's anti-Jewish writings influenced policy, or affected public views of prejudicial legislation and violence against the Jews. It is clear his writings on the subject, despite the constant accusations by the likes of Mathilde Ludendorff, Alfred Rosenberg, Wolf Meyer-Erlach, or Martin Sasse that they were being suppressed, found significant distribution, and not simply in scholarly editions. What is more difficult to parse is how much they were actually registered by a German public, a third of whom were Catholic, and many of whom were culturally Lutheran but not necessarily pious. In addition, as was noted by authors eager to see these works more widely recognized and consumed, the writings were crude and distasteful; were one a vehement anti-Semite they might be invigorating, but for those whose distaste for

---

[128] Schroth, *Luthers christlicher Antisemitismus*, 25.
[129] Schroth, *Luthers christlicher Antisemitismus*, 23.
[130] See Christopher Probst's insightful treatment of Schroth's work in *Demonizing the Jews*, 103–112. In addition, see Victoria Barnett. *For the Soul of the People. Protestant Protest against Hitler*. (New York and Oxford: Oxford University Press, 1992), chapter 7, "The Confessing Church and the Jews," for a discussion of the degree to which even within the Confessing Church negative attitudes concerning the Jews were given credence and shaped responses to the various attacks upon the Jews carried out by the regime.

the Jews was more passive, Luther's views may have well been the sort of thing one sought not to register, looked away from, just as was the case with the sort of violence that occurred on November 9–10, 1938. An article by Dorothea Wendebourg explores an interesting incident that made the rounds in the aftermath of so-called "Night of Glass."[131] The *Preußische Zeitung* of Königsberg, in the aftermath of the violent actions across Germany, published excerpts from Luther where he advocated measures very similar to what were carried out—the same type of passages cited by Meyer-Erlach and Sasse. The newspaper's purpose was to endorse the actions of the regime, but in the aftermath of the publication it heard back from the Königsberg Consistory that pastors had inquired as to the authenticity of the cited passages, being unfamiliar with this aspect of Luther's writing. The newspaper reported about this exchange, decrying that trained pastors of the Protestant church could be so ignorant of a critical aspect of the writings of their founder. Within the Protestant church this was greeted with embarrassment and led to an initiative to require local administrative units to develop training on Luther's anti-Jewish writings and report back. Wendebourg reports that almost nothing came of this effort, and that in general engagement with these writings seemed a low priority among the localities involved.[132]

The article pursues the question of the meaning of this incident by looking at the channels through which knowledge of Luther's anti-Jewish ideas and writing might have flowed into the Wilhelmine, Weimar, and Nazi eras, and also what we can know about how these ideas were consumed. Wendebourg concludes that, at least by 1938, if one were interested in Luther's anti-Jewish ideas, there was no problem accessing them in part or in whole, though also that the training of pastors put virtually no emphasis on Luther's views about the Jews. Whatever the prevalence of these writings in the public sphere, the incident in 1938 cited above suggests it was not the case that these writings and their content had become part of the mindset of the broader Protestant population beyond the DC and the anti-Semitic "movement." She concludes:

> Despite everything, *völkisch* ideologues, organs of the Party, and interested DC circles did not succeed in one thing: minting a sweeping new image of Luther that bundled together everything that the reformer had written and done in this message: the image of "Luther the anti-Semite." It seems to me it is frustration concerning this lack of success that stands behind the obsessively repeated accusation that the church had suppressed the true Luther. And this frustration was justified.[133]

---

[131] Dorothea Wendebourg, "Die Bekanntheit von Luthers Judenschriften im 19. Und frühen 20. Jahrhunderts." In *Protestantismus, Antijudaismus, Antisemitismus*, ed. Dorothea Wendebourg et al. (Tübingen: Mohr Siebeck, 2017): 147–80.

[132] Wendebourg, "Die Bekanntheit von Luthers Judenschriften," 147–50.

[133] "Eines aber gelang völkischen Ideologen, Parteiorganen und interessierten deutschchristlichen Kreisen trotz allem nicht: ein durchschlagendes neues Lutherimage zu prägen, das alles, was der

This raises an essential question about the degree to which Luther's image impacted the course of events unleashed by the Party against the Jews in the 1930s and '40s. To what degree was the willingness of Germans to participate, either actively or passively, in Jewish disenfranchisement, isolation, confiscation of property, mistreatment, and finally exile and extermination predicated on ideas about the Jews influenced by the image of Luther as an anti-Semite? Wendebourg's article suggests the complexity of the issue. Though there was no shortage of parties within the Protestant church eager to spread the news about aspects of Luther's legacy as an anti-Semite, these parties participated in a specific ideational circle within German Protestantism, the "German Christian" movement, and even within those circles there was some differences in how they imagined Luther. Some, such as Sasse or Meyer-Erlach, who stood very close to the ideological positions of the Alfred Rosenberg and the anti-Semitism of the Nazi Party, were ready to jettison the Old Testament, Paul, and those aspects of Jesus that suggested a Jewish heritage. This sort of radicalism had limited resonance, as the reaction to the Sports Palace event suggests, and cannot be taken as emblematic of a general sensibility.[134] And even within the party, which one might anticipate would welcome fellow travelers in the Protestant church, such an image of Luther was not necessarily uniformly greeted. Any honest engagement with his legacy would come up against his embrace of the Old Testament as a constitutive part of the Christian faith, revealed by any full reading of what he had to say in his late anti-Jewish writings and in the translation of the Old Testament into vernacular German. And the Party wanted a revolution that departed from the cultural legacy of Christianity; dependance on Luther for legitimizing the measures against the Jews delayed the day when the German *Volk* were weaned from their Christian heritage. So even among the most eager persecutors of the Jews, there was no unanimity in their understanding of Luther. And the radical views of the DC fed a backlash which sought to adjust the understanding of Luther's anti-Jewish profile, either by highlighting his earlier views that embraced converting the Jews by kindness and persuasion, or, with his later writings, insisting on their full theological matrices, where the argument was about the meaning of the Old Testament as a Christian witness, and harsh condemnations of the Jews who betrayed it and Christ.

Reformator geschrieben und getan hatte, in dieser Botschaft bündelte—das Image 'Luther der Antisemit.' Mir scheint, es ist die Frustration über diesen Mißerfolg, die hinter der obsessive wiederholten Anklage steht, daß die Kirche den wahren Luther unterschlagen habe. Und diese Frustration war begründet." Wendebourg, "Die Bekanntheit von Luthers Judenschriften," 179.

[134] Though, as Sussanah Heschel notes in her pathbreaking study, *The Aryan Jesus. Christian Theologians and the Bible in Nazi Germany*. (Princeton: Princeton University Press, 2008), the sort of views expressed by Krause in 1933, advocating the purging of Christianity root and branch of Jewish influences and which spurred a strong reaction against the DC, lost their ability to shock over time. As she documents, the work of the Jena Institute for the Study and Eradication of Jewish Influence in German Church Life, whose existence owed a good deal to the work of Wolf Meyer-Erlach in nazifying the theological faculty at Jena, was instrumental in spreading such views beyond the narrow confines of Jena and the DC. Among the leading theological lights at Jena was Walter Grundmann.

While such opposition did not provide an outlet for defending the civic rights of Jews, it at least treated Judaism as a religion, and not a biological pestilence, and rejected the ethnic cleansing of the church. Figures such as Schroth who defended such a position appear from our present perspective to fall disappointingly short of a full-throated defense of the Jews as innocent victims, yet in the context of the 1930s even this limited dissent took some courage. For the most part, one suspects that Luther's Jewish writings simply weren't of particular interest for many German Protestants, including those in the pastorate. Aside from the rabid passages excerpted in the writings of the anti-Semites, they were not especially accessible, dealing as they did with theological arguments about the Old Testament from four hundred years prior. If one were not a highly motivated anti-Semite, such writings lacked relevance for the current context. So among the images of Luther that were disseminated about Luther in the public culture of the 1930s, Luther the anti-Semite was, it would seem, not the most compelling. However, it is also the case that this image provided a disincentive to resist the attempts of the National Socialist regime to see the Jews expelled from the pastorate and the congregations, to see them isolated and apart, based solely on their genetic lineage and not their faith. That German Protestant Christianity was not heroic in its resistance to the inhumanity of the Nazi attack on the Jews, that one wing of the church even embraced and encouraged such brutality, is a legacy, in part, of the anti-Jewish views of its "heroic" forbearer; Luther legitimized a negative view of the Jews that, while not grounded in racialist and *völkisch* ideology, fed into the overall spectrum of anti-Jewish sentiment, from vague distaste and prejudices to rabid eliminationist anti-Semitism. In that regard, the image of Luther the anti-Semite, even if it was not his most compelling profile, played a not insignificant role in the destruction of the European Jews.

The Luther Myth: The Image of Martin Luther from Religious Reformer to Völkisch *Icon*. Patrick Hayden-Roy, Oxford University Press. © Patrick Hayden-Roy 2024. DOI: 10.1093/9780198930297.003.0008

8
Luther the Heathen

In 1937 a work was published, *Luther. Staat und Glaube* (Luther, state and belief) by Arno Deutelmoser (1907–1983)[1] that, despite the innocuous title, set off a wave of outrage among scholars of church history, and for a time became a focal point of intense engagement. In his work, Deutelmoser composed a picture of Luther as the inventor of a heathen understanding of history that was deeply woven into the fabric of the German spirit and society. And while posterity has mostly forgotten Deutelmoser's work, it only gaining attention in secondary literature on Luther and his views of the state when examples of the excesses of the 1930s are needed,[2] at the time it elicited an outpouring of responses, almost uniformly negative, from senior scholars of Luther. No less than three separate books were published exclusively dedicated to refuting Deutelmoser, and endless articles and reviews in leading journals took on the work. The name Deutelmoser came, for a time, to have an almost incantatory power, conjuring up an image of a profane scholarship so deranged that it dared call into question the piety of Germany's most revered church father. And yet, when considered in retrospect, Deutelmoser's work, while provocatively formulated, in fact represents a great deal of continuity with the methodologies and perspectives that had circulated within the study of Luther in the era after World War I. The work is in a sense the apotheosis of the Luther who was born in the aftermath of the Wars of Liberation, celebrated as the avatar of a new Germany, affirmed as the spiritual core of German identity, imagined as an existential hero of a new age, and exalted as a prophet of God who conceived and instigated the destiny of the German *Volk*. Though Deutelmoser situates the elements of this image somewhat differently, and will label its parts provocatively, his work posits nothing truly novel. The outrage against it stems not from the deficiencies of the work itself, though they are many, but the fundamental disjunctures and incoherence of the image of Luther promoted in Germany in the inter-war years, and by extension the religious culture that nurtured it, a type of collective cognitive dissonance. The image of Luther widely disseminated in Germany by the end of the 1930s was unmoored from the historical Luther, refracted as it was by the through-the-looking-glass culture of Nazi Germany. In this sense, the work and its response represent the final episode in the development of the mythic Luther of this era.

---

[1] Arno Deutelmoser, *Luther. Staat und Glaube* (Jena: Eugen Diederichs Verlag, 1937).
[2] See, for instance, the treatment by Horst Stephan, *Luther in den Wandlungen seiner Kirche*. 2nd ed. (Berlin: Alfred Töpelmann, 1951): 91ff.

Arno Deutelmoser was, in many ways, a recognizable figure of the inter-war era; a young radical who was active in the extremist right-wing socialist youth movement of the late Weimar period in Göttingen, though as part of a cell that was at odds with the Nazi movement, which led to his arrest once the Nazis gained power in 1933.[3] His incarceration lasted only a short time, and following his release he became attracted to the non-Christian Independent Free Church movement of Friedrich Hielscher (1902–1990), which also had its roots in the non-NSDAP right-wing socialism of the Weimar period; Deutelmoser remained a follower for the rest of his life.[4] He studied law, philosophy and history at Göttingen, and then later in the 1930s, at the instigation of Hielscher, completed a dissertation in religious history at Hamburg that was the basis for *Luther. Staat und Glaube*. The distinctive thesis Deutelmoser developed here drew heavily from earlier work by Hielscher, in particular his 1931 treatise *Das Reich* (later banned by the Nazis),[5] a fact which led Deutelmoser's critics to repeatedly accuse him of plagiarism.

Indeed Deutelmoser's study, while a good deal more conventional in its prose than Hielscher's abstract and philosophical work, borrowed heavily from Hielscher for its theoretical perspective.[6] Deutelmoser posited what might be termed an underground history of Germany, defined by a spiritual "Reich" or Empire[7] that first became manifest at the time of the Hohenstaufen, but then was suppressed and became latent with the advent of Roman and "Western" forces within the German world, which imposed upon the Germans a foreign culture which was Christian and individualistic, embodied in the Holy Roman Empire.

---

[3] There is very little scholarship on Deutelmoser. For an overview of his activities in the 1930s see Ina Schmidt, *Der Herr des Feuers: Friedrich Hielscher und sein Kreis zwischen Heidentum, neuem Nationalismus und Widerstand gegen den Nationalsozialismus* (Cologne: SH-Verlag, 2004): 75ff. Beyond *Luther. Staat und Glaube*, Deutelmoser published very little. He did produce a volume for the series "Stoffe und Gestalten der deutschen Geschichte (Substance and Form of German History)," Vol. 1, no. 4: *Reformation und Gegenreformation in Deutschland* (Leipzig: B. G. Teubner, 1938), which repeats some of the overview material from his earlier work, and somewhat mutes his distinctive thesis about Luther.

[4] Hielscher's movement, like Deutelmoser's work, was an idiosyncratic amalgam of the social and cultural movements that were generated between the wars, combining a non-Christian "Germanic" spirituality with hyper-nationalism, though with a much greater emphasis on the socialist elements than was the case by the 1930s with the National Socialists. Hielscher eschewed the racial nationalism of the Nazis, and his movement resisted the Nazis during the 1930s. Hielscher sought to situate his followers in positions of influence, and he was the one who encouraged Deutelmoser to pursue academic credentials, the result of which was *Luther. Staat und Glaube*. See Schmidt, *Der Herr des Feuers*.

[5] Friedrich Hielscher, *Das Reich* (Berlin: Das Reich Verlag, 1931).

[6] In fact Hielscher, who sought to control all aspects of what went on in his movement, required all work published by his followers to be approved by him before publication. Though, as noted, Deutelmoser's critics accused him repeatedly of plagiarism, it would seem the close tracking of Hielscher's theories that one finds in his book reflect Hielscher's guiding hand. See I. Schmidt, *Der Herr des Feuers*, 62ff.

[7] The term "das Reich" or "Empire" has a particular meaning for Hielscher and Deutelmoser. It refers specifically to the spiritual type of the Germanic world, and is basically interchangeable with terms such as "Deutschtum" (Germanity) or even simply "German". It does not refer to any specific German state or political formation.

Still, tendencies that drew upon the native spiritual identity of the Germans were active within German culture during the later Middle Ages, most strongly expressed in the mystical theology of Meister Eckhart and his epigones. It was Luther who revived the Germanic concept of the *Reich* in his theology, and insinuated it back into the development of German history, becoming manifest in the career of Gustavus Adolphus, and then the princes of Brandenburg and Prussia, and realizing itself fully in the Second Reich of Bismarck. In addition, the corresponding spiritual manifestation of Luther's vision can be traced in later German mystics, such as Böhme, Classical German literature, especially Goethe, German Idealist philosophy, and finally in the work of Friedrich Nietzsche.[8] While the views Deutelmoser developed to provide a theoretical matrix for his work are broadly speculative and abstracted from the material history to which they refer, in comparison to its source material in Hielscher's work, which avoided almost entirely any specific historical references or citations to the literary record, they present themselves as historical scholarship. Deutelmoser, unlike Hielscher, laid out an argument about Luther's theology which was grounded in copious citations of Luther's works—he included almost sixteen hundred endnotes—and rested on a detailed interpretation of specific aspects of Luther's teaching. So, whatever the idiosyncrasies of the theoretical matrix within which it was set, Deutelmoser's work presented itself as a serious piece of Luther scholarship.

Deutelmoser began his argument about Luther by emphasizing the critical role his faith played in breaking the hold of the Roman Church and its Christian viewpoint on German culture and politics by undermining it from within:

> Indeed Luther is only able to break the power of Rome by striking the first blow against the foundations of the Roman faith. And it's only because Luther starts his attack on Rome at the level of the most fundamental and deepest things that he is able to overcome Rome from its foundations upwards, also freeing the state from the Roman dominance. Correspondingly the particularity of the Lutheran understanding of the state results by necessity out of the singularity of its faith, out of which the struggle against Rome begins. In order to understand Luther's state one has to understand Luther's faith.[9]

On the one hand, we see here Deutelmoser extrapolating from the image presented by Holl and his students of an existential Luther drawing from experience

---

[8] This is a summary of the programmatic pieces that frame Deutelmoser's *Luther*, "Die Voraussetzungen," 9–17, and "Die Erben," 303–25.

[9] "In der Tat kann Luther die Macht Roms nur dadurch brechen, daß er den ersten Stoß gegen die Grundlagen des römischen Glaubens ansetzt. Nur weil Luther den Angriff gegen Rom bei den letzten und tiefsten Dingen beginnt, kann er, Rom von Grund aus überwindend, auch den Staat von der römischen Vorherrschaft befreien. Dementsprechend ergibt sich auch die Besonderheit des Lutherschen Staatsgedankens mit Notwendigkeit aus der Eigenart seines Glaubens, von dem aus er den Kampf gegen Rom beginnt. Um Luthers Staat zu verstehen, muß man Luthers Glauben kennen." Deutelmoser, *Luther*, 22.

the fundamental insights of his faith, which becomes the basis for his rebellion against a foreign Roman church. However, Deutelmoser depicted Luther as positing a world view that was fundamentally unchristian, a view that, as Deutelmoser aptly notes, had not as yet gained much currency. In fact, even in his theology, Deutelmoser claimed, Luther had departed from Christianity:

> Luther had indeed regarded himself throughout his life as a believing Christian, both when he spoke about God as well about the world and the state. In fact, however, when he thinks Christianity through to its very end, he goes well beyond it, arriving at the same faith that Meister Eckhart had already preached. Starting from the omnipotence of God, he finds the unfree will; and because he sees God at work in all things, he's able to sanctify the whole world. That doesn't have anything more to do with the Gospel. It is the faith of the Empire, on which basis Luther pronounces the autocracy [*Selbstherrlichkeit*] of the State.[10]

Though a bold thesis, even here there were parallels in the literature on Luther generated by Rosenberg as well as the DC figures such as Wolf Meyer-Erlach, who, though they don't necessarily frame Luther as unchristian, so transposed the meaning of his faith and rebellion against Rome as to essentially separate him from historic Christianity.

Deutelmoser, having asserted his basic position, pursued it further:

> The separation that Christianity posits between God and creation is not present in Luther. The distinction between God and things is merely a matter of form; God is the Whole and the One, the multiplicity of things is his individuation, his masks; in **essence** God and creation are one.[11]

With this Deutelmoser revealed his basic strategy. He would focus on Luther's teaching concerning the hidden God, the *deus absconditus*, relying particularly on his work *The Bondage of the Will*. And from here he would move to connect Luther's understanding of God to the state. Deutelmoser repeatedly insisted that Luther was compelled to see all of history as a product of God's working; everything that happens from the greatest to the most trivial is effected by God.

---

[10] "Luther selbst hält sich zwar zeit seines Lebens für einen gläubigen Christen, sowohl wenn er über Gott als auch wenn er über die Welt und den Staat spricht. Tatsächlich aber schreitet er, indem er das Christentum zu Ende denkt, darüber hinaus und kommt zu demselben Glauben, den schon Eckehart gepredigt hat. Ausgehend von der Allmacht Gottes, findet er zur Unfreiheit des Willens; und weil er Gott in allen Dingen wirksam sieht, kann er die ganze Welt heiligen. Das hat nichts mehr mit dem Evangelium zu tun. Es ist der Glaube des Reiches, aus dem heraus Luther die Selbstherrlichkeit des Staates verkündet." Deutelmoser, *Luther*, 23.

[11] "Der Abstand, den das Christentum zwischen Gott und der Kreatur sieht, ist bei Luther nicht vorhanden. Der Gegensatz zwischen Gott und den Dingen besteht nur der Form nach: Gott ist das Ganze und Eine, die vielfältigen Dinge sind seine Besonderungen, seine Masken. Aber dem **Wesen** nach sind beide eins." Deutelmoser, *Luther*, 24.

Between God and the world there is no distance. "Nothing in history occurs out of the strength of *Völker* or humans.... God brings about all greatness and baseness. He acts in the mask of heroes when, for example, through Hannibal or Alexander he destroys or constructs great empires."[12] Deutelmoser saw this view of God as reflecting Luther's move beyond the God of Christianity, which posited a world over which God rules, but within which humans function with free will, and into which God intervened on occasion. This was not Luther's God, according to Deutelmoser. Again, though the accents here are distinctive, one of the features of the Luther Renaissance was its interest in *The Bondage of the Will* and Luther's emphasis on the hiddenness of God in history;[13] in addition, Deutelmoser connects this to Luther's speculations about the heroic *Wundermänner* of history, another feature of the Luther scholarship that emerged in the 1930s.

Deutelmoser elaborated by unpacking Luther's understanding of the hidden God. He claimed that for Luther even the God revealed in Christ is subordinated to God in his hiddenness:

> Because Luther never doubts that in the Gospel we have the authoritative revelation of the hidden God before us, it is possible for him to retain the Holy Scriptures. But this occurs at the expense of dethroning the God who is proclaimed in the New Testament. For the God of compassion now is no longer the whole and true and real God. He is only a revelation of the real God, who in his boundless omnipotence is infinitely more magnificent. The compassionate God is, like every revelation, only a mask of the solely real, hidden God. The compassionate God is not the divine majesty itself; he is merely the foreground.[14]

He drove home his point by noting that if in Holy Scripture Jesus sits at the right hand of God, then Satan sits on his left hand.[15]

This view of God Deutelmoser saw as suited to the particular spiritual sensibilities of what he referred to as the "humanity of the Empire" (*Menschen des Reiches*). "From Switzerland to Sweden, from Flanders to Finland, the humanity of the Empire confessed the faith of Luther because in it they found their essence

---

[12] "Nichts in der Geschichte geschieht aus eigener Kraft der Völker und Menschen.... Gott wirkt alle Herrlichkeit und alle Niedrigkeit. Er handelt dabei in der Maske des Helden, wenn er etwa in Hannibal oder Alexander große Reiche vernichtet und errichtet." Deutelmoser, *Luther*, 26–7.

[13] See the discussion in Asel, *Der andere Aufbruch*, 84–6, 149–52.

[14] "Weil Luther nicht daran zweifelt, im Evangelium die für uns maßgebende Offenbarung des verborgenen Gottes vor sich zu haben, ist es ihm möglich, die Heilige Schrift beizubehalten. Aber es geschieht um den Preis einer Entthronung des in Neuen Testament verkündigten Gottes. Denn der Gott der Barmherzigkeit ist jetzt nicht mehr der ganze und wahre und wirkliche Gott. Er ist nur eine Offenbarung des wirklichen Gottes, der in seiner grenzenlosen Allmacht unendlich viel mehr und herrlicher ist. Der barmherzige Gott ist, wie jede Offenbarung, nur eine Maske des allein wirklichen verborgenen Gottes. Der barmherzige Gott ist nicht die göttliche Majestät selbst; er ist Vordergrund." Deutelmoser, *Luther*, 42.

[15] Deutelmoser, *Luther*, 43.

was given voice."[16] This is in contrast to the West and Rome, for whom this way of understanding was foreign. Though Deutelmoser did not take a racialist view of differences between peoples—in this he was the follower of Hielscher—he did ascribe to the widely held belief during this era that the differences between peoples rested upon fundamental differences between their basic inner structures. For Deutelmoser such differences were grounded in various spiritual-cultural groups, which he called "soul-doms" (*Seelentümer*), a term he borrowed from Hielscher. The "soul-doms" dictated such outward manifestations as culture and political organization. Luther's genius was to give expression to the fundamental spiritual disposition of the Germanic world, and to set it in motion. In the case of the West, by which Deutelmoser meant in particular England and its extensions, their God was materialism, with which Luther's and the Germanic spirit were at fundamental odds, a view widely echoed in the racialist views of Luther. In the case of Rome, Deutelmoser saw the fundamental difference between it and Luther, and by extension the Germanic world, to reside in the view of God; Rome's deity was limited by human freedom, while Luther's was unbounded and effected all that unfolded in the world, as well as within the human conscience. For Rome a set of outward rules regulated human behavior, and humans had placed upon them the responsibility to respond to such outward commands either positively or negatively. It is basically a reward/punishment system. For Luther, Deutelmoser asserted, the understanding of the human conscience was entirely different:

> Luther's conscience, in contrast, involves the efficacy of God in the soul. God is present, acts, and speaks directly.... Humans are finally bound to this divine command which appears in their conscience. For Luther there was no other prescriptions that would have validity before the conscience.[17]

He notes further that for Luther, "God himself and no one and nothing else is alive in the conscience, each person is exclusively bound by the law and standards which he finds in his own inner self."[18] Here Deutelmoser's depiction of Luther takes as its departure point Holl's understanding of Luther's *Gewissensreligion* (religion of conscience).

---

[16] "Von der Schweiz bis Schweden, von Flandern bis Finnland bekennen sich die Menschen des Reiches zu Luthers Glauben, weil sie darin ihr eigenes Wesen ausgesprochen finden." Deutelmoser, *Luther*, 44.
[17] "Luthers Gewissen dagegen ist die Wirksamkeit Gottes in der Seele. Im Gewissen west und wirkt und spricht Gott unmittelbar.... Diesem göttlichen Befehl, der im Gewissen erscheint, ist der Mensch im letzten verpflichtet. Es gibt für Luther keine anderen Vorschriften, welche vor dem Gewissen Geltung hätten." Deutelmoser, *Luther*, 49.
[18] "Weil Gott selbst und sonst niemand und nichts in der Seele lebendig ist, sind für jeden Menschen ausschließlich die Gesetze und Maßstäbe verpflichtend, die er in seinem eigenen Inneren vorfindet." Deutelmoser, *Luther*, 50.

Because Luther does away with the separation between God and humanity, he no longer had anything to do with Christianity, according to Deutelmoser. He had become the prophet of "*das Reich*." And in so doing, Luther made God responsible for all that occurred, even those things attributable to Satan, such that there is no longer any question of human guilt for what occurs. And though Luther continued to use the traditional language of Christianity, it can't mean the same thing as it did in the New Testament:

> Out of the doctrine of sin, which assumed the separation of God and humanity, emerges the doctrine of indemnity (*Haftung*), which sees a unity between God and the world. There is nothing more left of Christianity.[19]

Although Deutelmoser admitted that Luther continued to consider himself a Christian his whole life, this was only because, in order for Luther to break away to his true faith, he had to dig so deeply into Christianity that he overcame it. It is because of this we find contradictions in Luther's writings. Though Luther shied away from exploring too deeply the meaning of the hidden God, Deutelmoser saw in that a sign that Luther recognized the radicality of what he had accomplished.[20]

Deutelmoser developed his argument further by claiming that Luther's attitude toward Scripture revealed his questioning of revelation based on the outward letter of the Bible. For Luther, it isn't the outward letter of the word that is determinative, but the inward conscience; when the outward word is at odds with the inward witness, it is the outward text that is rejected: "Above the unalterably given Word of God Luther places, just as impartially and decisively, his own inner personal voice, in the same way he placed the omnipotent God above the compassionate God."[21] Though Deutelmoser emphasized Luther's indebtedness to Meister Eckhart and medieval German mysticism, Luther's mature theological speculations were not based on philosophical reflection, Deutelmoser noted, but on experience, which was key to his disposition; "Luther's lonely pride rests on the certainty that God speaks directly in his conscience and endows him with the pure truth.... The consciousness that God speaks in him and through him also endowed Luther with his vehement fighting spirit."[22] Luther's understanding was

---

[19] "Aus der Sündenlehre, welche den Abstand zwischen Gott und Menschen voraussetzt, ist die Lehre von der Haftung geworden, welche Gott und die Welt in Einheit sieht. Vom Christentum ist nichts mehr übriggeblieben." Deutelmoser, *Luther*, 53.

[20] Deutelmoser, *Luther*, 53.

[21] "Luther stellt über das unverrückbar gegebene Wort Gottes ebenso unbefangen wie entschieden seine eigene innere Stimme, genau so wie er über den barmherzigen Gott den allmächtigen gestellt hat." Deutelmoser, *Luther*, 56.

[22] "Aus der Gewißheit, daß Gott unmittelbar in seinem Gewissen spricht und ihm die reine Wahrheit schenkt, rührt Luthers einsamer Stolz.... Das Bewußtsein, daß Gott selbst in ihm und durch ihn redet und handelt, schenkt Luther auch die ungestüme Kampfeskraft." Deutelmoser, *Luther*, 76.

thus, according to Deutelmoser, grounded in the action of God within his conscience, once again following the basic narrative about Luther's breakthrough to faith as posited by Holl.

Having explored Luther's basic theological position, Deutelmoser turned to consider his doctrine of the state. This flowed directly from his theological views, where Luther affirmed all that happened in the world as instigated by God. Thus, as with all the human dispositions and orders placed within the world by God that directed its course, such as love, sex, marriage, food, drink and art, Luther also embraced the state:[23]

> As in all "creatures" and "gifts" God lives and is present also in the state. "Therefore, because it [the state] is God's authority and order, one must view it as if one is looking at God." Luther advocated this often, that one should immediately "see God in the ruling authorities".[24]

Among all the manifold masks of God, the state occupied a special place with Luther, because he saw power as the essence of God. For that reason Luther designated the rulers as saviors and deities, "not because they, too, as all creatures, are God's masks, but because they rule, which alone befits God."[25] And while Luther continued to insist on the importance of the church as well as the state, he did not set one over the other, and saw them working within one another.

Deutelmoser highlighted the implications of this view:

> With this doctrine [the sanctification of the state—"Heiligung des Staates"] however Luther created the inner prerequisites for the fulfillment of this old yearning for the power of Empire. For only based on Luther's faith does it become possible for the state, trusting in its own divinity, and freed from the Roman Church's dictates, to realize its own essence.[26]

Deutelmoser's representation of Luther's view of the state followed from this initial premise that the state is divine and therefore autocratic. While admitting that at times the echoes of Luther's rejected Christian understanding confuse or distort his presentation of the state, ultimately Luther affirms a state that is based on the

---

[23] Deutelmoser, *Luther*, 80–1.
[24] "Wie in allen 'Kreaturen' und 'Gaben' wohnt und west Gott auch im Staat. 'Darum, weil es Gottes Gewalt und Ordnung ist, muß man es ansehen, als ob man Gott sehe.' Luther fordert des öfteren, daß man unmittelbar 'Gott in der Obrigkeit sehen' soll." Deutelmoser, *Luther*, 87.
[25] "…nicht weil sie—wie alle anderen Kreaturen auch—Gottes Masken sind, sondern weil sie herrschen, was allein Gott zukommt." Deutelmoser, *Luther*, 88.
[26] "Mit dieser Lehre [the 'Heiligung des Staates'] aber schafft Luther erst die innere Voraussetzung für die Erfüllung jener alten Sehnsucht nach der Macht des Reiches. Denn erst aus dem Glauben Luthers heraus ist es möglich, daß der Staat im Vertrauen auf seine eigene Göttlichkeit frei von römisch-kirchlicher Bevormundung, sein eigenes Wesen entfaltet." Deutelmoser, *Luther*, 90.

exercise and expansion of power, apart from any other ethical norms,[27] which gives to the ruler unencumbered power to rule, and requires from the ruler's subjects unquestioning obedience. The state rules for the good of the state, not the individual, and the state is the ruling order of the entirety, serving the will of the collective, which is embodied in the ruler.[28] Though, Deutelmoser noted, Luther used the language of his time, what he was looking towards was the power of the state as it came to be realized by Gustavus Adolphus and the Prussian State. And as such, what Luther was conceptualizing was the German Empire, of which he was the German Prophet.[29] And the state intrudes legitimately with its influence into every part of the life of the individual, whether it be the family or economic life.[30] Deutelmoser here takes to its extreme an argument that was repeated persistently in DC circles about the implications of Luther's view of the state, which they conceive as anticipating the power claimed by Hitler, and has connections to the *Schöpfungstheologie* of Paul Althaus and others.

The autocracy of the state is especially pronounced in the area of law. Luther, Deutelmoser observed, did not give countenance to the idea of a natural law. Rather the sources for the law flowed through the great rulers, those figures whose genius stood above the common lot of humanity, and who through their intuition brought about a legal order. Such an order was not dependent on any intervention of the church into the affairs of the state. Luther also argued, Deutelmoser continued, that because the law is always placed under the interpretative mind of the ruler, "To the extent that and because the prince exercises rulership for the whole, he stands not under, but above the law of the state, which serves as a mediator of this rulership."[31] As with the law, when it comes to warfare, Deutelmoser claimed that Luther did not put a boundary on the prerogative of the ruler, and in those instances where he did, it was, as usual, only the desire to appear to stay within the realm of Christian teaching, when in fact the implications of his teaching had gone well beyond that.[32] And because Luther attributed to God ultimately the sources for such warfare, his will lying behind all that occurs in the world, Luther can be seen embracing war as godly:

> The decisiveness with which Luther, despite his detailed knowledge of the pacifism of the Gospel, speaks of the godliness of warfare betrays Luther's unchristian, warlike/martial being. From this being alone can Luther's powerful "yes" to war to be understood.

---

[27] See the section "Die Staat als Macht" (the state as power), Deutelmoser, *Luther*, 90ff.
[28] See the section "Die Selbstherrlichkeit des Staates" (the self-autocracy of the state), Deutelmoser, *Luther*, 100ff.
[29] Deutelmoser, *Luther*, 109.   [30] Deutelmoser, *Luther*, 131–51.
[31] "Weil und soweit der Fürst für das Ganze die Herrschaft ausübt, steht er nicht unter, sondern über dem staatlichen Recht als einem Mittel dieser Herrschaft." Deutelmoser, *Luther*, 157.
[32] "Die Staat und Krieg" (the state and war), Deutelmoser, *Luther*, 159ff.

>...As soon as Luther speaks of war, his joy in struggle breaks through everywhere. This goes for the relentless battle of the spirits as well as for the bloody slaughter of bodies.[33]

The bloody handwork of the warriors serves God, and in it God is immediately at work. This view of war, Deutelmoser argued, is an explicit representation of the way the spirit of the Empire has triumphed in Luther, and its expression in later epochs of German history, from the battles of Gustavus Adolphus to the First World War, make this manifest.[34] Though Deutelmoser has cast his image provocatively, both during and after World War I Luther was regularly brought forward by those wished to affirm the legitimacy and holiness of violence in the name of the divinely ordained order of the state.

When Deutelmoser turned to look at Luther's understanding of the church in relation to the state, he basically recapitulated the pattern that he had previously claimed to find in Luther. Though Luther insisted that the state could not coerce the inner conscience of the individual, in every other way it was placed over the church, and ruled both its outward form and the physical circumstances of its members, who were obligated to show unquestioning obedience to the state's dictates. Deutelmoser saw this developing in the course of time between 1520 and 1527, culminating with Luther's authorization of the church visitations in Brandenburg. Luther did this not at the direction of the princes, but on his own volition, imploring the princes to intervene in the affairs of the church. The implications of this were to give to the state the prerogative to govern over not only secular affairs but the church as well.[35] Deutelmoser extended this point by insisting that while Luther never explicitly stated it, he in fact gave the princes the right to use force in spiritual matters.[36] In the person of the prince is united church and state: "The prince is the highest bishop of the church. At the same time he is lord of the state. In his person is united the highest office of the church as well as the state. The coherence of inwardness and power find in this their visible manifestation."[37] Deutelmoser saw Luther's persistence in his theological battles with Zwingli not to stem primarily from a theological conviction, but rather from his concern that to concede a theological point for the sake of political

---

[33] "Die Entschiedenheit, mit welcher Luther trotz genauer Kenntnis der friedfertigkeit des Evangeliums von der Göttlichkeit des Krieges spricht, verrät das unchristlich-kriegerische Wesen Luthers. Nur aus diesem Wesen heraus ist Luther kräftiges Ja zum Krieg zu verstehen." Deutelmoser, *Luther*, 165. "Sobald Luther vom Kriege selbst spricht, kommt überall seine Freude am Kampf zum Durchbruch. Das gilt für den unerbittlichen Streit der Geister wie für die blutige Schlacht der Leiber." Deutelmoser, *Luther*, 166.
[34] Deutelmoser, *Luther*, 167–8.   [35] Deutelmoser, *Luther*, 185.
[36] Deutelmoser, *Luther*, 193.
[37] "Das Fürst ist der oberste Bischof der Kirche. Er ist zugleich der Herr des Staates. In seiner Person ist das höchste Amt sowohl der Kirche als auch des Staates vereinigt. Darin findet die Zusammengehörigkeit von Innerlichkeit und Macht ihren sichtbaren Ausdruck." Deutelmoser, *Luther*, 201.

expediency would ultimately damage the state.[38] For Deutelmoser, this highlighted how Luther placed reasons of state above all other considerations, even within his theological struggles.

Ultimately Deutelmoser's Luther saw the successful exercise of power as its own justification. Deutelmoser explored that side of Luther's thinking in comments regarding Luther's response to the peasant revolt:

> In the final view Luther didn't reject the uprising of the enthusiasts and peasants because they, in contradiction to the Gospel, used force, but because they were, in contrast to the princes, not authorized to administer force. They do not have the divine command for that. For they don't have the capability and the power to overthrow the old order and set a new order in its place. Power would have given them the right. For in this power would have been made manifest the divine command. That the enthusiasts and the peasant "have neither the order, power, right, nor command from God" was the decisive objection that Luther held against their uprising.[39]

Deutelmoser painted Luther as someone who valued any authority to the extent that it had the inner and outer means to impose order.[40] Luther's didn't reject armed revolt as such, and even in the actions of the peasants affirmed a view that saw God at work in the dialectic of the world; the judgment of God against the peasants was not a result of their revolt per se, but the fact that they were not sufficient to create a new order. On the other hand, Luther could support the princes' resistance against the Emperor because they did possess that force.[41]

Deutelmoser connected this point to Luther's teaching about the great heroes, or "*Wundermänner*": "Whoever has the power is permitted to destroy the old world and create a new one. The right of heroes rests on this divine power.... Luther distinguishes the moral or civic person on the one side from the heroic person on the other."[42] Deutelmoser made Luther appear to affirm a principle where the constant struggle of heroes, one against another, was the driving force behind

---

[38] Deutelmoser, *Luther*, 209.
[39] "Luther lehnt im letzten Grunde den Aufruhr der Schwärmer und der Bauern nicht deshalb ab, weil diese—im Widerspruch zum Evangelium—überhaupt Gewalt anwenden; sondern weil sie—im Gegensatz zu den Fürsten—zur Anwendung dieser Gewalt nicht befugt sind. Sie haben nicht den göttlichen Befehl dazu. Denn sie haben nicht die Fähigkeit und die Macht, die alte Ordnung zu stürzen und an ihre Stelle eine neue zu setzen. Die Macht würde ihnen das Recht geben. Denn in der Macht würde der göttliche Befehl erscheinen. Daß die Schwärmer und die Bauern 'von Gott weder Gebot, Macht, Recht noch Befehl haben', das ist der entscheidende Einwand, den Luther den Aufrührern entgegenhält." Deutelmoser, *Luther*, 238–9.
[40] Deutelmoser, *Luther*, 240–1.   [41] Deutelmoser, *Luther*, 270.
[42] "Wer die Macht dazu hat, der darf die alte Welt zerstören und eine neue dafür schaffen. Auf dieser göttlichen Macht beruht das Recht des Helden.... Luther unterscheidet moralische oder bürgerliche Menschen auf der einen Seite und heldische Menschen auf der anderen." Deutelmoser, *Luther*, 271.

world affairs, and that he saw his own struggle against the Church of Rome in that light.[43] He summed up toward the end of the study his image of Luther thusly:

> On the basis of the omnipotence of God, which Luther consistently understood as Gods efficacy in all things, he also sanctified the power of the state. For Luther, all earthly power is in and of itself divine, without it having to serve any other law or purpose outside itself. Luther believed not in the divine power of justice, but in the divine right of the powerful. By thinking through belief in divine omnipotence to its very end, Luther came to say a limitless "yes" to limitless power. Taking Rome's own point of departure, with this [Luther] overcame what for Rome was the characteristic conflict between power and law in favor of power.[44]

On this note, Deutelmoser finished the volume by tracing forward the influence of these views in the political formations of later German history, the behavior of its leaders, and the philosophical and literary figures whose works channeled Luther's ideas.

Given the extremity of the picture Deutelmoser painted of Luther, it is hardly surprising that the critical reaction among established Luther scholars to his book was decidedly negative. What is striking, however, is the preoccupation with Deutelmoser's book that developed almost immediately after its publication and persisted over the next couple of years. The initial reaction was led by Theodor Knolle (1885–1955), longtime leader within the Luther Society and Luther scholar, who, at the fall 1937 Conference of the Luther Society sounded a first warning to the gathered members about the appearance of a book which claimed Luther had departed from the foundations of Christianity, providing an hour-long synopsis of the book, an effort that was greeted with gratitude by the audience.[45] He followed this the next day with another presentation at the working session of the Conference, where he provided an overview of Luther's teaching about the masks of God, and a refutation of Deutelmoser's interpretation. This was merely a prelude to a series of reviews and publications channeled through Knolle that represented the official anathematizing of Deutelmoser's book. Most programmatically, he took Deutelmoser to task at book length in *Luthers Glaube: Eine Widerlegung*

---

[43] Deutelmoser, *Luther*, 275.
[44] "Von der Allmacht Gottes her, die Luther folgerichtig als Alleinwirksamkeit Gottes begreift, heiligt er aber auch die staatliche Macht. Alle irdische Gewalt ist für Luther aus sich selbst heraus göttlich, ohne daß sie dem Recht oder irgendeinem anderen außer ihr liegenden Zweck dient. Luther glaubt nicht an die göttliche Macht der Gerechtigkeit, sondern an das göttliche Recht des Mächtigen. Aus dem zu Ende gedachten Glauben an die göttliche Allmacht...kommt Luther also dazu, ein uneingeschränktes Ja zur uneingeschränkten Macht zu sagen. Damit ist der für Rom kennzeichnende Widerstreit zwischen Macht und Recht von Roms eigenem Ausgangspunkt her zugunsten der Macht aufgehoben." Deutelmoser, *Luther*, 288.
[45] Fritz Dosse, "Die Herbsttagung der Luther Gesellschaft 1937." *Luther* 20 (1938): 27.

(Luther's faith: a rebuttal), which appeared in 1938. The proportions of Knolle's abhorrence of Deutelmoser's study were apparent from the start:

> The obliviousness with which Deutelmoser expects the reader to put up with a Luther of such grotesque character is shocking. What a concept of the truthfulness of a German man, who allegedly means something entirely other than what he expresses with his affirmations and confessions! What duplicity is blithely attributed to a man, who under the pretense of authentic Christianity disguises his leap away from it! What a dance of fools is the history of an intellect [*Geist*] whose self-understanding over centuries was subject to a delusion! What mockery of German history, when one of its greatest so misconstrues his mission that he believes he was sent as Reformer of the Church but in fact is the destroyer and trailblazer of the Empire! What a vision of the great men, who are like the blind and possessed in their grandiose misconception of themselves. Out of the heroic course of history is made a satyr's play, out of the imprint of truth a counterfeit currency, out the teaching of Jesus the autocracy of power, out of Luther the Christian – Nietzsche the Antichrist! Nowhere does it become apparent that this inversion of the world, this reinterpretation of all values, this transposition of polarities, this quid pro quo, has caused Deutelmoser any sort of difficulties. It's as if he doesn't even notice what he's subjecting his reader to.[46]

This voice of outrage suffused the whole work. It is striking that Knolle's outrage is not exclusively, or even primarily, directed against Deutelmoser's theological sins, but rather the offense it represents against the German character of Luther and his authentic self. In that sense, he is seeking to defend another version of the heroic Luther than the one posited by Deutelmoser. Knolle did not fail, as well, to direct at Deutelmoser most every accusation of scholarly misconduct available—plagiarism, willful misconstruing of the obvious meaning of words, misuse of his sources, ignorance of secondary literature, among others. It is clear that Deutelmoser's

---

[46] "Die Selbstverständlichkeit, mit der Deutelmoser dem Leser einen Luther zumutet, dessen Charakter eine Groteske darstellt, ist erschütternd. Welche Vorstellung von der Wahrhaftigkeit eines deutschen Mannes, der etwas total anderes meinen soll als er mit seinen Beteuerungen und Bekenntnissen ausdrückt! Welche Doppelzüngigkeit, die man wie selbstverständlich einem Mann unterschiebt, der unter dem Vorgeben des echten Christentums seinen Absprung vom Christentum verhüllt! Welcher Narrentanz, die Geschichte des Geistes, dessen Selbstverständnis jahrhundertelang einer völligen Selbsttäuschung unterliegt! Welcher Hohn auf die deutsche Geschichte, wenn einer ihrer Größten seine Sendung so verkennt, daß er sich als Reformator der Kirche gesandt glaubt, in Wirklichkeit aber ihr Zerstörer und Bahnbrecher des Reiches ist! Welche Anschauung von den großen Männern, die wie blind und besessen sind im grandiosen Mißverständnis ihrer selbst! Aus dem Heldengang der Geschichte wird ein Satyrspiel, aus der Wahrheitsprägung Falschmünzerei, aus der Lehre Jesu die Selbstherrlichkeit der Macht, aus dem Christen Luther der Antichrist Nietzsche! Nirgend wird ersichtlich, daß diese Umkehrung der Welt, diese Umdeutung aller Werte, diese Vertauschung der Vorzeichen, dieses quid pro quo Deutelmoser irgendwelche Schwierigkeiten macht. Es ist, als ob er gar nicht spüre, was er damit seinen Lesern zumute." Theodor Knolle, *Luthers Glaube. Eine Wiederlegung* (Weimar: Böhlau, 1938): 8.

work had hit a nerve. Knolle, who was the main editor of the *Lutherjahrbuch*, also commissioned articles for the journal refuting Deutelmoser.[47] And the Luther Society published another volume beyond Knolle's taking on Deutelmoser.[48] Almost all the major Protestant theological and church-related journals and magazines published reviews of Deutelmoser, with most, though not all, taking their lead from Knolle and the Luther Society. One of the few of these denunciatory reviews that went beyond simply listing Deutelmoser's sins came from Hermann Schuster (1874–1965), who reflected on the question of why such a book would have come into being in the first place. And while he primarily repeated Knolle's dismemberment of Deutelmoser's book, and mostly just circled back to focus on the misguided approach of Deutelmoser himself, at the very end of the long review he included a self-critical observation almost completely absent from all the rest of the critical literature on the book:

> I've repeatedly asked myself how such a work, which, for anyone who considers Luther's Catechism or songs, is such a conspicuously and fully absurd misinterpretation of Luther, has become possible. There has to be a halfway plausible reason even for such nonsense. And the explanation repeatedly presented itself to me, that Protestant theology has some complicity in this folly. It didn't, to be sure, rediscover Luther's work on *The Bondage of the Will*, ... but highlighted it so one-sidedly, and overemphasized its darkest elements, namely the misunderstood doctrine of predestination, with its talk of the hidden God, praising it as the centerpiece of his faith, that such a misunderstanding was practically provoked. One could almost say that the Calvinizing, indeed the dechristianizing, of Luther that began with the dialectical theologians was thought out here to its logical conclusion.[49]

While the attribution of guilt in the distortion of Luther's theology to the circle of theologians around Karl Barth is untenable, Schuster's recognition that

---

[47] Martin Doerne, "Gottes Ehre am gebundenen Willen. Evangelische Grundlagen und theologische Spitzensätze in De servo arbitrio." *Luther-Jahrbuch* 20 (1938): 45–92; Johannes von Walter, "Luthers Christusbild." *Luther-Jahrbuch* 21 (1939): 1–26.

[48] Ernst Kinder, *Geistliches und weltliches Regiment Gottes nach Luther* (Weimar: Hermann Bohlaus Nachfolger, 1940).

[49] "Ich habe mich immer wieder gefragt, wie diese auffallende, für jeden, der an Luthers Katechismen und Lieder denkt, völlig absurde Mißdeutung Luthers möglich geworden ist. Irgendeinen halbwegs plausiblen Grund muß doch auch solch ein Unsinn haben. Und mir drängt sich immer wieder die Erklärung auf, daß die protestantische Theologie an diesem Unfug selber mitschuldig ist. Sie hat in der Nachkriegszeit Luthers Schrift 'De servo arbitrio' nicht freilich neu entdeckt (Scheel hat sie schon vorher in einem Ergänzungsband für die Berliner Lutherausgabe übersetzt und erläutert, 1905), aber so einseitig hervorgehoben und ihr dunkelstes Stück, die mißverständliche Prädestinationslehre mit der Rede vom verborgenen Gott so überbetont und als das Herzstück seines Glaubens gepriesen, daß solch ein Mißverständnis dadurch fast herausgefordert wurde. Man könnte sogar sagen, die von der dialektischen Theologie begonnene Calvinisierung, ja Entchristlichung Luthers ist hier folgerichtig zu Ende gedacht." Hermann Schuster, "Luther Christ oder Heide?" *Die Christliche Welt* 52 (1938): 637–46; 645.

Deutelmoser's work had deeper roots in the Luther literature of the period is perceptive. When one turns to consider what made the work distinctive, and so objectionable, there is little that Deutelmoser puts forward about Luther that was not already posited in some form or another in the contemporary literature, in most cases at great length and repeatedly.

What are the distinguishing features of Deutelmoser's Luther? First, the enormous metaphysical importance placed upon Luther as the instigator of history; Luther is the one who sets off the realization of the German spirit within German historical development. Second, for Deutelmoser, the center of Luther's theology lies in his mysticism, and his inner concept of a God who masks himself within the material world, but is immanently active, bringing about all that occurs. Third, that Luther himself advocated heroic leadership from rulers, whose legitimacy and power resided in their willingness to use violence to conform the world to their will. Power and the ability to exercise it successfully is its own justification, and creates its own moral legitimacy—this is perhaps most jarring in Deutelmoser's depiction of Luther as an enthused celebrant of organized violence. As a result, the state dominates all aspects of life, including the church, and in the material sphere there was no separation of church and state, but the latter directed the former. All this is grounded in the notion that the twists and turns of history are the working out of a divine providence whose rationality is hidden from human view. Finally, that Luther in the end went beyond the parameters of traditional Christian understanding, and challenged the authority of Popes, church teaching, and even scripture in order to realize his inner vision; in doing so, he undermined Christianity, and prepared the way for a new pagan German religiosity of power. What is particularly striking about this picture of Luther is that, aside from his explicit denial that Luther was a Christian, it all can be found within the literature on Luther that circulated in the 1930s, as has been chronicled so far in this study; far from representing some bizarre aberration, Deutelmoser's view of Luther connects remarkably well with much of what was being published about Luther at the time.

Let's take each of these features and explore how they connect to the Luther of this era, starting with the enormous emphasis that he placed on the person and ideas of Luther as the key element in setting off the advance of Germany as a cultural and political force. Deutelmoser stood firmly with the prevailing views concerning Luther's importance, and, while representing it in distinctive fashion, in fact seems no more outlandish than many other more "mainstream" representations of Luther. One of the most striking assumptions about Luther is that his spiritual experience and then actions that ensued therefrom instigated a movement of spiritual and material structures that remade the German universe. And Luther wasn't just an active agent of the past, but because of his spiritual potency and how his consciousness represented as a microcosm the macrocosm of Germanity as a whole, he lived on in the spiritual constellations of the present.

Hence Luther wasn't just a historical figure, but a living embodiment of Germanity. Deutelmoser's study makes no sense without this fundamental assumption about Luther as historical agent. And while such "great man" views of history were prevalent in many national historiographies, they were particularly prominent within Germany and in Luther scholarship. One thinks of the founder of the Luther Society, Rudolf Eucken, and his reflections in the very first edition of the *Lutherjahrbuch*, where he invoked the spirit of Luther for the new age.[50] Like Eucken, Deutelmoser situates this within Luther's spirit, which embodies the spiritual essence of a larger spiritual whole, and explicitly isn't racial. Luther spirit brings into focus a larger corporate Germanic identity, which is contrasted with the identities of other peoples, particularly those of the "West." This parallels the sort of structures posited by Paul Althaus in his 1927 work *Kirche und Volkstum* and his positing of a *Volkheit* within which resided the identity of the Germans, and which had been fundamentally shaped by Luther. Such ethnic sodalities are a distinctive feature of the Luther scholarship of the era, and enable the methodological approach in which the writings of Luther are deciphered not just for what they say about Luther but by extension their implications for the movements of the corporate spiritual identities of which they are a part. It is that approach that also makes Luther a world-historical spirit effecting change as he intuits the divine being, however that is imagined. Critics of the study object to Deutelmoser's penchant for finding implications and realities that clearly go beyond the letter of what Luther wrote, but in this way of reading Luther, he isn't really just an individual, but has become a construct, subject to being remade in the image of the concepts that can be extrapolated from his experiences, actions, and words.

For Deutelmoser, a major conceptual focal point is Luther's conception of God. As was common with many who took an interest in non-Christian "Germanic" spirituality, medieval mysticism, particularly the figure of Meister Eckhart, had a special draw. It represented a way of knowing that affirmed inner experiences as the breeding ground for divine knowledge that came out of the spiritual structures that shaped the self, which could be posited as racial in character, or in the shape of the *Seelentümer* of Deutelmoser. Though the specifics of Luther's connection to mysticism were the subject of controversy, they were also

---

[50] "Für uns Deutsche bedarf es dessen dringend, daß wieder der echte Luthergeist kräftig auf uns wirke, alles Scheinhafte austreibe und verjüngend in unseren Seelen walte. Nur von da aus kann uns wieder eine feste Zuversicht, eine Unerschrockenheit, eine Fröhlichkeit des Lebens inmitten aller der Gefahren und Nöte kommen. Wenn in diesem Geist die Luther-Gesellschaft entstehen wird, kann Luther abermals ein Erretter für uns Deutsche werden." (For us Germans it is of pressing concern that the true spirit of Luther work again in us, driving out all that is false, and rejuvenate us through its rule. Only only on this basis can come a solid confidence, a fearlessness, a joy in life in the midst of dangers and emergencies... if the Luther Society is founded in this spirit, then can Luther once again become a savior for us Germans.) Rudolf Eucken, "Weshalb bedürfen wir einer Luther-Gesellschaft." *Lutherjahrbuch* 1 (1919): 5–8; 5. See Chapter 3 (p. 49ff.).

the subject of renewed interest in this era. Mystical revelation within the inner self was, in some accounts, at the root of Luther's own evangelical breakthrough; prior to the encounter with scripture was the encounter with the hidden God of history as he struggled in the monastery with his sense of sin and perdition. For Karl Holl, for example, it was the experience of the sinful self in the conscience, as manifested in his early writings, that reflected the initial breakthrough to the knowledge of a merciful God, prior to encountering that God in Christ as revealed in scripture. This idea of a revelation grounded in experience also suggests that God's revelation works outside the channels of scripture; the hidden God manifests himself in nature, in the actions of the great heroes, in the state structures that emerge from violence and conflict; all of this could be imagined as suggested by Luther's inner experiences and speculation about the nature of the hidden God. When one played with a Luther who is separated from the Lutheran Confessions and from his rootedness in scripture, that Luther could well affirm a great deal that was antithetical to traditional Christian belief, and, if taken to an extreme, emerge as a Luther who celebrated a heathen God of power rather than the God of Christ on the cross.[51]

Deutelmoser has Luther affirming the actions, violent or otherwise, of heroic leaders who impose their dominance and will on the saeculum. In doing so, they exercise the providential destiny given to them by God. Indeed, this was an element of Luther's writings little noted until the 1930s, but then repeatedly referenced as authors sought to make sense of the new authoritarian order in Germany, and to affirm the leadership cult surrounding Hitler. While Deutelmoser himself wasn't attracted to Nazism, he was a participant in another movement focused around the leadership claims of Friedrich Hielscher, and affirmed the notion that whatever historical actor could render order, whatever the means, this bespoke providential election. Deutelmoser's Luther affirms the formula "might makes right," predicated on the notion that God places into creation the order of the state based on its ability to render order in time. Where that is the case, Luther countenances whatever violence is necessary to make it come about; like Paul Althaus as discussed in Chapter 3 (pp. 70–4), Deutelmoser sees this admirably exemplified in Luther's response to both the princes and the peasants at the time of the Peasants' War.

Deutelmoser's Luther is the prophet of a new world that affirms the all-encompassing power of the state over every other entity, a heathen religiosity of a new German *Reich*. This is the most provocative aspect of Deutelmoser's work, and the one that most incites those such as Knolle who see it as not simply mistaken or invented, but an affront to Luther and the church that bore his name. But in fact, the DC movement, which came out of the Lutheran church tradition, more or less crafted an understanding of Luther that parallels in many ways

---

[51] One is reminded of Hans Preuß's comparison of Luther to Thor; see Chapter 5 (p. 109).

Deutelmoser's. First, though the Reformation was incomplete, Luther as part of his prophetic calling foresaw a church grounded in the *Volk*, predicated on an intuited racial consciousness that he himself was not able to articulate, but which was manifested in other ways in his writings and actions. This Luther affirmed violence in order to achieve the realization of this new *völkisch* order, to be led by a heroic figure who embodied the providentially ordained leadership affirmed by Luther. This was not realized in Luther's day, but he foresaw it, and in Hitler it was now coming to pass. While the accents are different, the lineaments are just as creatively constructed and parallel those of Deutelmoser.[52] Of course, there were those in the Protestant church, including Knolle, who found the Luther of the DC almost as untenable as that of Deutelmoser. But almost all Luther scholarship in one way or another was rooted in an image of Luther that gave sustenance to Deutelmoser's views; Hermann Schuster's intuition that Protestant theology shared some complicity in the creation of Deutelmoser has more than a little truth to it.

This becomes even clearer with a few responses to his work which take a measured and in part affirming approach to its conclusions. One such response was published in the *Zeitschrift für Kirchengeschichte*, one of the leading church historical scholarly journals in Germany. Its author, Johannes Oberhof (1905–1987), sees Deutelmoser's study to have broached a pressing problem within the understanding of Luther in relationship to Christ, as it is related to his understanding of God, which Oberhof sees not simply as a question about Luther, but about the Christian character of the current world view. Oberhof concedes "what Deutelmoser has rightly seen and what the theologians mostly play down, is the raging dynamic in Luther's concept of God. Deutelmoser's thesis regarding Luther's pantheistic metaphysics notes what normally is overlooked: the character of Luther's powerful intuition of the absolute, which explodes the modern idea of personality."[53] This sense of the potency of Luther's concept of the divine

---

[52] It is noteworthy that at the same time Deutelmoser's work was being pilloried in the Lutheran press, another study with strikingly similar features was published, Helmuth Kittel's, *Religion als Geschichtsmacht* (discussed in chapter 6) and elicited nothing like the storm of criticism that surrounded Deutelmoser's study. Kittel's work, while grounded in the racialist mentality of DC theology, more or less made the same argument as Deutelmoser concerning the larger implications of Luther's work for the relationship of the state to the church. For instance, the passage of Kittel's quoted in chapter 6, pp. 143–5, makes strikingly similar claims about Luther's view of the church and state in relationship to the will of God. He, too, calls upon Luther's theory of the *Wundermänner* to affirm the dignity of the state and also notes Luther affirming such power regardless of the status of the ruler as a Christian, highlights his actions in the context of the Peasants' War, has a long passage on Luther's affirmation of violence in service to the state and its order, and closes imagining a church that is thoroughly deinstitutionalized and in service to *Volk* and state. While the work is clearly imbued with the spirit of the DC, such that it makes no claims that Luther is a non-Christian heathen, the portrait it paints is remarkably parallel to that of Deutelmoser. See chapter 6 (pp. 143–5).

[53] "Was Deutelmoser richtig gesehen hat und was die Theologen meist verharmlosen, ist die reißende Dynamik in Luthers Gottesbegriff. Deutelmosers These von der pantheistischen Metaphysik Luthers sieht zwar, was in der Regel übersehen wird: den die moderne Persönlichkeitsvorstellung sprengenden Charakter der gewaltigen Intuiton Luthers vom Unbedingten." Johannes Oberhof,

as conceived by Deutelmoser is given credence by Oberhof, though he notes that Deutelmoser fails to account for the dialectic of immanence and transcendence that can be found in Luther's conceptualization of God—he references Erich Seeberg's recent study of Luther's view of Christ as a better take on the implications of Luther's view. Nevertheless, Oberhof doesn't reject out of hand the relevance of Deutelmoser's representation of Luther, finding that it articulates the conundrum of relating the past to the present, as well as making the past relevant to the present. In a way, Oberhof is articulating the problem of studying Luther in general in this era, where the present ideological preoccupations so powerfully affect the ability to perceive the figure or ideas of Luther. Though Oberhof's piece is somewhat ambiguous in its final conclusions, and he certainly refrains from endorsing Deutelmoser's study as a whole, it is one of the few responses that acknowledges that Deutelmoser captures something real about the Luther image of the present.

This type of modulated response is even more clearly expressed in a review by Erich Vogelsang in the *Archiv für Reformationsgeschichte*. Titled "Der gefährliche Luther" (the dangerous Luther), Vogelsang clearly had a somewhat conflicted response to Deutelmoser. On the one hand, he fully acknowledges all the flaws in the study as enumerated by Theodor Knolle, whose work he cites in the course of his review. On the other hand, Vogelsang clearly wishes to use one central element of Deutelmoser's argument to affirm his own view of Luther, emphasizing much more robustly Luther's embrace of the hidden God than would be countenanced by Luther scholars such as Knolle. What comes through clearly here are the deep tensions in the image of Luther of the 1930s. Vogelsang wants to situate Luther in a dialectic that gives equal play to the idea of revelation that comes through history, custom, the state, and the *Volk*, the Luther who was seen as the prophet of the *völkisch* religiosity by a goodly portion of German Protestantism. Knolle, who wished to bracket the hidden God of Luther within the revelation that comes through Christ, thoroughly denounces this aspect of Deutelmoser's depiction. Vogelsang isn't so sure, and, regardless of all scholarly shortcomings, would like to embrace at least part of Deutelmoser's representation:

> What Deutelmoser calls - erroneously and misleadingly, to be sure – "unchristian" in Luther is not so entirely absurd as it sounds to pious Christian ears. This so-called unchristian aspect is in truth the pre-Christian understanding of God, which also comes to a stop for Luther beneath the Gospel as dangerous truth: as the fathomless mystery of the high divine majesty.[54]

"Die Christlichkeit Luthers und der Begriff der Geschichte." *Zeitschrift für Kirchengeschichte* 57 (1938): 96–109; 108–9.
[54] "Was Deutelmoser fehlerhaft und mißverständlich genug das 'Unchristliche' an Luther nennt, ist also nicht ganz so absurd wie es frommen christlichen Ohren zunächst klingt. Das sog. Unchristliche ist in Wahrheit das vorchristliche Gottesverständnis, das für Luther auch unter dem Evangelium als

Vogelsang sees in scholars such as Knolle an unwillingness to confront those elements of Luther that disturb their traditionalist representation of him as a church father and man of conventional Lutheran piety. While, Vogelsang concedes, Deutelmoser's larger study is untenable, he contests Knolle's insistence that for Luther an understanding of God only comes through the Word, which is Christ:

> But Luther's theology is not only that! In fact Luther emphasized against Erasmus that even the heathens, as well as our folk wisdom, history, experience, and natural reason all know, within the limits of human knowing, about providence and predestination, about the sole efficacy of God and the bondage of the human will, and that this knowledge is part of the law written in every heart, which is confirmed by scripture as true. Luther's discussion about the hidden God is not based on impertinent speculation, but also not primarily on the revelation of scripture, but is compelled through reason, experience, and history. Therefore, one justifiably...speaks here of a continuation of the natural, Germanic idea of fate in Luther.[55]

Vogelsang situates this "dangerous Luther" as an expression, as did Deutelmoser, of the continuing spiritual resonance of a pre-Germanic religiosity within him, which Vogelsang sees as having been betrayed by Melanchthon. In an earlier section of the review he affirmed Rudolf Thiel's indictment of Melanchthon as having falsified Luther's Gospel with his rejection of Luther's hidden God.[56] One gets the sense that Vogelsang finds Knolle's objections to Deutelmoser, while understandable, too fussy, overly pious, and unwilling to face up to the hard truth about Luther's untamable God. For Vogelsang, Deutelmoser is a convenient vehicle to goad those guardians of Lutheran orthodoxy who have not wholly absorbed the Luther for this new age.

The most incisive look into Deutelmoser came in a study by Harald Diem of Luther's teaching on the two kingdoms published in 1938.[57] Diem, along with his

---

gefährliche Wahrheit stehenbleibt: als unerforschliches Geheimnis der hohen göttlichen Majestät." Erich Vogelsang, "Der gefährliche Luther." *Archiv für Reformationsgeschichte* 35 (1938): 162–71; 168.

[55] "Aber Luthers Theologie ist nicht nur das! Luther betont doch gerade gegen Erasmus, daß schon die Heiden, gleichwie unsere Volksweisheit, Geschichte, Erfahrung und natürliche Vernunft von der Vorsehung und Vorherbestimmung, von der Alleinwirksamkeit Gottes und Gebundenheit des menschlichen Willens wissen, und daß dies Wissen zu dem in allen Herzen geschriebenen Gesetz gehört, welches von der Schrift als wahr bestätigt wird. Luthers Rede von dem verborgenen Gott gründet also nicht in vorwitziger Spekulation, aber auch nicht erst in der Offenbarung der Schrift, sondern wird durch Vernunft, Erfahrung und Geschichte erzwungen. Darum darf man hier auch mit Recht...von einem fortwirken des natürlichen germanischen Schicksalsgedankens bei Luther reden." Vogelsang, "Der gefährliche Luther," 167.

[56] Vogelsang, "Der gefährliche Luther," 164. The vilification of Melanchthon as perpetrator of a humanistic and deracinated religiosity, of having highjacked Luther's Reformation and purged it of its vital Germanic elements, is a commonplace in the literature of many who advocate for a *völkisch* Lutheranism.

[57] Harald Diem, *Luthers Lehre von den zwei Reichen* (Munich: Chr. Kaiser Verlag, 1938).

brother Hermann, was deeply involved in the Confessing Church in Württemberg, and wrote his study as his dissertation. His larger project was to reframe Luther's teaching on the two kingdoms to address the common interpretation that Luther more or less placed the church under the authority of the state, thereby prohibited it from questioning its authority. Such views suffused the literature of Luther from the DC, in particular. But to frame his study, Diem starts by commenting on the prevailing image of Luther since World War I, and uses Deutelmoser as a vehicle to frame his critique. He starts by noting that Luther has become, as is to be expected, the forum around which differences in the church have been contested. He objects to those images of Luther that depict him as something other than a Doctor of Scripture and preacher of the Gospel:

> It's not acceptable to distort the prophet of the Germans into the herald of the German racial type, the confessor of Worms into the 'Germanic Protestant character' (as if it were merely 'his Nordic blood that had rebelled against southern, Roman blood!'), the champion of the priesthood of all believers into the forefather of a faith in God accessible through a kind of "imperial immediacy". All such reinterpretations are so unambiguously propagandistic as to preclude there being any real interest in the real Luther here.[58]

He names, among others, Wolf Meyer-Erlach's work *Verrat an Luther* (the betrayal of Luther)[59] as a work whose treatment of Luther led to the publication of Deutelmoser's work, and exemplifies the general problem with the image of Luther as it currently stands.

> In fact our interest in such a thorough review of this book is purely paradigmatic. But it is, despite all, a shameful paradigm for Luther scholarship, of which Deutelmoser himself should have been ashamed when considering how carelessly he interprets Luther (an issue we will point out repeatedly in the course of this study). But did he come to that result entirely by chance? Don't we in the church of the Reformation have reason to give account—earnestly and without respect of person—as to whether such negligence hasn't been cropping up here and there within Luther scholarship now for quite some time? Must we not understand this historian theologically better than he is able to understand himself? Must we not help him and his friends return to an understanding of the

---

[58] "Es geht nicht an, den Propheten der Deutschen in den Künder deutscher Art, den Bekenner von Worms in den 'germanischen Charakterprotestanten' [he inserts a note here: "Als habe bloß 'sein nordisches Blut gegen das südländische römische rebelliert'!"], den Verfechter des allgemeinen Priestertums in den Ahnherrn einer reichsunmittelbaren Gottgläubigkeit umzufälschen. Alle solche Umdeutungen geben sich heute zu eindeutig propagandistisch, als daß hier noch ein wirkliches Interesse am wirklichen Luther auch nur zu vermüten wäre." Diem, *Luthers Lehre von den zwei Reichen*, 5–6.

[59] See Chapter 5 (117–24).

real Luther, even if that will only happen through much repentance and through substantial corrections of our currently accepted images of Luther? Questions of prestige are not allowed in the church of Jesus Christ.[60]

Diem moves from here to highlight many of the ways he sees the Luther image of the present having gone seriously astray, pointing out Wilhelm Stapel's depiction of Luther subordinating the church to the state as anticipating Deutelmoser,[61] and noting that even Ernest Troeltsch's view of the church had the makings of such a subordination. Turning to another major development in the image of Luther, he looks at Karl Holl, whom he praises for putting the focus back onto Luther's actual writings, but notes that his idiosyncratic understanding of Luther's theory of justification, which defined Luther's religion as a *Gewissensreligion*, opened things up for Deutelmoser as well: "how are we supposed prevent a Deutelmoser, from making such unbridled use of the 'autocracy [*Selbstherrlichkeit*] of the conscience' so long as we let him define Luther's conscience as 'God's efficacy in the soul. In the conscience God is and works and speaks without mediation?'"[62] He transitions into the main section of his study with the following observation:

Deutelmoser's book had to open our eyes to the fact that right from his initial question—where does God reveal himself?—the decisive battle between the kingdom of God and that 'Empire', between Gospel and myth, was being fought. Whoever doesn't dare to take a stand against the enemy here and wrest Luther from him has lost the battle forever, and not just to the historian Deutelmoser. However, as long as we Lutherans haven't definitively clarified among ourselves that initial question, we will be poorly armed for battle with those who, lacking all inhibition, see Christendom overthrown on its own turf by Luther and now wish to lay claim to Luther against the church.[63]

---

[60] "Wir haben wirklich nur paradigmatisches Interesse an solch ausführlichem Referat dieses Buches. Aber es ist ein für die Lutherforschung beschämendes Paradigma trotz allem, wessen sich Deutelmoser selber an Leichtfertigkeiten der Lutherinterpretation—wir werden im Verlauf dieser Arbeit immer wieder darauf hineweisen—zu schämen hätte. Kommt er denn so ganz von ungefähr zu jenem Ergebnis? Haben wir in der Kirche der Reformation nicht Grund, uns mit allem Ernst und ohne Ansehen der Person Rechenschaft darüber zu geben, ob nicht schon seit geraumer Zeit diese und jene Fahrlässigkeit in der Erforschung Luthers vorgekommen ist? Müssen wir jenen Historiker nicht theologisch besser verstehen, als er sich selbst zu verstehen vermag? Müssen wir ihm und seinen Freunden nicht zum Verständnis des wirklichen Luther zurückhelfen, auch wenn das nur mit viel Buße und mit beträchtlichen Korrekturen an unseren gängigen Lutherbildern abgehen wird? Es darf in der Kirche Jesu Christi keine Prestigefragen geben." Diem, *Luthers Lehre von den zwei Reichen*, 9.
[61] He cites Stapel's *Christliche Staatsmann* (Hamburg, 1932), quoting at some length and noting that from the views of Stapel one only needs to modify slightly a couple of terms and you arrive at Deutelmoser's version of Luther. Diem, *Luthers Lehre von den zwei Reichen*, 10.
[62] "Wie sollen wir es einem Deutelmoser wehren, von der 'Selbstherrlichkeit des Gewissens' jenen hemmungslosen Gebrauch zu machen, solange wir ihn Luthers Gewissen definieren lassen als: 'Gottes wirksamkeit in der Seele. Im Gewissen ist und wirkt und spricht Gott unmittelbar'?" Diem, *Luthers Lehre von den zwei Reichen*, 16.
[63] "Deutelmoser's Buch mußte uns die Augen dafür öffnen, daß wirklich schon an dem ersten Einsatz: wo offenbart sich Gott? die Entscheidungsschlacht zwischen der basileia tou deou und jenem

From here Diem moves into his explication of Luther's two kingdoms theory by looking at Luther's exegesis of the Sermon on the Mount. Diem is unique among scholars of Luther in the 1930s in identifying the genesis of a work as outlandish as Deutelmoser's not in some flaw in Deutelmoser's approach, or knowledge of the secondary sources, but in the substance of the image of Luther that had developed over the last decades. Though Diem's rear-guard action will not bear fruit, and his career will be cut short before it began when in 1941 he was one of the first to fall on the newly opened Eastern Front, he correctly diagnoses the challenge of seeing Luther's image free from the distorting lens of the Nazi era.[64]

In a way, Deutelmoser's Luther is an apt image to close out this era, coming as it does at that point where the Nazi state had established its full control over German society, when Hitler had achieved the sort of popular legitimacy that allowed him to move forward to pursue his true aims, which were territorial expansion and the elimination of racial enemies. Deutelmoser's Luther and his God of power and violence would, for a time, have celebrated Hitler's mastery of the times, affirming Hitler's providential calling that seemed manifest in the events of the late 1930s and first couple of years of the 1940s. Soon, however, it would become clear that the providential wheel was turning once more, and, at least in the terms established by Deutelmoser's study, divine favor was dramatically withdrawn. And with the turn of events, the portrayal of Luther that had played out over one hundred years would come to a close, lost in the destruction of the Nazi state and the willful forgetfulness of the times that would follow.

The Luther Myth: The Image of Martin Luther from Religious Reformer to Völkisch Icon. Patrick Hayden-Roy, Oxford University Press. © Patrick Hayden-Roy 2024. DOI: 10.1093/9780198930297.003.0009

'Reich', zwischen Evangelium und Mythus geschlagen wird. Wer sich dem Feind nicht hier zu stellen und ihm Luther zu entreißen wagt, der hat die Schlacht für immer, und nicht bloß an den Historiker Deutelmoser verloren. Aber bevor wir Lutheraner uns untereinander nicht endgültig Klarheit verschaffen über jenen Einsatz, sind wir schlecht gerüstet zum Kampf mit denjenigen, die, aller Hemmungen vollends ledig, das Christentum auf dessen eigenem Boden von Luther überwunden sehen und jetzt Luther gegen die Kirche in Anspruch nehmen möchten." Diem, *Luthers Lehre von den zwei Reichen*, 17.

[64] Renate Brandt, "Hermann Diem (1900–1975) und Harald Diem (1913–1941)." *Wir konnten uns nicht entziehen: 30 Porträts zu Kirche und Nationalsozialismus in Württemburg*, ed. Ranier Lächele and Jörg Thierfelder (Stuttgart: Quell-Verlag, 1998): 481–504, esp. 495–504. The circumstances of both Diem brothers, who were active in the Confessing Church, represent the increasing pressure that was placed upon those in the church who resisted the insistent demands of the state and party for conformity. The outbreak of the war and wartime suppression of any dissent only increased such persecution.

9
Luther the Perpetrator?

The war years did not add anything new to Luther's nationalist image in Germany, given the restrictions on publications and the dire circumstances that ensued after 1942. Many publications ceased altogether, and the dynamic of the war did not lend itself to the patriotic nationalism that fueled the engagement with Luther that marked World War I. When the end came, it involved the destruction of German cities, the loss of millions of lives, millions of refugees, the occupation of the country, and a defeat so thorough that it seemed to cut the present off from the past decisively. Yet, as is always the case, the movement of events carried forward the legacy of the past, however damaged. In the case of Luther, he was caught up in the coming-to-terms process that shadowed all considerations of Germany's past. As with World War I, the issue of guilt was one of the most immediate concerns for the Allied victors, exponentiated in its proportions given the massive loss of lives, especially on the Eastern Front, and, with the uncovering of the concentration and death camps, the decimation of the Jews and other "racial enemies." Inevitably, the figure of Luther was drawn into this process, and for a time there was a sharp debate over the degree to which he, or his teachings, bore guilt for what happened, and, if so, what the implications of that would be. Similar to the process of trials and punishments that followed the war, this indictment of Luther died down fairly quickly, and then much of the legacy of the pre-war image of Luther was forgotten, although many of the practitioners of church history in West Germany were figures whose careers went back to the 1920s and '30s. The *völkisch* Luther of the pre-war era was an embarrassment, and other issues related to the ensuing Cold War and division of Germany, as well as the renewed economic vitality that emerged in Germany in the 1950s, made that image unsightly and unusable. Though Luther continued to loom large as a figure of the German past, he was no longer the progenitor of the German self and embodiment of its spirit; rather, he was a figure whose vexing dichotomies were a rich store for scholarly exploration and reflection about Germany's heritage. But he was mostly returned to his past realities, no longer charging up the sensibilities of *völkisch* nationalists.[1]

---

[1] "Der umstrittene Luther," the introduction to Walther von Loewenich's 1982 study *Martin Luther. Der Mann und das Werk* (Munich: List Verlag, 1982): 13–20, provides an instructive example of how one Luther scholar who cut his teeth in the 1930s had, by the 1980s, taken stock of the meaning of Luther in the post-war world.

The issue of Luther's guilt emerged already during the war among concerned observers living outside of Germany. It was perhaps most cogently and thoughtfully expressed by Karl Barth, who was forcibly expelled from Germany in 1934, but never ceased in his engagement with the German church from his Swiss homeland. In December 1939, Barth wrote to a French pastor a letter in which, among other themes, he broached the issue of how to explain the susceptibility of the Germans to the attractions of Hitlerism.[2] The German *Volk* as a whole, he noted, are not evil, or no more so than any other, so the thought that they bear a corporate guilt is misplaced. It is Hitlerism, he continues, where we observe, though, an "expression of uncommon political folly, confusion, and helplessness of the German *Volk*."[3] The English, Dutch, or Swiss are no more or less a "Christian" *Volk* than the Germans, but are not afflicted with this national madness. He explains why this would be with reference to Luther:

> The German *Volk* suffer, however, from an inheritance of an especially profound and consequently especially wild, unwise, life-ignorant paganism. And it suffers from the inheritance of the greatest Christian German: from the errors of Martin Luther regarding the relationship between Law and Gospel, between secular and spiritual order and power, through which their natural paganism became not so much limited and restricted as it was ideologically transfigured, confirmed, and strengthened.

He continues, "Hitlerism is the present evil dream of the German pagan who was first Christianized in the Lutheran form. It is, for the Germans themselves and for all of us, an especially life-endangering dream."[4] In a second letter written to colleagues in the Netherlands in February 1940, he commented upon his earlier missive and refined what he intended with his diagnosis:

> Hitlerism as "the present evil dream of the German pagan, who was first Christianized in Lutheran form." Naturally I don't mean to say that a 'nihilistic

---

[2] Karl Barth, "Ein Brief nach Frankreich," *Eine Schweizer Stimme 1938–1945* (Zürich: Evangelischer Verlag, 1945): 108–17. The letter was published in this collection of pieces Barth has produced between 1938 and 1945 and published in 1945, and was meant to share work that would have been inaccessible to Germans during the war.

[3] "Es ist aber der Hitlersche Nationalsozialismus der allerdings böse Ausdruck der ungewöhnlichen politischen Torheit, Verworrenheit und Hilflosigkeit des deutschen Volkes." Barth, *Eine Schweizer Stimme*, 113.

[4] "Es leidet aber das deutsche Volk an der Erbschaft eines besonders tiefsinnigen und gerade darum besonders wilden, unweisen, lebensunkundigen Heidentums. Und es leidet an der Erbschaft des größten christlichen Deutschen: an dem Irrtum Martin Luthers hinsichtlich des Verhältnisses von Gesetz und Evengelium, von weltlicher und geistlicher Ordnung und Macht, durch den sein natürliches Heidentum nicht sowohl begrenzt und beschränkt als vielmehr ideologisch verklärt, bestätigt und bestärkt worden ist.... Der Hitlerismus ist der gegenwärtige böse Traum des erst in der lutherischen form christianisierten deutschen Heiden. Er ist ein besonders böser, für die Deutschen selbst und für uns andern alle besonders lebensgefährlicher Traum." Barth, *Eine Schweizer Stimme*, 113.

revolution' is only possible in Germany as a Lutheran land, or indeed in every Lutheran land as such. It is quite clear that all sorts of corresponding evils—there are certainly many other diabolical possibilities—could also be possible in other lands, without any connection with Lutheranism. And, moreover, it is completely clear that other Lutheran lands could perhaps resist such other possibilities of nihilistic revolution just as monumentally, as Lutheran Germany succumbed to it. I was thinking with this sentence very concretely about the special, National-Socialist form of nihilistic revolution, about its get-up and disguise as a construction of legitimate governmental authority. And I specifically had in mind the connection of Lutheranism and German paganism. Here I do see—naturally, with the relative perspective to perceive such things—a connection: Lutheranism provided German heathenism with a certain amount of breathing room (with its segregation of creation and the law from the Gospel), and assigned it something akin to its own sacral space. Thus, the German pagan is able to use the Lutheran teaching on the authority of the state as a Christian justification for National Socialism, and using this same teaching the Christian German feels invited to recognize National Socialism. Both these things have occurred. I think, moreover, that this combination is only possible in Germany, and would request consequently that one not draw any generalizing conclusion from it. And one must consider that those sentences in my letter stand in a context, where I wanted to **explain and excuse** the German *Volk*, not accuse them.[5]

As is clear, Barth here is seeking to diagnose a phenomenon that he sees as specific to Germany with its particular interpretation of Luther's teaching on law and Gospel, and not as a theory in general of how to understand Luther's teaching.

---

[5] "Der Hitlerismus als 'der böse gegenwärtige Traum des erst in der lutherischen Form christianisierten deutschen Heiden.' Ich will natürlich nicht behaupten, daß eine 'nihilistische Revolution' nur in Deutschland als einem lutherischen Land oder gar daß die in jedem lutherischen Land als solchem möglich sei. Es ist ganz klar, daß allerlei Entsprechendes (es gibt da gewiß noch viele ander teuflische Möglichkeiten) auch in andern Ländern und ohne allen Zusammenhang mit dem Luthertum möglich werden könnte. Und wiedrum ist es klar, daß andere lutherische Länder solchen andern Möglichkeiten nihilistischer Revolution vielleicht ebenso gewaltig widerstehen könnten, wie ihr das lutherische Deutschland nun eben erlegen ist. Ich habe bei jenen Sätzen schon ganz konkret an die besondere, die nationalsozialistische Form der nihilistischen Revolution gedacht, an ihre Aufmachung und Tarnung als Aufrichtung wahrer obrigkeitlicher Autorität. Und ich habe konkret an die Verbindung des Luthertums nun eben mit dem deutschen Heidentum gedacht. Hier sehe ich allerdings—natürlich in der Relativität, in der man so etwas allein sehen kann—eine Beziehung: das Luthertum hat dem deutschen Heidentum gewissermaßen Luft verschafft, ihm (mit seiner Absonderung der Schöpfung und des Gesetzes vom Evangelium) so etwas wie einen eigenen sakralen Raum zugewiesen. Es kann der deutsche Heide die lutherische Lehre von der Autorität des Staates als christliche Rechtfertigung des Nationalsozialismus gebrauchen und es kann der christliche Deutsche sich durch dieselbe Lehre zur Anerkennung des Nationalsozialismus eingeladen fühlen. Beides ist tatsächlich geschehen. Ich denke aber, daß es in dieser Kombination nur in Deutschland möglich ist und möchte darum bitten, keine verallgemeinernden Folgen daraus zu ziehen. Und man muß bei jenen Sätzen meines Briefes beachten, daß sie in einem Zusammenhang stehen, in welchem ich das deutsche Volk **erklären und enschuldigen** und nicht etwa anklangen wollte." Barth, *Eine Schweizer Stimme*, 122.

But as a diagnosis, it suggested that the issue was connected to the reception of this teaching within German history and culture, and would naturally lead one to look back at the legacy of that reception, to try to connect Luther to Hitler in the processes of the German cultural and political past. And in the course of the war, that is just what other commentators started to do.

One of the earliest diagnostic works that sought to trace such a line from Luther to Hitler was the work of William Montgomery McGovern (1897–1964), whose colorful Indiana-Jones-like career led to his nomination as a possible model for the fictional hero. In 1941, McGovern, who taught at Northwestern University, published a long study which sought to explain the origins of what he termed the "Fascist-Nazi tradition" by reference to a genealogy of ideas that he took back to Luther. In justifying his study, McGovern argued that "neither Mussolini nor Hitler is the creator of a new political philosophy":

> Both men are merely popularizers of doctrines which began four centuries ago, which slowly developed and were transformed during the subsequent period, and which received their final formulation during the opening years of the twentieth century. If we would seek to understand the true nature of Fascism and National-Socialism, therefore, we cannot be content to study merely the speeches and writings of Mussolini and Hitler and their immediate followers, but must strive to understand the underlying political philosophy of which the Fascist and Nazi doctrines are concrete expressions.[6]

The concept with which McGovern worked, namely that Nazism resulted from long-term, processes within a German culture that developed fundamentally differently from the West, parallels in striking ways the theories of right-wing Germans about the roots of their *völkisch* German identity, which they attribute to the exertions of Luther to free himself from the chains of a foreign religiosity. Obviously in the latter case this was thought to redound to Luther's glory, while for McGovern Luther stands at the source of what poisoned German political ideology.

Like his German counterparts, McGovern contrasts an "Anglo-Saxon" way of understanding with what pervades Germany, and sees in ideas the roots of struggle for dominance of one system of belief versus another. To that end he begins his study with a definition of liberalism over and against the Fascist-Nazi tradition.[7] He sees the Fascist-Nazi tradition grounded in a combination of assumptions, the first being authoritarianism, or the right of the one or few to rule over the many,

---

[6] William Montgomery McGovern, *From Luther to Hitler: The History of Fascist-Nazi Political Philosophy* (London: George G. Harrap: 1946): 7–8; 1st ed. (Boston: Houghton Mifflin, 1941).

[7] "Chapter I: The Liberal and Fascist Traditions: a Study in Contrasts." McGovern, *From Luther to Hitler*, 3–17.

and the second etatism, or the unquestioned dominance of the state over all other institutions and individuals. McGovern posed Luther's legacy as follows:

> In many ways the political philosophy of Martin Luther (1483–1546) must be regarded as an amazing paradox. Luther started with a plea for reform in the concept of the church and ended with a reform in the concept of the state. He started with a plea for individual liberty and for freedom of conscience; yet his doctrines led directly to a belief in the divine right of kings and to the belief that monarchs have a right to dictate religious dogmas to the private individual. He started as an internationalist with a message to the peoples of all nations; he ended by formulating the doctrine that all men should be subject to the iron will of their secular lord.[8]

McGovern's formulation of Luther's "doctrines" is strikingly devoid of any actual reference to Luther's writings or actions, but despite this lack his argument proved to have surprising resonance. The notion that German behavior in the twentieth century was rooted in the teachings of Luther worked its way into a viewpoint widely acknowledged within the English-language world. Unlike Barth, who looked at a particular doctrine as specifically interpreted among German theologians, McGovern posited a demiurge that shaped the German political universe.

Such broad *Sonderweg* ideas about German history, while for the most part losing their influence in scholarly circles over time, were widely disseminated in popular literature, most prominently in 1960 in William L. Shirer's epic *The Rise and Fall of the Third Reich*, a surprise best-seller which posited in even starker terms the idea broached by McGovern that it all went back to Luther.[9] It is emblematic that Herman Wouk, in his best-seller *The Winds of War*, has his highly educated American diplomat diagnose the source of German authoritarianism and anti-Semitism as a cultural infection that goes back to Luther.[10] Perhaps the most egregious instance of this view was put forward by Peter Wiener, expatriate German living in England, whose 1945 work *Martin Luther: Hitler's Spiritual Ancestor*, put forward the most aggressively negative portrait of Luther in this tradition, attributing to him severe moral failings and serious mental unfitness in addition to the baleful influence of his ideas on the course of German history. One unique

---

[8] McGovern, *From Luther to Hitler*, 31.
[9] William L. Shirer, *The Rise and Fall of the Third Reich: A History of Nazi Germany* (New York: Simon and Schuster, 1960). Shirer emphasizes the contradictions of Luther's character as fateful for Germans, seeming to have taken at face value the literature on Luther from the 1930s which sees him as the embodiment of the German self. In addition, he assigns Luther responsibility for the disposition of Germans to authority: "But tragically for them, Luther's siding with the princes in the peasant risings, which he had largely inspired, and his passion for political autocracy ensured a mindless and provincial political absolutism which reduced the vast majority of the German people to poverty, to a horrible torpor and a demeaning subservience" (91).
[10] Herman Wouk, *The Winds of War*. (New York: Pocket Books, 1973), 254–59. First edition (New York: Little, Brown & Co., 1971).

feature of Wiener's work was to look beyond just Luther's teachings on obedience to authority and to highlight as well his writings against the Jews.[11] Wiener's book elicited a defense from the noted English Luther scholar E. Gordon Rupp, who felt compelled by the favorable reception the book received to produce a rejoinder, *Martin Luther, Hitler's Cause or Cure?*, noting the wide credence this decidedly negative portrayal, and by extension the attendant image of Luther, received.[12] It was clear that, in the English language world, searching for a theory to explain the success of a system in a country that was widely credited with some of the greatest minds and artists of modernity, the narrative that it went back to Luther seemed apt; such a potent historical force must have correspondingly deep and distinguished roots. Though it is unlikely that these authors were reliant on the literature generated in Germany in the previous decades, it is striking how it freights Luther with an equally potent, albeit negative, impact.

The end of the war in Europe let loose the debate about Germany's guilt. Some publications released immediately after the war repeated the "Luther to Hitler" formula. Two works published in the Soviet occupation zone mark the construction of a Luther whose eagerness to enhance the power of the princes created the basis for the authoritarian system of rule that would prevail in Germany. The first of these, Ernst Niekisch (1889–1967), *Deutsche Daseinsverfehlung* (the German aberration of existence), portrays Luther as intentionally bringing into being the fateful subordination of religion to the state:

In order to excuse the fateful progress of events, the Protestant theologians love to pose Luther as a *homo religiosus,* or exclusively religious man, who stood clueless in the face of all societal and political developments. Nothing could be more false or misleading that this attempt to whitewash things. Luther had, we find, an absolutely wonderfully developed sensitivity for the true social and political power relationships in the Empire. He grasped sooner and better than anyone else that the real masters of the situation were the territorial princes and that anyone who wanted get anything done in Germany had to throw in their lot

---

[11] Peter Wiener, *Hitler's Spiritual Ancestor* (London: Hutchinson Co., 1945; republished by American Atheist Press, 1999); "Martin Luther and the Jews," 69–77. Wiener was no atheist, and explains his highly polemical attack on Luther as a means to confront Christians with their shortcomings. The editorial comments of the 1999 edition explain the republication as a vehicle for pointing out the fundamental immorality of all Christianity in the figure of Luther. This odd publication history highlights further the labile character of his image, as well as the persistence in the popular culture of the "Luther to Hitler" idea.

[12] "Why trouble to write a reply? After all, those of us who know him [Wiener] to be wrong can go on reading and learning from Martin Luther. So many lies have been told about Luther that a few more or less can hardly make much difference. There were many reasons why I should have preferred to hoard my pearls. But the favourable reviews by writers of repute in two responsible journals showed how plausible the Luther caricature could be to those who, unable to verify the facts, were intellectually predisposed to its acceptance." Gordon Rupp, *Martin Luther, Hitler's Cause or Cure. In reply to Peter F. Wiener* (London: Lutterworth Press, 1945): 5.

with them. He drew the consequences from this insight and allied himself for better or worse with the territorial princes who were rebelling against the Emperor and the Empire. The princes strove after sovereign power; they were very great manorial lords, who wished to organize their lands according to the principles of manorialism and be rid of the sovereignty of the Emperor. The structure that had to develop out of this was the authoritarian state. Luther had understood this, and everyone knows how assiduously he went to work to strengthen and fortify the authority of the princely "rulers."[13]

This Machiavellian representation of Luther was echoed in another work published in the Soviet occupation zone, Wolfram von Hanstein (1899–1965), *Von Luther bis Hitler: Ein wichtiger Abriss deutscher Geschichte* (from Luther to Hitler: an important outline of German history) published in 1947. Von Hanstein sees Luther as a political calculator who aimed to invest the princes with power, apparently because he himself was power-hungry. Similar to Niekisch, he sees Luther falsely portrayed as a religious reformer:

Luther was no reformer. He never wanted to play this role that German scholars – consciously or unconsciously – falsely attribute to him, in order to create the foundation for German mercenary politics needed for the pursuit of imperialistic, predatory doctrines – all the while stultifying the *Volk*. Luther was a politician. For him, it was all about politics. It was he who first proclaimed German Imperialism; it was he who preached German chauvinism; he was the true destroyer of European unity. All political consequences and conclusions that pulled Germany into the abyss go back to Luther.[14]

---

[13] "Die protestantischen Theologen lieben es, um dem verhängnisvollen Fortgang der Ereignisse zu entschuldigen, Luther als einen homo religiosus, d. h. ausschließlich religiösen Menschen darzustellen, der allem gesellschaftlichen und politischen Geschehen ahnungslos gegenübergestanden sei. Nichts wohl ist falscher und irreführender als dieser Reinwaschungsversuch. Luther hatte, so finden wir, ein geradezu wunderbar entwickeltes Feingefühl für die wahren gesellschaftlichen und politischen Machtverhältnisse im Reiche. Er erfaßte, besser und früher als jeder andere daß die wirklichen Herren der Lage die Territorialfürsten waren und daß sich jeder, der es in Deutschland zu etwas bringen wollte, auf deren Seite schlagen müsse. Er zog die Konsequenz aus dieser Einsicht und verbündete sich auf Gedeih und Verderb mit dem gegen Kaiser und Reich rebellierenden Landesfürstentum. Die Landesfürsten erstrebten die Souveränität; sie waren sehr große Grundherren, die ihre Länder nach den Prinzipien der Grundherrschaft organisieren und der Oberherrlichkeit des Kaisers sich entschlage wollten. Das Gebilde, das auf diesem Wege entstehen mußte, war der Obrigkeitsstaat. Luther hatte es begriffen und man weiß, mit welche Fleiß er ans Werk ging, die Autorität der fürstlichen 'Oberkeit' zu stärken und zu befestigen." Ernst Niekisch, *Deutsche Daseinsverfehlung* (Berlin: Aufbau Verlag, 1946): 11.
[14] "Luther war kein Reformator. Er hat nach niemals diese Rolle spielen wollen, die ihm deutsche Gelehrte bewußt oder unbewußt falsch zuerkannten, um so der deutschen Landsknechtspolitik das Fundament zu schaffen, das sie in Verfolg ihrer imperialistischen Raubdoktrinen, das eigene Volk verdummend, benötigte. Luther was Politiker. Nur um Politik war es ihm tun. Er ist es gewesen, der den deutschen Imperialismus als erster verkündete; er war es, der den deutschen Chauvinismus predigte; er war der eigentliche Zerstörer europäischer Einheit. Auf ihn gehen alle politischen Folgen

As with many of the interpretations of Luther in racial nationalist literature, the author is not especially interested in actual writings or actions, except to the extent they suggest political goals. Much time is devoted to the Peasants' War and his betrayal of the peasants, and brief mention is made of his attitude toward the Jews. Luther is depicted as having absorbed the mindset of the "Landesknecht," by which von Hanstein means to typify the territorial princes as mercenary robbers, whose mentality flows down through German history. Both works are devoted to tracing a path through the Thirty Years War, Frederick the Great, Bismarck, the Weimar Republic, coming to a close with Hitler. These two works seem to anticipate the view of Luther that prevailed in the East German state up into the 1970s where Luther was seen as the tool of feudal territorial princes who strike down the forces of the peasants and their early attempt to bring about revolution in the name of the bourgeoisie. Certainly it is a strikingly negative portrayal of Luther as a political manipulator.[15]

In some sense these schematic representations of Luther represent the interest of the victorious Allied powers to provide an explanation of German history that convicted it of corrupted ancestry, justifying a thorough-going remodeling of Germany through denazification and political restructuring. In this sense, the attribution of guilt to Luther was the first crude sketch of an argument, later to be refined, about the course of German history that will come to be known as the *Sonderweg*, or special path, debate.[16] In seeking to explain Nazism, Germany's development into the modern world is contrasted with that of the "West." Germany, it is argued, followed a special route, one in which, unlike the West, the political formation reflected the influence of a mentality that privileged the rights of rulers over that of their subjects—individual rights were sacrificed to the power of the state. McGovern's book is an early attempt at articulating such a theory, and Luther gets caught up in these theories. Prior to the war, German scholars of many stripes had argued something similar, with the major difference that they lionized that development, and used it as the basis for rejecting, among other things, the constitutional order of the Weimar Republic, which was argued to be a foreign intrusion into the Germanic order of political life. Luther, in that view,

---

und Folgerungen zurück, die Deutschland schließlich in den Abgrund rissen." Wolfram von Hanstein, *Von Luther bis Hitler: Ein wichtiger Abriss deutscher Geschichte* (Dresden: Voco Verlag, 1947): 22.

[15] Such a view has a lineage back to Friedrich Engels, whose representation of the Peasants' War valorized Thomas Müntzer, and cast Luther as the antagonist who did the dirty work of the princely oppressors. Friedrich Engels, "Der deutsche Bauernkrieg." In *Marx Engels Werke*. Vol. 7 (Berlin: Akademie Verlag, 1973): 327–413. This work stimulated a historiography up into the period of the divided Germanies. See Roland Boer, "Luther im Marxismus." In *Martin Luther: Ein Christ zwischen Reformen und Moderne (1517–2017)*, ed. Alberto Melloni. Vol. II (Berlin: de Gruyter, 2017): 1003–15. For a broader treatment of Luther in the GDR, see Martin Roy, *Luther in der DDR: Zum Wandel des Lutherbildes in der DDR-Geschichtsschreibung* (Bochum: Winkler Verlag, 2000).

[16] See Jürgen Kocka, "German History before Hitler: The Debate about the German Soderweg." *Journal of Contemporary History* 23 (1988): 3–16.

was also the creator of German authoritarianism, but this was credited to him as a heroic accomplishment; after the war, this was widely seen as his original sin.

In the broader responses to Luther among other sectors of German opinion, the idea that he contributed to the tendency of Germans to submit to authority had many other defenders, though framed less polemically than von Hanstein or Niekisch. Where Luther was seen as part of the problem, it was typically his failure to provide a basis for resistance to ruling authority that was highlighted. This was often contrasted with the Calvinist tradition, which was viewed as providing a basis for an ideology of resistance within the Anglo-Saxon world.[17] Perhaps no indictment of Luther generated as much negative reaction within Germany in the post-war years as Thomas Mann's (1875–1955) lecture at the Library of Congress in 1945 on "Germany and the Germans."[18]

Mann had, like many German literary figures, a long engagement with Luther, though by War's end he had come to a decidedly negative, if complicated, understanding of Luther. He labels him "a gigantic incarnation of the German spirit," but confesses "I do not love him."[19] He views Luther's "Germanism in its unalloyed state" as "separatist, anti-Roman, anti-European," which "shocks and frightens" him, "even when it appears in the guise of evangelical freedom and spiritual emancipation; and the specifically Lutheran, the choleric coarseness, the invective, the fuming and raging, the extravagant rudeness coupled with the tender depth of feeling and with the most clumsy superstition and belief in demons, incubi, and changelings, arouses my instinctive antipathy."[20] He admits he would not have liked sharing a dinner with Luther, preferring Leo X, the Medici Pope against whom Luther's initial rebellion was directed. Still, he continues:

> …no one can deny that Luther was a tremendously great man, great in the most German manner, great and German even in his duality as a liberating and at once reactionary force, a conservative revolutionary. He not only reconstituted the Church; he actually saved Christianity.[21]

He compares Luther's work with that of the New Deal in the United States at the time, seeking to save capitalist economics though unappreciated by the practitioners of said system. Luther was great, he notes, in his translation of the Bible, the renovation of the conscience, creating a direct relationship of the individual to God. "He was a liberating hero,—but in German style, for he knew nothing of

---

[17] See the discussion in Barbro Eberan, *Luther? Friedrich "der Große"? Wagner? Nietzsche? Wer war an Hitler schuld? Die Debatte um die Schuldfrage 1945–1949*. 2nd ed. (Munich: Minerva, 1985): esp. 48–9, 110–15.

[18] Thomas Mann, *Germany and the Germans* (Washington, DC: Library of Congress, 1945). Published in German as *Deutschland und die Deutschen* (Berlin: Suhrkamp, 1947).

[19] Mann, *Germany and the Germans*, 6.   [20] Mann, *Germany and the Germans*, 6.

[21] Mann, *Germany and the Germans*, 7.

liberty."[22] This was obvious in his response to the Peasants' War, which Luther perceived as a "distortion of his work of spiritual liberation and therefore he fumed and raged against it as only he could do."[23] Mann depicts this as fateful for the history of Germany, which would have been better and freer had the peasants succeeded. Luther's inward form of spiritual liberty led to the outward servility to the princes, Mann argues, "sundering...the national impulse and the ideal of political liberty."[24] This leads Mann into a sweeping assessment of other implications of this primal event, and its connection to the broader cultural and political history of Germany. Like most of the literature up to this point, the issue of anti-Semitism does not emerge as a topic; Mann focuses instead on the corruption of the understanding of freedom in Luther. It is striking how his depiction of Luther's antinomies parallels Heine's description,[25] though Heine, unlike Mann, celebrated the irreducible elements of Luther's personality. Mann, having experienced the political and religious developments of the 1920s and '30s, was filled with revulsion at what he felt were its implications.

Mann's address, when disseminated in Germany, elicited broad revulsion itself among many, and was rejected out of hand by most Protestant commentators. Heinrich Bornkamm, even at the distance of 1970, still reacted strongly to Mann's representation, contrasting "the intensive historical, biographical and theological work that led to the transition of Luther's image since the nineteenth century" with the embarrassingly immoderate views of Mann, who was "apparently entirely untouched by them."[26] Though Bornkamm protests that he is not responding personally to Mann's views, it is striking how heated his repudiation is:

Lest I be misunderstood: that he [Mann] doesn't personally like him [Luther] is his own business; how he expressed this distaste was something he had to sort out for himself. What concerns us here are only the non-private elements of his views: in praise and rebuke, a horrific tangle of elements stemming from liberal and socialist sources, from Nietzsche and Troeltsch, and from Catholic polemical writings; a fun-house mirror in which he collected what has been said critically about Luther in the last century.[27]

---

[22] Mann, *Germany and the Germans*, 7. [23] Mann, *Germany and the Germans*, 8.
[24] Mann, *Germany and the Germans*, 9. [25] See Chapter 1 (pp. 15–16).
[26] "Von der intensive historischen, biographischen und theologischen Arbeit, die zu dem Wandel des Lutherbildes seit dem 19. Jahrhundert geführt hatte, stechen einige, offenbar von ihr ganz unberührte, ja maßlose Äusserungen *Thomas Manns* peinlich ab." Heinrich Bornkamm, *Luther im Spiegel der deutschen Geistesgeschichte*. 2nd ed. (Göttingen: Vandenhoeck & Ruprecht, 1970): 140. The first edition was published in 1955, but the section on Mann in the second edition is essentially the same.
[27] "Um nicht mißverstanden zu werden: daß er ihn persönlich nicht mag, ist seine Sache; wie er diese Abneigung ausdrückte, mußte er mit sich selbst ausmachen. Uns beschäftigt hier nur das Nichtprivate seiner Auffassung: in Lob und Tadel ein erschreckender Wirwarr liberaler und sozialistischer, von Nietzsche, Troeltsch und aus katholischen Kampfschriften stammender Elemente; ein Zerrspiegel, in dem er sammelte, was im letzten Jahrhundert an Kritik über Luther geäußert worden war." Bornkamm, *Luther im Spiegel*, 140.

He confesses that the views expressed in the Washington, DC, lecture of 1945 are too unpleasant to repeat, and generally condemns Mann for learning nothing substantial about Luther in all of his long career.[28] Bornkamm reflects the general tenor of the response to Mann's views from the 1940s, a response that was all the more heated given that it came from one in exile, and who praised the culture of his exile home in the United States. The reception of Mann's speech parallels in general the reaction to criticism of Luther within Lutheran circles, where critical viewpoints often were caught up in other issues that divided Protestant Germans.[29]

Given this developing narrative about Luther, the discussion of Luther's legacy was inevitably drawn into larger issues of German guilt. Such discussions were fraught. Most Germans remembered vividly the provision of the Versailles Treaty that assigned guilt for World War I to Germany, the rejection of which by Germans as an indictment of German honor united them across social and political boundaries.[30] The issue presented itself somewhat differently after World War II, given the widespread destruction of Germany, its occupation by the Allied powers, the misery of immediate post-war existence, and the revelations that came in the Nuremberg Trials. Gerrman guilt was not categorically denied, although to whom it was to be assigned, and how to conceive of its meaning and implications, raised issues of enormous complexity. For the Protestant church the debate about the issue was modulated by circumstances specific to its situation. For one, the church in Germany was seeking with the end of the war to reconnect with Protestantism worldwide. The 1930s and especially the war had cut the German church off from the larger oikumene. And the end of the war, and the insistence that German institutions "denazify," impacted the church as well and brought into positions of leadership those who could plausibly pose as having resisted, mostly those who had been within the circle of the Confessing Church.[31] It was in the interests of those who had in one way or another participated in the resistance to the coordination of the Protestant church to present themselves as a resistance movement, even though for the most part that resistance was at the level of the church and its institutions, and did not involve resistance to the political

---

[28] Bornkamm, *Luther im Spiegel*, 141.
[29] Those critical of Mann were particularly fixated on what they perceived to be his temerity to judge Germans who had stayed rather than gone into exile, from whence he could not fathom the suffering either during the regime or after. The whole episode, which stretched over many years, reflects the same forces at work with the animosity of Protestant church figures toward Karl Barth. See the discussion in Kurt Sontheimer, *Thomas Mann und die Deutschen* (Munich: 1961): 137–53. For an overview of the landscape of debate about Luther after World War II, see Hartmut Lehmann, "Katastrophe und Kontinuität: die Diskussion über Martin Luthers historische Bedeutung in den ersten Jahren nach dem Zweiten Weltkrieg." In *Luthergedächtnis 1817–2017* (Göttingen: Vandenhoeck & Ruprecht, 2012): 189–212; first published in 1974. He gives a brief overview of the controversy surrounding Mann, 207–8.
[30] See Ulrich Heinemann, *Die verdrängte Niederlage: politische Öffentlichkeit und die Kriegschuldfrage in der Weimarer Republik* (Göttingen: Vandenhoek & Ruprecht, 1983).
[31] See the discussion in Harry Noormann, *Protestantismus und politisches Mandat 1945–1949*, Vol. 1: *Grundriß* (Gütersloh: Gerd Mohn, 1985): 32–41.

changes that were being effected in Germany: as Karl Barth noted after the war: "one stood generally in a relationship to National Socialism, also in the Confessing Church, which can be captured in the unfortunate formula: "worldview no, politics yes!"[32] The motives for confessing a measure of guilt for the war were tied up with the need to portray outwardly a credible image of contrition and rejection of the legacy of the immediate past, mixed together with a genuine desire among some to explore this guilt as a means to move forward.

These motives were present in the impulses that led to the so-called Stuttgart Confession of Guilt of October 1945.[33] Leading figures of the post-war church—among others Bishops Wurm of Württemberg, Bishop Meiser of Bavaria, Hans Asmussen, Martin Niemöller—signed this brief document, which admitted guilt and expressed deep contrition for the destruction and suffering brought by Germany. Part of the audience for the statement were the ecumenical colleagues from abroad who participated in the discussions leading to its adoption, whose frame of reference would more likely be the international view of Germany as a pariah given its culpability for the conflict. However, what emerged in Germany with the dissemination of the statement was a vehement blowback from laity and pastors, most of whom responded with a sense of outrage about the assigning of guilt without reference to the complicity of the Allies in bringing about the Third Reich through their unfair treatment of Germany in the Versailles Treaty, the need to explore the crimes committed by the Allies against the Germans, and the general sense that one hadn't done anything but was carried along by forces one couldn't combat. In general the German public as a whole was more focused on their own immediate suffering in the context of military occupation, and more abstract issues of guilt seemed, at best, constructs of little use, if not affronts to German honor. In this sense, the response in the immediate post-war environment had parallels to the aftermath of World War I.[34]

The reaction to the Stuttgart Confession highlighted the fact that the war had certainly not changed the reality that, prior to the war, the Confessing Church's sentiments only represented perhaps a quarter of the larger church-members within the German Protestant church, and that after the war this broader church membership was looking for consolation during hard times, and not reminders of previous culpability. And even among those who had been part of the Confessing Church, and who now had a leading voice in the reemergence of the Protestant church after the war, there were serious fissures between those, such as Barth and

---

[32] Quoted in Noorman, *Protestantismus und politisches Mandat*, 36; originally in Karl Barth, *Die evangelische Kirche in Deutschland nach dem Zusammenbruch des Dritten Reiches* (Stuttgart: 1946): 27.
[33] On the events and literature surrounding the *Stuttgarter Schuldbekenntnis* see Martin Greschat, ed., *Der Schuld der Kirche: Dokumente und Reflexionen zur Stuttgarter Schulderklärung vom 18./19. Oktober 1945* (Munich: Chr. Kaiser, 1982): 91–109 for the development of the text of the Confession. See also Noorman, *Protestantismus und politisches Mandat*, 50–8.
[34] For reactions to the Confession, see Greschat, ed., *Der Schuld der Kirche*, 120–55.

his circle, who had advocated for a much more thoroughgoing rejection of Nazism root and branch, and others, such as the bishops of the so-called intact churches, Wurm in Württemberg and Meiser in Bavaria, who had sought a modus vivendi with the regime.[35] The reaction to Luther plays out in this divided landscape, with a majority of responses to the criticisms of Barth, not to mention the more undifferentiated indictments of Luther-to-Hitler theoreticians, from within the Protestant church taking a decidedly aggressive defensive posture. As it happened, February 1946 marked the four-hundredth anniversary of Luther's death; as with past commemorations, this one provided the forum for exploring the legacy of Luther, and for debates about his complicity in the disaster of Nazism and, by extension, his relevance for the current challenges for faith and the church.

The four-hundredth anniversary of Luther's death was commemorated with the recent Nazi era and its consequences lurking beneath the surface, though mostly not explicitly confronted; the most common message was that Luther was not to blame. Of course, there was a flurry of publications on Luther, and for the most part they were not interested in exploring issues of Luther's guilt, or even any shortcomings in the reception of Luther in the pre-war era.[36] As noted, the post-war environment in Germany did not incline most in the Protestant church toward self-critical appraisal of the legacy of Luther, whether one was deeply engaged with the Confessing Church or not. For instance, Paul Althaus contributed

---

[35] Noormann quotes a telling passage from a piece published by Hermann Diem in 1947. Diem was active in the Confessing Church in Württemberg in the 1930s, where he often fell into tensions with the church administration under Wurm. "Ich denke an die im Sommer 1938 von der Kirchenleitung angeordnete Vereidigung auf Hitler, die wir ablehnten, obwohl wir damals annehmen mußten, daß uns das mindestens unser Amt kosten werde, und die Kirchenleitung uns ausdrücklich vorher sagte, sie werde uns nicht schützen können. Ich denke an so manche Kanzelansprache, Fürbittenordnungen, die wir wegen ihres unmöglichen Inhalts ignorieren mußten, obwohl die Parteistellen uns nachher dafür belangten. Ich denke an die begeisterte Zustimmung zur 'Heimkehr Österreichs' ins Reich, an die kirchenamtliche Wahlpropaganda für Hitlers 'Volksabstimmungen'... Fürbitte für Hitlers Geburtstag usw. Einmal stellte mich mein Ortsgruppenleiter zur Rede warum ich zur Feier eines 'Wahlsieges' das von Dr. Wurm angeordnete Glockengeläute unterlassen hätte, und ich mußte ihm sagen, daß ich für den größten Betrug, den die deutsche Geschichte kennt, nicht auch noch die Glocken läuten werde." (I think back on the Summer of 1938 and the oath to Hitler ordered by the church leadership, which we rejected even though we knew that it would cost us at the very least our clerical office, and the church leadership telling us ahead of time explicitly that they wouldn't be able to protect us. I think about so many required messages from the pulpit and prescribed intercessory prayers, which we had to ignore because of their impossible content, although the Party authority prosecuted us afterwards. I think of the enthused affirmation of the 'return home of Austria' into the Empire, and the election propaganda for Hitler's 'Volk elections'...prayers for Hitler's birthday, etc. Once my regional group leader took me to task about why I had failed to ring the bells, as ordered by Dr. Wurm, to celebrate an 'electoral victory' [one of Hitler's staged votes to endorse the regime], and I had to tell him that I just couldn't let the bells ring for the greatest fraud known to German history). Noorman, *Protestantismus und politisches Mandat*, 40. Originally Hermann Diem, "Zur Kontroverse über den deutschen Kirchenkampf." *Kirchenblatt für die reformierte Schweiz* 103.21 (1947): 328. The passage captures tellingly the disposition reflected also in the quote from Barth above.

[36] For an overview of the Luther reception in the immediate post-war era, see two articles by Harmut Lehmann, "'Muss Luther nach Nürnberg?' Deutsche Schuld im Lichte der Lutherliteratur 1946/47," and "Katastrophe oder Kontinuität: Die discussion über Martin Luthers historische Bedeutung in den ersten Jahren nach dem Zweiten Weltkrieg." In *Luthergedächtnis 1817–2017* (Göttingen: Vanderhoeck & Ruprecht, 2012): 176–88; 189–212.

a work, "Luther und das öffentliche Leben" (Luther and the public life), where he raised the issue of Luther's relevance to the current situation.[37] Clearly Althaus was conscious of the issues raised concerning the effect of Luther's two kingdoms teaching on the readiness of Lutherans to submit to the rule of the Nazis, and felt compelled to explore it in the course of his piece. Though he notes to begin the current crisis in broad terms, in fact, there are few specifics about any of the historical particulars that are clearly the reference point for his reflections on Luther.[38] He sketches Luther's teachings in clear and compelling outline, making sure to emphasize that Luther's understanding of Christians in relationship to the state in no way compels them to act against their Christian conscience. Quite to the contrary, Althaus highlights passages in Luther that explicitly endorse refusal to follow commands that violate the Christian conscience.[39] In the end he concludes that Luther himself had nothing to do with the readiness of German's to follow the dictates of Nazism, but that rather it was the legacy of the kind of absolutism that was part of Germany's history, and the teachings of Hegel, who divinized the state.[40] The current situation, notes Althaus, lays bare the autonomy of modern politics and its horrific consequences, but that is not a product of Luther's teaching.

In some ways, Althaus piece represents an implicit admission not of the shortcomings of Luther, but a repudiation of some of the legacy of which Althaus was a participant, namely of the traditional relationship of the church to politics and the state captured in the formula "throne and altar" that was embodied in Bismarck's Reich, and which Althaus, as a German nationalist in the 1920s, had yearned to restore. Further, the reference to Hegel's complicity might be interpreted as a repudiation of the *völkisch* nationalism that Althaus promoted in his writings of the 1920s and '30s. It is noteworthy that in the lecture Althaus nowhere makes reference to the *völkisch* discourse and the connected "orders of creation" (*Schöpfungsordnungen*) theology that pervaded his works from 1920s and '30s. So there are potentially some new accents to Althaus' reflections on Luther, though he rejects decisively the idea that Luther himself bears responsibility; in fact, Althaus strongly endorses the continued engagement with Luther as a restorative for Germany.

While Althaus represents someone whose publications in the 1920s and '30s brought him under the critical gaze of the occupying powers,[41] being briefly suspended from his position at Erlangen for his publications, even those with

---

[37] Paul Althaus, "Luther und das öffentliche Leben." *Zeitwende* 18 (1946/7): 129–42.
[38] Althaus, "Luther und das öffentliche Leben," 129–30.
[39] Althaus, "Luther und das öffentliche Leben," 140.
[40] Althaus, "Luther und das öffentliche Leben," 140.
[41] Gehard Jasper, *Paul Althaus*, 320–36, describes the complicated set of circumstances that surrounded Althaus' status after the war. Late in 1946 a combination of factors brought him to the attention of those overseeing denazification, and though his removal from his position was brief, it was also stress-laden, and may explain some of his reaction to the work of Ernst Wolf discussed below, where Althaus was identified among those who had created a theological justification for the embracing the Nazi state in 1933 and following.

impeccable credentials of resistance to the Nazis took a distinctly defensive posture when it came to Luther's culpability. Gerhard Ritter (1888–1967), Confessing Church member and Nazi resister,[42] published in the same volume of *Zeitwende* where Althaus' article appeared an exploration of Luther's responsibility for the success of the Nazis.[43] Ritter had published in 1925 an influential study of Luther[44] that dressed him in German *völkisch* nationalist colors, though his successive reediting of the work in editions from 1933, 1943, 1947, and finally in 1959 progressively weakened the nationalist theme.[45] As a historian, Ritter's focus in "Luther and the Political Education of Germany"[46] was, unlike Althaus', directly on the political catastrophe of 1945 and the need for stock taking. He notes to start the necessity of evaluating the legacy of German history and culture to assess the degree that certain elements had led them into the arms of National Socialism, that one should not shy away from scrutiny of even "the greatest spiritual leaders of our *Volk*, indeed not sparing the prophetic religious figures," in whom, Ritter suggests, "certain dangerous, basic elements of German being might appear with particular clarity".[47] One anticipates with such language that we will be taking stock of Luther.

Ritter notes that hard charges have been brought against Luther, primarily but not exclusively from abroad, portraying him as Machiavellian in his political views. More specifically he is charged with being responsible for the separation of politics from Christian morality, a la Machiavelli, and of making Germans passive and obedient subjects to political authority through his teachings.[48] He mentions that even from the Evangelical Protestant camp, from Barth, one hears this theory, noting, that this is connected to Barth's desire to teach Germans Swiss

---

[42] Ritter combined a German nationalist perspective with traditional Lutheranism, but was also an engaged participant in the Confessing Church as well as with circles connected with Carl Goerdeler who planned resistance to the influence of Nazism, for which Ritter was imprisoned and was scheduled for trial and undoubted execution, surviving only because of the timing of Germany's defeat. See Claudia Lepp, "Konservativ-christlicher Widerstand: Das Beispiel Gerhard Ritter." *Jahrbuch für badische Kirchen- und Religionsgeschichte* 2 (2008): 69–89, as well as the overview by Ulrich Bayer, "Gerhard Ritter (1888–1967)." In *Lebensbilder aus der evangelischen Kirche in Baden im 19. und 20. Jahrhundert: Vol. 2: Kirchenpolitische Richtungen*, ed. Johannes Ehmann (Heidelberg: verlag regionalkultur, 2010): 390–415.

[43] The same volume of *Zeitwende*, 18, had another piece by Ritter, this a lecture delivered for the Luther commemoration and which also defended Luther's legacy: Gerhard Ritter, "Luthertum, katholisches und humanistisches Weltbild." *Zeitwende* 18 (1946/7): 65–84.

[44] Gerhard Ritter, *Luther, Gestalt und Symbol* (Munich: Bruckmann, 1925); *Luther der Deutsche* (Munich: Bruckmann, 1933); *Luther: Gestalt und Tat* (Munich: Bruckmann, 1943, 1947, and 1959).

[45] See Hartmut Lehmann, "Katastrophe oder Kontinuität," 200–3. Lehmann notes that Ritter's publications after 1946 were even more decisive in absolving Luther's legacy of responsibility for the disaster of Nazism.

[46] Gerhart Ritter, "Luther und die Politische Erziehung der Deutschen." *Zeitwende* 18 (1946/7): 592–607.

[47] "Eine solche Selbstbesinnung wird grundsätzlich auch nicht vor den größten geistigen Führern unseres Volkes, ja nicht einmal vor den religiösen Prophetengestalten haltmachen. Es könnte ja doch sein, daß gerade in solchen Geistesgrößen gewisse gefährliche Grundzüge deutschen Wesens besonders deutlich in Erscheinung träten…." Ritter, "Luther und die Politische Erziehung," 592.

[48] "Luther und die Politische Erziehung," 593.

democracy. Not surprisingly, given what he has already said, Ritter decisively rejects this somewhat stylized critique, which itself misapprehends Barth's views. He sees these developments attributed to Luther as not specifically German but rather coming out of the Renaissance, and becoming a feature of the modern world.[49] Luther was a realist who knew that the political sphere would never conform to some utopian dream of a kingdom of God constructed within the material political order of this world, though always insisting the prince must carry out his office according to principal of love over those he rules.[50] Like Althaus, Ritter sees the growth of the absolutist state as not a Lutheran phenomenon, and not even especially German, but a European tendency. According to Ritter, Luther himself did not aim for such a state as a goal of his teachings but merely reflected the realities that surrounded him at the time as he worked on what was his project of religious reform. Luther constantly admonished the rulers with whom he had influence, and spoke hard truths to them. In general Ritter seeks to set Luther back in the sixteenth century in terms of his political thinking and influence, though emphasizing his heroism within context:

> When one accuses Lutheranism of having taught the Germans a groveling servility, this accusation finds in the behavior of the reformer himself, as we have seen, no support. That is not to deny that the epigones of Luther did not long sustain their master's heroic manliness and proud sense of mission in the face of the secular rulers. Such behavior would also have been difficult for them, given the social and economic dependency of the Lutheran clergy on noble patrons and princely authorities, which up to most recent times can be considered the gravest weakness of this church.[51]

Ritter points to the inexperience of German Lutherans with the sort of freedom given the church in the 1920s as an explanation for their desire to return to a church subordinated to the state and the enthusiasm in 1933 for Nazism, rather than any sort of effect of Luther's teaching on the subject. He seeks to deflect blame further by pointing to the Bavarian origins of the Nazi Party, and also to the fact that Protestants didn't make up the entirety of the German population, and notes in the end, fairly enough, that the causes are all very complex. And when

---

[49] During the war Ritter had published a work connected to this theme, *Machstaat und Utopie* (Munich: Bruckmann, 1940).

[50] "Luther und die Politische Erziehung," 598–9.

[51] "Wenn man dem Luthertum vorwirft, die Deutschen zu kriechender Servilität erzogen zu haben, findet diese Anklage in der Halting des Reformators selbst, wie wir gesehen haben, keine Stütze. Aber nicht zu leugnen ist, daß die Epigonen Luthers die heroische Männlichkeit und das stolze Sendungsbewußtsein ihres Meisters den irdischen Machthabern gegenüber nicht lange bewahrt haben. Eine solche Haltung wurde ihnen auch erschwert durch die soziale und wirtschaftliche Abhängigkeit des lutherischen Klerus von adeligen Patronen und fürstlichen Obrigkeiten, die man wohl die bedenklichste Schwäche dieses Kirchentums bis auf die neueste Zeit nennen darf." "Luther und die Politische Erziehung," 604.

the mask fell away Lutheranism was shaken out of its passivity, which, he assures his readers, goes for the church in the post-war setting.[52] He concludes by pointing back to Luther as the model:

> This new Lutheranism [meaning the post-war church] could be of danger to the church if it leads to immortalizing the temporal, purely historical aspects of Luther, especially of his political attitudes. It can, however, become a source of new strength, if it means a renewal of that heroic stance of faith, which, without ambition for outward, visible successes, will not let up in preserving the basic principles of Christian morality, also in the struggle surrounding the structuring of public life.[53]

Ritter's resistance to exploring any element of responsibility within Lutheranism reflects the conservative nature of his resistance to the Nazis; he wishes to ground any new German state firmly in the moral order of traditional Protestant Christianity, and for that a deep encounter with the teachings of Luther are, to his mind, essential.

This emphasis on a continuing engagement with Luther runs throughout much of the literature of 1946. Rudolf Hermann (1884–1976), associated with the Luther Renaissance but nevertheless a member of the Confessing Church in the 1930s, provides another example of the insistent attraction of Luther.[54] His lecture "Luther's historical and theological meaning as a problem of the present," delivered in February 1946 as part of the observances related to the Luther commemoration, highlights the issue of how to approach Luther in the immediate post-war context. He introduces his talk by noting how common it is to treat Luther either as a historical figure, or as a theologian of his time:

---

[52] "Luther und die Politische Erziehung," 606. In 1946 Ritter would not have the benefit of postwar historiography that has convincingly demonstrated the greater receptivity of Protestant Christians for Nazism as compared to German Catholics.

[53] "Dieses Neuluthertum könnte ihr zur Gefahr werden, wenn es dazu führen sollte, auch des Zeitbedingte, rein Historische an Luther, zumal an seiner politischen Haltung, zu verewigen. Es kann aber dann zur Quelle neuer Kraft werden, wenn es eine Erneuerung jener heroischen Glaubenshaltung bedeutet, die ohne den Ehrgeiz äußerlich sichtbarer Erfolge nicht abläßt, die Grundsätze christlicher Sittlichkeit auch im Kampf um die Gestaltung des öffentlichen Lebens zu bewähren." "Luther und die Politische Erziehung," 607.

[54] Hermann is a figure of particular interest given the differences between him and Emanuel Hirsch in how they worked out the implications of Luther's teaching on justification as opened up with the work of Karl Holl. Heinrich Assel in his study of the Luther Renaissance, *Der andere Aufbruch*, contrasts Hirsch's subjective and existential approach with Hermann's language-based approach. While Hirsch connected his understanding of Luther's religion of conscience to *völkisch* politics, Hermann's approach formed the basis for a more individualistic interpretation of Luther's teaching, and consequently led away from the *völkisch* politics of the 1920s and '30s. Hermann, long-time professor of systematic theology at Greifswald, was an active participant in formulating the Barmen Declaration and in the Confessing Church during much of the 1930s.

However, in the face of the division of these two sides, it is especially important today, in the still powerful ferment of our fatherland's history, to join our view of one of the greatest men in the history of our *Volk* with an immersion into his understanding of faith. If we in our whole fatherland wish to survive our fate, we will need the treasures which lie hidden in [Luther's] theology.[55]

Hermann notes that the time is especially ripe for this reengagement, though the somewhat unexpected reason he provides is that, given the changes in Catholic historiography on Luther in the last decade, there no longer is the danger of offending the sensibilities of Catholics by engaging the *Volk* with Luther's gifts to the present age.[56] But this reference is one of the few to any specific events of the most recent historical developments. Luther is treated, both in terms of his teachings concerning the outward world or the inner world of faith, in somewhat timeless fashion.

Like Ritter, he raises the issue of misunderstanding Luther, and connects this in particular with the theme of the hiddenness of God in history, an element of Luther that was repeatedly used to sacralize the profane history of the Third Reich by not a few eminent Luther scholars. But the specific example that Hermann picks out is the much reviled study of Deutelmoser, who, while no doubt guilty of misusing Luther's teaching on the hidden God, unlike most did not use it to affirm the providential credentials of Adolf Hitler.[57] And while Hermann's piece is thoughtful, and reflects his deep engagement with the individual consolations that are provided with Luther's understanding of justification, as well as its difficulties, it leaves aside entirely, as did Ritter and Althaus, the concrete and extensive misuse of Luther during the 1930s as the basis for Protestant engagement with or submission to the criminal Nazi regime. In the end, Hermann recommends keeping one's gaze fixed on *sola fides*.[58] It is difficult to say whether Hermann intentionally directed attention away from the glaring flaws of the Luther image of the immediate past, or why, but it is emblematic of much of what was written about Luther in 1946,

---

[55] "Aber gegenüber dieser Trennung der beiden Seiten ist es heute, in der noch mächtig gärenden Geschichte unseres Vaterlandes, besonders wichtig, den Blick auf einen der Größten in der Geschichte unseres Volkes mit der Vertiefung in sein Glaubensverständnis zu verbinden. Wenn wir in unserem Gesamtvaterlande unser Schicksal bestehen wollen, tun uns die Schätze Not, die in seiner Theologie verborgen liegen." Rudolf Hermann, "Luthers geschichtliche und theologische Bedeutung als Gegenwarsproblem." In Rudolf Hermann, *Gesammelte Studien zur Theologie Luthers und der Reformation* (Göttigen: Vandenhoeck & Ruprecht, 1960): 330–41; 330.

[56] Hermann, "Luthers geschichtliche und theologische Bedeutung," 330–1.

[57] It is of note that in Paul Althaus' lecture the only specific work he identifies in his exploration of Luther's teachings on church and state is Deutelmoser, who stands in for the errors of its interpretation; Althaus, "Luther und das öffentliche Leben," 136. Standing outside the Lutheran theological circle, Deutelmoser was a safe target. As we'll see below, Ernst Wolf also references Deutelmoser, though in his case to yoke him to the errors of Protestant Luther interpretation stemming from the Luther Renaissance.

[58] Hermann, "Luthers geschichtliche und theologische Bedeutung," 341.

whether from one, such as Althaus, who extolled a *völkisch* reading of Luther, or one like Hermann, who did not, or one like Ritter who took great risks in opposing the regime. Clearly the commemoration of 1946 was seen as an opportunity to reassert the relevance of Luther for the issues of the day, to keep Luther front and center before the German church, in a context where at least some were calling for a more vigorous reevaluation of his legacy.

Of those who called for a more critical view, the most aggressive stock-taking came from Ernst Wolf (1902–1971), like Ritter and Hermann a member of the Confessing Church, but unlike them a close associate of Karl Barth. His lecture, "Luther's Legacy," which was also delivered as part of the 1946 commemoration, takes on explicitly the legacy of Luther's theology and image as it was transmitted over time, in particular through the Luther Renaissance. Though recognizing all the complexity and pitfalls that are involved in seeking to capture and to carry on a legacy, Wolf indicts the Luther Renaissance as a movement for misinterpreting and misappropriating Luther's legacy, and in doing so having opened it up for misuse during the 1930s. He notes three basic features of Karl Holl's work that he sees as having set the program for the Luther Renaissance. The first, and the one he affirms, is grounding Luther research in a rigorous philological/historical methodology, though he notes that not all those who followed Holl always fulfilled the strictures of the methodology.[59] The two other features he sees as having opened up Luther for endless misappropriation.

First, says Wolf, Holl saw the consequences of Luther's career to lie in the way he created new spiritual trajectories in all areas of culture: "Holl showed how the Reformation of Luther introduced a new historical understanding of the nature of reality, a new concept of personality, and with it a new sense of community."[60] From here, Wolf argues, one could connect Luther's legacy to just about anything— great political questions like the relationship of church and state, the law, the ethics of economic life, as well as science, philosophy, music, and art. By interpreting Luther this way, Holl found that Luther had something binding to say about all such areas because he was the original inspiration. Wolf cites a representative selection of "Luther and..." article titles.[61] This, he says, leads into incessant Luther apologetics, and well as generating what he terms a "strained Luthermania."[62] One must look skeptically at this literature, he notes, despite some significant insights:

---

[59] Ernst Wolf, "Luthers Erbe." In *Peregrinatio* II (Munich: Chr. Kaiser Verlag, 1965): 52–81; 62. The piece was first published in 1947.

[60] "Holl zeigt, wie die Reformation Luthers sein neues Verständnis der natürlichen Wirklichkeit, einen neuen Persönlichkeitsbegriff, damit ein neues Gemeinschaftsgefühl in die Geschichte eingeführt." Wolf, "Luthers Erbe," 63.

[61] Wolf, "Luthers Erbe," 63. He cites innumerable studies which connect Luther to all variety of historical figures—Böhme, Hamann, Goethe, Nietzsche, and finally Hitler.

[62] "Das Thema: 'Luther und', Luther und Böhme, Luther und Kant, Luther und Nietzsche und so weiter wurde in höchstem Maße aktuell, bis hin zu einer da und dort auftauchenden untentwegten Lutherapolotetik neuen Stils und zu einer verkrampften *Lutheromanie*." Wolf, "Luthers Erbe," 63.

"When a passion thus ignited overpowers critical distance, then one wishes to have, and could have everything from this Luther, whatever one needs and desires for oneself. Luther began from here on out to play a not so innocuous role in the contemporary struggles over world view."[63]

As the second of these negative features, Wolf brings forward Holl's interpretation of Luther's Reformation Gospel as a theocentric and personal "Gewissensreligion" or "religion of the conscience":

> The integration of Luther's Gospel message into a concept of religion determined by the conscience, be that concept either ethical or religious, can lead to the Gospel message being constructively dissolved into a religion for the human needs, which are ever being historically shaped, to the extent one believes that one should take such needs into account, with, for example, an overarching concept of culture or comprehensive world view.[64]

In other words, Wolf sees Holl's concept of Luther basically setting him up to be drawn in and used by movements of the present to achieve some goal that serves their ideological needs.

And the evidence for this effect is the scholarship that lays itself out over the twenty years that followed the publication of Holl's Luther book in 1921. Though Holl was consciously seeking to depart from the liberal Protestantism of Albert Ritschl and the nineteenth century, what he accomplished, says Wolf, was to allow a new sort of equating of the Gospel with social or political developments: "In the place of the historical pantheism of liberal theology stepped an authoritarian historical theology. The excesses of Holl's assessment of the cultural achievements of the Reformation translated itself now into such Luthermaniacal claims (*lutheromanen Anspruch*)... *The legacy was turned into booty.*"[65] He highlights his point with reference to Bornkamm's article on *Volk* and race in Martin Luther,[66] as well as Paul Althaus' "German Hour of the Church,"[67] noting how in each case they "find" elements such as race and orders of creation that fit their present needs.

---

[63] "Wo die hier entzündete Leidenschaft die kritische Zurückhaltung überwältigt, da wollte und könnte man von diesem Luther alles haben, was man brauchte und sich wünschte. Luther begann von da aus seine nicht unbedenkliche Rolle im Weltanschauungskampf der Gegenwart zu spielen." Wolf, "Luthers Erbe," 64.

[64] "Die Hereinziehung von Luthers Evangeliumsbotschaft in einen von Gewissen her, sei es sittlich, sei es religiös bestimmten Religionsbegriff kann dazu führen, die Evangeliumsbotschaft konstruktiv in Religion für die je und je geschichtlich gestalteten Bedürfnisse der Menschen aufzulösen, so weit man, etwa in einem übergreifenden Kulturbegriff oder Weltanschauungszusammenhang, meint, mit solchen Bedürfnissen rechnen zu sollen." Wolf, "Luthers Erbe," 65.

[65] "An die Stelle des Geschichtspantheismus der liberalen Theologie tritt eine authoritäre Geschichtstheologie. Die Übersteigerung in Holls Beurteilung der Kulturleistung der Reformation setzt sich jetzt um in solchen lutheromanen Anspruch... *Das Erbe wurde zum Raub.*" Wolf, "Luthers Erbe," 68.

[66] See Chapter 7 (pp. 181–4).   [67] See Chapter 4 (pp. 81–5).

242   THE LUTHER MYTH

Their work, he argues, leads right into that of Arno Deutelmoser, the apotheosis of this misappropriation of Luther.[68] Wolf uses the issue raised by Deutelmoser of the Empire (*das Reich*) to explore what Luther did have to say about such issues, and demonstrates that his viewpoint was contained within his sixteenth-century understanding of such concepts, and also was connected intimately to his scriptural exegesis. Luther's legacy, Wolf emphasizes, must be understood with sober consideration of the specifics of his time and his meaning, and not transposed through enthusiasm into ideological decorations for the Third Reich.[69]

He identifies as particularly culpable in this regard the extrapolation of orders of creation (*Schöpfungsordnungen*) from Luther's teaching about the state in order to situate the realization of faith in the racial/nationalist order of the state. Wolf calls for a critical engagement with Luther's legacy, which is conscious of where he goes astray and where he leaves off. "Continuous critique of the adoption of Luther's legacy…shall serve to secure it from misinterpretation and misuse; and connected with this is the effort to understand his works correctly, which is required if his legacy is to be acquired legitimately."[70] He closes his address by proclaiming:

> All ideology is at its base an attempt by humans to openly or secretly justify themselves before God. The freedom of conscience preached by Luther lives, however, from the faith in the justification of humanity through God in Christ. That is the signature of the *libertas Christiana*, of the "Freedom of a Christian," of the life of the Christian in the world. The Reformation was about this freedom alone and exclusively; it is its essential legacy.[71]

Wolf in his address held back from naming the names of the theologians whose works he highlighted, but that did not prevent his piece from raising hackles. Paul Althaus, among others, complained about his tactless approach, and Wolf was accused of cherry-picking quotes out of context to make the views seem egregious.[72] Wolf notes, as well, that some saw his lecture as providing solace for

---

[68] Wolf, "Luthers Erbe," 69–72. On Deutelmoser, see Chapter 8 (pp. 199–210).

[69] Wolf, "Luthers Erbe," 73.

[70] "Die immer wieder zu vollziehende Kritik an der Übernahme von Luthers Erbe…soll der Sicherung dienen vor Mißdeutung und Mißbrauch; und die mit ihr verbundene Bemühung, den Reformator in seinem Werk richtig zu verstehen, ist die Voraussetzung dafür, sein Erbe legitim zu erwerben." Wolf, "Luthers Erbe," 79.

[71] "Alle Ideologie ist zutiefst ein Versuch des Menschen zu offener oder heimlicher Selbstrechtfertigung gegen Gott. Die von Luther gepredigte Freiheit der Gewissen lebt aber von dem Glauben der Rechtfertigung des Menschen durch Gott in Christus. Das ist die Signatur der *libertas Christiana*, der 'Freiheit des Christenmenschen', des Lebens des Christen in der Welt. Um diese Freiheit allein und ausschließlich ist es der Reformation gegangen; sie ist ihr wesentliches Erbe." Wolf, "Luthers Erbe," 81.

[72] Wolf notes these criticisms in an article he published in 1947, "Politia Christi. Das Problem der sozialethik im Luthertum," *Peregrinatio I* (Munich: Chr. Kaiser Verlag, 1962): 214–42, in a footnote, 219–21, where he makes some of the same points as in "Luthers Erbe," and quotes from Althaus in particular. In the "Vorwart" to *Peregrinatio II* he notes that he had, in the first volume of *Peregrinatio*, held back "Luthers Erbe" because it had caused such hard feelings, but that he decided to include it in the second volume after receiving requests to make it available. He adds the following comment:

those abroad who were blaming everything on Luther, the thought being, it would seem, that Luther scholars should be drawing the wagons around Luther's endangered reputation. Wolf's forthright engagement with the Luther of the pre-war era was the exception in the years immediately after the war, and the reaction to his piece provides some sense why that was. Even within the circles of those who were part of the Confessing Church, the operative stance was defensive, seeking to preserve the heroic Luther, and deflect blame onto other culprits, be it the legacy of Renaissance humanism, Enlightenment reason, Hegelian idealism, or simply the legacy of a soulless modern industrial society.[73]

The tone of the debate about Luther's responsibility for the sins of the Nazi state paralleled the response within the church to policies of the occupying powers related to denazification, as well as the economic circumstances of the post-war years. The winter of 1946-7 was especially hard on the native German population, and in particular heating and food were in short supply. Though this was not, as was perceived by many, including many in the Protestant church, a deliberate effort to punish Germans, it created a mood that was increasingly resistant to messages about German guilt. On the contrary, the hardships led many in leading positions in the church to address the issue of guilt much more defensively, and to highlight the sins of the Allies, both in terms of their occupation policies, but also in terms of their guilt.[74] In 1946-7 denazification efforts were carried through with some earnestness in the American zone, and were a particular focus for criticism among leaders of the newly constructed Evangelical Church of Germany. It is within this context that one of the sharpest exchanges

"Es sieht so aus, als ob auch im Bereich der 'Lutherranaissance' die Neigung zur 'Restauration' wirksamer gewesen ist als diejenige zur angekündigten 'Revision'. Vielleicht ist das aber auch ein Grund dafür, daß Luther nicht mehr so oft und so leidenschaftlich als Helfer in Gegenwartsnöten beschworen wird wie damals" (It appears as if in the circles of the 'Luther Renaissance,' too, the inclination to 'restoration' is more operative than any formerly announced 'revision.' Perhaps that is the reason why Luther is no longer so frequently and so passionately invoked as a helper for present needs as used to be the case). Wolf, "Vorwart," *Peregrinatio II*, 7. This is a pointed reference to the oft repeated aspiration of the literature generated from the 1946 commemoration of Luther's death that he continue to be the aid needed by Germans in their time of need.

[73] For an broader overview of these themes see Helmut Lehmann, "Katastrophe und Kontinuität," esp. 193ff.

[74] See, for instance, the volume published in 1948, Hermann Diem, *Die Schuld der Anderen: Ein Briefwechsel zwischen Helmut Thielicke und Hermann Diem* (Göttingen: Vandenhoeck & Ruprecht, 1948). It contains a sermon delivered by Thielicke on Good Friday, 1947, in which, with great pathos, he highlighted the sins committed against Germans as a result of the policies of the occupation powers, which constituted, he preaches, a policy of *Seelenmord*, spiritual murder. The sermon elicited a great deal of positive response, as well as criticism from Hermann Diem, whose correspondence with Thielicke makes up the majority of the volume. The title's focus on the "guilt of others" captures a critical issue about the relevance of other's guilt when Germans considered the legacy of their past. Thielicke, in his reply to Diem's criticism, also raises the issue of needing to address the suffering of his congregation, and to speak to their concerns, or risk failing to carry out his pastoral duties and being cut off from his congregants. The fact that the work was published indicates the resonance of the issue of guilt, and also the increasing resistance to it within the church. For context, see Martin Greschat, *Die evangelische Christenheit und die deutsche Geschichte nach 1945: Weichenstellungen in der Nachkriegzeit* (Stuttgart: Kohlhammer, 2002): 162-3.

came forward from the criticism of Wolf and Barth of Luther's legacy. The trigger for the exchange came from Barth's criticism of the disposition of church leadership in the aftermath of the Stuttgart Confession of Guilt. Barth, who persistently advocated for a forthright admission of guilt, criticized how some responded by framing the horrific crimes of the regime against the Jews within the context of the powers of the demonic in the world:

> I have, even in the circles of the Confessing Church, where one would liked to have heard this simple concession, first heard much talk, with a suspicious amount of ardor, about the demonic, with whose deceptive powers one had made acquaintance in these last twelve years.[75]

This is coupled, he adds, with the tendency to develop fantasies about the guilt of others. Barth published his thoughts shortly after the emergence of the Stuttgart Confession, disappointed with what he felt was the lack of follow up to the document, which he saw as only a first step.

His comments, however, clearly targeted the figure of Hans Asmussen (1898–1968), his long-time colleague in the Confessing Church, and key formulator of the Stuttgart Confession, who had written about the demonic just in the manner described by Barth. Asmussen reacted sharply to these views, which led to a further exchange of letters that only exacerbated the conflict, Asmussen feeling that Barth was questioning the sincerity of his work on the Stuttgart Confession.[76] In was in this context that Asmussen delivered a lecture in Flensburg in October 1947 that was then published under the title "Does Luther have to go to Nuremburg?"[77] Asmussen's title obviously puts Luther in the shoes of the high-level figures who were tried in Nuremberg after the war, playing off of the accusations of those who would assign Luther primary guilt for the coming of the Nazi regime.[78] Asmussen sets up his discussion by asking "is the church of Luther

---

[75] "Ich habe aber auch in den Kreisen der Bekennenden Kirche, wo man gerne jenes simple Zugeständnis gehört hätte, zunächst viel und mit einer verdächtigen Inbrunst von den Dämonen reden hören, mit deren verführerischer Gewalt man in Deutschland in diesen zwölf Jahren Bekanntschaft gemacht habe." Greschat, Die Schuld der Kirche, 88.

[76] See the exchange of letters in Greschat, Die Schuld der Kirche, 212–15, which captures the sharpness, and perhaps somewhat overblown, criticism by Barth, and the raw emotions in Asmussen's response. This exchange marked a break between their long-time collaboration.

[77] Hans Asmussen, "Muß Luther nach Nürnberg?" Nordwestdeutsche Hefte 1947 (Heft 11/12): 31–7.

[78] In one sense, Asmussen's question already been answered when Julius Streicher, the notorious anti-Semite and publisher of Der Stürmer, raised the issue of Luther while on the stand at Nuremberg. Asked by the interrogator about other anti-Jewish weekly newspapers in Germany during the 1930s, Streicher answered by raising up Martin Luther's work "The Jews and their Lies," and stated that if they took this book into account, Luther would be sitting on the bench in his place, clearly seeking to deflect blame for his own views back onto Luther. The interrogator, unimpressed with Streicher's attempt to change the topic, admonished him to answer the question. International Military Tribunal. Trial of the Major War Criminals Before the International Military Tribunal. Vol. 12, Proceedings, 18 April 1946–2 May 1946. (Nuremberg: International Military Tribunal, 1947): 318.

responsible for National Socialism, the idolization of the state and its collapse?"[79] But the attribution that it was Luther's influence that led to the receptivity for Hitler rests, Asmussen notes, on a misunderstanding of what lay behind the church's willingness to embrace the new state, which stemmed from a desire to turn the national revival into a religious revival.[80] Barth and his school took this up in 1945, says Asmussen, using the German Christians to claim that the Germans themselves recognized their guilt: "You Lutherans have recognized yourselves for a long time that you're responsible for Hitler. You are anti-democratic, you're crypto-capitalists, you're reactionaries, you're anti-Socialists, you're National Socialists."[81] This somewhat heated expostulation reveals the sense of mistreatment that fueled Asmussen at this point. He does admit that Barth's critique is a bit more refined than this, but, Asmussen contends, Barth essentially blames Luther for the fact that Germans in the church saw that things were happening that were wrong, and they didn't do anything about it. Asmussen defends Luther vigorously, noting that the Hohenzollern weren't Lutheran, that the roots of things are always complicated, and if you are looking for guilty parties, what about Kant, the French Revolution, or Karl Marx and Socialism?[82] Luther himself was neither a fascist nor an anti-fascist, Asmussen asserts, and he had admonished the rulers of his time like few others. One finds neither in Luther or the Lutheran Confessions any trace of National Socialism, Asmussen continues, and while there may be those who did take a wrong turn, this was because of elements that came from in and outside Germany. And as long as one had not done anything criminal, one should not be put on trial.[83] And why doesn't Barth, Asmussen asks, look at himself, and ask if his criticism of liberalism in the 1920s wasn't also a cause of the rise of Hitler. In any case, Lutherans had addressed the issue of guilt before Karl Barth had.[84]

Asmussen's article brought to the surface a political divide among the members of the Confessing Church that previously had been more submerged. Barth had always been more skeptical of Luther than most German Lutherans, and many who came to associate with him in the 1930s did so in a common front against the

---

[79] "Ist die Kirche Luthers für Nationalsozialismus, Staatsvergottung und Zusammenbruch verantwortlich?" Asmussen, "Muß Luther…," 31.
[80] "Dahinter stand jenes unselige volksmissionarische Mißverständnis, als ob es darauf ankäme, der Welt zu einem besseren Verständnis iher selbst und also dem Nationalsozialismus zu einem christlichen Verhältnis seiner selbst zu helfen und so den 'Aufbruch der Nation', wie man es damals nannte, zu einem religiösen Aufbruch zu machen" (Behind this [embrace of the state] stood this unholy mission-to-the-*Volk* misunderstanding, as if it was all about helping the world to a better understanding of itself and in this way helping National Socialism find its own Christian connection, thus making the "national awakening," as it was then termed, into a religious awakening). "Muß Luther…," 32.
[81] "Ihr Lutheraner habt es ja selbst schoin seit langer Zeit anerkannt, dass ihr an Adolf Hitler schuldig seid. Ihr seid Antidemokraten, ihr seid verkappte Kapitalisten, ihr seid Reaktionäre, ihr seid Antisozialisten, ihr seid Nationalsozialisten." "Muß Luther…," 31.
[82] "Muß Luther…," 34.   [83] "Muß Luther…," 35.   [84] "Muß Luther…," 36.

greater threat of the coordination of the churches by the Nazis. But Barth's Reformed and Swiss background, as well as his Socialism, had always made most traditionalist German Lutherans suspicious. And Barth was immune to the nationalist sentiments that were especially powerful among many German theologians. Someone like Asmussen was defensive about Luther because, for him as for many German theologians of his generation, they saw Luther still as the embodiment of a religiosity that was a pillar of German identity. For most German Protestants after World War II, there was no fundamental change in their nationalist sentiments, which, while mostly stripped of their *völkisch* vocabulary, still looked for a Christianity that connected back to the legacy of Luther. Rather than see the key to Germany's future lying with nurturing democratic sensibilities, they rather saw their project to protect the German church, and by extension German culture, from secularizing tendencies that they associated with individualism and materialism. Continuing to root German religiosity in Luther, and to connect that religiosity to the German people would bring about the real corrective that Germany needed. In that regard, they were not as interested in denazification as they were defending their religious heritage from accusations of some sort of Nazi penumbra, and maintaining a vital connection to the Germans as a whole. For that reason, they were so protective of Luther, continued to extol his virtues and legacy, and turned away from admissions of guilt and toward defending Germans and German culture from wholesale indictment by deflecting guilt back onto the occupying powers. The experience of the war had certainly broken the hold of the Nazi state and the German Christian movement, but the sentiments that had pervaded German Protestantism in the 1930s continued, in a more muted fashion, to shape attitudes after the war. And it would be unrealistic to expect the conditions of military defeat simply to wash away the patterns of past religious culture. It would take decades for the sort of coming to terms that Barth or Hermann Diem envisioned to come about, and then only with the very changed circumstances that developed from the 1950s to the 1990s. As for Asmussen's question about Luther going to Nuremberg, that too took decades, but the most recent Luther commemorations of 1983 and especially 2017 reflect a sea change in the relationship to Luther, who, though still a figure of great fascination and interest among Germans, no longer holds the cultural power that he exercised with past generations of Germans.

The Luther Myth: The Image of Martin Luther from Religious Reformer to Völkisch *Icon*. Patrick Hayden-Roy, Oxford University Press. © Patrick Hayden-Roy 2024. DOI: 10.1093/9780198930297.003.0010

Conclusion

Dietrich Bonhoeffer, in his 1937 work *Nachfolge* (discipleship), in discussing Luther's understanding of grace and how it had been cheapened, noted the ubiquity of his words, but also their consistent distortion: "Luther's words are everywhere, but twisted from their truth into self-delusion."[1] Certainly no era of German history was more saturated with Luther's words than the era covered in this study; Luther was everywhere. Yet as Bonhoeffer suggests, perhaps at no time was Luther as Luther less attended to, more willfully distorted. Luther became whatever was needed to affirm the preexisting needs and assumptions of an era which searched for legitimizing authority. The need to refashion Luther in the garb of the *Volk*, to have him affirm the radical politics of the present, suggested the vacuum of meaning that could be drawn from tradition and doctrinal formula. Luther was everywhere, but wrenched from his time and place, from his actual words so as to reside in and speak to a latter-day reality. Though it was a common trope to have Luther affirm the *Führer* and all that was being done, looked on from the outside one imagines that Luther would have been as perplexed by the fulgent realities of the 1930s as are those who look back on it from ninety or so years down the road of time. Such a strange world, such strange ideas, and such a strange Luther. And yet it is just that oddity and its appalling consequences that stands in need of explanation, how the present remakes the past, reshapes it for new purposes.

The story of Luther's image as it emerged in the aftermath of the Napoleonic Wars, and then evolved in the course of the nineteenth and twentieth centuries, highlights how historical developments imprint themselves on the figures of the past. The outline of this image was provided by ideas, carried over from the Enlightenment, of a Luther who stood for freedom of conscience, but transposed in the nationalist sentiment that took root with the victories over the French that brought the Wars of Liberation, as they were known among Germans, to a close.

---

[1] "Überall Luthers Worte und doch aus der Wahrheit in Selbstbetrug verkehrt." Dietrich Bonhoeffer, *Nachfolge*. In *Dietrich Bonhoeffer Werke*. Vol. 4 (Munich: Chr. Kaiser Verlag, 2002): 40. English in Dietrich Bonhoeffer, *Discipleship*. In *Dietrich Bonhoeffer Works*. Vol. 4 (Minneapolis: Augsburg Fortress, 2001): 53. The work has been more commonly known in English as *The Cost of Discipleship*. The aptness of this quote to capture the environment within which Luther was apprehended in the 1930s is represented by their use for an exhibition that took place in 2017 in Berlin to commemorate the five-hundredth anniversary of the Reformation: *"Überall Luthers Worte..." Martin Luther in Nationalsozialismus / "Luther's Words are Everywhere..." Martin Luther in Nazi Germany* (Berlin: Topographie des Terrors/Gedenkstätte Deutscher Widerstand, 2017).

The Luther of the 1817 celebration of the onset of the Reformation was for the first time posed as a figure of virtues encompassing a spectrum of features—freedom, bravery, *völkisch* nationalism, faith—that were associated with a German identity and its freedom from foreign influences. This was a new Luther, one who anticipated the course of German liberalism with its advocacy both of political freedoms but also for the realization of those freedoms in a national state, one for which Luther could stand as a symbol. Luther came out of the church and into the public square in the course of the nineteenth century, literally with the public statuary and other public commemorations, but also as his legacy was taken up into Idealist projections of spiritual influences ostensibly set into motion by Luther and generative of the dialectical processes that would bring into being the Germanity of the nineteenth century. This idea was transposed in the history of the Reformation as imagined by Leopold von Ranke, and, after German unification, in the celebration of his birth in 1883, most memorably in the encomium of Heinrich von Trietschke, where, shorn of its Enlightenment elements, Luther emerges as the soul of the new Germany, stripped of his doctrinal baggage, and promoted as the father of unified German identity.

While such a secularized Luther offended the sensibilities of traditionalists, such was its insistent appeal that by the time of World War I and its traumas, the Luther of faith and the Luther of the nation could be combined to produce a potent symbol of spiritual, martial, and national commitment. The crucible of the war would forge an image that, in the trauma of the post-war, would be subsumed into a new culture of Luther mythology, where his living spirit was invoked as the source for revival and authentic renewal of a German identity that was strongly resistant to the appeal of democracy and individualism as embodied in the Weimar Republic. This newly minted *völkisch* Luther gains both scholarly legitimacy in the 1920s, as well as becoming the cornerstone of a German Protestantism where his image can confirm a sense of alienation from the broader state and society that emerged from the war. Luther, the existential man of conscience, who realizes his authentic self in his rebellion against and struggles with the foreign religiosity of Rome, defines as well the possibilities for a *völkisch* Germanity of the present in its struggles to emerge spiritually and materially from the shame of defeat and foreign enslavement. The success of National Socialism as a mass political movement was especially due to its appeal for middle-class Protestants, whose value system and sensibilities as embodied in Luther were particularly susceptible to the invidious ideological stylings of Nazism as "positive Christianity." The broadly positive response of the Protestant church to the Nazi seizure of power can be seen in the almost universal embrace of the new regime, and the eager coupling of its leader with Luther in the four-hundred-fiftieth anniversary of his birth in 1933. Luther's image could be seamlessly transposed to dress in brown and sport the swastika, and as the spiritual *Führer* provided a compelling doppelgänger for the *Führer* of the reborn nation. Luther's image under the Nazis provided legitimation for the regime and its drive to coopt all sources of cultural and material authority. It is a testament to the insatiability of Nazism for control that even the servile attempts of the German Christians to shape Luther in the image of the party were treated with indifference. Even a compliant church was insufficient as long as it sought to maintain any sort of institutional and ideological autonomy, so that even where Luther, with his vitriolic late anti-Jewish writings, provided the greatest amount of affirmation for the party's goals, he fell short of fulfilling their needs. It is one of the ironies of the history of this era that the Protestant church, one of the most significant sources of support for Nazism, became after the seizure of power one of the most vexing challenges for Nazi attempts at coordination. While Luther certainly was remade in the image of the times, as a signifier it was not possible to fully integrate him into the mentality of the Nazi movement with authenticity. The Luther of the Nazi era was profoundly incoherent, and represents the cultural contradictions of the era. In reading the rhetoric that surrounded Luther, one has the impression of stepping through the looking glass, and entering a world whose logic and ideals had become unmoored from reality. The present etched itself so deeply on Luther that the faith that animated him and the historical reality within which he resided became almost inaccessible. It is only in such a context that a learned study could pose with a straight face the proposition that Luther's great achievement was to formulate an anti-Christian philosophy of religion. While this was a bridge too far for most contemporaries, they were mostly oblivious to the fact that the features of this Luther were for the most part drawn from the existing stock images. Looking back, one is surprised how seriously this obviously deeply flawed study was taken, but that response indicates that it hit a nerve, it resonated disturbingly, because it cast into relief the ideological environment that gave it birth. In that sense, it provided a fitting final episode for the portrayal of Luther, brought to a close by the disaster of the Second World War. Though after the war there will be an effort to reestablish Luther as a symbol of national regeneration, he had been too strongly associated with the sources of Germany's ills to retake center stage as a symbol of German identity. The scholarship of the post-war years would mostly return him to his own world, and while still a figure of enormous fascination, his image could no longer claim the mythic significance attributed to it in the previous epoch.

What light does this account of Luther's image shed on the development of German history up into the era of National Socialism? First, it suggests some of the continuities of development from the end of the Napoleonic Wars up through the Second World War. The image of Luther was reshaped by the nationalist impulses over that period of time, and many of the specific features of that nationalism are embodied in Luther: its idiosyncratic definition of freedom, its *völkisch* essentialism, its xenophobia, its sense of providential destiny and spiritual superiority, its bellicosity, its middle-class self-satisfaction, its anti-Semitism, among others. Luther, as the putative symbol of the nation, not only embodied all of these elements, but their presence within the German soul was attributed to his spiritual agency. As early as 1817 one can see these elements coming together in the projections of him, and then evolving over the course of time. But while there are clear lines of continuity that can be traced with the development of his image across the nineteenth and into the twentieth century, it is also the case that this image of Luther only really comes into full focus in the context of the First World War and its aftermath. The fervent reception of Luther in the years immediately after World War I provide the impetus for the development of the *völkisch* Luther, paralleling the similar emergence of *völkisch* political movements in this context. In many ways the success of Luther's *völkisch* image in the 1920s and 1930s parallels the growth and success of Nazism, and is itself a factor in that success. The symbiosis of the two suggest the degree to which ideas about Luther served to legitimate the political program of National Socialism; the linkages are numerous. And the insistence that the ideological sources of German *völkisch* identity go back to Luther forms a *Sonderweg* theory of a sort meant to affirm the deep roots of the *völkisch* state; like the *Sonderweg* debate after the war, this idea only makes good sense if one accepts the premise that there is something uniquely different about German identity and German history, whether one views it in terms of essential virtues or vices. The Luther of nineteenth and twentieth centuries that has been traced here is a construction of that era, and while there are always lines of continuity back in time, the most striking feature of the Luther of this more modern era is how disconnected he becomes with the historical figure, how idiosyncratic is the image that develops. Tracing Luther's image in this era affirms the general consensus that the sources and success of Nazism are rooted in the nineteenth and twentieth centuries, and especially in the conditions that resulted from the outcome of World War I. The remarkable contingencies of this history overshadow any long-term essential unfolding of a uniquely German genius or daemon.

Within the field of Luther studies, the genesis of this image of Luther happens in the context of the so-called Luther Renaissance. While this revival of Luther scholarship was grounded in the principle of going to the sources, which meant the enormous corpus of Luther's works made readily accessible in the Weimar Edition, its basic premises allowed Luther to be disentangled from his biblicism in order to make him relevant to an era which no longer shared Luther's understanding of scripture. A whole generation of scholars whose works shaped the study of Luther up at least into the 1970s were trained under the influence of Karl Holl and his school. They were grounded in the works of Luther as never before. Yet under their tutelage Luther learned to speak with the voice of the *Volk*, to find a racial consciousness, to find God's revelation in nature and history, and do and think many other things that made him a man not of his time but of the Germany of the Luther Renaissance. And aspects of his writing that were not much noted before, such as his anti-Jewish writings, or his speculation about *Wundermänner*, emerged into the center of his legacy. While not all of this scholarship is marked by this remarkable present-mindedness, it is one of the striking features of these scholars that they found in Luther what they needed to affirm their political and cultural commitments. While all historical scholarship is a negotiation of the present with the past, this era of scholarship was particularly blind to, or willfully uninterested in, how it imposed the present onto the past. Rather than serving as a corrective to overly ideological interpretations of Luther, the Luther Renaissance provided tools for sculpting the Luther to fit the times. The scholarship of this era is heavily compromised by this desire to make Luther relevant, to make him speak to the times, which over time creates the context for the extreme make-over of Luther in the 1930s.

Theologically, there were a number of ways in which the approach to Luther that developed in the 1920s paved the way for the embrace of Nazism. While much attention has been paid to Luther's teaching on the two kingdoms, in fact the more fateful misapprehension of his work comes through the embrace of the orders of creation (*Schöpfungsordnungen*), the over-extension of his understanding of the hiddenness of God (*Deus absconditus*), and his teaching about *Wundermänner*. The first of these, *Schöpfungsordungen*, was particularly carried forward in the work of Paul Althaus. Though Althaus recognized that he was building an edifice on a very thin base when it came to things Luther actually taught, nevertheless he argued continually for the legitimacy of this way of connecting God to creation as faithful to Luther's legacy. By making the *Volk* an order of creation founded by God prior to the Fall, that is, founded not as a response to the need for order of a sinful humanity, but as an order to provide for the goodness of creation, he elevated its status as a sphere within which the divine will would be worked out in the material world. Althaus, though always noting that the *Volk* wasn't the vehicle through which humanity gained salvation, nevertheless gave it an emphasis within his theological arguments that affirmed *völkisch* nationalism as a divinely ordained movement, a vehicle to bring the Gospel into the world. This resulted in equating the political order brought into being in 1933 with the will of God. Similarly, the notion of God working mysteriously through the processes of history and its political orders as the *Deus absconditus*, the hidden God of providence, again equated the *völkisch* Nazi state with a divinely ordained working out of destiny. And applying Luther's teaching about *Wundermänner*, whose peculiar genius makes them the architects of world-historical turning points, to Hitler furnished the *Führer* with even further legitimacy and unbridled prerogative. None of these theological positions was a fair extrapolation of Luther's teachings, but the hermeneutical approach enabled by the Luther Renaissance legitimized "strong" readings and creative extensions of his works.

One major issue raised by the image of Luther in this era is his culpability in the Holocaust. It is probably most difficult to decipher the role of Luther in enabling the assault upon the Jews in Nazi Germany. In this instance, the scholarship of the 1920s and '30s does not invent, or creatively extrapolate, from his writings an anti-Jewish profile. It is there in the works of his later years, ready to be deployed in the environment of anti-Semitic racial nationalism of Wilhelmine, Weimar, and Nazi Germany. Luther's anti-Jewish writings become a fixture in the literature advocating prejudicial treatment of the Jews. And in the 1930s within the Protestant German Christian movement this aspect of Luther's teachings is embraced and celebrated. So Luther is certainly useable and made use of. Yet the degree to which this impacts the public support for measures against the Jews is ambiguous. On the one hand it cannot have failed to mute voices that might have been raised against the mistreatment of the Jews. It is a striking fact that amidst the controversies over the Arian paragraph and the exclusion of converted Jews from clergy and congregation, there is almost no protest raised against the policies as they were applied to the larger Jewish population, to unconverted Jews. That such treatment was in keeping with Luther provided powerful justification, and was used by the German Christians accordingly. But the German Christians wished to go farther, to eliminate Judaism from Christianity entirely, expunging the Old Testament, remaking Jesus as an Aryan, and creating a *völkisch* Germanic Christianity. For that radical project Luther didn't provide any sustenance, and in fact one had to ignore a good part of his anti-Jewish tracts since they were grounded in an argument about the Old Testament as uniquely connected to Christian faith. So, while one could choose simply to ignore that aspect of his works, it made the historical Luther awkward. And despite the attempts to bring Luther's writings to the attention of the broader church, evidence would suggest that they didn't connect with a broader public consciousness. While there is little doubt that prejudicial views of Jews were commonplace in Germany, and certainly had spread in the environment of the Third Reich, what seems most common was a passive anti-Jewish sentiment, which viewed Jews with distaste, found their customs foreign, and held stereotyped prejudices about their character. The Nazi policies of the 1930s with boycotts, removal from the civil service, removal of citizenship, and separation from "Aryans" were designed to enhance this sense of difference. Yet evidence that Luther's anti-Jewish writings translated into direct support for the sort of eliminationist anti-Semitism that stirred the emotions of the party faithful isn't extensive. Luther's writings on the Jews seem to have been limited in their influence both because of their arcane argumentation, but also because even when one excerpted the "good" parts that called for harsh punishment, the material didn't connect with the immediate concerns of many Germans, and within the church didn't seem to meet an existing need. Not that this absolves Luther of complicity, but it suggests that his impact may have been more indirect than seems the case on the surface.

Finally, we come to the larger issue of Luther's role in enabling the Third Reich overall. To what degree did the mythic *völkisch* Luther of this era pave the way and enable the successful seizure and consolidation of power by Hitler and the Nazis? There is no simple way to track that impact. In his magisterial two-volume biography of Hitler, Ian Kershaw poses the phenomenon of "working toward the *Führer*" as a key to understanding the functioning of the Nazi system and the role of Hitler in it.[2] Kershaw and others have noted that Hitler was a hands-off leader, a visionary who eschewed engagement with the daily drudgery of bureaucratic government. He allowed a striking degree of conflict to exist within the institutional structures of the regime, an environment within which subordinates were constantly seeking to fulfill the unstated will of the *Führer*, that is, working toward what he would want them to do. In so doing, they created out of his overarching ideological vision an actual working out of policy. In a way, one can see this operative at the level of the church, especially among the German Christians who were the most eager to make the church be what they thought the state wanted it to be. And it wasn't just among the German Christians where this was operative. Even in those parts of the church resistant to being coopted institutionally, there was an eagerness to find a working relationship with the regime. In that environment, the image of Luther becomes a tool to work toward the *Führer*. Luther whose ethos embraces the *völkisch* ideal, who himself is an embodiment of such an ideal; Luther whose theology accommodates and christens the sort of power structure desired by the regime; Luther whose image affirms the *Führer* because of the many congruencies between the one and the other; Luther who hates the Jews and would mistreat them, just as the *Führer* advocates and is doing; Luther, who, were he here today, would be marching lockstep with the *Führer*. It is clear that Luther was an ideal vehicle for indicating the degree to which the church wished to fulfill the needs of the new regime and its leader, to work toward the *Führer*. Though the Protestant church did resist the regime at some points, and part of the church, the Confessing Church, took that to somewhat greater lengths (and part of the Confessing Church resisted at a theologically deeper level), not much of that resistance rested on the figure of Luther. While Dietrich Bonhoeffer may have drawn much from Luther in his lonely resistance to the regime, those who resisted the most within the circle around Karl Barth found it hard to use Luther for their purposes. It was hard to think about Luther outside of the image that had been cast for him, and outside of the Luther who so usefully exemplified the willingness of the church to work cooperatively with the regime. Protestants didn't support the regime in larger numbers because of Luther, but in projecting this image of Luther, they enhanced the legitimacy of the regime in the eyes of Protestants, and made it less likely that they would turn to resistance at those points where conflict emerged. The image of Luther served a legitimating function

---

[2] Ian Kershaw, *Hitler, 1889–1936: Hubris* (London: Penguin Press, 1998): ch. 13, "Working toward the *Führer*."

that helps explain, in part, the passivity of much of the church in the face of Nazism, and the enthusiasm of part of the church for the regime over its years of power. It is instructive that this image of Luther did not survive the downfall of the regime, representing the degree that this image was sustained only in the environment of racist nationalism that was the life blood of Nazism. In that sense, the *völkisch* Luther died in the onslaught that brought Nazi Germany to an end, and he exists now as a peculiar artifact of that unlamented past.

The Luther Myth: The Image of Martin Luther from Religious Reformer to Völkisch Icon. Patrick Hayden-Roy, Oxford University Press. © Patrick Hayden-Roy 2024. DOI: 10.1093/9780198930297.003.0011

Bibliography

Primary Sources

Althaus, Paul. "Der Krieg und unser Gottesglaube II." *Allgemeine Evangelisch-Lutherische Kirchenzeitung* XXVII (July 2, 1915): 629.
Althaus, Paul. *Luther und das Deutschtum*. Leipzig: A. Deichertsche Verlag, 1917.
Althaus, Paul. "Theologie und Geschichte: zur Auseinandersetzung mit der dialektischen Theologie." *Zeitschrift für Systematische Theologie* 1 (1923): 741–86.
Althaus, Paul. "Luthers Haltung im Bauernkrieg." *Lutherjahrbuch* 7 (1925): 1–39.
Althaus, Paul. *Evangelium und Leben: gesammelte Vorträge*. Gütersloh: Bertelsmann, 1927.
Althaus, Paul. *Kirche und Volkstum: der völkische Wille im Lichte des Evangeliums*. Gütersloh: Bertelsmann, 1928.
Althaus, Paul. *Die deutsche Stunde der Kirche*. 3rd ed. Göttingen: Vanderhoek and Ruprecht, 1934.
Althaus, Paul. "Der Geist der Lutherbibel." *Lutherjahrbuch* 16 (1934): 1–26.
Althaus, Paul. *Kirche und Staat nach lutherischer Lehre*. Leipzig: A. Deichert, 1935.
Althaus, Paul. *Politisches Christentum: ein Wort über die Thüringer "Deutschen Christen."* Leipzig: A. Deichert, 1935.
Althaus, Paul. *Theologie der Ordnungen*. Gütersloh: C. Bertelsmann, 1935.
Althaus, Paul. *Obrigkeit und Führertum: Wandlungen des evangelischen Staatsethos*. Gütersloh: Bertelsmann, 1936.
Althaus, Paul. *Luther und die politische Welt*. Weimar: Verlag H. Böhlaus Nachfolger, 1937.
Altmann, Ulrich. *Martin Luther, deutschgläubig oder Christ?* Neudettelsau: Freimund Verlag, 1939.
Aner, Karl. *Das Luthervolk: ein Gang durch die Geschichte seiner Frömmigkeit*. Tübingen: J. C. B. Mohr [Paul Siebeck], 1917.
"Ansbacher Ratschlag." In Gerhard Niemöller, *Die erste Bekenntnissynode der Deutschen Evangelischen Kirche zu Barmen*. Vol. 1: *Geschichte, Kritik und Bedeutung der Synode und ihrer theologischen Erklärung*. Göttingen: Vandenhoeck & Ruprecht, 1959: 143.
Asmussen, Hans. "Muß Luther nach Nürnberg?" *Nordwestdeutsche Hefte* 1947, Heft 11/12: 31–7.
Baetke, Walter. "Germanentum und Christentum." *Deutsche Evangelische Erziehung* 45 (1934): 491–5.
Barth, Karl. *Lutherfeier 1933*. Munich: Chr. Kaiser Verlag, 1933.
Barth, Karl. *Eine Schweizer Stimme 1938–1945*. Zurich: Evangelischer Verlag, 1945.
Barth, Karl. *Die evangelische Kirche in Deutschland nach dem Zusammenbruch des Dritten Reiches*. Stuttgart: 1946.
Beckmann, Joachim. *Verrat an Luther?* [Barmen]: Theologische Amt der evang. Bekenntnissynode im Rheinland, [1937?].
Berger, Arnold E. "Luther und der deutsche Staatsgedanke." *Lutherjahrbuch* 1 (1919): 34–56.
"Betheler Bekenntnis." Dietrich Bonhoeffer, *Gesammelte Schriften*. Vol. II, Eberhard Bethge, ed. Munich: Christian Kaiser Verlag, 1959: 90–119. English translation in *Dietrich Bonhoeffer Works*. Vol. 12: *Berlin 1932–1933*. Minneapolis: Fortress Press, 2009: 374–424.
Beyer, Hermann Wolfgang. *Luther und das Recht: Gottes Gebot, Naturrecht, Volksgesetz in Luthers Deutung*. Munich: Chr. Kaiser Verlag, 1935.
Bezzel, Hermann von. *Luther, Bismarck: von Dr. von Bezzel*. Munich: Müller & Fröhlich, 1917.
Bluth, Hugo Gotthard. "Luthers Kampf gegen die Juden." *Deutsches Pfarrerblatt* 40 (1936): 175–6, 194–5, 214.

Böhme, Klaus ed. *Aufrufe und Reden deutscher Professoren im Ersten Weltkrieg*. Stuttgart: Reclam, 1975.
Boll, Carl. *Der politische Katholismus und seine Bundesgenossen—Ein Briefwechsel zwischen Landesbischof Meiser und Landesbischof Weidemann: wer Steht eigentlich bei Luther?* Bremen: Hauschild, 1935.
Bonhoeffer, Dietrich. *Discipleship*. In *Dietrich Bonhoeffer Works*. Vol. 4. Minneapolis: Augsburg Fortress, 2001.
Bonhoeffer, Dietrich. *Nachfolge*. In *Dietrich Bonhoeffer Werke*. Vol. 4. Munich: Chr. Kaiser Verlag, 2002.
Bornkamm, Heinrich. "Volk und Rasse bei Martin Luther." In *Volk, Staat, Kirche: ein Lehrgang der Theologischen Fakultät Gießen*. Giessen: Alfred Töpelmann, 1933: 5–19.
Bornkamm, Heinrich. "Christentum. Vortrag an einem SA-Sturmabend." *Glaube und Volk in der Entscheidung* 3 (1934): 45–52.
Bornkamm, Heinrich. *Luther und der deutsche Geist: Rede bei der Lutherfeier der Universität Gießen am 19. November 1933*. Tübingen: Mohr, 1934.
Bornkamm, Heinrich. "Wirkliche Kirche." *Glaube und Volk in der Entscheidung* 3 (1934): 122–33.
Bornkamm, Heinrich. *Gott und Geschichte nach Luther*. Lüneburg: Heliand Verlag, 1947.
Brachmann, Wilhelm. *Alfred Rosenberg und seine Gegner. Zur Auseinandersetzung mit den "Protestantischen Rompilgern."* Munich: Hoheneichen Verlag, 1938.
Brandenburg, Erich. *Martin Luther als Vorkämpfer deutschen Geistes*. Leipzig: Quelle und Meyer, 1917.
Brinkmann, Heinrich. "Zur Theologie der Ordnungen." *Deutsche Theologie* 3 (1936): 29–33.
Bruder, Otto. *Luther der Kämpfer: ein chorisches Feierspiel*. Munich: Chr. Kaiser Verlag, 1933.
Buchhorn, Josef. *Wende in Worms*. Cottbuss: Heine, 1937.
Chamberlain, Houston Stewart. *Grundlagen des neunzehnten Jahrhunderts*. Munich: Bruckmann, 1899.
Die Christus Bekennende Reichskirche. Eine Schriftenreihe. Landesbischof Lic. Dr. Weidemann, Bremen, ed. Bremen: Haushild, 1935-Heft 1–11.
Craemer, Rudolf. *Reformation als politische Macht*. Göttingen: Vandenhoeck & Ruprecht, 1933.
Cramer, Karl. "Kirche in der Entscheidung." *Glaube und Volk in der Entscheidung* 3 (1934): 153–63.
Deutelmoser, Arno. *Luther. Staat und Glaube*. Jena: Diederichs, 1937.
Deutelmoser, Arno. *Reformation und Gegenreformation in Deutschland*. Leipzig: Teubner, 1938.
Deutschchristentum auf rein-evangelischer Grundlage. 95 Leitsätze zum Reformationsfest 1917. Friedrich Andersen, Adolf Bartels, Ernst Katzer, and Hans Paul Freiherrn von Wolzogen, eds. Leipzig: Theodor Weicher, 1917.
Diem, Harald. *Luthers Lehre von den zwei Reichen*. Munich: Chr. Kaiser Verlag, 1938.
Diem, Hermann. *Die Schuld der Anderen: ein Briefwechsel zwischen Helmut Thielicke und Hermann Diem*. Göttingen: Vandenhoeck & Ruprecht, 1948.
Doerne, Martin. "Gottes ehre am gebundenen Willen. Evangelische Grundlagen und theologische Spitzensätze in De servo arbitrio." *Lutherjahrbuch* 20 (1938): 45–92.
Dörries, Hermann. *Luther und Deutschland*. Tübingen: J. C. B. Mohr [Paul Siebeck], 1934.
Dosse, Fritz. "Die Herbsttagung der Luther Gesellschaft 1937." *Luther: Zeitschrift der Luther Gesellschaft* 20 (1938): 27.
Dreß, W. "Wider das falsche Luther-Bild." *Die Junge Kirche* 5 (1937): 932–40.
Duken, Johann. "In der Entscheidung." *Glaube und Volk in der Entscheidung* 3 (1934): 3–13.
Eggers, Kurt. *Revolution um Luther. Ein Spiel*. Munich: Chr. Kaiser, 1935.
Das Eisleber Lutherbuch 1933. Hermann Etzrodt and Kurt Kronenberg, eds. Eisleben: Ernst Schneider, 1933.
Elert, Werner. *Morphologie des Luthertums*. Munich: C. H. Beck, 1931.
Elert, Werner. *Bekenntnis, Blut und Boden. Drei Theologische Vorträge*. Leipzig: Dörffling & Francke, 1934.
Engels, Friedrich. "Der deutsche Bauernkrieg." In *Marx Engels Werke*. Vol. 7. Berlin: Akademie Verlag, 1973: 327–413.

Eucken, Rudolf. "Aufruf zur Gründung einer Luthergesellschaft." *Deutscher Wille. Des Kunstwarts* 31 (1917): 182–4.
Eucken, Rudolf. *Die Lebensanschauungen der grossen Denker: eine Entwicklungsgeschichte des Lebenproblems der Menschheit von Plato zur Gegenwart*. Leipzig: Veit, 1918.
Eucken, Rudolf. "Luther und die geistige Erneurung des deutschen Volkes." *Lutherjahrbuch* 1 (1919): 27–34.
Eucken, Rudolf. "Weshalb bedürfen wir einer Luther-Gesellschaft." *Lutherjahrbuch* 1 (1919): 5–8.
Evangelisch-Sozialien Preßverband für die Provinz Sachsen. *Was Luther uns heute noch ist! Eine Sammlung von zeitgenössischen Original Aussprüchen, Abhandlungen und Gedichten im 400 Gedächtnisjahr der Reformation 1917*. Halle, 1917.
Falb, Alfred. *Luther und die Juden*. Munich: Deutscher Volksverlag, D. E. Boepple, 1921.
Falb, Alfred. *Luther und die Juden*. 2nd ed. Munich: Deutscher Volksverlag, 1936.
Fausel, Heinrich. *Luther und die deutsche Nation*. Munich: C. Kaiser, 1935.
Fleisch, P. "Luther und die Eindeutschung des Christentums." *Die Junge Kirche* 3 (1935): 498–501.
Foertsch, Karl. *Luther als Begründer und Vorbild der deutschen Familie*. Berlin: Evang. Pressverband für Deutschland, 1934.
Fritsch, Theodor, *Handbuch der Judenfrage*. 28th ed. Hamburg: Sleipner-Verlag, 1919.
Fritsch, Theodor. *Der Falsche Gott (Beweis-Material gegen Jahwe)*. 7th ed. Leipzig: Hammer Verlag, 1920.
Fronemann, Wilhelm. *Der deutsche Luther*. Leipzig: Fr. Schneider, 1933.
Gebhardt, Florentine. *Luther, der deutsche Mann und Streiter Gottes*. Berlin: N. B. Buchvertrieb, 1933.
Gogarten, Friedrich. "Luther als Theologe." *Deutsche Theologie*. Sonderheft: *Luther* (Nov. 1933): 1–10.
Gogarten, Friedrich. "Offenbarung und Geschichte." *Deutsche Theologie* 2 (1935): 115–31.
Grisar, Hartmann. *Der Deutsche Luther im Weltkrieg und in der Gegenwart*. Augsburg: Haas & Grabherr, 1924.
Grünagel, Friedrich. *Rosenberg und Luther: Rosenberg's Mythus des 20. Jahrhunderts und die theologischen Probleme*. Bonn: Gebr. Scheur, 1934.
Grundmann, Walter. "Die Neubesinnung der Theologie und der Aufbruch der Nation." *Deutsche Theologie* 1 (1934): 39–46.
Güldenberg, O. "Luther und seine Deutschen: Stoffe für Andachten." *Deutsche Evangelische Erziehung* 46 (1935): 393–4.
[Hahn, Gerhard]. "Von den Jüden und ihren Lügen." *Die Christus Bekennende Reichskirche. Eine Schriftenreihe*. Landesbischof Lic. Dr. Weidemann, Bremen, ed. Bremen: Haushild. Heft 7 (1937): 1–16.
Hanstein, Wolfram von. *Von Luther bis Hitler: Ein wichtiger Abriss deutscher Geschichte*. Dresden: Voco Verlag, 1947.
Hashagen, Justus. "Die apologetische Tendenz der Lutherforschung und die sogenannte Lutherrenaissance." *Historische Vierteljahrschrift* 31 (1936): 625–50.
Hermann, Rudolf. *Gesammelte Studien zur Theologie Luthers und der Reformation*. Göttingen: Vandenhoeck & Ruprecht, 1960.
Hesselbacher, Karl. *Martin Luther, der Held Gottes*. Hamburg: Agentur des Rauhen Hauses, 1933.
Heussi, Karl. *Luthers Deutsche Sendung*. Jena: Frommann, 1934.
Hielscher, Friedrich. *Das Reich*. Berlin: Das Reich Verlag, 1931.
Hilbert, Gerhard. *Wie ward Luther der "Deutscheste der Deutschen"? Ein Vortrag*. Leipzig: Hensius, 1933.
Hildebrant, Gustaf. *Lutherdramen: Dramen der Luther Renaissance von der Jahrhundertwende bis zur Gegenwart*. Cottbus: Heine, 1937.
Hirsch, Emanuel. "Luthers Berufung." *Deutsche Theologie*. Sonderheft: *Luther* (Nov. 1933): 24–34.
Hirsch, Emanuel. "Die Lage der Theologie." *Deutsche Theologie* 3 (1936): 36–66.
Hirsch, Emanuel. *Leitfaden zur christlichen Lehre*. Tübingen: J. C. B. Mohr [Paul Siebeck], 1938.
Hirsch, Emanuel. *Lutherstudien I &2*. Gütersloh: Bertelsmann, 1954.
Hitler, Mein Kampf. Eine kritische Edition. Vol. 1. Christian Hartmann et al., eds. Munich/Berlin: Institut für Zeitgeschichte, 2016.

Holl, Karl. *Gesammelte Aufsätze zur Kirchengeschichte*. Vol. 3: *Der Westen*. Tübingen: J. C. B. Mohr [Paul Siebeck], 1928.
Holl, Karl. *Gesammelte Aufsätze zur Kirchengeschichte*. Vol. 1: *Luther*. 6th ed. Tübingen: J. C. B. Mohr [Paul Siebeck], 1932.
Holstein, Günther. *Luther und die deutsche Staatsidee*. Tübingen: Mohr, 1926.
Islebiensis. *Dr. Martin Luther und das Judenthum*. Berlin: Im Commissions-Verlag von Oscar Lorentz, [1882].
Johst, Hanns. *Propheten: Schauspiel*. Munich: Albert Langen/Georg Müller, 1922.
Kern, Franz. *Der Bergmann Gottes; ein Lutherspiel in 6 bildern*. Eisleben-Lutherstadt: Mansfelder Heimatverlag E. Schneider, 1933.
Kibler, Max. "An alle Lutherischen: Ein Brief Martin Luthers im Jubeljahr 1933." *Glaube und Volk in der Entscheidung* 3 (1934): 34–37.
Kinder, Ernst. *Geistliches und weltliches Regiment Gottes nach Luther*. Weimar: Hermann Böhlaus Nachfolger, 1940.
Kittel, Gerhard, *Die Judenfrage*. Stuttgart: W. Kohlhammer, 1933.
Kittel, Helmuth. *Religion als Geschichtsmacht*. Leipzig: B. G. Teubner, 1938.
Knolle, Theodor. *Luthers Glaube. Eine Wiederlegung*. Weimar: Böhlau, 1938.
Knolle, Theodor. "Luthers Stellung zu den Juden." *Luther: Zeitschrift der Luther Gesellschaft* 20 (1938): 117–24.
Knolle, Theodor, ed. *Luther in der deutschen Kirche der Gegenwart*. Gütersloh: Bertelsmann, 1940.
Kohlmeyer, Ernst. *Gustav Adolf und die Staatsanschauung des Altluthertums*. Halle (Saale): Max Niemeyer Verlag, 1933.
Kölli, Josef Georg. *Martin Luthers Entscheidung: Ein Spiel*. Weimar: Böhlaus Nachf., 1938.
König, Karl. *Vom Geiste Luthers des Deutschen*. Jena: Diederichs, 1917.
Kühn, Hugo, ed. *Das Wartburgfest am 18. Oktober 1817. Zeitgenössische Darstellungen, archivalische Akten und Urkunden*. Weimar, 1913.
Künneth, Walter. "Luthertum und Deutschtum." *Zeitwende* 10.1 (1934): 116–19.
Laible, Wilhelm. *Luther als Prophet des deutschen Hauses vor dem Tribunal des Krieges*. Leipzig: A. Deichertsche Verlag, 1917.
Lamparter, Eduard. *Evangelische Kirche und Judentum: Ein Beitrag zu christlichem Verständnis von Judentum und Antisemitismus*. Gotha?: Leopold Klotz?, 1928.
Lau, Franz. *Das Heil des Volkes und das Evangelium, geistlicher und leiblicher Segen: ein Beitrag zu dem Thema: Luther und die Gegenwart*. Leipzig: A. Deicherische Verlagsbuchhandlung, 1937.
Leisegang, Hans. *Luther als deutscher Christ*. Berlin: Junker und Dünnhaupt, 1934.
Lerche, Otto. *Martin Luther deutscher Kämpfer. Bilder aus seiner Zeit und seiner Welt*. Berlin: Mittler und Sohn, 1933.
Linden, Walter. *Luthers Kampfschriften gegen das Judentum*. Berlin: Klinkhardt und Biermann, 1936.
Lorentz, Paul. "Luthers Glaubensgehorsam als christlich-deutsche Gefolgstreue." *Die Christliche Welt* 49 (1935): 652–7.
Lorentz, Paul. *Der deutsche Luther tut not! Was jeder von Luthers deutscher Religiosität wissen müßte*. Bonn: Verlag Gebr. Scheur, 1935.
Lorentz, Paul. "Die Offenbarung Gottes in Natur und Vernunft bei Luther." *Deutsche Evangelische Erziehung* 49 (1938): 452–61.
Lother, Helmut. *Neugermanische Religion und Christentum: eine kirchengeschichtliche Vorlesung*. Gütersloh: Bertelsmann, 1934.
Lother, Helmut. "Christentum und Deutschtum: Grundsätzliche Bemerkungen zu einem kirchengeschichtlichen Thema." *Zeitschrift für Kirchengeschichte* 57 (1938): 1–18.
Luther, Johannes. "Die Bedeutung Martin Luthers für seine und unsere Zeit." *Lutherjahrbuch* 1 (1919): 8–27.
Luther, Martin. *D. Martin Luthers Werke: Kritische Gesammtausgabe*. Weimar: Hermann Böhlau, 1889–.
Mann, Thomas. *Germany and the Germans*. Washington, DC: Library of Congress, 1945. Published in translation as *Deutschland und die Deutschen*. Berlin: Suhrkamp, 1947.

Martin Luther: dass Jesus Christus ein geborener Jude sei und andere Judenschriften. Matthias Morgenstern, ed. Berlin: Berlin University Press, 2019.
Martin Luther in der deutschen bürgelichen Philosophie 1517–1845. Eine Textsammlung. Werner Schuffenhauer and Klaus Steiner, eds. Berlin: Akademie-Verlag, 1983.
Martin Luther: Judenfeindliche Schriften. Vol. 2, Karl-Heinz Büchner et al., eds. Aschaffenburg: Alibri Press, 2017.
Martin Luther: Judenfeindliche Schriften. Vol. 3, Karl-Heinz Büchner et al., eds. Aschaffenburg: Alibri Press, 2018.
Martin Luther und die Kabbala: Vom Schem Hamephorasch und vom Geschlecht Christi. Matthias Morgenstern, ed. Berlin: Berlin University Press, 2019.
Martin Luther: Von den Juden und ihren Lügen. Karl-Heinz Büchner et al., eds. Aschaffenburg: Alibri Press, 2016.
Martin Luther: Von den Juden und ihren Lügen. Matthias Morgenstern, ed. Berlin: Berlin University Press, 2016.
Maurenbrecher, Max. *Der Heiland der Deutschen.* 2nd ed. Göttingen: Vandenhoek & Ruprecht, 1933.
McGovern, William Montgomery. *From Luther to Hitler: The History of Fascist-Nazi Political Philosophy.* Boston: Houghton Mifflin, 1941.
Merz, Georg. "Gesetz Gottes und Volksnomos bei Martin Luther." *Lutherjahrbuch* 16 (1934): 51–82.
Meyer-Erlach, Wolf. *Juden, Mönche und Luther.* Weimar: D.C. Verlag, 1937.
Meyer-Erlach, Wolf. *Verrat an Luther.* Weimar: D.C. Verlag, 1937.
Müller, Hans Michael. *Die Verleugnung Luthers im heutigen Protestantismus.* Stuttgart: Kohlhammer, 1936.
Nazi Ideology before 1933: A Documentation. Barbara Miller Lane and Leila J. Rupp, eds. Austin: University of Texas Press, 1978.
Niekisch, Ernst. *Deutsche Daseinsverfehlung.* Berlin: Aufbau Verlag, 1946.
Oberhof, Johannes. "Die Christlichkeit Luthers und der Begriff der Geschichte." *Zeitschrift für Kirchengeschichte* 57 (1938): 96–109.
Pabst, Carl. *Volkskirche und Freikirche.* Gütersloh: Bertelsmann, 1933.
Pauls, Theodor. *Luthers Auffassung von Staat und Volk.* Halle (Salle): Waisenhaus, 1927.
Pauls, Theodor. "Martin Luthers Geschichtsauffassung." *Deutsche Evangelische Erziehung* 45 (1934): 264–71.
Pauls, Theodor. "Blut und Boden bei Luther." *Deutsche Evangelische Erziehung* 46 (1935): 408–14.
Pauls, Theodor. *Luther Wille zur Volkskirche.* Bonn: Universität Druckerei, 1936.
Pauls, Theodor. *Luthers Anschauung vom Menschentum des Christen.* Bonn: Bonner Universität Druckerei, 1937.
Pauls, Theodor. *Luther und die Juden.* Bonn: Universität Druckerei, 1939.
Preuß, Hans. *Unser Luther.* Leipzig: Deichert, 1917.
Preuß, Hans. *Luther und Hitler.* Erlangen: Freimund Verlag, 1933.
Preuß, Hans. *Martin Luther, der Prophet.* Gütersloh: Bertelsmann, 1933.
Preuß, Hans. *Martin Luther, der Deutsche.* Gütersloh: Bertelsmann, 1934.
Preuß, Hans. *Martin Luther, der Deutsche und Christ.* Leipzig: Bertelsmann, 1940.
Riethmüller, Otto. *Martin Luthers Ruf an die Deutsche Nation.* Berlin: Burckhardthaus Verlag, 1933.
Ritter, Gerhard. *Luther, Gestalt und Symbol.* Munich: Bruckmann, 1925.
Ritter, Gerhard. *Luther der Deutsche.* Munich: Bruckmann, 1933.
Ritter, Gerhard. "Die 16. Jahrhundert als Weltgeschichtliche Epoche." *Archiv für Reformationsgeschichte* 35 (1938): 8–31.
Ritter, Gerhard. *Luther: Gestalt und Tat.* Munich: Bruckmann, 1943.
Ritter, Gerhard. "Luthertum, katholisches und humanistisches Weltbild." *Zeitwende* 18 (1946/7): 65–84.
Ritter, Gerhart. "Luther und die Politische Erziehung der Deutschen." *Zeitwende* 18 (1946/7): 592–607.
Ritter, Gerhard. *Luther: Gestalt und Tat.* Munich: Bruckmann, 1947.
Ritter, Gerhard. *Luther: Gestalt und Tat.* Munich: Bruckmann, 1959.

Rosenberg, Alfred. *Der Mythus des zwanzigsten Jahrhunderts*. Munich, 1930.
Rosenberg, Alfred. *Protestantische Rompilger: Der Verrat an Luther und der Mythus des 20. Jahrhunderts*. Munich: Hoheneichen Verlag, 1937.
Rückert, Hanns. "Luther der Deutsche." *Deutsche Theologie*. Sonderheft: *Luther* (Nov. 1933): 10–23.
Rückert, Hanns. *Der völkische Beruf des Theologen: ein theologisches Kolleg, gehalten in Tübingen zu Beginn des Sommersemesters 3. Mai 1933*. Tübingen: Osiander, 1933.
Rückert, Hanns. *Das Wiedererwachen reformatorischer Frömmigkeit in der Gegenwart*. Stuttgart: Kohlhammer, 1933.
Rupp, E. Gordon. *Martin Luther: Hitler's Cause or Cure*. London: Lutterworth Press, 1945.
Sasse, Martin. *Martin Luther über die Juden: Weg mit ihnen!* Freiburg i.B.: Sturmhut-Verlag, 1938.
Scharfe, Siegfried. *Verrat an Luther?* Halle: Deutsche Bibeltag, [1938?].
Scheel, Otto. *Evangelium, Kirche und Volk bei Luther*. Leipzig: M. Heinsius Nachfolger, 1934.
Scheel, Otto. "Die Volksgedanke bei Luther." *Historische Zeitschrift* 161 (1940): 477–97.
Schmidt, Hans. *Führer und Gefolgschaft nach dem Regentenspiegel Martin Luthers vom Jahre 1534*. Halle: Max Niemeyer Verlag, 1935.
Schneider, Georg. *Völkische Reformation: eine Wegweisung zu christdeutscher Einheit*. Stuttgart: W. Kohlhammer, 1934.
Scholz, Hermann. *Was wir der Reformation zu verdanken haben*. Berlin: Evangelischer Bund, 1917.
Schroth, Hansgeorg. *Luthers christlicher Antisemitismus heute*. Witten: Lutherverlag, 1937.
Schulze, Otto. *Doktor Martinus: Ein Buch für das deutsche Volk zum Reformationsjubelfest 1917*. Gotha: Perthes, 1917.
Schulze-Maizer, Friedrich. "Der untheologische Luther." *Die Tat* 28 (1936): 45–58.
Schuster, Hermann. *Der Prophet der Deutschen: Luthers Art und Glaube*. Frankfurt a. M.: Diesterweg, 1936.
Schuster, Hermann. "Luther, Christ oder Heide." *Die Christliche Welt* 52 (1938): 637–46.
Seeberg, Erich. "Gedächtnisrede des 450. Geburtstages Martin Luthers." *Zeitschrift für Kirchengeschichte* 52 (1933): 525–44.
Seeberg, Reinhard. *Christentum und Germanentum*. Leipzig: Dieterisch'sche Verlagsbuchhandlung Theodor Weicher, 1914.
Seeberg, Reinhold. "Die kirchengeschichtliche Bedeutung der Reformation Luthers." *Zeitschrift für Kirchengeschichte* 37 (1918): 61–88.
Sertorius, L. "Luther, der Deutsche." *Catholica* 4 (1935): 61–75.
Shirer, William L. *The Rise and Fall of the Third Reich: A History of Nazi Germany*. New York: Simon and Schuster, 1960.
Simon, Hermann. *Luther, der deutsche Mann*. Halle: Schroedel, 1933.
Sommerlad, Theo. *Martin Luther und der deutsche Sozialismus*. Halle a.d. Saale: Gebauer-Schwetschke, 1934.
Sommerlad, Theo. "Luther und der deutsche Sozialismus." *Deutsche Evangelische Erziehung* 46 (1935): 99–104.
Stange, Carl. "Die Bedeutung Luthers für die Gegenwart." *Zeitschrift für systematische Theologie* 11 (1933–4): 298–307.
Stange, Carl. "Richtlinien für das Verhältnis von Kirche und Staat." *Zeitschrift für systematische Theologie* 11 (1933–4): 147–8.
Stapel, Wilhelm. *Die Kirche Christi und der Staat Hitlers*. 2nd ed. Hamburg: Hanseatische Verlagsanstalt, 1933.
Steinlein, Hermann. *Frau Dr. Ludendorffs Phantasien über Luther und die Reformation*. Leipzig: A. Deichertsche Verlagsbuchhandlung, 1932.
Steinlein, Hermann. "Luthers Stellung zur Frage der Judentaufe." *Die Junge Kirche* 3 (1935): 842–6.
Steinlein, Hermann. "Kennt Luther einen 'deutschen Glauben'?" *Luther: Zeitschrift der Luther Gesellschaft* 21 (1939): 17–24.
Stoll, Heinrich. "Der germanische Schicksalsglaube und Luthers Lehre vom verborgenen und offenbaren Gott." *Allgemeine Evangelisch-Lutherische Kirchenzeitung* 69 (1936): 754–9, 770–3, 822–5.
Thiel, Rudolf. *Luther, von 1522 bis 1546*. Berlin: P. Neff, 1935.
Thiel, Rudolf. "Staat und Kirche bei Luther." *Glaube und Volk in der Entscheidung* 4 (1935): 161–77.

Thiel, Rudolf. *Luther antwortet*. Berlin: Eckhart-Verlag, 1936.
Thulin, Oscar, ed. "450 Jahre Luther." Sonderausgabe der *Illustrirten Zeitung*. 1933.
Treitschke, Heinrich von. "Unsere Aussichten." *Preußiche Jahrbücher* 44 (1879): 559–76.
Treitschke, Heinrich von. "Luther und die Deutschen." *Preußische Jahrbücher* 52 (1883): 469–86.
Vesper, Will. *Martin Luthers Jugendjahre; Bilder und Legendum*. Gütersloh: C. Bertelsmann, 1935 [1st ed. 1918].
Vogelsang, Erich. *Luthers Kampf gegen die Juden*. Tübingen: J. C. B. Mohr [Paul Siebeck], 1933.
Vogelsang, Erich. "Der gefährliche Luther." *Archiv für Reformationsgeschichte* 35 (1938): 162–71.
Vogelsang, Erich. "Die Unio Mystica bei Luther." *Archiv für Reformationsgeschichte* 35 (1938): 63–80.
Volgelsang, Erich. "Das Deutsche in Luthers Christentum." *Lutherjahrbuch* 16 (1934): 83–102.
Walter, Johannes von. "Luthers Christusbild." *Lutherjahrbuch* 21 (1939): 1–26.
Walther, Wilhelm. *Luthers Charakter*. Leipzig: Deichert, 1917.
Werdermann, Hermann. *Martin Luther und Adolf Hitler: Ein geschichtliche Vergleich*. 3rd ed. Gnadenfrei in Schlesien.: Winter, 1938.
Wieneke, Friedrich. *Deutsche Theologie im Umriss*. Soldin: H. Madrasch, 1933.
Wiener, Peter F. *Martin Luther: Hitler's Spiritual Ancestor*. London: Hutchinson, 1945. Republished Cranford, NJ: American Atheist Press, 1999.
Witte, Johannes. *Doktor Martin Luther als rechter Christ und echter Deutscher*. Berlin: Evangelischer Bund, 1934.
Wolf, Ernst. *Martin Luther, das Evangelium und die Religion*. Munich: Chr. Kaiser Verlag, 1934.
Wolf, Ernst. "Politia Christi. Das Problem der sozialethik im Luthertum." *Peregrinatio I*. Munich: Chr. Kaiser Verlag, 1962: 214–42.
Wolf, Ernst. "Luthers Erbe." In *Peregrinatio* II. Munich: Chr. Kaiser Verlag, 1965: 52–81.
Wolff, Otto. *Die Haupttypen der neueren Lutherdeutung*. Stuttgart: Kohlhammer, 1938.

Secondary Literature

Aland, Kurt. "Der 'deutsche' Luther." *Luther: Zeitschrift der Luther Gesellschaft* 51 (1980): 115–29.
Albrecht, Christian. "Zwischen Kriegstheologie und Krisentheologie. Zur Lutherrezeption im Reformationsjubiläum 1917." In *Luther Zwischen den Kulturen: Zeitgenossenschaft—Weltwirkung*. Hans Medick and Peer Schmidt, eds. Göttingen: Vandenhoeck & Ruprecht, 2004: 482–99.
Arnold, Claus. "Heinrich Suso Denifle OP (1844–1905): Die Wirkungen einer historischen Polemik gegen Luther." In *Martin Luther: Monument, Ketzer, Mensch: Lutherbilder, Lutherprojektionen und ein ökumenischer Luther*. Andreas Holzem and Volker Leppin, eds. Freiburg: Herder, 2017: 247–68.
Assel, Heinrich. *Der Andere Aufbruch: Die Lutherrenaissance—Ursprünge, Aporien und Wege. Karl Holl, Emanuel Hirsch, Rudolf Hermann (1910 bis 1935)*. Göttingen, Vandenhoeck und Ruprecht, 1994.
Assel, Heinrich. "Politische Theologie im Protestantismus 1914–1945." In *Politische Theologie: Formen und Funktionen im 20 Jahrhundert*. Jürgen Brokoff and Jürgen Fohrmann, eds. Paderborn: Ferdinand Schöningh, 2003: 67–80.
Assel Heinrich. "The Use of Luther's Thought in the Nineteenth Century and the Luther Renaissance." In *The Oxford Handbook of Martin Luther's Theology*. Robert Kolb et al., eds. Oxford: Oxford University Press, 2014: 551–72.
Assel, Heinrich, ed. *Karl Holl: Leben-Werke-Briefe*. Tübingen: Mohr Siebeck, 2021.
Baeumer, Max. "Lutherfeiern und ihre politische Manipulation." In *Deutsche Feiern*. Reinhold Grimm and Jost Hermand, eds. Wiesbaden 1977: 46–61.
Baird, Jay W. *Hitler's War Poets: Literature and Politics in the Third Reich*. Cambridge: Cambridge University Press, 2008.
Barnett, Victoria. *For the Soul of the People. Protestant Protest against Hitler*. New York and Oxford: Oxford University Press, 1992.
Basse, Michael. "Luthers Geschichtsverständnis und dessen Rezeption im Kontext der Reformations-jubiläum 1817 und 1917." *Lutherjahrbuch* 69 (2002): 47–70.
Baumgärtner, Raimund. *Weltanschauungskampf im Dritten Reich: Die Auseinandersetzung mit Alfred Rosenberg*. Mainz: Matthias Grünewal-Verlag, 1977.

Bayer, Oswald. "Uns voraus. Bemerkungen zur Lutherforschung und Lutherrezeption." *Lutherjahrbuch* 84 (2017): 170–89.
Bayer, Ulrich. "Gerhard Ritter (1888–1967)." In *Lebensbilder aus der evangelischen Kirche in Baden im 19. und 20. Jahrhundert*, Vol. II: *Kirchenpolitische Richtungen*. Johannes Ehmann, ed. Heidelberg: verlag regionalkultur, 2010: 390–415.
Becker, Frank. "Protestantische Euphorien 1870/71, 1914, 1933." In *Nationalprotestantische Mentalitäten*. Manfred Galius and Hartmut Lehmann, eds. Göttingen: Vandenhoeck & Ruprecht, 2005: 19–44.
Becker, Thomas. *Zwischen Diktatur und Neubeginn: Die Universität Bonn im "Dritten Reich" und in der Nachkriegszeit*. Göttingen: Vandenhoeck & Ruprecht, 2009.
Bergen, Doris. "Christianity and Germanness: Mutually Reinforcing, Reciprocally Undermining?" In *Religion und Nation, Nation und Religion: Beiträge zu einer unbewältigten Geschichte*. Michael Geyer and Hartmut Lehman, eds. Göttingen: Wallstein Verlag, 2004: 76–98.
Bergen, Doris. "Nazism and Christianity: Partners and Rivals? A Response to Richard Steigmann-Gall, *The Holy Reich: The Nazi Conceptions of Christianity*." *Journal of Contemporary History* 4 (2007): 25–33.
Bergen, Doris L. *Twisted Cross: The German Christian Movement in the Third Reich*. Chapel Hill: University of North Carolina Press, 1996.
Bering, Dietz. *War Luther Antisemit?: Das deutsch-jüdische Verhältnis als Tragödie der Nähe*. Berlin: Berlin University Press, 2015.
Bering, Dietz. *Luther im Fronteinsatz: Propagandastrategien im Ersten Weltkrieg*. Göttingen: Wallstein Verlag, 2018.
Beutel, Albrecht. "Martin Luther in Urteil der deutschen Aufklärung: Beobachtungen zu einem epochalen Paradigmenwechsel." In *Martin Luther: Monument, Ketzer, Mensch*. Andreas Holzem and Volker Leppin, eds. Freiburg: Herder, 2017.
Boer, Roland. "Luther im Marxismus." In *Martin Luther: Ein Christ zwischen Reformen und Moderne (1517–2017)*. Alberto Melloni, ed. Vol. II. Berlin: de Gruyter, 2017: 1003–15.
Böhm, Susanne. *Deutsche Christen in der Thüringer evangelischen Kirche (1927–1945)*. Leipzig: Evangelische Verlagsanstalt, 2008.
Bollbuck, Harold. "Martin Luther in der Geschichtsschreibung zwischen Reformation und Aufklärung." In *Luthermania: Ansichten einer Kultfigur*. Hole Rößler, ed. Wiesbaden: Harrassowitz, 2017: 47–68.
Bornkamm, Heinrich. *Luther im Spiegel der deutschen Geistesgeschichte*. 2nd ed. Göttingen: Vandenhoeck & Ruprecht, 1970.
Brakelmann, Günter. *Protestantische Kriegstheologie im 1. Weltkrieg. Reinhold Seeberg als Theologe des deutschen Imperialismus*. Bielefeld: Luther Verlag, 1974.
Brakelmann, Günter. "Der Krieg 1870/71 und die Reichsgründung im Urteil des Protestantismus." In *Kirche zwischen Krieg und Frieden. Studien zur Geschichte des deutschen Protestantismus*. Wolgang Huber and Johannes Scherdtfeger, eds. Stuttgart: Ernst Klett Verlag, 1976: 293–320.
Brakelmann, Günther. *Der deutsche Protestantismus im Epochenjahr 1917*. Witten: Luther Verlag, 1974.
Brakelmann, Günther. *Hitler und Luther 1933*. Bochum, 2008.
Brakelmann, Günther. *Protestantische Kriegstheologie 1914–1918*. Kamen: Spenner Verlag, 2015.
Brandt, Renate. "Hermann Diem (1900–1975) und Harald Diem (1913–1941)." In *Wir konnten uns nicht entziehen: 30 Porträts zu Kirche und Nationalsozialismus in Württemburg*. Rainer Lächele and Jörg Thierfelder, eds. Stuttgart: Quell-Verlag, 1998: 481–504.
Bräuer, Siegfried. "Das Lutherjubiläum 1933 in den deutschen Universitäten I." *Theologische Literaturzeitung* 108 (1983): 641–62.
Bräuer, Siegfried. "Der 'Deutsche Luthertag 1933' und sein Schicksal." In *Martin Luther: Leistung und Erbe*. Horst Bartel, ed. Berlin: Akademie Verlag, 1986: 423–34.
Bräuer, Siegfried. "Der säkularisationsfähige Reformator: Studien zur Lutherrezeption in 20. Jahrhundert." Habilitationsschrift, Kirchlichen Hochschule Naumberg, 1991.
Bräuer, Siegfried. "'Wir erheben aufs tiefste entrüstet Einspruch': Die Lutherehrung der Deutschen Christen 1933 in Sachsen und der Protest von Dresdner Schülerinnen." *Neues Archiv für Sächsische Geschichte* 64 (1993): 151–74.

Bräuer, Siegfried. "Der urdeutsche und tief christliche Reformator. Zur Planung und Vorbereitung der Wittenberger Luther-Festtage 1933." In *700 Jahre Wittenberg: Stadt, Universität, Reformation.* Stefan Oehmig, ed. Weimar: Böhlau, 1995: 545–63.

Bräuer, Siegfried. "'Martin Luther und Adolf Hitler—die Träger des deutschen Schicksal' (Kurt Thieme): das Lutherbild der 'Deutschen Christen' unter besonderen Berücksichtigung der Ereignisse in Altenburger Land." *Altenburger Geschichts- und Hauskalender* 6 (1997): 579–86.

Bräuer, Siegfried. "Die Lutherwoche vom 19. bis 27. August 1933 in Eisleben." In *Lutherinszenierung und Reformationserrinerungen.* Stefan Laube and Karl-Heinz Fix, eds. Leipzig: Evangelische Verlagsanstalt, 2002: 391–451.

Brennecke, Hans-Christof. "Zwischen Luthertum und Nationalismus: Kirchengeschichte in Erlangen." In *Geschichtswissenschaft in Erlangen.* Helmut Neuhaus. ed. Erlangen: Palm & Enke, 2000: 227–68.

Brosseder, Johannes. *Luthers Stellung zu den Juden im Spiegel seiner Interpreten: Interpretation und Rezeption von Luthers Schriften und Äußerungen zum Judentum im 19. und 20. Jahrhundert vor allem im deutschsprachigen Raum.* Munich: Max Hueber Verlag, 1972.

Burkhardt, Johannes. "Reformations- und Lutherfeiern: die Verbürgerlichung der reformatorischen Jubiläumskultur." In *Öffentliche Festkultur: Politische Feste in Deutschland von der Aufklärung bis zum Ersten Weltkrieg.* Dieter Düding, ed. Reinbek bei Hamburg, 1988: 212–36.

Buss, Hansjörg. "Deutsche und Luther Reformationsjubilaen im 19. und 20. Jahrhundert." In *Luther: zeitgenössisch, historisch, kontrovers.* Richard Faber and Uwe Puschner, eds. Frankfurt a.M.: Peter Lang, 2017: 29–46.

Dathe, Uwe. "Reform des Glaubens? Reform der Kirche? Reform des Lebens!: Rudolf Euckens lebensphilosophische Luther-Interpretation." In *Luther Denken: Die Reformation im Werk Jenaer Gelehrter.* Christopher Spehr, ed. Leipzig: Evangelische Verlagsanstalt, 2019: 221–38.

DeJonge, Michael P. *Bonhoeffer's Reception of Luther.* Oxford: Oxford University Press, 2017.

Deppermann, Klaus. "Gerhard Ritters Lutherbild." In *Protestantische Profile von Luther bis Francke: sozialgeschichtliche Aspekte.* Klaus Deppermann and Thomas Baumann, eds. Göttingen: Vandenhoeck & Ruprecht, 1992: 22–30.

Dingel, Irene. "Luther's Authority in the Late Reformation and Protestant Orthodoxy." In *The Oxford Handbook of Martin Luther's Theology.* Robert Kolb et al., eds. Oxford: Oxford University Press, 2014: 524–39.

Düfel, Hans. "Das Lutherjubuläum 1883." *Zeitschrift für Kirchengeschichte* 95 (1984): 1–94.

Ebeling, Gerhard. "Karl Barths Ringen mit Luther." In *Lutherstudien*, vol. 3, *Begriffsuntersuchungen, Textinterpretationen, Wirkungsgeschichtliches.* Tübingen: J. C. B. Mohr [Paul Siebeck], 1985: 428–573.

Ebeling, Gerhard. "Über die Reformation hinaus? Zur Luther-Kritik Karl Barths." In *Zeitschrift für Theologie und Kirche*, Beiheft 6, *Zur Theologie Karl Barths: Beiträge aus Anlaß seines 100. Geburtstags.* Eberhard Jüngel, ed. Tübingen: J. C. B. Mohr [Paul Siebeck], 1986: 33–75.

Eberan, Barbro. *Luther? Friedrich "der Große"? Wagner? Nietzsche?: Wer war an Hitler Schuld. Die Debatte um die Schuldfrage 1945–1949.* 2nd ed. Munich: Minerva, 1985.

Ehling, Kay. "Der deutscheste der Deutschen: Luther im Krieg 1917." In *Luther Imagines 17.* Kay Ehling, ed. Munich, 2017: 115–28.

Ericksen, Robert. *Theologians under Hitler: Gerhard Kittel, Paul Althaus, Emanuel Hirsch.* New Haven: Yale University Press, 1985.

Ericksen, Robert P. "Emanuel Hirsch—Intellectual Freedom and the Turn toward Hitler." *Kirchlich Zeitgeschichte/Contemporary Church History* 24 (2011): 74–91.

Friedländer, Saul. *Nazi Germany and the Jews*, Vol. I: *The Years of Persecution, 1933–1939.* New York: Harper Collins, 1997.

Gäbe, Lüder. "Fries, Jakob Friedrich." In *Neue Deutsche Biographie.* Vol. 5. Berlin: Duncker & Humboldt, 1961: 608–10.

Gailus, Manfred. *Protestantismus und Nationalsozialismus.* Cologne: Bohlau Verlag, 2001.

Gailus, Manfred. "1933 als protestantisches Erlebnis. Emphatische Selbsttransformation und Spaltung." *Geschichte und Gesellschaft* 29 (2003): 481–511.

Gailus, Manfred. "'Nationalsozialistiche Christen' und 'christliche Nationalsozialisten': Anmerkungen zur Vielfalt synkretistischer Gläubigkeiten im 'Dritten Reich.'" In *Nationalprotestantische Mentalitäten*. Manfred Galius and Hartmut Lehmann, eds. Göttingen: Vandenhoeck & Ruprecht, 2005: 223-61.

Gailus, Manfred. "Martin Luthers 'Judenschriften' und der protestantische Antisemitismus im 'Dritten Reich.'" In *Luther: zeitgenössisch, historisch, kontrovers*. Richard Faber and Uwe Puschner, eds. Frankfürt a.M.: Peter Lang, 2017: 363-76.

Gailus, Manfred. *Gläubige Zeiten: Religiosität Im Dritten Reich*. Freiburg: Herder, 2021.

Gailus, Manfred and Armin Nolzen, eds. *Zerstrittene "Volksgemeinschaft": Glaube, Konfession und Religion im Nationalsozialismus*. Göttingen: Vandenhoeck & Ruprecht, 2011.

Geck, Albrecht. "Luthererinnerung im Zeichen von Aufklärung und Emanzipation." In *Ketzer, Held und Prediger: Martin Luther im Gedächtnis der Deutschen*. Marcel Nieden, ed. Darmstadt: Wissenschaftliche Buchgesellschaft, 2017: 83-117.

Graf, Friedrich Wilhelm. *Der heilige Zeitgeist: Studien zur Ideengeschichte der protestantischen Theologie in der Weimar Republik*. Tübingen: Mohr Siebeck, 2011.

Graf, Gerhard. *Gottesbild und Politik: eine Studie zur Frömmigkeit in Preußen während der Freiheitskriege 1813-1815*. Göttingen, Vandenhoeck und Ruprecht, 1993.

Gremmels, Christian, ed. *Bonhoeffer und Luther: Zur Sozialgestaltung des Luthertums in der Moderne*. Munich: Chr. Kaiser, 1983.

Greschat, Martin, ed. *Der Schuld der Kirche: Dokumente und Reflexionen zur Stuttgarter Schulderklärung vom 18./19. Oktober 1945*. Munich: Chr. Kaiser, 1982.

Greschat, Martin, ed. *Der Deutsche Protestantismus im Revolutionsjahr 1918-1919*. Stuttgart: W. Kohlhammer, 1997.

Greschat, Martin. "Der Held der Nation. Die Gestalt Luther im Kaiserreich." In *Luther in seiner Zeit*. Martin Greschat, ed. Stuttgart, 1997: 107-26.

Greschat, Martin. *Die evangelische Christenheit und die deutsche Geschichte nach 1945: Weichenstellungen in der Nachkriegzeit*. Stuttgart: Kohlhammer, 2002.

Haag, Norbert. "Der umstrittene Luther: Martin Luther als Referenzgröße in den kirchenpolitischen Auseinandersetzungen in the der württembergischen Landeskirche 1933-1934." In *Martin Luther: Monument, Ketzer, Mensch: Lutherbilder, Lutherprojektionen und ein ökumenischer Luther*. Andreas Holzem and Volker Leppin, eds. Freiburg i.B: Herder, 2017: 323-59.

Hamm, Berndt. "Schuld und Verstrickung der Kirche: Vorüberlegungen zu deiner Darstellung der Erlanger Theologie in der Zeit des Nationalsozialismus." In *Kirche und Nationalsozialismus*. Wolfgang Stegemann, ed. Stuttgart: Kohlhammer, 1990: 11-56.

Hamm, Berndt. "Werner Elert als Kriegstheologe. Zugleich ein Beitrag zu Diskussion Luthertum und Nationalsozialismus." *Kirchliche Zeitgeschichte/Contemporary Church History* 11 (1998): 206-54.

Hakamies, Ahti. *"Eigengesetzlichkeit" der natürlichen Ordnungen als Grudproblem der neuren Lutherdeutung: Studien zur Geschichte and Problematik der Zwei-Reiche-Lehre Luthers*. Witten: Luther-Verlag, 1971.

Hayden-Roy, Patrick. "Unmasking the Hidden God: Luther's *wundermänner*." *Lutherjahrbuch* 82 (2015): 66-105.

Hering, Rainer. "In Luthers Namen. Protestantischer Kirchenbau im 'Dritten Reich.'" In *Luther: zeitgenössisch, historisch, kontrovers*. Richard Faber and Uwe Puschner, eds. Frankfürt a.M.: Peter Lang, 2017: 343-61.

Heschel, Susannah. "The Theological Faculty at the U. of Jena as 'Stronghold of National Socialism.'" In *"Kämpferische Wissenschaft": Studien zur Universität Jena im Nationalsozialismus*. Uwe Hoßfeld et al., eds. Cologne: Böhlau, 2003: 452-70.

Heschel, Sussanah. *The Aryan Jesus. Christian Theologians and the Bible in Nazi Germany*. Princeton: Princeton University Press, 2008.

Hetzer, Tanja. *"Deutsche Stunde": Volksgemeinschaft und Antisemitismus in der politischen Theologie Paul Althaus*. Munich: Alitera Verlag, 2009.

Hoffmann, Peter. *Heinrich Arminius Riemann. Lehrer, Pastor, Demokrat* (Friedland: Steffen, 2006). Available online at https://www.burschenschaftsgeschichte.de/pdf/hofmann_riemann.pdf

Hofmann, Andrea. "Martin Luther in First World War Sermons." *Kirchliche Zeitgeschichte/ Contemporary Church History* 31 (2018): 118–30.
Hofmeister, Björn. "Protestantismus, deutsche Kriegsgesellschaft und Mobilisierungspolitik zwischen Erstem Weltkrieg und Weimarer Republik 1914–1933." In *Luther: zeitgenössisch, historisch, kontrovers*. Richard Faber and Uwe Puschner, eds. Frankfürt a.M.: Peter Lang, 2017: 47–72.
Hölscher, Lucian. "'Die Legende vom frommen Reichsgründer Bismarck: Neue Überlegungen zu Bismarcks Religiosität." In *"Got mit uns: Nation, Religion, und Gewalt im 19. und früh 20. Jahrhundert*. Gerd Krumreich and Hartmut Lehmann, eds. Göttingen: Vandenhoeck & Ruprecht, 2000: 173–92.
Ingen, Ferdinand van and Gerd Labroisse, eds. *Luther Bilder im 20. Jahrhundert: Symposien an der Freien Universität Amsterdam*. Amsterdam: Rodopi, 1984.
Jasper, Gotthard. *Paul Althaus (1888–1966): Professor, Prediger und Patriot in seiner Zeit*. Göttingen: Vandenhoeck & Ruprecht, 2013.
Kampmann, Jürgen. "Das Lutherbild der evanglischen Kirche in der nationalsozialistischen Zeit." In *Martin Luther: Monument, Ketzer, Mensch: Lutherbilder, Lutherprojektionen und ein ökumenischer Luther*. Andreas Holzem and Volker Leppin, eds. Freiburg i.B: Herder, 2017: 293–321.
Karttunen, Tomi. "Die Luther-Lektüre Bonhoeffers." In *Bonhoeffer und Luther: Zentrale Themen ihrer Theologie*. Klaus Grünwalt et al., eds. Hannover: Amt der VEKLD, 2007: 9–31.
Kaufmann, Thomas. "Werner Elert als Kirchenhistoriker." *Zeitschrift für Theologie und Kirche* 47 (1996): 193–242.
Kaufmann, Thomas. "Anmerkungen zu generationsspezifischen Bedingungen und Dispositionen." In *Evangelische Kirchenhistoriker im "Dritten Reich*." Thomas Kaufmann and Harry Oelke, eds. Gütersloh: Kaiser Verlag, 2002: 32–54.
Kaufmann, Thomas. "Die Harnacks und die Seebergs. 'Nationaltprotestantische Mentalitäten' im Spiegel zweier Theologenfamilien." In *Nationalprotestantische Mentalitäten*. Manfred Galius and Hartmut Lehmann, eds. Göttingen: Vandenhoeck & Ruprecht, 2005: 165–222.
Kaufmann, Thomas. *Luthers "Judenschriften*." Tübingen: Mohr Siebeck, 2011.
Kaufmann, Thomas. *"Hier Stehe Ich!" Luther in Worms-Ereignis, mediale Inszenierung, Mythos*. Stuttgart: Anton Hiersemann, 2021.
Kaufmann, Thomas. "Antisemitische-Lutherflorilegien." In Thomas Kaufmann, *Aneignungen Luthers und der Reformation: Wissenschaftsgeschichtliche Beiträge zum 19.-21. Jahrhundert*. Tübingen: Mohr Siebeck, 2022: 3–36.
Kaufmann, Thomas. "Protestantisch-theologische Wurzeln des 'Personenkultes' im 19. Jahrhundert?" In Thomas Kaufmann, *Aneignungen Luthers und der Reformation: Wissenschaftsgeschichtliche Beiträge zum 19.-21. Jahrhundert*. Tübingen: Mohr Siebeck, 2022: 36–57.
Keßler, Martin. "Das Luthertum um 1918 im Spiegel seiner Zeit." *Lutherjahrbuch* 86 (2019): 174–228.
Keinhorst, Willi. *Wilhelm Stapel-Ein evangelischer Journalist im Nationalsozialismus*. Frankfurt a.M.: Peter Lang, 1993.
Kershaw, Ian. *The Hitler Myth: Image and Reality in the Third Reich*. Oxford: Oxford University Press, 1987.
Kershaw, Ian. *Hitler, 1889–1936: Hubris*. London: Penguin Press, 1998.
Kocka, Jürgen. "German History before Hitler: The Debate about the German Sonderweg," *Journal of Contemporary History* 23 (1988): 3–16.
König, Almut. "Der Krieg von der Kanzel." *Studia Germanistica* 19 (2016): 45–52. https://dokumenty. osu.cz/ff/journals/studiagermanistica/2016-19/SG_19_4_Konig.pdf [accessed 8/4/22].
König, Christopher. *Zwischen Kulturprotestantismus und völkischer Bewegung. Arthur Bonus (1864–1941) als religiöser Schriftsteller im wilhelminischen Kaiserreich*. Tübingen: Mohr Siebeck, 2018.
Kranich, Sebastian. "Das Dresdner Lutherjubiläum 1883." In *Spurenlese: Reformationsvergegenwärtigung als Standortbestimmung (1717–1983)*. Klaus Tanner und Jörg Ulrich, eds. Leipzig: Evangelische Verlagsanstalt, 2012: 101–44.

Kremers, Heinz, ed. *Die Juden und Martin Luther: Martin Luther und die Juden: Geschichte, Wirkungsgeschichte, Herausforderung*. Neukirchen-Vluyn: Neukirchener Verlag, 1985.
Krippner, Friederike. "Der 'deutscheste Mann unserer Geschichte.' Luther im nationalen Diskurs zu Beginn der 19. Jahrhundert." In *Das Imaginäre der Nation. Zur Persistenz einer politischen Katagorie im Literatur und Film*. Katharina Grabbe et al., eds. Bielefeld: transcript Verlag, 2012: 105–30.
Krumwiede, Hans-Walter. *Glaubenszuversicht und Weltgestaltung bei Martin Luther: mit einem Ausblick auf Dietrich Bonhoeffer*. Göttingen, Vandenhoeck und Ruprecht, 1983.
Krumwiede, Hans-Walter. "Dietrich Bonhoeffers Luther-Reziption und seine Stellung zu Luthertum." In *Die lutherischen Kirchen und die Bekenntnissynode von Barmen*. W.-D. Hauschild et al., eds. Göttingen: Vandenhoeck und Ruprecht, 1984: 206–23.
Küllmer, Björn. *Die Inszenierung der Protestantischen Volksgemeinschaft*. Berlin: Logos Verlag, 2012.
Kurz, Roland. *Nationalprotestantisches Denken in der Weimarer Republik: Voraussetzungen und Ausprägungen des Protestantismus nach dem Ersten Weltkrieg in seiner Begegnung mit Volk und Nation*. Gütersloh: Gütersloher Verl.-Haus, 2007.
Laube, Stefan. "Lutherbrief an den Kaiser—Kaiserbrief an die Lutherhalle." In *Lutherinszenierung und Reformationserinnerung*. Stefan Laube and Karl-Heinz Fix, eds. Leipzig: Evangelische Verlagsanstalt, 2002: 265–86.
Lehmann, Hartmut. "Das Lutherjubiläum 1883." In *Luthers Bleibende Bedeutung*. Jürgen Becker, ed. Hosum: Husum Verlag, 1983: 93–116.
Lehmann, Hartmut. "Martin Luther als deutscher Nationalheld im 19. Jahrhundert." *Luther: Zeitschrift der Luthergesellschaft* 55 (1984): 53–65.
Lehmann, Hartmut. "Anmerkungen zur Entmythologisierung der Luthermythen 1883–1983." *Archiv für Kulturgeschichte* 68 (1986): 457–77.
Lehmann, Hartmut. "The Germans as a Chosen People." *German Studies Review* 14 (1991): 261–73.
Lehmann, Hartmut. "'God Our Old Ally': The Chosen People Theme in Late Nineteenth, Early Twentieth Century German Nationalism." In *"Many are Chosen": Divine Election and Western Nationalism*. William R. Hutchison and Harmut Lehmann, eds. Cambridge, MA: Harvard University Press, 1994: 85–113.
Lehmann, Hartmut. "Hitlers evangelische Wähler." In *Protestantische Weltsichten*. Hartmut Lehmann, ed. Göttingen, Vandenhoeck und Ruprecht, 1998: 130–52.
Lehmann, Hartmut. "Katastrophe und Kontinuität. Die Diskussion über Martin Luthers historische Bedeutung in den ersten Jahren nach dem Zweiten Weltkrieg." In Hartmut Lehmann, *Protestantische Weltsichten*. Hartmut Lehmann, ed. Göttingen, Vandenhoeck und Ruprecht, 1998: 174–203.
Lehmann, Hartmut. "Luther als Kronzeuge für Hitler: Anmerkungen zu Otto Scheels Lutherverständnis in den 1930er Jahren." In *Protestantische Weltsichten*. Hartmut Lehmann, ed. Göttingen, Vandenhoeck und Ruprecht, 1998: 153–73.
Lehmann, Hartmut. "Hans Preuß 1933 über 'Luther und Hitler.'" *Kirchliche Zeitgeschichte: Contemporary Church History* 12 (1999): 287–96.
Lehmann, Hartmut. "'Er ist wie selber: der ewige Deutsche': Zur Langanhaltenden Wirkung der Lutherdeutung von Heinrich von Treitschke." In *"Gott mit uns": Nation, Religion und Gewalt im 19. und frühen 20. Jahrhundert*. Gerd Krumreich and Hartmut Lehmann, eds. Göttingen: Vandenhoeck & Ruprecht, 2000: 91–103.
Lehmann, Hartmut. "Heinrich Bornkamm im Spiegel seiner Lutherstudium von 1933 und 1947." In *Evangelische Kirchenhistoriker im "Dritten Reich."* Thomas Kaufmann and Harry Oelke, eds. Gütersloh: Kaiser Verlag, 2002: 367–80.
Lehmann, Hartmut. "Martin Luther und der 31. Oktober 1517." In *Luthergedächtnis 1817–2017*. Hartmut Lehmann, ed. Göttingen: Vandenhoeck & Ruprecht, 2012: 16–34.
Lehmann, Hartmut. "Die Lutherfaszination der Deutschen 1817–2017." In Hartmut Lehmann, *Das Reformationsjubiläum 2017: Umstrittenes Erinnern*. Göttingen: Vandenhoeck & Ruprecht, 2021: 69–84.
Lehmann, Hartmut. "Die Nationalsozialisten und Luther." In Hartmut Lehmann, *Das Reformationsjubiläum 2017: Umstrittenes Erinnern*. Göttingen: Vandenhoeck & Ruprecht, 2021: 107–20.

Lepp, Claudia. "Konservativ-Christlicher Widerstand: Das Beispiel Gerhard Ritter." *Jahrbuch für badische Kirchen- und Religions Geschichte* 2 (2008): 69–89.
Leppin, Volker. "In Rosenbergs Schatten: Zur Lutherdeutung Erich Vogelsangs." *Theologische Zeitung* 61 (2005): 132–42.
Leppin, Volker. "Mystik und Neuzeit: Die Lutherinterpretationen der Holl-Schule in den theologischen Debatten der Weimarer Republik." In *Martin Luther: Monument, Ketzer, Mensch: Lutherbilder, Lutherprojektionen und ein ökumenischer Luther*. Andreas Holzem and Volker Leppin, eds. Freiburg: Herder, 2017: 269–91.
Liedtke, Barbara. *Völkisches Denken und Verkündigung des Evangeliums. Die Rezeption Houston Stewart Chamberlain in evangelischer Theologie und Kirche während der Zeit des "Dritten Reichs."* Leipzig: Evangelische Verlagsanstalt, 2012.
Loewinich, Walther von. *Luther und der Neuprotestantismus*. Witten: Luther-Verlag, 1963.
Loewinich, Walther von. "Paul Althaus als Lutherforscher." *Lutherjahrbuch* 35 (1968): 9–47.
Loewinich, Walther von. *Martin Luther. Der Mann und das Werk*. Munich: List Verlag, 1982.
Löfgren, David. *Die Theologie der Schöpfung bei Luther*. Göttingen: Vandenhoeck & Ruprecht, 1960.
Lorentzen, Tim. "19. Jahrhundert Nationale, Konfessionelle und Tourist Errinnerugskulturen." In *Ketzer, Held und Prediger: Martin Luther im Gedächtnis der Deutschen*. Marcel Nieden, ed. Darmstadt: Wissenschaftliche Buchgesellschaft, 2017: 119–69.
Maron, Gottfried. "Luther 1917: Beobachtung zur Literatur des 400. Reformationsjubiläums." *Zeitschrift für Kirchengeschichte* 93 (1982): 1–45.
Maron, Gottfried. "Luther und die 'Germanisierung des Christentums'. Notizen zu einer fast vergessenen These." *Zeitschrift für Kirchengeschichte* 94 (1983): 313–37.
Meding, Wichman von. "'Jubel ohne Glauben?' Das Reformationsjubiläum von 1817 in Württemberg." *Zeitschrift für Kirchengeschichte* 93 (1982): 119–60.
Mehnert, Gottfried. *Evangelische Kirche und Politik 1917–1919: die politischen Strömungen im deutschen Protestantismus von der Julikrise 1917 bis zum Herbst 1919*. Düsseldorf: Droste Verlag, 1959.
Müller, Christine-Ruth. *Bekenntnis und Bekennen: Dietrich Bonhoeffer in Bethel (1933), ein lutherischer Versuch*. Munich: Chr. Kaiser Verlag, 1989.
Nipperdey, Thomas. *Deutsche Geschichte 1800–1866. Bürgerwelt und starker Staat*. Munich: C. H. Beck, 1985.
Nipperdey, Thomas. *Religion im Umbruch: Deutschland 1870–1918*. Munich: C. H. Beck, 1988.
Nipperdey, Thomas. *Deutsche Geschichte 1866–1918*. Vol. 1: *Arbeitswelt und Bürgergeist*. Munich: C. H. Beck, 1990.
Nipperdey, Thomas. *Deutsche Geschichte 1866–1918*. Vol. 2: *Machtstaat vor der Demokratie*. Munich: C. H. Beck, 1993.
Noormann, Harry. *Protestantismus und politsches Mandat 1945–1949*. Vol. 1: *Grundriß* Gütersloh: Gerd Mohn, 1985.
Oelke, Harry, ed. *Martin Luthers "Judenschriften." Die Rezeption im 19. und 20. Jahrhundert*. Göttingen, 2015.
Ohst, Martin. "Der I. Weltkrieg in der Perspektive Emanuel Hirschs." In *Evangelische Kirchenhistoriker im "Dritten Reich."* Thomas Kaufmann and Harry Oelke, eds. Gütersloh: Chr. Kaiser Verlag, 2002: 64–121.
Ohst, Martin. "Antisemitismus als Waffe im weltanschaulichen und politischen Kampf: Adolf Stoecker und Reinhold Seeberg." In *Protestantismus, Antijudaismus, Antisemitismus*. Dorothea Wendebourg et al., eds. Tübingen: Mohr Siebeck, 2017: 275–308.
Osten-Sacken, Peter von der. "Der Nationalsozialistische Lutherforscher Theodor Pauls: Vervollständigung eines fragmentarischen Bildes." In *Das mißbrauchte Evangelium: Studien zu Theologie und Praxis der Thüringer Deutschen Christen*. Peter von der Osten-Sacken, ed. Berlin: Inst. Kirche und Judentum, 2001: 136–66.
Osten-Sacken, Peter von der. *Martin Luther und die Juden: neu untersucht anhand von Anton Margarithas "Der gantz Jüdisch glaub" (1530/31)*. Stuttgart: Kohlhammer, 2002.
Pawlas, Andreas. "Mit Luther durch aufgewühlte Zeiten-Theodor Knolle und die Luther-Gesellschaft." In *Luther-Gesellschaft 1918–2018*. Johannes Schilling and Martin Treu, eds. Leipzig: Evangelische Verlagsanstalt, 2018: 83–128.

Piper, Ernst. *Alfred Rosenberg, Hitlers Chefideologe*. Munich: Karl Blessing Verlag, 2005.
Pöder, Christine Svinth-Vaerge. "Die Lutherrenaissance im Kontext des Reformationsjubiläums: Gericht und Rechtfertigung bei Karl Holl, 1917-1921." *Kirchliche Zeitgeschichte / Contemporary Church History* 26 (2013): 191-200.
Postert, André. "'Lieber fahre ich mit meinem Volk in die Hölle als ohne mein Volk in Deinen Himmel.' Wolf Meyer-Erlach und der Antiintelliktualismus." In *Für ein artgemäßes Christentum der Tat: Völkische Theologen im "Dritten Reich."* Manfred Gilus and Clemans Vollnhals, eds. Göttingen: Vandenhoeck & Ruprecht, 2016: 219-38.
Pressel, Wilhelm. *Die Kriegspredigt 1914-1918 in der evangelischen Kirche Deutschlands*. Göttigen: Vandenhoeck & Ruprecht, 1967.
Probst, Christopher J. *Demonizing the Jews: Luther and the Protestant Church in Nazi Germany*. Bloomington: Indiana University Press, 2012.
Raschzok, Klaus. "Wolf Meyer-Erlach und Hans Asmussen: ein Vergleich zwischen der praktischen Theologie der Deutschen Christen und der Bekennende Kirche." In *Zwischen Volk und Bekenntnis: Praktische Theologie im Dritten Reich*. Klaus Raschzok, ed. Leipzig: Evangelische Verlagsanstalt, 2000: 167-202.
Reichelt, Silvio. *Der Erlebnisraum Lutherstadt Wittenberg. Genese, Entwicklung und Bestand eines protestantischen Errinerungsortes*. Göttingen: Vandenhoeck & Ruprecht, 2013.
Reichelt, Silvio and Sebastian Kranich. "Martin Luther als evangelischer Schutzheiliger: die Reformationsfeiern an der Universität Halle-Wittenberg 1927-1941." In *Spurenlese: Reformationsvergegenwärtigung als Standortbestimmung (1717-1983)*. Klaus Tanner and Jörg Ulrich, eds. Leipzig: Evangelische Verlagsanstalt, 2012: 145-94.
Rhein, Stefan. "Wittenberg und die Anfänge der Luther-Gesellschaft." *Die Luther-Gesellschaft 1918-2018*. Johannes Schilling and Martin Treu, eds. Leipzig: Evangelische Verlagsanstalt, 2018: 9-33.
Rickers, Folkert. *Zwischen Kreuz und Hakenkreuz: Untersuchungen zur Religionspädagogik im "Dritten Reich."* Neukirchen-Vluyn: Neukirchener Verlag, 1995.
Rieger, Reinhold. "Der biographische Luther: Stationen der Geschichte biographischer Luther-Konstruktionen." *Lutherjahrbuch* 88 (2021): 220-85.
Rinnen, Anja. *Kirchenmann und Nationalsozialist: Siegfried Lefflers ideelle Verschmelzung von Kirche und Drittem Reich*. Weinheim: Deutscher Studien Verlag, 1995.
Roos, Daniel. *Julius Streicher und der Stürmer, 1923-1945*. Paderborn: Ferdinand Schöningh, 2014.
Roy, Martin. *Luther in der DDR: zum Wandel des Lutherbildes in der DDR-Geschichtsschreibung*. Bochum: Winkler Verlag, 2000.
Ruff, Mark. "The Nazis' Religionspolitik: An Assessment of Recent Literature." *Catholic Historical Review* 92.3 (2006): 252-67.
Schjørring, Jens Holger. *Theologische Gewissensethik und politische Wirklichkeit: Das Beispiel Eduard Geismars und Emanuel Hirsch*. Göttingen: Vandenhoek & Ruprecht, 1979.
Schmidt, Georg. "Luther und die Freiheit seiner 'lieben Deutschen.'" In *Der Reformator Martin Luther 2017*. Heinz Schilling, ed. Oldenbourg: de Gruyter, 2014: 173-94.
Schmidt, Georg. "Der 'deutsche' Luther." In *Luther: Zankapfel zwischen den Konfessionen und "Vater im Glauben."* Mariano Delgado and Volker Leppin, eds. Stuttgart: Kohlhammer, 2016: 163-81.
Schmidt, Ina. *Der Herr des Feuers: Friedrich Hielscher und sein Kreis zwischen Heidentum, neuem Nationalismus und Widerstand gegen den Nationalsozialismus*. Cologne: SH-Verlag, 2004.
Schmidt, Johann M. "Heine und Luther: Heines Lutherrezeption in der Spannung zwischen den Daten 1483-1933." *Heine-Jahrbuch* 24 (1985): 9-79.
Scholder, Klaus. *Die Kirchen und das Dritte Reich*, Vol. 1: *Vorgeschichte und Zeit der Illusionen, 1918-1934*. Frankfurt a.M.: Ullstein, 1986.
Scholder, Klaus. "Neure deutsche Geschichte und protestantische Theologie." In *Die Kirchen zwischen Republik und Gewaltherrschaft: Gesammelte Aufsätze*. K. O. v. Aretin and Gerhard Besier, eds. Berlin: Siedler Verlag, 1988: 75-97.
Scholder, Klaus and Gerhard Besier. *Die Kirchen und das Dritte Reich*, Vol. 2: *Das Jahr der Ernüchterung 1934: Barmen und Rome*. Frankfurt a.M.: Ullstein, 1988.

Schreiner, Klaus. "Wann 'Kommt der Retter Deutschlands?': Formen und Funktionen von politischem Messianismus in der Weimarer Republik." *Saeculum* 49 (1998): 107–60.

Schuchard, Jutta. "Luther auf dem Postament: Gedanken und Überlegungen zu Lutherdenkmälern." In *"Der fühlt der Zeiten ungeheuren Bruch und fest umklammert er sein Bibelbuch…": zum Lutherkult im 19 Jahrhundert*. Hardy Eidam and Gerhard Seib, eds. Berlin: Schelzky & Jeep, 1996: 73–88.

Selge, Kurt-Victor. "Heinrich Bornkamm (1901–1977) als Kirchenhistoriker und Zeitgenosse." *Heidelberger Jahrbücher* 23 (1979): 101–22.

Siegele-Wenschkewitz, Lenore. "Die Geschichtsverständnis angesichts des Nationalsozialismus: Die Tübingener Kirchenhistoriker Hanns Rückert in der Auseinandersetzung mit Karl Barth." In *Theologische Fakultäten im Nationalsozialismus*. Lenore Siegele-Wenschkewitz and Carsten Nicolaisen, eds. Göttingen: Vandenhoeck & Ruprecht, 1993: 113–44.

Siems, Gisela. "Hauptpastor Friedrich Andersen, Bund für Deutschkirch—ein Wegbereiter des Nationalsozialismus in der Stadt Flensburg." In *Kirche und Nationalsozialismus. Beiträge zur Geschichte des Kirchenkampfes in den evangelischen Landeskirchen Schleswig-Holsteins*. Klauspeter Reumann, ed. Neumünster: Karl Wachholtz Verlag, 1988: 13–34.

Slenczka, Notger. *Selbstkonstitution und Gotteserfahrung. Werner Elerts Deutung der neuzeitlichen Subjektivität im Kontext der Erlanger Theologie*. Göttingen: 1998.

Smid, Marikje, *Deutscher Protestantismus und Judentum 1932/33*. Munich: Ch. Kaiser Verlag, 1990.

Sontheimer, Kurt. *Thomas Mann und die Deutschen*. Munich: Nymphenburger Verl.-Handlung, 1961.

Stayer, James M. *Martin Luther, German Saviour*. Montreal: McGill and Queen's University Press, 2000.

Steffens, Martin. *Luthergedenkstätten im 19. Jahrhundert. Memoria-Repräsentation-Denkmalpflege*. Regensburg: Schnell & Steiner, 2008.

Stegmann, Andreas. "Der Berliner Antisemitismusstreit 1879/80." In *Protestantismus, Antijudaismus, Antisemitismus*. Dorothea Wendebourg et al., eds. Tübingen: Mohr Siebeck, 2017: 239–74.

Steigmann-Gall, Richard. *The Holy Reich: The Nazi Conceptions of Christianity, 1933–1945*. New York: Cambridge University Press, 2003.

Stephan, Horst. *Luther in den Wandlungen seiner Kirche*. Berlin: Alfred Töpelmann, 1951.

Stroup, John. "Political Theology and Secularization Theory in Germany, 1918–1939: Emanuel Hirsch as a Phenomenon of His time." *Harvard Theological Review* 80 (1987): 321–68.

Sucher, C. Bernd. *Luthers Stellung zu den Juden: ein Interpretation aus germanistischer Sicht*. Nieuwkoop: B. de Graaf, 1977.

Tafilowski, Ryan. *"Dark, Depressing Riddle": Germans, Jews and the Meaning of the Volk in the Theology of Paul Althaus*. Göttingen: Vandenhoeck & Ruprecht, 2019.

Thadden, Rudolf von. "Bismarck—ein Lutheraner?" In *Luther in der Neuzeit*. Bernd Moeller, ed. Gütersloh: Gerd Mohn, 1983: 104–20.

Tiefel, Hans. "The German Lutheran Church and the Rise of National Socialism." *Church History* 41 (1972): 326–36.

Treu, Martin. "'…ihr steht auf heiliger Erde.' Lutherverehrung im Mansfelder Land des 19. Jahrhundert." *Lutherinszenierung und Reformationserinnerung*. Stefan Laube and Karl-Heinz Fix, eds. Leipzig: Evangelische Verlagsanstalt, 2002: 85–96.

Tümperl, Christian. "Zur Geschichte der Luther-Denkmäler." In *Luther in der Neuziet*. Bernd Moeller, ed. (Gütersloh: Gerd Mohn, 1983): 227–47.

"Überall Luthers Worts…": Martin Luther im Nationalsozialismus. Stiftung Topographie des Terrors, ed. Berlin: Topographie des Terrors, 2017.

"Volk, Nation, Nationalismus, Masse." In *Geschichtliche Grundbegriffe: Historisches Lexikon zur politisch-sozialen Sprache in Deutschland*. Vol. 7. Otto Brunner, Werner Conze, and Reinhart Koselleck, eds. Stuttgart: Clett-Cotta, 1992: 141–431.

Walkenhorst, Peter. "Zur religiösen Dimension nationalistischer Ideologie im Kaiserreich." In *Religion im Kaiserreich: Milieus—Mentalitäten—Krisen*. Olaf Blashke and Frank-Michael Kuhlemann, eds. Munich: Chr. Kaiser, 1996: 503–30.

Wallmann, Johannes. "Karl Holl und seine Schule." In *Zeitschrift für Theologie und Kirche*, Beiheft 4: *Tübinger Theologie in 20. Jahrhundert*. Eberhard Jüngel, ed. Tübingen: J. C. B. Mohr [Paul Siebeck], 1978: 1–33.

Wallmann, Johannes. "Ein Vermächtnis Kaiser Wilhelms II: Was hat Walter Grundmanns Eisenacher 'Entjudungsinstitut' mit Martin Luther zu tun?" *Zeitschrift für Theologie und Kirche* 114 (2017): 289–314.

Wallmann, Johannes. *Martin Luthers Juden Schriften*. Bielefeld: Luther Verlag, 2019.

Weber, Wolfgang E. J. "'Es ist eine merkwürdige Tatsache, daß die protestantische Leben-Jesu-Forschung viel weniger apologetisch war und ist als die Lutherforschung': Lutherbild und Geschichtswissenschaft im 19. und 20. Jahrhundert." In Richard Faber and Uwe Puschner, eds. *Luther: zeitgenössisch, historisch, kontrovers*. Frankfürt a.M.: Peter Lang, 2017: 317–42.

Wendebourg, Dorothea. "Die Bekanntheit von Luthers Judenschriften im 19. Und frühen 20. Jahrhunderts." In *Protestantismus, Antijudaismus, Antisemitismus*. Dorothea Wendebourg et al., eds. Tübingen: Mohr Siebeck, 2017: 147–80.

Wendebourg, Dorothea. *So viele Luthers...: Die Reformationsjubiläen des 19. und 20. Jahrhunderts*. Leipzig: Evangelische Verlagsanstalt, 2017.

Wiese, Christian. "'Unheilsspuren': zur Rezeption von Martin Luthers 'Judenschriften' im Kontext antisemitischen Denkens in den Jahrzehnten vor der Schoah." In *Das mißbrauchte Evangelium: Studien zu Theologie und Praxis der Thüringer Deutschen Christen*. Peter von der Osten-Sacken, ed. Berlin: Inst. Kirche und Judentum, 2001: 91–135.

Wiese, Christian. "Überwinder des Mittelalters? Ahnherr des Nationalsozialismus?: Zur Vielstimmigkeit und Tragik der jüdischen Lutherrezeption im wilhelminischen Deutschland und in der Weimarer Republik." In *Lutherinszenierung und Reformationserinnerung*. Stefan Laube and Karl-Heinz Fix, eds. Leipzig: Evangelische Verlagsanstalt, 2002: 165–97.

Willenberg, Nicola. "'Mit Luther und Hitler für Glauben und Volkstum.'" In *Spurenlese: Reformationsvergegenwärtigung als Standortbestimmung (1717–1983)*. Klaus Tanner and Jörg Ulrich, eds. Leipzig: Evangelische Verlagsanstalt, 2012: 195–238.

Winckler, Lutz. *Martin Luther als Bürger und Patriot: das Reformationsjubiläum von 1817 und der politische Protestantismus des Wartburgfestes*. Lübeck, Hamburg: Matthiesen, 1969.

Winkler, Markus. *Mythisches Denken zwischen Romantik und Realismus: zur Erfahrung kultureller Fremdheit im Werk Heinrich Heines*. Tübingen: Max Niemeyer Verlag, 1995.

Wolff, Jens. "Erich Vogelsang." In *Biographisch-Bibliographischeslexikon* 17, Ergänzungen IV. Herzberg: Verlag Traugott Bautz, 2000: 1507–21.

Wolgast, Eike. *Die Wahrnehmung des Dritten Reiches in der unmittelbaren Nachkriegszeit*. Heidelberg: Winter, 2001.

Zeeden, Ernst Walter. *Martin Luther und die Reformation in Urteil des deutschen Luthertums: Studien zum Selbstverständnis des lutherischen Protestantismus von Luthers Tode bis zum Beginn der Goethezeit*, Vol. 1: *Darstellungen*; Vol. 2: *Dokumente*. Freiburg i.B.: Herder, 1950.

Index for *The Luther Myth*

Since the index has been created to work across multiple formats, indexed terms for which a page range is given (e.g., 52–53, 66–70, etc.) may occasionally appear only on some, but not all of the pages within the range.

Adolphus, Gustavus 200–1, 206–8
Aleander 152–3
Althaus, Paul 28–9, 39–43, 62–3, 69–79, 81–7, 89, 93–4, 97–100, 103–5, 107, 122, 146–7, 181, 183–4, 206–7, 213–15, 234–7, 239–43, 251
  and 1917 400th Anniversary Reformation celebration tract 39–43
  and Karl Holl 62–3, 69–71
  and Luther's *Gewissensreligion* 70–2
  and *Schöpfungsordnungen* 69–70, 74, 100, 235
  and *Schöpfungstheologie* 74, 81–2, 207
  and *völkisch* theology 74–8
  Die Deutsche Stunde der Kirchen ("The German Hour of the Church,") 81–6, 241–2
  Post-War view of Luther 234–6, 241–2
Andersen, Friedrich 39–40, 165
Arndt, Ernst Moritz 6, 8–9
Asmussen, Hans 233, 244–6
Assel, Heinrich 57–8, 63 n.44, 69 n.61, 238 n.54
Augustine 143–4

Barmen Declaration 97–8, 238
Barth, Karl 57–8, 93–7, 103, 112–13, 115, 118, 126, 150, 212–13, 223–6, 232–4, 236–7, 240, 243–6, 252–4
  Lutherfeier 1933 93–7
Baumgärtner, Raimund 125 n.67
Beckmann, Joachim
  Verrat an Luther? ("Betrayal of Luther?") 128–30
Berger, Arnold E. 51–6, 61
Bering, Dietz 29 n.5
Bethel Confession (*Betheler Bekenntnis*) 93, 97–103
  on "non-Aryan" Christians 101
Birt, Theodor 33–5
Bismarck, Otto von 6–7, 18, 34, 52, 91–3, 165–6, 200–1, 229, 235
Bodelschwingh, Friedrich von 97–8, 103
Böhme, Jacob 200–1, 240–1
Bonhoeffer, Dietrich 97–103, 112–13, 247, 252–4
Bonus, Arthur 25–7, 35

Bora, Katherina von 89–90
Bornkamm, Heinrich 6, 14–15, 18, 181–4, 231–2, 241–2
Brakelmann, Günter 18 n.39
Bruder, Otto 150–2
Burschenschaften 10
Buchhorn, Josef 152–4
Butzer, Martin (Martin Bucer) 150–1

Chamberlain, Houston Stewart 25–7, 169
Charlemagne 134
Church Struggle (*Kirchenkampf*) 93, 113–14, 180–1
Confessing Church 100, 104–5, 115–18, 126, 128–30, 180–1, 184–7, 195, 218, 220, 232–6, 238, 240, 242–5, 252–4

DeJonge, Michael 103 n.58
Delitzsch, Friedrich 168–72
Der Stürmer 157, 186–7, 244–5
Deutelmoser, Arno 48–9, 199–221, 239–42
  Luther, Staat und Glaube ("Luther, the State and Belief") 199–210
  reaction to 210–21
Deutsche Christen (= DC, also German Christians) 26–7, 35, 81–2, 85–7, 89, 91–4, 97–8, 100, 104–5, 114, 116–18, 121, 125–6, 128–9, 135, 146–7, 154, 165–7, 179–81, 183–9, 191, 193, 195–8, 202, 206–7, 215–16, 218–19, 248–9, 251–4
Deutschtum 6, 8, 34, 37, 39–40, 44, 105–6, 141–2, 178, 200–1 *see also* (Germanity)
Diem, Hermann 218–19, 221, 233–4, 243–6
Diem, Harald 218–21

Eckart, Dietrich 131 n.1
Eggers, Kurt 148–50
Engels, Friedrich 229 n.15
Ericksen, Robert P. 64 n.47
Eucken, Rudolf 47–51, 55, 213–14

Alfred Falb 167–73, 175, 184–6
Fichte, Johann Gottlieb 8–9, 64–5, 67

Four Hundredth Anniversary of the
    Reformation, 1917 29–31
Franke, C.J. 141–2
Frederick the Great 131–2, 134, 229
Frick, Wilhelm 111–12
Fries, Jakob Friedrich 10–11
Fritsch, Theodor 160–5, 169, 175, 184–6,
    187 n.108
Fronemann, Wilhelm 154

Gailus, Manfred 104 n.2
Gebhardt, Florentine 87–91
German Christians (see *Deutsche Christen*)
German nationalism 6, 14, 24, 27, 39–40, 165
German National People's Party
    (DNVP/*Deutsche
    Nationalvolkspartei*) 79–80
Germanity 5–6, 23, 33–4, 37, 39–40, 44, 65,
    70–1, 105–6, 109, 112–13, 130, 141–2, 165–7,
    178, 200–1, 213–14, 247–9 see also
    (*Deutschtum*)
Goethe, Johann Wolfgang von 9–10, 91–3,
    200–1, 240–1
Gogarten, Friedrich 47 n.1
Goerdeler, Carl 235–6
Greschat, Martin 19 n.45, 243 n.74
Grundmann, Walter 142–3

Hahn, Gerhard 186–9
Hanstein, Wolfram von 228–30
Harnack, Adolf von 39–40
G.F.W. Hegel 14–15, 18, 47–8, 61, 234–5, 242–3
Heinrich Heine 15–16, 111, 230–1
Herder, Johann Gottfried 5
Hermann, Rudolf 238–40
Hielscher, Friedrich 200–1, 203–4, 215
    Das Reich 200
Hirsch, Emanuel 62–70, 72, 85–6, 95–6, 107, 120,
    175–6, 238
    and Luther's *Gewissensreligion* 63–7, 72
Hitler, Adolf 2–3, 62–4, 68–9, 79–82, 85–93, 97,
    102, 104–6, 108–9, 113–14, 123–4, 131–8,
    140–3, 146–7, 150, 152–5, 160, 172–3, 186–8,
    186 n.106, 206–7, 215–16, 221, 224–5, 227,
    229, 233–4, 239–41, 244–5, 251–4
    Mein Kampf 113–14, 131–2
Holl, Karl 54–65, 69–71, 95–6, 99, 103, 107, 120,
    143, 175–6, 201–2, 204–6, 214–15, 220,
    238, 240–2, 250–1
    concept of *Gewissensreligion* (religion of
        conscience) 58–9, 70–1, 95–6, 103, 204,
        220, 241
    Gesammelte Aufsätze I 58 n.28
    Review in the *Lutherjahrbuch* 62–3
    Influence on Emanuel Hirsch 63–5

Influence on Paul Althaus 69–71
view of World War I 56–7
Hossenfelder, Joachim 154–5

Islebiensis, *Dr. Martin Luther und das
    Judenthum* 157–60, 162

Jasper, Gerhard 235 n.41

Kant, Immanuel 166–7, 240–1
Kaufmann, Thomas 16 n.33
Kern, Franz 150–2
Kerrl, Hanns 143
Kershaw, Ian 2–3, 132 n.3, 134 n.17, 252–4
Kittel, Helmuth 143–5, 216 n.52
Knolle, Theodor 48–9, 80
    reaction to Arno Deutelmoser, *Luther, Staat
        und Glaube* 210–12, 215–18
Karl König 35–9, 89
Krause, Reinhold 184–6
Künneth, Walter 128 n.75

Lamparter, Eduard 173–5, 177–8
Leo X 230
Lehmann, Hartmut 4–5, 19–20, 80 n.3, 132–3,
    183 n.100
Loewenich, Walther von 222 n.1
Ludendorff, Mathilde 186 n.106, 193–6
Luther Renaissance 47, 50–1, 54–5, 57–8,
    76, 78, 176, 203, 238–40, 242–3,
    250–1
Luther Society (*Luther-Gesellschaft*) 47–9,
    80–1, 210–14
Luther, Martin
    and anti-Semitism 136, 156–7, 175–9, 193–5
    Image in late 19th century anti-Semitic
        nationalism 25–7, 157–60
    Image in 1917 Reformation celebration
        anti-Semitic literature 39, 165–7
    Distribution and knowledge of
        Luther's anti-Jewish writings,
        1930s 195–6
    Luther's early sympathy for the Jews
        (*That Jesus Christ was born a Jew*) 162,
        169, 173–4
    On the Jews and Their Lies 156–7, 162, 174,
        183, 187, 189, 192
    *On the Unknowable Name of God and the
        Generations of Christ* 156–7, 162, 174, 192
    and *Gewissensreligion* (religion of
        conscience) 58–61, 63–4, 66–7, 69–73,
        107, 201–2, 220, 241
    and the hiddenness of God (*Deus absconditus*)
        59–61, 73–4, 139–41, 202–3, 206, 212,
        214–15, 218, 239–40

and the order of nature 108–9, 119–20, 133
and the Peasant's War 70–4, 209
and the Two-Kingdoms Theory (*Zwei-Reich Lehre*) 73–4, 223–5
as cultural symbol 1–2
as embodiment of the *Volk* 25–7, 29, 72, 78, 80, 85, 88–9, 138, 151–2, 203–4
as *Führer* 54, 106–11, 138–9, 141–2, 148, 153
as heathen 199–210
as messianic figure 35–7, 50, 89, 137–8, 149–50
as "most German of all Germans,"/as defining "Germanity" 5, 15–16, 31–2, 35–6, 105–8, 111
as responsible for the Third Reich 223–31, 237, 244–5
as spiritual presence 4–5, 36, 49–50, 90, 239
compared to Adolf Hitler 91–3, 132–8, 141–2, 152, 187–8
East German view of 229
Enlightenment views of 7
Heinrich von Treitschke's image of Luther, 1883 19–24
Image in the celebration of the 300th anniversary of the Reformation, 1817 8–14, 247–8
Image in the celebration of the 400th anniversary of the Reformation, 1917 29–43
Image in the 400th birthday celebration, 1883 18–24
Image in the 400th anniversary commemorations of his death, 1946 234–43
Image in the 450th birthday celebration, 1933 86–93
in Karl Barth, *Lutherfeier 1933* 93–7
Image in World War I 29
Public memorials, 19th century 16–17, 24–5
Racial consciousness 109–11, 171–2, 178, 181–3, 241–2
Thomas Mann's view of 230–1
View of the Bible 119–20
View of the "miracle man (*Wundermann*)" 53–4, 131–2, 134–5, 139–41, 144–7, 154–5, 209–10
View of the Old Testament 163–4
View of the state 51–4, 122–4, 143–5, 206–10, 227–9

Mann, Thomas 230–2
Maron, Gottfried 30 n.7
McGovern, William Montgomery 225–7, 229
Meiser, Hans 233–4
Meister Eckhart 200–3, 214–15

Melanchthon, Philip 94–5, 218
Merz, Georg 97–8, 103
Meyer-Erlach, Wolf 128–30, 192, 195–8, 202, 219
 Juden, Mönche, Luther ("Jews, Monks, Luther") 189–91
 Verrat an Luther ("Betrayal of Luther") 117–25
Mosheim, Johann Lorenz 7
Müller, Ludwig 97–8, 134
Müntzer, Thomas 70–1, 229

Niekisch, Ernst 227–8, 230
Niemöller, Martin 232–3
Nietzsche, Friedrich 200–1, 211, 231, 240–1
Nipperdey, Thomas 28 n.1
Noormann, Harry 234 n.35

Oberhof, Johannes 216–17
Ohst, Martin 63 n.44

Pauls, Theodor 140–1
Piper, Ernst 113 n.35, 117 n.48
Positive Christianity 79–80, 108, 111–12, 125–6, 130, 137–8, 248–9
Preuß, Hans 113–14, 130–2, 214–15
 Luther der Deutsche ("Luther the German") 105–13
 Luther und Hitler 132–8
Probst, Christopher 175 n.73
Protestant response to Germany's defeat in World War I 43–5

Racial nationalism 2–3, 5, 26–8, 38, 74, 77–9, 97, 124, 200, 235, 248–9, 251–2, *see also* (*Völkisch* nationalism)
Rade, Martin 56–7
Ranke, Leopold von 18–20, 55, 61, 247–8
Rhein, Stefan 51 n.12
Riemann, Heinrich 12
Ritschl, Albrecht 241–2
Ritter, Gerhard 235–40
Rosenberg, Alfred 111, 113–14, 116–18, 124–32, 143, 169–70, 172–3, 180–1, 184–6, 195–8, 202
 Protestantische Rompilger 114–16
Rupp, E. Gordon 227

Sasse, Hermann 97–8, 103
Sasse, Martin 195–8
 Martin Luther über die Juden: Weg mit ihnen! ("Martin Luther on the Jews: Throw them out!") 191–2
Scharfe, Siegfried
 Verrat an Luther? ("Betrayal of Luther?") 125–8

Schjørring, Jens Holger 65 n.53
Schlatter, Adolf 103
Schleiermacher, Friedrich 94–5
Schmidt, Georg 3 n.7
Schmidt, Ina 200 n.3, 200 n.4
Schöpfungsordnungen (order of creations) 48–9, 57, 69–70, 74, 100, 191, 235, 242, 251
Schöpfungstheologie 74, 81–2, 206–7
Scholder, Klaus 45 n.51, 63 n.44, 93 n.32, 97 n.47
Scholz, Hermann 7 n.5
Schroth, Hansgeorg, *Luthers christlicher Antisemitismus heute* ("Luther's Christian anti-Semitism today") 193–5, 197–8
Schuster, Hermann 212–13, 215–16
Seeberg, Erich 138–41, 216–17
Seeberg, Reinhard 26–7, 28 n.2, 43 n.46, 138
Shirer, William L. 226–7
Simon, Hermann 147–8
Sonderweg ideas about German history 226–7, 229, 249–50
Sontheimer, Kurt 232 n.29
Spieker, Christian Wilhelm 13
Sports Palace scandal 93–4, 184–5
Stapel, Wilhelm 220
Stoecker, Adolf 157–9
Streicher, Julius 157 n.3, 187 n.108, 244 n.78
Stuttgart Confession of Guilt 233–4, 243–4

Thiel, Rudolf 145–7, 218
Thielicke, Helmut 244 n.74

Treitschke, Heinrich von 18–24, 61, 89–90, 157
and anti-Semitism 19–20, 157
Troeltsch, Ernst 39–40, 70–1, 220, 231

Vogelsang, Erich 63–4, 175–81, 183–4
review of *Luther, Staat und Glaube* 217–18
Völkisch nationalism 2–3, 5, 26–8, 38, 74, 77–9, 97, 124, 200, 235, 248–9, 251–2,
see (racial nationalism)

Wagner, Richard 91–3, 131–2, 165
Warmuth, Kurt 31–3
Wars of Liberation 6, 8–10, 199, 247–8
Weidemann, Heinrich 186–7
Weimar Republic 2–4, 46, 79–80, 114, 170, 229–30, 252–4
Protestant views of 24–5, 28, 43, 62, 81–2, 248–9
Wendebourg, Dorothea 196–8
Werdermann, Hermann 131–2, 138
Martin Luther und Adolf Hitler 134–8
Wiener, Peter 226–7
Winckler, Lutz 9–10
Wittenberg as *Lutherstadt* 16–17, 24–5
Wolf, Ernst 235, 239–43
Wouk, Herman 226–7
Wurm, Theophil 232–3

Zumbini, Massimo Ferrari 160 n.15
Zwingli, Huldrych 108–9, 208